American Furniture

AMERICAN FURNITURE 2002

Edited by Luke Beckerdite

Published by the CHIPSTONE FOUNDATION

Distributed by University Press of New England

Hanover and London

CHIPSTONE FOUNDATION BOARD OF DIRECTORS
Dudley Godfrey, Jr.
Charles Hummel
W. David Knox, II   *President*
Jere D. McGaffey
John S. McGregor
Jonathan Prown   *Executive Director*
Philip L. Stone
Allen M. Taylor   *Chairman*

EDITOR
Luke Beckerdite

BOOK AND EXHIBITION REVIEW EDITOR
Gerald W. R. Ward

EDITORIAL ADVISORY BOARD
Glenn Adamson, *Curator, Chipstone Foundation*
David Barquist, *Associate Curator for American Decorative Arts, Yale University Art Gallery*
Edward S. Cooke, *Charles F. Montgomery Professor of American Decorative Arts, Department of the History of Art, Yale University*
Wendy Cooper, *Curator of Furniture, Winterthur Museum*
Leroy Graves, *Upholstery Conservator, Colonial Williamsburg Foundation*
Peter Kenny, *Curator of American Decorative Arts and Administrator of the American Wing, Metropolitan Museum of Art*
Jack Lindsey, *Curator of American Decorative Arts, Philadelphia Museum of Art*
Alan Miller, *Conservator and Independent Furniture Consultant, Quakertown, Pennsylvania*
Robert F. Trent, *Independent Furniture Consultant, Wilmington, Delaware*
Gerald W. R. Ward, *Katharine Lane Weems Senior Curator of Decorative Arts and Sculpture, Art of the Americas, Museum of Fine Arts, Boston*
Philip Zea, *Vice President for Museums and Collections, Society for the Preservation of New England Antiquities*

Cover Illustration: Detail of the carved shell on a high chest by George Claypoole, Jr., Philadelphia, Pennsylvania, 1754. (Private collection; photo, Gavin Ashworth.)

Design: Wynne Patterson, Pittsfield, VT
Copyediting: Alice Gilborn, Mt. Tabor, VT
Typesetting: Aardvark Type, Hartford, CT
Printing: Meridian Printing, East Greenwich, RI

Published by the Chipstone Foundation, 7820 North Club Circle, Milwaukee, WI 53217
Distributed by University Press of New England, Hanover, NH 03755
© 2002 by the Chipstone Foundation
All rights reserved
Printed in the United States of America   5 4 3 2 1
ISSN 1069–4188
ISBN 1–58465–057–5

Contents

Editorial Statement *Luke Beckerdite*	VII
Preface *Allen M. Taylor*	IX
Introduction *Luke Beckerdite*	XI
Survival of the Fittest: The Lloyd Family's Furniture Legacy *Alexandra Alevizatos Kirtley*	2
Furniture Fakes from the Chipstone Collection *Luke Beckerdite and Alan Miller*	54
Pennsylvania Clouded Limestone: Its Quarrying, Processing, and Use in the Stone Cutting, Furniture, and Architectural Trades *R. Curt Chinnici*	94
Manuscripts, Marks, and Material Culture: Sources for Understanding the Joiner's Trade in Seventeenth-Century America *Peter Follansbee*	125
The Claypoole Family Joiners of Philadelphia: Their Legacy and the Context of Their Work *Andrew Brunk*	147
The Politics of the Caned Chair *Glenn Adamson*	174
The Quiet Canon: Tradition and Exclusion in American Furniture Scholarship *Jonathan Prown and Katherine Hemple Prown*	207
An Early Cupboard Fragment from the Harvard College Joinery Tradition *Robert F. Trent and Michael Podmaniczky*	228

Book Reviews 243

The Furniture of Sam Maloof, Jeremy Adamson; *Made In Oakland: The Furniture of Garry Knox Bennett,* Ursula Ilse-Neumann, et al.; review by Glenn Adamson

Encyclopedia of Furniture Materials, Trades and Techniques, Clive Edwards; *One Good Turn: A Natural History of the Screwdriver and the Screw,* Witold Rybczynski; review by Gerald W. R. Ward

Willard's Patent Time Pieces: A History of the Weight-Driven Banjo Clock, 1800–1900, Paul J. Foley; review by David Wood and Robert C. Cheney

An American Vision: Henry Francis du Pont's Winterthur Museum, Wendy A. Cooper; review by Kenneth L. Ames

Recent Writing on American Furniture: A Bibliography 260
Gerald W. R. Ward

Index 271

Editorial Statement

American Furniture is an interdisciplinary journal dedicated to advancing knowledge of furniture made or used in the Americas from the seventeenth century to the present. Authors are encouraged to submit articles on any aspect of furniture history, essays on conservation and historic technology, reproductions or transcripts of documents, annotated photographs of new furniture discoveries, and book and exhibition reviews. References for compiling an annual bibliography also are welcome.

Manuscripts must be typed, double-spaced, illustrated with black-and-white prints or transparencies, and prepared in accordance with the *Chicago Manual of Style*. Computer disk copy is requested but not required. The Chipstone Foundation will offer significant honoraria for manuscripts accepted for publication and reimburse authors for all photography approved in writing by the editor. Low resolution digital images are not acceptable.

Luke Beckerdite

Preface

The Chipstone Foundation was organized in 1965 by Stanley Stone and Polly Mariner Stone of Fox Point, Wisconsin. Representing the culmination of their shared experiences in collecting American furniture, American historical prints, and early English pottery, the foundation was created with the dual purpose of preserving and interpreting their collection and stimulating research and education in the decorative arts.

The Stones began collecting American decorative arts in 1946, and by 1964 it became apparent to them that provisions should be made to deal with their collection. With the counsel of their friend Charles Montgomery, the Stones decided that their collection should be published and exhibited.

Following Stanley Stone's death in 1987, the foundation was activated by an initial endowment provided by Mrs. Stone. This generous donation allowed the foundation to institute its research and grant programs, begin work on three collection catalogues, and launch *American Furniture*.

Allen M. Taylor

Introduction

Luke Beckerdite

In 1993, the Chipstone Foundation established *American Furniture* with the goal that it would become the journal of record for its field. Since that date ten volumes have appeared containing a total of eighty-six articles, fifty book and exhibition reviews, and bibliographies on hundreds of publications in the field. The articles in *American Furniture* have always presented the latest research, and we have endeavored to make the journal useful to a broad and diverse audience. Today, many museum professionals, academics, conservators, craftsmen, collectors, and individuals in the trade consider *American Furniture* essential reading.

Like most of its predecessors, this volume includes articles that are about discovery and reassessment. Andrew Brunk's "The Claypoole Family Joiners of Philadelphia: Their Legacy and the Context of Their Work" breaks new ground in attributing furniture to the shops of Joseph Claypoole, his son George, and his grandson George, Jr. Because the Claypooles' work spanned several decades, the furniture attributed to them provides an index of stylistic shifts in Philadelphia as well as a model for understanding how designs, construction features, and patronage passed from father to son and master to apprentice in family shops. Similarly, Robert F. Trent and Michael Podmaniczky focus on a seventeenth-century cupboard fragment to clarify and expand previous interpretations of a shop tradition associated with various joiners employed by Harvard College in Cambridge, Massachusetts. They show how the earliest phase of that tradition, distinguished by the use of mannerist carving, gradually gave way to an applied ornament style emanating from Boston. This pattern echoed earlier stylistic developments in London and other urban areas of the British Empire.

R. Curt Chinnici's "Pennsylvania Clouded Limestone: Its Quarrying, Processing, and Use in the Stone Cutting, Furniture, and Architectural Trades" is a much needed addition to decorative arts scholarship. For centuries, marble, limestone, and other types of figured rock have been used as furniture components, and in many instances these materials were more valuable than the wooden forms they embellished. Chinnici's discussion of tools and techniques will assist scholars in determining the originality and production date of stones used for furniture and architecture during the eighteenth and nineteenth centuries.

In "Furniture Fakes from the Chipstone Collection," Alan Miller and I argue that the "prevalence and persistence of fakery are intimately linked to the demands and expectations in the marketplace." The authors document the techniques and marketing strategies used by a small group of fakers during the mid-twentieth century, and contrast evidence on fraudulent objects with that found on period work. Much of our study will be accessible on the Chipstone Foundation's web site next year.

Jonathan Prown and Katherine Hemphill Prown's "The Quiet Canon: Tradition and Exclusion in American Furniture Scholarship" is a constructive critique of traditional decorative arts installations. According to the authors, "the display of early American furniture—and the scholarship on which it is based—remains largely dependent on a specialized interpretive model crafted over a century ago." They contend that decorative arts scholars need to take a more transdisciplinary approach in order to provide "an experience for visitors that is more intellectually and emotionally inclusive."

There is little doubt that contemporary attitudes affect the way we perceive the past. Peter Follansbee's "Manuscripts, Marks, and Material Culture: Sources for Understanding the Joiner's Trade in Seventeenth-Century America" suggests that many scholars and collectors continue to maintain romantic notions about historic trades. Using a variety of documentary sources, physical evidence on surviving furniture, and information gleaned from the use of period tools in reproduction work, Follansbee demonstrates that the lives of most seventeenth-century American furniture makers "were far more challenging than we imagine today."

As Glenn Adamson's "The Politics of the Caned Chair" reveals, *American Furniture* continues to provide a forum for presenting new and alternative interpretive models. This insightful article reveals how the makers and marketers of caned chairs exploited middle-class aspirations regarding fashionability and taste to create a commodity that fit perfectly into Britain's mercantilist scheme. In colonial America, this approach gave rise to Boston's dominance in the furniture export trade, a status that it enjoyed for more than half a century.

In "Survival of the Fittest: The Lloyd Family's Furniture Legacy," Alexandra Alevizatos Kirtley illustrates and discusses a range of furniture and household goods acquired and preserved by several successive generations of the Lloyd family of Talbot County, Maryland. She contends that family "assemblages" often represent a more direct and more informative link with the past than do institutional and private collections because the former reveal how "each generation reassesses and reorders objects and ephemera based on their own views regarding aesthetics, personal and family identity, historical significance, and sentiment."

To make *American Furniture* available to a broader audience, issues will eventually be posted on the Chipstone Foundation's web site. This site will also provide access to the highly acclaimed journal *Ceramics in America* as well as virtual exhibitions. Visit us at <www.chipstone.org>.

American Furniture

Figure 1 Wye House, Talbot County, Maryland, ca. 1787. (Photo, Gavin Ashworth.)

Alexandra Alevizatos Kirtley

Survival of the Fittest: The Lloyd Family's Furniture Legacy

▼ OBJECTS ARE WHAT MATTER. *Only they carry the evidence that throughout the centuries something really happened among human beings.*

Claude Levi-Strauss

The survival of objects can be the result of either random or purposeful acts, whereas collections are by definition intentional. Most institutions have mandates and policies governing acquisitions, but their collections invariably reflect the interests and goals of successive curators, administrators, and donors. In contrast, private collections generally embody the tastes, interests, and aspirations of one or two individuals. Groups of objects acquired and preserved by consecutive generations of a single family are often described as "collections," but they are actually assemblages because each generation reassesses and reorders objects and ephemera based on their own views regarding aesthetics, personal and family identity, historical significance, and sentiment. By revealing what specific consumers and their progeny deemed important and valuable, family assemblages often represent a more direct and more informative link with the past than do institutional and private collections.[1]

The furniture and furnishings of the Edward Lloyd family of Wye House (fig. 1) in Talbot County, Maryland, provide a unique opportunity to consider possessions that descended in an important American family. These objects raise several intriguing questions: Where, how, and why did their original owners acquire them? In what context were these objects used, and what do they say about the Lloyds' wealth, tastes, social status, and self-perception? Why do these objects survive?

The history of the Lloyd family of Maryland began in 1659, when Edward Lloyd I (ca. 1610–1696) acquired 3,500 acres of land in Talbot County with the intention of establishing a tobacco farm. He named the property and the river adjacent to it Wye, after the Wye River in his native Wales. Edward I and his descendants accumulated power and money through political positions, the establishment of lucrative trade routes, and politically and socially advantageous marriages. By the 1770s, the Lloyds were one of the wealthiest and most powerful families in America.[2]

Built in 1787 by the fifth proprietor, Edward Lloyd IV (1744–1796), the present Wye House is presumably the fourth house built on the property. The previous ones fell victim to their proprietor's desire to build a newer and more current residence. Just as Edward IV's Wye house is the only dwelling surviving on the estate, the furniture that remains there is merely a fractional representation of what each proprietary family owned. For at least four generations (1718–1834), elder sons rose to power in the wake of their father's death. They dispersed possessions to siblings, purged vast quantities of household goods, and bought anew. Successive generations used the cultural criterion of their own time to decide what to save and what not to save from the patrimony of previous generations. Throughout this period, the old furnishings preserved by the Lloyds and the new objects acquired by each patriarch served as vehicles for conveying power and social status and defining respective proprietorships.

Financial reversals contributed to the survival of some furnishings and the loss of others. By the 1850s, income from agricultural products grown at Wye had declined, reducing the family's ability to maintain the house and outbuildings and acquire new furnishings and interior decorations. Although the Lloyds were less active consumers during the mid-nineteenth century, they remained intensely interested in their family's legacy. These sentiments continued long after the Centennial, propelled by the colonial revival and the Lloyds' awareness of their place in local and national history.

By the first decade of the twentieth century, debts at Wye were mounting, and many buildings on the property were in dire need of repair. The Lloyds had sold thousands of acres of land since the Civil War, but the proceeds were quickly exhausted. In 1906, Wye ceased to pass from father to eldest son when Edward Lloyd VIII (1857–1948), a commodore in the United States Navy, realized that he could not afford the taxes due upon the death of his father Edward VII (1825–1907). To maintain family control of the estate, Mary Donnell Lloyd (1865–1943)—the wife of Edward VIII's younger brother Charles Howard Lloyd (1859–1929) (fig. 2)—purchased Wye House, its outbuildings and contents, and several thousand acres of land from Edward VII for $2,726.80 with money she had inherited from her family. Charles and Mary lived in Baltimore, residing at Wye House

Figure 2 Circa 1896 photograph showing (left to right) Elizabeth Phoebe Key Howard, Charles Howard Lloyd, Joanna Leigh Lloyd, and Mary Lloyd Howard Lloyd.

only seasonally. In 1943, their daughters Joanna Leigh Lloyd Singer (1895–1972) and Elizabeth Key Lloyd Schiller (1897–1993) inherited the property, and Elizabeth and her husband Morgan B. Schiller moved there. Joanna's daughter, Mary Donnell Tilghman (neé Singer) (b. 1919), inherited Wye in the 1990s and has used the latest and most careful methods of conservation to preserve the house, its outbuildings, and its furnishings.[3]

Although early proprietors routinely sold household goods through auctions and direct transactions, Charles Howard Lloyd, his wife Mary, and their daughter Elizabeth Lloyd Schiller were the most aggressive. Their efforts to preserve and restore Wye House were strongly influenced by colonial revival attitudes, which tended to romanticize the past. Charles, Mary, and Elizabeth made significant strides in improving the appearance of Wye House and oversaw the division of objects to Charles' seven siblings after Edward VII died and sold unwanted furnishings as well. To re-create a semblance of the house's colonial grandeur, they kept only what they perceived to be "true antiques" and replaced objects not fitting this criteria with colonial revival reproductions made by the Potthast brothers in Baltimore. The fact that the furnishings surviving at Wye House endured so many generations of taste and perception makes them even more rare, more evocative, more iconic.[4]

A strong tradition of patriarchy and primogeniture allowed Wye to descend from father to eldest son into the twentieth century—when ownership passed to the second son, and then to his two daughters—and the property remains in the possession of the eleventh generation today. Because furniture and other decorative arts associated with the Lloyd family have not entered the public domain, they have not captured the attention of scholars to the same degree as those that descended in many less

Figure 3 Charles Willson Peale, *The Edward Lloyd Family*, Maryland, 1771. Oil on canvas. 48" x 57½". (Courtesy, Winterthur Museum.)

Figure 4 Benjamin West, *Richard Bennett Lloyd*, London, ca. 1773. Oil on canvas. 36" x 28". (Photo, Gavin Ashworth.)

influential families. It was, after all, the Lloyd family's wealth that purchased the lavish and well-documented furnishings of John (1742–1786) and Elizabeth (Lloyd) (1742–1776) Cadwalader.[5]

Edward Lloyd III

Edward Lloyd III (1711–1770) is often remembered today as the wealthy father-in-law of Philadelphia merchant John Cadwalader (1742–1786), but in the eighteenth century he was a prosperous planter and a stalwart member of the Maryland General Assembly and Governor's Council who supported Tory politics with diehard fortitude. Edward III's death in January 1770 spared his family from the political, financial, and social demise that befell other Maryland loyalists after the revolution. His will, written eighteen years earlier, left half of his considerable estate to his eldest son Edward IV (1744–1796) (fig. 3) and divided the remaining half equally beween his youngest son Richard Bennett (1750–1787) (fig. 4) and his daughter Elizabeth or her husband (fig. 5). This document conflicted with Edward III's verbal, bedside instructions that his estate be divided in equal thirds. The discrepancy between the written and oral mandates ignited a major quarrel, which played itself out in heated correspondence between Edward IV and John Cadwalader, who represented Elizabeth's and Richard's interests as well as his own. By early 1771, Edward IV succumbed to his angry siblings and agreed to divide the estate equally between the three heirs. The only documents pertaining to the house and furnishings of Edward III are two inventories, though neither may be complete. His probate inventory lists objects room by room and notes their values, and a private inventory designated who inherited what by the initials "JC" (John Cadwalader), "EL" (Edward Lloyd IV), and "RL" (Richard Bennett Lloyd).[6]

Both of Edward III's inventories begin by listing his lavish silver equipage, all procured through London agents and lending a palpable reminder of the Lloyds' London-based wealth. The rooms are designated by function, color, and location, except for the bedrooms, which are identified by the names of family members who traditionally slept there. It is clear that furniture had been shuffled and removed by the heirs since the parlor contained no chairs and the dining room contained no table.[7]

John Cadwalader received most of the furnishings in the large bedroom over the passage, designated "The Colonel's" (Edward III's). This room contained a high-post mahogany bedstead with blue silk furniture, matching window curtains, a bottle stand and basin, two Wilton bedside carpets, prints, a settee bed, a dressing table with a cover and corresponding glass, and a pair of andirons with shovel and tongs. The only object that Edward IV received from his father's bedroom was a close stool easy chair valued at £4.8.[8]

Richard Lloyd inherited the contents of the small passage, two bedrooms, and the dressing room over the dining room. The passage furnishings included two settees with covers, a large round table, a tea table, a breakfast table "eight square," two floor mats (one large and one small), a large old map, and thirteen paintings. A small mahogany bedstead with furniture,

Figure 5 Charles Willson Peale, *The Family of John Cadwalader*, Philadelphia, 1771. Oil on canvas. 51½" x 41¼". (Courtesy, Philadelphia Museum of Art.)

two dressing tables with glasses, a japanned tea table, six chairs, a bottle stand, and two pairs of andirons with shovels and tongs were in the bedroom over the parlor and the dressing room over the dining room. The other bedroom, formerly occupied by Richard's mother Anne Rousby Lloyd (1721–1769), had a variety of expensive furnishings: a mahogany bedstead with yellow silk furniture, two matching window curtains, six chairs with yellow silk damask "bottoms," two armchairs, a chimney glass, a japanned cupboard, two brackets with porcelain pots painted with flowers, a print of John Wilkes, a mahogany stand, and a fire screen. Richard subsequently sold the settees with covers from the passage and the side chairs and one armchair from his mother's bedroom to Edward IV.[9]

An English walnut armchair (fig. 6) in Wye House may be the latter seating form. It appears to date about 1760, which is too early to have been commissioned by any of Edward III's children. Edward Lloyd III's inventory lists an armchair valued at £10, an amount sufficient for an example with an upholstered back, seat, and arms. This armchair may also be the "large" one valued at £2.5 in the 1796 inventory of Edward IV. Referred to as "cabriole," "French," or "elbow" chairs in English design books, such armchairs were considered appropriate for both parlors and bedrooms.[10]

Figure 6 Upholstered armchair, England, ca. 1760. Walnut with beech. H. 37¾", W. 28¼", D. 23". (Photo, Gavin Ashworth.)

With the exception of the silk window curtains, which went to Edward IV, all of the parlor furnishings passed to the Cadwaladers. The couple received a large looking glass, a chimney glass and two sconces, a marble slab (presumably with a wooden frame), an old carpet, and a pair of andirons with shovel and tongs. Edward IV inherited the contents of the dining room and "Great Passage." The dining room furnishings included two large gilt pier glasses, two silk damask window curtains, twelve chairs with silk bottoms and covers, four paintings, two fire screens, a tea table, a japanned tea table, a card table, four flower pots on brackets, and a pair of andirons with shovel and tongs; and the passage had a large and a small painted and gilt screen and eight flag bottom chairs.[11]

Random furniture not considered as part of a suite or for a specific room appears separately in the inventories. Cadwalader received ten mahogany side chairs and two mahogany armchairs with carpet bottoms, a Wilton carpet, and a shagreen case with silver handled knives and forks. Richard Bennett Lloyd inherited six chairs with damask bottoms, a broken mahogany card table, a broken tea table, a broken round table, mattresses, and a Wilton carpet. Edward IV received a sideboard table, a sideboard, a bureau, two leather armchairs, eight chairs with yellow damask bottoms, two fire screens, two sets of silk window curtains, an old clock, a Wilton carpet, and a shagreen case with silver mounts and five bottles. The three heirs divided twenty "common" and "low mahogany" beds and mattresses.[12]

A tall clock case at Wye House (fig. 7) has an eight-day movement by English clockmakers Daniel Quare and Stephen Horseman, who were in partnership from 1709 to 1720. This movement probably came from the "old clock" inherited by Edward IV, who replaced the original case with a more up to date, locally made one. The date range attributable to the movement suggests that the original owner was Edward II (1670–1718). Family photographs indicate that the clock has been secured to the passage wall since at least the late nineteenth century.[13]

The proceeds from two auctions recorded in Edward III's estate ledger reveal that his heirs sold unwanted household furnishings. Each heir received £478.8.11 from a sale held in Philadelphia on September 6, 1770, and Edward IV and Richard received £113.9.2 from a sale of their unwanted goods held in Annapolis a year later. The Annapolis auction included textiles, kitchen utensils, chinaware, foodstuffs, and furniture, although only "a looking glass" was specified. Buyers from various social and economic strata vied for these goods. Among the successful bidders were royal governor Robert Eden (1728–1804), architect William Buckland (1734–1774), silversmith William Farris, ship captain, merchant and cabinetmaker Joseph Middleton, cabinetmaker Archibald Chisholm (d. 1810), cabinetmaker William Tuck, the Lloyds' agent Arthur Bryan, merchant Richard McCubbin, and Thomas, "the servant man at the Middleton's."[14]

Many of the furnishings retained by the heirs document Edward III's patronage of London tradesmen and his and his progeny's familiarity with mid-eighteenth-century, European court styles. Silver served as one of the most potent symbols of the Lloyds' wealth, social status, and taste. Much of the equipage listed in Edward III's inventory was given to later generations of Lloyds, most often as wedding gifts. Of the silver that survives, two pieces are remarkable for their ownership and survival in an American context. The large tea waiter, or salver, valued at £242 features a cast rim with decorative allusions to the Lloyds' wheat farming and an elaborately engraved "shield" with the arms of Lloyd impaling Rousby (figs. 8, 9). London silversmith Jacob Marsh made the waiter in 1754, but the name of the engraver is not known. The appraiser's assessment of this monumental

Figure 7 Tall clock case, probably Easton, Maryland, ca. 1790. Walnut with tulip poplar, yellow pine, and oak. H. 91", W. 19", D. 10". (Photo, Gavin Ashworth.) The movement is by Daniel Quare and Stephen Horseman of London and dates about 1715.

Figure 8 Salver by Jacob Marsh, London, 1754. Silver. H. 3½", Diam. 28". (Photo, Gavin Ashworth.)

Figure 9 Detail of the engraving on the salver illustrated in fig. 8.

Figure 10 Bread basket by John Wirgman, London, 1754. Silver. H. 12½", L. 13½". (Photo, Gavin Ashworth.)

Figure 11 Platter, Chinese export for the British market, 1755–1760. Porcelain. 18" x 15". (Photo, Gavin Ashworth.)

waiter was more than twice what Philadelphia cabinetmaker Thomas Affleck charged John Cadwalader for making eighteen major pieces of furniture, two window cornices, and two knife trays, and performing sundry repairs and services between October 13, 1770, and January 14, 1771. Maryland and Pennsylvania currency had almost equal value during the early 1770s. Besides effectively conveying the Lloyd family's wealth, the waiter is steeped in lore. Family tradition maintains that during the late eighteenth and early nineteenth centuries newborn Lloyd children were placed on the salver and presented to their father.[15]

Edward III's inventory also notes that Richard Bennett Lloyd sold Edward IV a bread basket for £88. Made by John Wirgman in 1754, this imposing object (fig. 10) also has trophies pertaining to wheat farming. The reticulated nautilus shape alludes to fertile ground—the source of Edward III's immense wealth—and the handle depicts the goddess of the harvest, Demeter (Greek) or Ceres (Roman), holding a shield engraved with the Lloyd coat of arms. John Cadwalader and Richard Bennett Lloyd divided a set of four large candelabra, each of which held twelve candles and had sixteen "savealls." None of these objects are known to have survived, nor did they appear on any of the inventories of Edward III's heirs. Given the fact that they were valued £118 each, the candelabra must have rivaled the magnificence of Edward III's surviving silver.[16]

Numerous English, French, and Chinese porcelain dining services complemented Edward III's silver, but only the tobacco leaf set remains at Wye (see fig. 11). Comprised of several hundred pieces, this service was described as "Ribb[d]," "Enamel[d]," and "Enamel[d] china" in his inventory. Edward IV inherited one-third of the tobacco leaf porcelain and purchased the remaining two-thirds from Cadwalader and Richard Bennett Lloyd. No other porcelain, either useful or ornamental, survives from the elder Lloyd's proprietorship.[17]

9 LLOYD FAMILY'S FURNITURE LEGACY

Figure 12 Cannon, England, ca. 1720. Bronze, iron, steel, and wood. L. 26". (Photo, Gavin Ashworth.)

Figure 13 Coat-of-arms of the Lloyd family, England, ca. 1785. Watercolor on paper. 12¾" x 15¾". (Photo, Gavin Ashworth.)

Unlike most of his peers, Edward III controlled every facet of his business—thousands of acres of land, hundreds of slaves, several mills and drying houses, and a fleet of schooners that transported wheat and tobacco from Maryland to London. The family's connection to the water and involvement in transatlantic commerce may have prompted Edward III's heirs and their progeny to preserve a pair of deck cannons (see fig. 12) from his private schooner. Edward III used the cannon to "thunderously report" his arrival in port as did Edward IV, V, and VI, the latter having transferred the two pieces of artillery to their own private schooners. According to family tradition, the cannons were last discharged in 1865 when Admiral Franklin Buchanan (1800–1878), who was married to Edward V's daughter Anne Catherine Lloyd (1808–1892), repelled Union deserters attempting to burglarize Wye House.[18]

The dispersal of Edward III's estate and redecorating by generations of his extended family has left only a small amount of furniture that can be associated with his proprietorship. At present, it is unclear where the furniture inherited by Richard Bennett Lloyd and the Cadwaladers ended up. It is possible that John and Elizabeth decorated their Kent County, Maryland, estate—Shrewsbury Farm—with some of her father's furnishings. At the very least, Edward III and Anne's interiors inspired those that the Cadwaladers created in the Philadelphia townhouse Edward III urged them to purchase. The silk curtains and upholstery fabrics in John and Elizabeth's principal first floor rooms were yellow and blue like those in Wye House. Edward III and Anne's color choices may have been inspired by the Lloyd family coat-of-arms, which is azure and gold (see figs. 13, 14). These colors would also have resonated with John Cadwalader, whose crest features a

Figure 14 Coat-of-arms of the Lloyd family, England, ca. 1785. Watercolor on paper. 9¾" x 7½". (Photo, Gavin Ashworth.)

Figure 15 Side chair attributed to the shop of Benjamin Randolph, Philadelphia, Pennsylvania, ca. 1769. Mahogany with white cedar. H. 36¾", W. 21¾" (seat), D. 17⅞" (seat). (Chipstone Foundation; photo, Hans Lorenz.)

gold cross formé fiché against an azure ground. The Cadwaladers also had the ten mahogany side chairs and two armchairs they inherited recovered by Philadelphia upholsterer Plunkett Fleeson, and they augmented the Wilton carpets from Wye House with others purchased through their London agent Mathias Gale. Although the side chairs and armchairs are not known to have survived, it is conceivable that they served as models for the well-known ribbon-back set that the Cadwaladers commissioned about 1769 (see fig. 15).[19]

The Wye House of Edward Lloyd IV
After the revolution, Edward IV became less active in politics and moved from Annapolis to Wye in hopes that country life would remedy the gout that debilitated him. Like other enlightened men of his era, he studied art and architecture and amassed a large and useful library. Many of the architectural design books he acquired remain in his house today. In fact, entries in Edward IV's ledgers suggest that he designed and supervised the construction of the surviving residence at Wye.[20]

In 1781, Edward IV instructed his overseer James Burke to move the contents remaining in his father's house to Forrest Plantation, a neighboring Lloyd plantation. These items included a writing desk with papers, several mahogany chairs, a large mahogany couch with a check cover, a mahogany stand, two large gilt pier glasses, two "fincured" knife cases, window blinds, tea china, glass, chimney-piece ornaments, andirons, fender grates, shovels and tongs, bird cages, a drum and a pair of drum sticks, six guns and six barrels, and nine pieces of flagstone. The following year, Edward IV demolished his father's residence and commissioned engineer Charles Gardiner to survey the site to establish a perfect north-south axis for his new Wye House (fig. 16). Entries in Edward IV's ledgers

Figure 16 Circa 1935 photograph showing part of the Wye House estate. The house, gardens, and greenhouse are oriented on a north-south axis.

from 1781 to 1788 document expenditures for building materials—wood for the framing and weather boarding and brick (some fired at Wye) for wall filler. On March 13, 1787, joiner William Eaton received £9.3.4 for "shifting the studs of the main house to prepare for weatherboarding."[21]

Construction must have been nearing completion the following year. A docket from Edward IV's Baltimore agent dated March 1788 lists furnishings and other goods shipped aboard the former's schooner to Wye. Included were powder yellow, boiled oil, raw oil, whiting, turpentine, fat oil, vitriol, litharge of gold, twenty books of gold leaf, twelve paint brushes, and nine other paint tools, presumably for re-gilding the pier glasses moved from Forrest Plantation to Wye House. Formerly thought to date from the late eighteenth century, these remarkable glasses (figs. 17, 18) show how profoundly Edward III's furnishings influenced the material world of his children.[22]

The large north parlor in Edward IV's residence was designed specifically to accommodate the pier glasses, which are the same height, but differ in width (fig. 17). Although earlier scholars believed that these objects were neoclassical imports, documentary evidence and microscopy

Figure 17 Pier glasses, London, ca. 1755. Woods not identified. Left: H. 104" (not including appliqué), W. 41½". Right: H. 104" (not including appliqué), W. 56¾". (Photo, Gavin Ashworth.)

Figure 18 Detail of the appliqué and guilloche on the left pier glass illustrated in fig. 17.

Figure 19 "Moldings for Tabernacle Frames" illustrated on pl. 78 of Batty and Thomas Langley's *The Builder's Jewell, or Youth's Instructor* (1741). (Courtesy, Winterthur Museum Library: Printed Book and Periodical Collection.)

suggest that they are the two pier glasses Edward IV inherited from his father's dining room and that the materials listed in the docket were for re-gilding them. Leaf and ribbon appliqués similar to those on the Lloyd examples are illustrated in architectural design books such as William Jones' *Builders Companion* (1739) and occur on British looking glass frames from the second quarter of the eighteenth century. The guilloche borders of the pier glasses also have architectural parallels. Plate 78 of Batty and Thomas Langley's *The Builder's Jewell* (1741) shows a popular variant in the upper right corner (fig. 19).[23]

As centerpieces of the most prominent room in Wye House and unable to be closeted, the pier glasses survived the purges of Edward IV and seven consecutive generations of his family. From the late 1780s to the present, the Lloyds have referred to this room as the "parlor," but Edward IV and his descendants also used it for large dinner parties. With the dining table placed on the north-south axis and the pier glasses reflecting the candlelight, the room undoubtedly made a dazzling impression. The glasses hung just above the chair rail with their tops canted forward until 1823 when Edward V installed a wider cornice and lowered them. The distance between the two sets of screw holes on each frame equals the amount that they were lowered and the amount they presently hang below the chair rail (see figs. 17, 18). Neither glass appears to have been moved since 1823.[24]

A third pier glass presumably obtained by Edward IV to complement the two he inherited from his father does not survive, but it is described in the younger Lloyd's inventory as "a gilt frame looking glass . . . £15." The value of this object and its listing adjacent to the "pair [of] large Gilt frame looking glasses . . . £100" suggests that all three were in the same room. Edward V's account and subsequent dispute with the London mercantile firm Thomas Eden, Christopher Court & Company also confirms the use

Figure 20 Bedstead with foot posts dating 1755–1770. The mahogany posts are probably British, although similar examples were made in Philadelphia. The bed that the posts came from probably had a carved or molded cornice and elaborate curtains.

Figure 21 Design for a "Canopy Bed" with gothic posts illustrated on plate 30 in the first edition of Thomas Chippendale's *The Gentleman and Cabinet-Maker's Director* (1754). (Courtesy, Winterthur Library: Printed Book and Periodical Collection.)

of a third looking glass in the north parlor. In 1810, the former ordered "three" pairs of cut crystal girandoles to stand in front of the parlor glasses (see fig. 17).[25]

Edward V may have displayed the girandoles on tables in front of the pier glasses. The 1861 inventory of his son Edward VI documents this practice, as do later photographs of the north parlor of Wye House. During the late nineteenth and early twentieth centuries, the D-shaped ends of a large classical dining table (see fig. 55) supported the girandoles while the other sections remained assembled for dining in the adjacent "withdrawing room." Elizabeth Lloyd Schiller replaced the D-ends with elliptical table sections (see fig. 17) she rescued from a barn loft. These sections may comprise all or part of one of the seven dining tables belonging to Edward IV.

Since the proprietorship of Edward Lloyd III, the pier glasses have defined the most important room in Wye House. Given their presence and the fact that they dictated the placement of other furniture forms and lighting devices, it is remarkable that these fragile objects endured the refurnishing and redecorating of subsequent generations. For the Lloyd family, these pier glasses have always represented a tangible connection with the grandeur of their eighteenth-century past.

In the Wye Houses of Edward III and Edward IV, bedsteads also provided a framework for lavish displays of wealth, primarily in the form of imported textiles. Edward III and his wife Anne both had bedsteads with silk furniture that matched the window curtains in their respective bedrooms. Edward IV and Elizabeth had comparable fabrics. In 1780, they paid £720 for eighteen yards of pink silk ordered from France. In the early twentieth century, Charles and Mary Lloyd sold a large quantity of furniture including several bedsteads. Only one early bedstead (fig. 20) remains in Wye, having been rescued from a tenant house by Elizabeth Lloyd Schiller in 1950. Related to both British (see fig. 21) and Philadelphia examples from the third quarter of the eighteenth century, it has gothic foot-posts and large Marlborough feet.[26]

Edward IV: Conspicuous Consumption

The inventories of Edward IV's houses at Wye and Annapolis paint a picture of a man who proudly earned the appellation his descendants bestowed upon him—"Edward the Magnificent." Excluding real estate, the value of his personal effects totaled £38,785.12.6, £11,000 of which were household furnishings (almost exactly ten percent of his entire wealth). Many of his possessions reflected personal interests, intellectual pursuits, and leisure activities. He had a library comprised of 2,500 volumes and owned a camera obscura, a mahogany compound microscope, surveying instruments, spy glasses, physics scales, a mahogany case of instruments for the recovery of drowning persons, several pairs of silver mounted pistols, 640 bottles of Madeira, 1822 bottles of sweet wine, sixty-nine pints of port wine, three demi-johns of apple brandy, a case of gin and brandy in cut glass bottles, and a cask of whiskey. He also maintained a park with sixty-one fallow deer and a small personal fleet consisting of barges, phaetons, and a schooner. The furniture in his residences included 103 side chairs, twenty-two armchairs, six settees, a sofa, nine Pembroke tables, seven card tables, six dining tables, five dressing tables, three writing tables, six washstands, three fire screens, eight bureaus, six desk-and-bookcases, six desks, one secretary bookcase, two bookcases, four clothes presses, and three sideboards. Although Edward V sold £10,956 worth of his father's household goods at auction in Baltimore in 1797, many of the finest furnishings acquired by Edward IV remain in Wye House along with more utilitarian objects that served the needs of Lloyd descendants' daily lifestyles.[27]

Immediately after his father's death, Edward IV and his wife Elizabeth (Tayloe) (1750–1825) set up residence in Annapolis, a town noted for "the quick importation of fashions from the mother country." The couple purchased a house that Annapolis lawyer Samuel Chase (1741–1811) had begun to build and hired London-trained, house joiner William Buckland to design their new home (fig. 22). Buckland had previously worked on Mount Airy, the home of Elizabeth's parents in Richmond County, Virginia. To augment Buckland's workforce, Edward IV imported carvers and plasterers from London. The result was the first three-story structure in Annapolis—an imposing residence with interiors that combined late baroque massiveness with the delicacy of the new neoclassical style. Charles Carroll of Carrollton, Edward IV's distant cousin, estimated that the interior details and furnishings comprised a substantial portion of the total cost. The townhouse "has cost ye Colonel upwards of £3000 cur^y and I think when the offices are finished and the house compleatley furnished it will cost him £6000 more."[28]

Although Edward IV was loyal to the revolutionary cause and the first member of his family to sell agricultural products to American markets, his cultural and economic ties to London spurred his desire to decorate his townhouse, and later residence at Wye, like the homes of English nobility. Unlike his brother-in-law John Cadwalader, who procured fashionable furnishings from Philadelphia artisans, Edward IV ordered most of his furniture and interior decorations from London agents. Because Elizabeth

Figure 22 Chase-Lloyd House, Annapolis, Maryland, ca. 1773. Architect William Buckland was responsible for the interior and exterior design. He had previously worked on Mt. Airy, the home of Elizabeth Tayloe's parents in Richmond County, Virginia.

Figure 23   "French chair," London, ca. 1772. Beech with oak. H. 34½", W. (seat) 24", D. 20" (seat). (Photo, Gavin Ashworth.)

Figure 24   Bureau bookcase, London, 1750–1760. Mahogany with cedrella, oak, and an unidentified conifer. H. 101", W. 47", D. 24". (Photo, Gavin Ashworth.) The gilding is modern.

Tayloe Lloyd retreated to Annapolis shortly after her husband's death, the furnishings in the townhouse were not dispersed until her death in 1825.[29]

Edward IV ordered twelve British armchairs (fig. 23), often referred to during the period as "French chairs," for his Annapolis townhouse. Sets of armchairs were ubiquitous in the homes of English and French nobility and were intended to subordinate issues of precedence. The wooden elements of the Lloyd chairs, as well as those of the settee that once accompanied them, were originally painted white with gilt decoration, and each piece in the suite had its seat, arms, and back (both front and rear) covered in silk. These seating forms are described in Edward IV's 1796 inventory as "12 Arm Chairs with silk damask lining . . . £45" and "1 large Settee with do. do. do. . . . £25." Thirteen "stuff covers" valued at two pounds protected the upholstery on the chairs. Edward IV moved the suite to Wye in 1791, but Elizabeth took it back to Annapolis five years later. After Elizabeth's death in 1825, her son Edward V returned the chairs to Wye House, where they remain today. Although the rococo style of these chairs was in many respects the antithesis of the late classical taste that held sway during Edward V's proprietorship, he clearly appreciated the historical and family associations of these important seating forms. The same can be said of his son Edward VI (1798–1861), who hired Baltimore cabinetmakers John and James Williams to make a new settee (see fig. 17) in 1844. The original must have been damaged or destroyed earlier.[30]

The London bureau bookcase and bookstand illustrated in figures 24 and 25 were also among the original furnishings of Edward IV and Elizabeth's Annapolis residence. Dating from the 1750s or early 1760s, these imposing objects were probably wedding gifts from Edward's parents, who gave a London silver tea service (Philadelphia Museum of Art) to

Figure 25 Bookstand, London, 1750–1760. Mahogany. H. 29", W. 24", D. 19". (Photo, Gavin Ashworth.)

Elizabeth and John Cadwalader when they married. With its scrolled pediment and lavish rococo carving, the bureau bookcase would have complemented the door friezes (see fig. 26), chimneypieces, and other architectural details in the Lloyds' townhouse. Edward's ledger indicates that Buckland received £62.0.6 for ornaments in the large first floor parlor, which included bold, gadrooned door and window surrounds, carved trusses, and frieze appliqués with bird heads and leafage based on designs by British architect Abraham Swan. Buckland's London-trained carver, Thomas Hall, was probably responsible for both the design and execution of this work. The practice of integrating furniture and interior architectural details was over a century old by the time the Lloyds began furnishing their townhouse.[31]

Like the silver and pier glasses commissioned by Edward Lloyd III, the bureau bookcase is one of the most extravagant and expensive London imports associated with an American owner. Although the leaves that rose from the scroll volutes are missing, the pediment design is related to that of a desk-and-bookcase illustrated on plate 78 in the first edition of Thomas Chippendale's *The Gentleman and Cabinet-Maker's Director* (1754) (fig. 27). No piece of Chippendale furniture with an American provenance is known, but the design, construction, and carving on the Lloyd bureau bookcase suggest that it came from the upper echelon of London's cabinet-making trade.

Figure 26 Detail showing one of the doors in the principal first floor room of the Chase-Lloyd House. The carving is attributed to Thomas Hall.

Figure 27 Design for a "Desk and Bookcase" illustrated on plate 78 in the first edition of Thomas Chippendale's *The Gentleman and Cabinet-Maker's Director* (1754). (Courtesy, Winterthur Museum Library: Printed Book and Periodical Collection.) This plate also illustrates leaves bound with ribbon as an optional frieze ornament on the left side. This motif, which occurs on the pier glasses ordered by Edward Lloyd III, was extremely popular in British furniture and architectural carving.

Figure 28   Desk-and-bookcase, Annapolis, John Shaw (active 1771–1819), 1797. Mahogany and light wood inlays with yellow pine and tulip poplar. H. 98½", W. 41¼", D. 23½". (Photo, Gavin Ashworth.) The design of the pediment is based on plate 57 of Thomas Sheraton's *The Cabinetmaker and Upholsterer's Drawing Book* (1793).

Figure 29   Detail of the pediment of the desk-and-bookcase illustrated in fig. 28. (Photo, Gavin Ashworth.)

Like the aforementioned French chairs, the bureau bookcase and bookstand were physical manifestations of the Lloyd family's wealth and taste. Edward IV moved both objects from Annapolis to Wye House, and his widow left them there when she returned to live in their townhouse. Later inventories and photographs of Wye indicate that during most of the nineteenth century, the bureau bookcase stood either in the "withdrawing room" to the left of the front door or in the "passage." Edward V may have used this case piece primarily for display after receiving the desk-and-bookcase he ordered from Annapolis cabinetmaker John Shaw (1745–1829) in 1797 (fig. 28). Shaw made the latter example specifically to fit between the windows of the office to the right of the front door. It is forty-one inches wide, a dimension narrow in proportion to the overall height. Although Shaw used one of his shop patterns to lay out the pierced tympanum, he reduced the width to accommodate his patron's specifications. This resulted in a somewhat awkward juncture of the cornice and scroll moldings (fig. 29).[32]

From the late eighteenth century to the early nineteenth century, the Shaw desk-and-bookcase functioned as the nucleus of business at Wye House. During that period, each proprietor used the desk for corresponding and record keeping, as indicated by the words "Bills" and "Receipts" written on two of the pigeonhole valances. Later members of the Lloyd family preserved the desk-and-bookcase as an heirloom and as an example of the refined work of an important Annapolis cabinetmaker. Shaw's illustrious reputation emanated not only from his skill, but also from his frequent use of labels, a practice that ensured his notoriety among early antiquarians and regional historians.[33]

Few objects purchased by Edward IV and preserved by his progeny have received attention from decorative arts scholars. Between 1770 and 1788, Edward IV ordered a relatively restrained pair of London neoclassical card tables (see fig. 30) for his Annapolis townhouse. Although the light and

Figure 30 Card table, London, ca. 1772. Mahogany, satinwood and mahogany veneer, ebony and other unidentified inlays with beech and an unidentified soft wood. H. 29½", W. 35¾", D. 16¾". This table is one of a pair remaining in Wye House. (Photo, Gavin Ashworth.)

dark inlays and flat surfaces of these tables contrast with the asymmetrical carving and sweeping curves of the bureau bookcase and bookstand that Edward IV received from his father (see figs. 24, 25), these stylistically disparate forms complemented the interior architecture of the younger Lloyd's townhouse. Most of the period carving in Edward IV's townhouse is rococo, but the plaster ornaments made and installed by John Rawlings and James Barnes are predominantly neoclassical. These two London emigrés received £603.1.6½ for their work, which was one the earliest expressions of neoclassicism in the colonies.[34]

The card tables stayed in fashion during the decade following Edward IV's death. His 1796 inventory lists "2 elegant fincerd card tables" valued at £21. Both remained at the Annapolis townhouse in the same room as the French chairs (see fig. 23) until Elizabeth Tayloe Lloyd's death in 1825 and were among the furniture Edward V chose to keep and return to Wye House.[35]

Like his father, Edward IV clearly imported most of his formal furniture from London. Both men sold their agricultural products in England, thus a good deal of their wealth was based there. Although most of the surviving furnishings associated with Edward III and Edward IV are British, the sheer quantity of furniture listed in their inventories indicate that they also patronized American artisans. Edward IV probably purchased a higher percentage of American-made objects than his father. The younger Lloyd was the first proprietor to exploit the colonial market by selling tobacco and grain in Annapolis beginning in 1770 and eventually adding Baltimore by the late 1770s as it eclipsed the capitol in economic, social, and cultural importance.

Figure 31 Shaving table, probably Annapolis, Maryland, ca. 1777. Mahogany with tulip poplar and yellow pine. H. 29¼", W. 19¾", D. 19¾". (Photo, Gavin Ashworth.)

Figure 32 Writing table, probably Annapolis, Maryland, ca. 1773. Mahogany with tulip poplar and yellow pine. H. 33", W. 36", D. 17½". (Photo, Gavin Ashworth.)

The shaving table illustrated in figure 31 may be from the shop of Archibald Chisholm, an Annapolis cabinetmaker patronized by Edward IV during the late 1770s, when he and Elizabeth lived in town. Were it not for its yellow pine and tulip poplar secondary woods, this object could easily be mistaken for a British shaving table from the 1760s or 1770s. Chisholm immigrated to Annapolis in the early 1760s and may have trained fellow Scot John Shaw, with whom he formed a partnership in 1772. Although no documented furniture by Chisholm is known, it is likely that he introduced some of the urban British designs and construction details now associated with Shaw's work. The shaving table and two chamber stands remained in use in Wye House until Charles Howard Lloyd installed plumbing in 1917. Clearly, these objects survived because they were useful.

The same can be said of the writing table shown in figure 32, which later generations of the Lloyd family used for storing silver flatware. Edward IV's inventory lists a "mahogany writing table with six drawers" valued at £4.10 between a "Mahogany [bureau] with glass doors and bookcase a little out of repair . . . £25" (fig. 24) and a "reading table stand" valued at £4.10 (fig. 25). The sequence of entries suggests that this relatively simple writing table stood in the same room with two overtly rococo forms. Although this may seem unusual from a modern perspective, eighteenth-century patrons often combined the lavish with the simple. Many wealthy patrons from the Chesapeake Bay region ordered "neat and plain" furniture from British merchants as well as from local tradesmen. The "neat and plain" style is best understood as restrained, structurally sound, and correct in proportion and adaptation of classical detail. Even leading British designers like Thomas Chippendale illustrated and produced forms in this mode.

Figure 33   Desk, Eastern Shore or Annapolis vicinity of Maryland, 1765–1780. Walnut with yellow pine. H. 38", W. 35½", D. 18½". (Photo, Gavin Ashworth.)

Figure 34   Side chair, England, ca. 1792. Mahogany with beech. H. 35½", W. 21", D. 19". (Photo, Gavin Ashworth.) During the late eighteenth and early nineteenth centuries, Baltimore chair makers produced their own version of this splat design. Imported chairs like those ordered by Edward Lloyd IV probably influenced local production.

Edward IV's inventory also listed several walnut desks. A Maryland example (fig. 33) in Wye House probably dates from his proprietorship and relates to other desks found on the Eastern Shore. Although the Lloyd desk could have been made on the Eastern Shore, it is also possible that Edward IV purchased it from a cabinetmaker in the Annapolis area and subsequently brought it to Wye. With its old-fashioned interior, this desk would most likely have served as "backstairs furniture." Edward IV's brother-in-law, John Cadwalader, commissioned simple walnut furniture from Philadelphia cabinetmaker William Savery for secondary spaces in his townhouse. The Lloyd desk fits perfectly in a small niche in a second floor bedroom once occupied by several members of the Wye House community, in particular a children's tutor. Edward IV's gardener, whom they brought over from England, may also have used the desk. It has resided in the same bedroom for more than a century.[36]

Beginning in the 1790s, Edward and Elizabeth became much more active in furnishing Wye House. In orders placed with their London agents, Edward specified furniture "procured of the best and most fashionable Materials." Correspondence survives for several large orders, six in 1791, six in 1792, and one in 1793. On August 6, 1791, he requested that Thomas Eden send a variety of foodstuffs, medicines, furnishings, and objects and animals associated with the leisurely activities of a wealthy planter:

22   ALEXANDRA ALEVIZATOS KIRTLEY

2 best Pastelion Velvet Caps wth Gold Band and Tassels
14 handsome Mahogany Chairs for a Dining Room Covered wth the best black Morocco leather. NB. two of these chairs to be Armed Chairs
Small Skiff wth two sets of Oars and Rudder to the Skiff. See Capt. Dunnes as to this Boat
2 dozen Sets of the best Guitar Strings
The Works in English of Emmanuel Swedenburg
2 d^oz. Hills Pictorial Balsome
2 d^o. Papers of Dr. James's Powders—NB None must be sent but that are Warranted genuine
2 dozen finest handsome coloured bordered Cambric Hankerchiefs
2 Pieces of Cambric cash Sterling 3 Pr Yds
2 D^o finest Linen Cash Sterling   4/ Yard
2 D^o   D^o   D^o   "   5/ P^r d^o
100 Wt. of best and Choicist Pickle Beef
2 Dozen best   d^o   d^o   Tongues
1 Pot Bird Lime
1 Puk of fresh Canary Bird Seed and graval d^o d^o d^o
4 Canary Birds Paired
a small Collection of the best English Birds
1 double Gloucester Cheese}
1 d^o Cheshire   D}   Send none but of the finest Quality
12 dozen finest old Porter in Casks of four dozen each well Secured NB. Attend to this Porters being of the best Quality
2 Thorough broke springing Spaniel Dogs—NB They must be under perfect Command as none others will do ~ Collars with my Name Must be sent with them.
a handsome fashionable Mahogany Settee covered with the black Morocco leather six feet long and the width in Proportion—with two cushions or Pillows at each end of black Morocco leather to suit the 14 chairs ordered above—NB. The Pillows to be filled with the Softist and finist Materials, the Settee and bottoms of the Chairs Neatly Stuffed with the best Curled hair and it is hoped that Particular Attention will be paid in executing this Order as will the whole of the above Articles inclosed in this Invoice
2 Chests of the finist Sweet Oranges from Lisbon well and securely put up
½ dozen dog Leather Collars Strongly fitted for Padlocks with my Name Thereon
½ dozen good Strong Padlocks and Keys for d^o [37]

Figure 35 Side chair by Potthast Bros., Baltimore, Maryland, ca. 1917. Mahogany. H. 40", W. 24", D. 19". (Photo, Gavin Ashworth.)

When Edward VIII conceded his birthright and sold Wye to Charles Howard Lloyd in 1906, he took the dining room chairs ordered from Eden (see fig. 34). Charles replaced the twelve English neoclassical side chairs with two sets of six chairs (fig. 35) made by Potthast Brothers (active 1892 to 1975) of Baltimore. The Potthast chairs were based on a Philadelphia example from the 1760s formerly in the collection of Dr. William Crim, a famous Baltimore antiquarian. This model, commonly referred to as the "Crim chair," was the most popular reproduction in the Potthast's line. Not only were these Potthast chairs sturdier than the neoclassical ones they replaced, they were, in the eyes of Charles Howard Lloyd, more "colonial."[38]

Numerous sets of six or more chairs are listed in Edward IV's inventory, and while the set of twelve armchairs and one of the sets of dining chairs with morocco leather seats survives, parts of others were also preserved. Charles Howard Lloyd paid Baltimore furniture restorers J. W. Berry &

Figure 36 Armchair, England, ca. 1795, modified by J. W. Berry & Sons of Baltimore, Maryland, ca. 1920. Mahogany. H. 37½", W. 22", D. 20". (Photo, Gavin Ashworth.)

Sons to modify several English chairs from Wye House for his daughter, Elizabeth Lloyd Schiller. One chair from an altered set has period arms, arm supports, legs, and stretchers. Its twentieth-century upholstered back and seat suggest that J. W. Berry & Sons replaced a damaged back and the seat rails with components that were more comfortable to modern sitters (fig. 36). An insurance inventory taken by Elizabeth Lloyd Schiller in 1948 describes the chairs as "made into usable chairs by Berry & Sons in 1920."[39]

Other furnishings imported by Edward IV and Elizabeth fared better over the years. On January 17, 1792, they placed an order with Oxley Hancock & Co. of London that included a large quantity of furniture, clothing, and foodstuffs:

> 1 Handsome Mahogany Bedstead and Cotton Furniture Compleat of a drab or dark Coloured ground. The Cornice to be Painted Wood with two Window Curtains to D⁰ The Chamber about 13 feet Pitch ready fixt with Cornice Pr" Pr" Pr" to the Window Curtains . . . }
> 1 Bed Bunt Bolster and two Pillows to fit this Bedstead.
> 1 Mattrass for D⁰ of the best Materials: ~
> 1 Pair of the best and Softist Blankets for D⁰—NB. Send those Blankets of Extraordinary quality
> 1 best Counterpane for—D⁰ ~ ~
> 1 Dressing Table. D⁰ Glass with drawers wᵗʰ best Locks & Keys to D⁰ ~
> 1½ dozen Strong Mahogany Chairs to D⁰
> 1½ dozen Cotton Covers for the Chairs to suit the Bed furniture & to take off and on—NB. Send as much of the Cotton as will cover a Chair seat & back} about 10 Yards with trimmings will be sufficient}
> 2 Chamber dressing Table Glass's wᵗʰ drawers
> a Handsome Mahogany Side Board Table Complete in every Respect
> a Sett of fashionable Elegant Ornaments to Place over Mantel of a Chimney Piece to Cost about 20 Guineas
> 1 ditto ditto to Cost about 6 Guineas
> Fashionable Ornamental decoration to set off a Dining or Supper Table, that will accomodate 20 People wᵗʰ a Sketch of the Table with the Images Pr" Pr" Pr" thereon Plain and full Directions showing how the Ornaments are to be Placed there—NB. These decorations not to exceed 100 Guineas

The sideboard table listed above does not survive, but a five-part plateau and twelve classical figures "to set off a Dining or Supper table" remain part of the Wye House furnishings (fig. 37). Described in Edward IV's inventory as "1 Case with silver and glass Ornaments for a Table & 29 Alabaster Images . . . £75," these objects show how he and his family emulated the most sophisticated European dining fashions. Throughout the nineteenth and twentieth centuries, various members of the Lloyd family continued to use these decorations like their ancestors, arranging the figures to depict scenes from classical mythology.[40]

Figure 37 Silver and glass plateau by William Pitts and Joseph Preedy with alabaster figures, London, 1792–1793. (Photo, Gavin Ashworth.) The three sections shown here are 52" long. With the two missing sections in place, the plateau measures 89½".

Figure 38 Chest of drawers, England, ca. 1790. Mahogany and light wood inlay with oak and an unidentified soft wood. H. 35", W. 37", D. 22". (Photo, Gavin Ashworth.)

A chest of drawers with a linen slide under the top (fig. 38) may be the "dressing table" that Edward and Elizabeth purchased from Oxley Hancock & Co. in 1792. George Hepplewhite illustrated "dressing drawers" with linen slides and French feet in the first edition of *The Cabinet-Maker and Upholsterer's Guide* (1788), but all of his designs included "a top drawer [with compartments for]...the necessary...equipage." Edward IV's inventory lists "1 mahogany dressing table with drawers inlaid" valued at £8.15; however, he may have owned more than one example since Oxley Hancock & Co. furnished him with "2 Chamber dressing Table Glass's wth drawers."[41]

In April 1792, Edward IV instructed Thomas Eden to send "Broderips finest tuned Organized Pianoforte," an expensive instrument and a conspicuous symbol of wealth and refinement. Valued in the proprietor's inventory at £75 with its music and chair, the piano survived until the twentieth century. Along with the piano, he requested a subscription:

> For Boydells Prints of Shakespeare which have handsomely framed in Glass and forwarded as Published ~ Send also a Collection of the best Coloured and most approved Prints in elegant frames sufficient for a Withdrawing Room of about 20 feet square ~ It is particularly requested that some person of Judgement be employed in Selecting this Collection as none but the most pleasing and best impressions will answer ~ NB. Coloured Prints are Meant those that have a variety of Tints in the same Print in Water Colors.

Both Edward IV and V ordered several sets of the Boydell brothers' immensely popular prints. Ten prints depicting scenes from Shakespeare's plays survive in their original gilt and paper lined frames, including one from Edward IV's 1792 order (figs. 39, 40), whereas portfolios of loose prints remained in a large pine bookcase in the library at Wye House until the early twentieth century. Loose and framed prints are listed in the inventories of several members of the Lloyd family taken during the nineteenth century, and some are visible in late nineteenth- and early twentieth-century photographs of Wye House.[42]

Figure 39 John and Josiah Boydell, *Richard III Act V Scene II*, London ca. 1792. Etching and engraving on wove paper. Frame dimensions: 22½" x 30½". (Photo, Gavin Ashworth.)

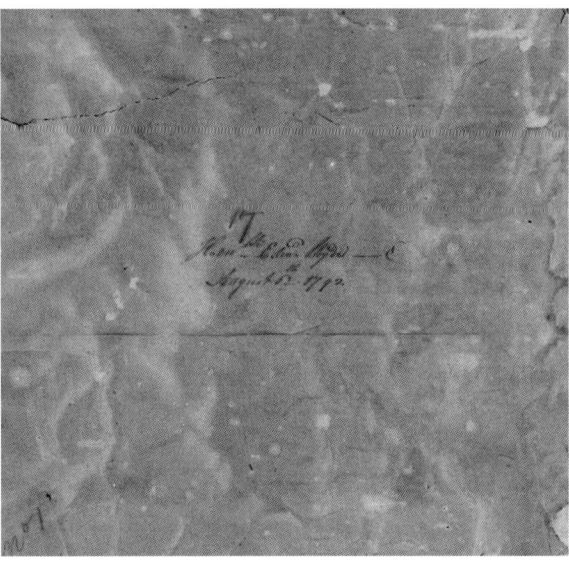

Figure 40 Detail of the back of the print illustrated in fig. 39. The inscription indicates that the print was part of a shipment to Edward Lloyd IV.

Figure 41   Balls for lawn bowling, England, 1785–1800. (Photo, Gavin Ashworth.)

Although Edward IV and Elizabeth were diligent in their efforts to build and furnish Wye, they found ample time to indulge their passion for formal gardening and outdoor leisure activities. Edward, for example, owned several sporting guns and pistols, badminton shuttle cocks, backgammon boards, lawn bowling balls, and a barn full of race horses that he imported from England and raced in Annapolis and at his own track along the Wye River. In 1792, he ordered from Thomas Eden:

> a Marquis Sufficiently large to hold a dozen People and . . . [private] appartments for lodging sufficient for half a dozen People ~ Bedsteads and Beding Complete in every article Tables and Seats to accommodate a dozen People all of which to be so constructed as to be capable of packing up into as Small a Compass as Possible ~ it is intended to be used occassionally on Fishing Parties on the Shores of the Chesapeake Bay.

Out of all of Edward IV's sporting equipment, only a few guns and the lawn balls (fig. 41), rolled on the green between the house and the greenhouse, survive.[43]

For Edward III, IV, and V the pursuit of leisure activities was a sign of refinement, gentility, and an enlightened mind—qualities the Lloyds were bred to possess and those that helped propel them to their social and political positions. The family's private graveyard (figs. 42, 43) and greenhouse

Figure 42   View of the graveyard at Wye. (Photo, Gavin Ashworth.)

Figure 43   View of the graveyard at Wye. (Photo, Gavin Ashworth.)

(fig. 44) define the boundaries of the garden, which evolved during the proprietorships of the aforementioned men. In the 1740s, Edward III built the central pavilion of the greenhouse, oriented on the north–south axis of the Wye House he built and his son later razed. Edward IV enlarged the greenhouse in 1786, when he paid William Eaton £148 for "repairing the G House and adding hot house wings." The wings (or furnaces) kept his fruit trees warm during the winter.[44]

Although the greenhouse remained in use for decades, it eventually housed one of the most expensive and important pieces of furniture that

Figure 44 Greenhouse at Wye, Talbot County, Maryland, 1740s and 1786. (Photo, Gavin Ashworth.)

Figure 45 Billiard table by John Shaw, Annapolis, Maryland, ca. 1800. Mahogany and light and dark inlays with tulip poplar and yellow pine. H. 38", L. 139½", W. 72¾". (Courtesy, Winterthur Museum.)

descended in the Lloyd family—a billiard table that Edward V purchased from John Shaw for $150 on December 29, 1800 (fig. 45). Two weeks later the young proprietor paid Baltimore merchant James P. Maynard for balls and cue sticks—the first and only set that accompanied the table. This costly sporting equipage suited the lifestyle of Edward V, whose orders to London in the early years of his proprietorship included sterling silver cock spurs and "a fashionable sattin cloak with silver bear or any other most fashionable fur with a muff and toppet to suit."[45]

The billiard table also speaks to the genteel tradition of gambling—a pastime at which all of the Lloyds excelled. In 1777, John Adams (1735–1826) described Maryland as a place where "planters and Farmers . . . hold their Negroes . . . Convicts . . . [and] laboring People and Tradesmen, in such Contempt, that they think themselves a distinct order of Beings. Hence they never will suffer their Sons to labour, or learn any Trade, but they bring them up in Idleness or what is worse in Horse Racing, Cock fighting, and Card Playing." Although Adams' comments seem harsh, Chesapeake planters were imminently conscious of their place in society. Unrestrained by the prudish attitudes maintained by many of their northern counterparts, the scions of the elite participated in all sorts of gambling activities. In fact, gambling was so ingrained in Edward V's lifestyle that he kept records of his opponents' scores and registered the winnings from his billiard games in his ledgers as legitimate income.[46]

Billiard tables were present in the homes of other wealthy Americans in the early nineteenth century, but no example comparable to Edward V's is known, much less one commissioned for use in a greenhouse. The fact that the billiard table was located there—away from the center of activity—during the nineteenth and early twentieth centuries may have contributed to its survival. By 1861, it had fallen into disrepair. Edward VI's inventory taken in that year valued the billiard table at only $5. Later generations of Lloyd children, many of whom inscribed their names on the window surrounds and panes of the greenhouse, reminisced about playing underneath the relic. The table remained in the greenhouse until 1958 when Elizabeth Lloyd Schiller decided that the microclimate was destroying it and that it would never be restored. When Henry Francis du Pont, founder of the Winterthur Museum, expressed his interest in purchasing the table, Elizabeth Schiller negotiated for the return of Charles Willson Peale's painting of Edward Lloyd IV and his family (fig. 3). The painting had descended to Edward's daughter Anne (Lloyd) Lowndes (1769–1840), whose great, great grandson sold it to du Pont in the 1940s. Although du Pont refused to sell the original, he acquired the billiard table for cash and commissioned a copy of the painting (fig. 46) from Jonathan Fairbanks, at that time a student in the Winterthur Program in Early American Culture. To

Figure 46 Jonathan Fairbanks after Charles Willson Peale, *The Edward Lloyd Family*, 1959. Oil on canvas. 43¾" x 52". (Photo, Gavin Ashworth.)

Figure 47 John Beale Bordley (1800–1882), *Governor Edward Lloyd V*, Maryland, 1828. Oil on canvas. 28¾" x 23¾". (Photo, Gavin Ashworth.)

prevent Fairbanks' painting from being confused with the original, the reproduction is eleven inches narrower and thirteen inches shorter. Much to the pleasure of Mrs. Schiller and her descendants, the copy is deceivingly fine and lends an air of ancestral presence to the interiors of Wye House. Other paintings that survive at Wye House include a Benjamin West portrait of Richard Bennett Lloyd (fig. 4) and four Dominc Serres marine paintings dated 1776.[47]

Edward V: Patriarch and Agriculturist

At the death of his father in 1796, seventeen-year-old Edward V (fig. 47) inherited over 20,000 acres of land, 320 slaves, the Annapolis townhouse, Wye House, and part of the furnishings of both residences. As the new family patriarch, Edward V also assumed responsibility for his mother and two unmarried sisters, Elizabeth (1774–1849) and Mary (1784–1859). Elizabeth subsequently married Henry Hall Harwood (1774–1839), and Mary married Francis Scott Key (1779–1843). On October 30, 1797, Edward V married Sarah (Sally) Scott Murray (1775–1854) of Annapolis, and fourteen months later the couple had their first child, Edward VI. During the same time frame, Edward V sold nearly £11,000 worth of his father's household furnishings and undertook a major redecoration of Wye House.

Edward V was a celebrated equestrian, the youngest man ever elected Governor of Maryland (1809–1811), and a United States congressman (1805–1809) and senator (1819–1826). More than twice as much furniture survives from his proprietorship than that of his father and grandfather. Because the industrial revolution fostered an economy less conducive to slave-based wheat farming, Edward V left his son and six siblings an estate that was proportionally smaller than those received by earlier proprietors. Consequently, Edward VI did less redecorating and continued to use a large percentage of the furnishings acquired by his father along with the heirlooms of earlier generations. In 1836, Edward VI's wife died prematurely, and his mother Sally resumed the role of proprietress. Sally was less inclined to make drastic changes to the home she and her husband had made, and she lived in Wye House until her death in 1854. By the time Edward VI died in 1861, the plantation economy that had fueled the Lloyd family's lifestyle was one month away from its demise. In the wake of Edward VI's death, his descendants' concern about the consequences of the impending war eclipsed any desire to sell furnishings and redecorate.[48]

No public inventory of Edward V's estate is known. A September 19, 1834, notation in the docket book of the Register of Wills for Talbot County stated that Edward V's administrators posted a $500,000 bond in lieu of paying the taxes due on his estate and that "No inventory is to be returned in this case." A small, private inventory of Wye House taken about 1834 describes some of the objects he owned, but it is skeletal at best.[49]

Unlike his ancestors, Edward V conducted most of his business in Baltimore, a city with a thriving cabinetmaking community capable of producing furniture that rivaled the finest imported wares. Edward V only purchased from London those items he deemed unobtainable from American craftsmen—silver cutlery, silk hose, shoes, certain flower seeds, subscriptions to Boydell's Shakespeare prints, and the three crystal girandoles mentioned earlier.[50]

Because neoclassicism was popular during the proprietorships of Edward IV and Edward V, it is often difficult to determine who was the original owner of certain pieces in that style. Nevertheless, the neoclassical furniture in Wye House documents the Lloyds' patronage of Maryland artisans and the family's retention and appreciation of these objects as heirlooms. A mahogany secretary (fig. 48), or "bureau" as the form was called in Edward IV's inventory, is part of a group of related Baltimore examples that mimic

Figure 48 Secretary, Baltimore, Maryland, 1790–1800. Mahogany and light and dark wood inlays with yellow pine, tulip poplar, and white pine. H. 43", W. 42", D. 22". (Photo, Gavin Ashworth.)

Figure 49 Clothes press, probably by James Martin, Baltimore, Maryland, 1797. Mahogany with tulip poplar and white pine. H. 82½", W. 53¾", D. 24". (Photo, Gavin Ashworth.)

contemporary English furniture. This object may have been used by the many scribes, accountants, and clerks that Edward IV and V hired to manage their accounts, ledgers, and correspondence. The secretary stood in the office opposite the Shaw desk-and-bookcase (fig. 28) during the nineteenth and twentieth centuries. Most recently, the secretary stored seventeenth-century maps and deeds.[51]

In 1797, Edward V began redecorating Wye House by purchasing vast quantities of textiles from Annapolis merchant Lewis Neth and commissioning a new desk-and-bookcase from John Shaw. Shortly thereafter, Edward paid Baltimore cabinetmaker James Martin (active 1790–1816) £22.12.6 for "a mahogany clothes press" (fig. 49). Unable to closet all their clothing, table linens, and bedding, presses and wardrobes were an essential part of the Lloyds' furnishings. Seven examples of this form survive at Wye House, but this is the only one from the eighteenth century. Because of the broad width of the case, the cabinetmaker used central muntins to support the bottoms of the linen trays and two lower drawers. This technique made the drawer frames more rigid, allowed the bottom boards to expand and contract seasonally, and enabled the drawers and trays to support more weight without sagging or coming apart. Richard Folwell's *The Philadelphia Cabinet and Chair-Maker's Book of Prices* (1796) lists a clothes press at £4, less than a quarter of the cost of the Lloyd example. The expensive mottled mahogany of the latter object and Maryland's inflated currency probably account for much of the price difference.[52]

Several card tables in Wye House are roughly contemporary with the clothes press. Circular tables like the one illustrated in figure 50 were pop-

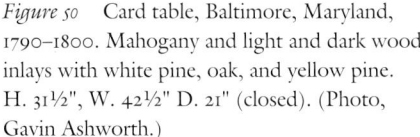

Figure 50 Card table, Baltimore, Maryland, 1790–1800. Mahogany and light and dark wood inlays with white pine, oak, and yellow pine. H. 31½", W. 42½" D. 21" (closed). (Photo, Gavin Ashworth.)

Figure 51 Card table, Baltimore Maryland, 1790–1800. Mahogany and light and dark wood inlays with white pine, oak, and tulip poplar. H. 29½", W. 36", D. 18" (closed). (Photo, Gavin Ashworth.) One of the inlay woods is Botany Bay oak, an exotic from Australia.

Figure 52 Armchair attributed to William Singleton (active 1790–1803), Baltimore, Maryland, ca. 1800. Mahogany and light wood inlays with tulip poplar, ash, and maple. H. 38", W. 21", D. 19". (Courtesy, Colonial Williamsburg Foundation.)

ular in Baltimore during the late eighteenth and early nineteenth centuries, although the Lloyd example is unusually wide—a trait more in keeping with British work. The original top must have been lost or severely damaged, for in September 1930 Elizabeth Lloyd Schiller paid the exorbitant sum of $198.90 to have it restored and fitted with a new top made of old wood. The fact that the table survived in its dilapidated state is significant, since most families discarded damaged relics.

Another card table from the same era has a square top with an elliptical front (fig. 51). It is distinguished by having a secret drawer concealed on the straight section of the front rail adjacent to right leg. Of the seven card tables listed on Edward IV's 1796 inventory and the untold number purchased by Edward V, a pair of English card tables and these two Baltimore examples are all of the neoclassical pieces that remain in Wye House. Given the number of tables the Lloyds acquired throughout the nineteenth century, that level of survival is remarkable.[53]

Only one armchair (see fig. 52) remains from the set (ten sides and two arms) Edward V purchased from Baltimore cabinetmaker William Singleton for $108 in 1801. The Lloyds used these seating forms as occasional chairs during the last half of the nineteenth century because they were no longer fashionable. The splat, which is almost identical to those on chairs made by Gillows & Co. of Lancaster, England, has an inherent weakness that likely contributed to the loss of other chairs from the set. After this example had broken several times, Elizabeth Lloyd Schiller gave it to Baltimore furniture restorer Harry Berry in exchange for work.[54]

In 1808, Edward V paid Baltimore fancy furniture painters John and Hugh Finlay for unspecified work commissioned by his mother. Although Edward V placed six additional orders between 1809 and 1833, only a frag-

Figure 53 Card table with decoration attributed to John and Hugh Finley, Baltimore, Maryland, 1808–1815. Tulip poplar with oak, white pine, and maple. H. 28¾", W. 36", D. 18". (Photo, Gavin Ashworth.)

Figure 54 Cornice by John and Hugh Finley, Baltimore, Maryland, 1828. Tulip poplar. H. 8", L. 59". (Photo, Gavin Ashworth.) The festoon is missing.

ment of a card table (fig. 53) and a window cornice (fig. 54) survive at Wye. Edward V ordered the latter on April 3, 1828. Painted furniture was used indoors and outdoors, and it served as a fashionable and less expensive alternative to comparable mahogany, walnut, maple, and rosewood forms. By the late nineteenth century, neoclassical painted furniture had passed out of fashion, and many pieces had suffered significant losses to the decoration. Given its condition, it is not surprising that the table was relegated to the barn. In fact, it is remarkable that the table survives at all.[55]

Because no original textiles remain in Wye House, the window cornices that Edward V ordered from Hugh Finlay in April 1828 and the card table are the only objects that allude to interior color schemes during the proprietorship of Edward V. The black and gold decoration on the table is sophisticated but restrained when compared to the color palette available on other fancy furniture produced in Baltimore during the 1810s. It is possible that other objects commissioned by Edward V were more vivid. The cornice, for example, has a guilloche with red and green leaves and a frieze with an Etruscan red ground. This somewhat capricious composition is in keeping with the less academic style of classicism prevalent in Baltimore in the late 1820s.

33 LLOYD FAMILY'S FURNITURE LEGACY

Figure 55 End of a three-part dining table attributed to Edward Priestley (active 1801–1837), Baltimore, Maryland, ca. 1812. Mahogany with tulip poplar and oak. H. 28½", W. 56¾", L. 164" (with all sections assembled). (Photo, Gavin Ashworth.)

Edward V returned to Wye House after living in Annapolis while he was governor from 1809 to 1811. In 1812 and 1813, he paid Baltimore cabinetmaker Edward Priestley (1778–1837) a total of $793.87 for furniture. During the 1810s, urban cabinetmakers in Maryland and their patrons began to embrace a later phase of neoclassicism, referred to today as "classical" or "empire." Priestley's furniture replaced many objects purchased for Wye House by Edward V shortly after his father's death. Later generations saved this furniture because it remained functional and relatively stylish, and large-scale household makeovers had become too expensive.[56]

Referred to in inventories as an "extension dining table," the size of the three-pedestal dining table (fig. 55) likely dictated its survival more than its dramatically figured mahogany top. Family tradition maintains that the table accommodated as many as twenty guests when used in the large par-

lor, but that it more often stood in the small parlor with the center section removed and the ends pushed together. Late nineteenth-century photographs show that the sections were used to support the girandoles underneath the pier glasses in the large parlor. In the 1940s, Elizabeth Lloyd Schiller sold the table, which she disliked, to her niece, the current proprietress, who returned it to Wye in the 1990s.[57]

Figure 56 Sofa attributed to Edward Priestley, Baltimore, Maryland, ca. 1812. Mahogany with tulip poplar. H. 35", W. 96", D. 24¼". (Photo, Gavin Ashworth.)

Figure 57   Card table attributed to Edward Priestley, Baltimore, Maryland, ca. 1812. Mahogany with white pine, tulip poplar, oak, and beech. H. 28¾", W. 36", D. 17½". (Photo, Gavin Ashworth.)

In early twentieth-century photographs, the Grecian sofa (fig. 56) and swivel-top card table (fig. 57) attributed to Priestley are pictured in the passage. The word "sofas" on the abbreviated 1834 inventory and the phrase "pair of sofas" in the 1861 inventory suggest that the surviving example had a mate. Similarly, the design of the radiating veneer on the top leaf of the card table suggests that it was one of a pair.[58]

The sideboard Edward V ordered from Priestley does not survive, but it is visible in a circa 1915 photograph (fig. 58). Soon after the picture was taken, Charles Howard Lloyd replaced the sideboard with a nearly identical reproduction made by Potthast Bros. During the colonial revival era,

Figure 58   Circa 1915 photograph showing a sideboard attributed to Edward Priestley, Baltimore, Maryland, 1810–1815. (Photo, Gavin Ashworth.)

Figure 59 Pair of knife vases, England, ca. 1800. Mahogany with oak and an unidentified conifer. H. 29", Diam. 12½". (Photo, Gavin Ashworth.)

Figure 60 Writing table attributed to Edward Priestley, Baltimore, Maryland, 1810–1815. Mahogany with tulip poplar and white pine; blue baize writing surface. H. 36", W. 36", D. 17¾". (Photo, Gavin Ashworth.)

Figure 61 Section of handrailing by Edward Priestley, Baltimore, Maryland, 1826. Mahogany. (Photo, Gavin Ashworth.)

sideboards with tall tapered legs were more popular evocations of the form than those with pedestal ends, but Charles chose to duplicate the family heirloom. As decorative arts scholar Catherine Rogers Arthur has shown, the Potthast firm took pride in reproducing furniture from Maryland's most illustrious families and, given the similarity of the original to the reproduction, it is possible that they copied the Priestley example exactly. In contrast, Charles Howard Lloyd chose to repair the knife vases (fig. 59) that sat on the sideboard rather than discard them. However, the vases were in such deplorable condition that the restorer essentially remade them. Edward IV's meticulous inventory includes knife cases, but does not list knife vases. The examples illustrated here are British and may have been ordered by Edward V after he received two dozen table spoons and dessert spoons (engraved "ELL") from London agent Thomas Eden & Co. in 1798. Knife vases were appropriate for a pedestal sideboard, whereas knife cases often accompanied earlier forms.[59]

A writing table (fig. 60) in Wye House has feet similar to those visible in the photograph of the sideboard. It is one of eight attributed to Priestley's shop, all of which have similar construction features and bear a resemblance to contemporary New England examples. Priestley used the term "portable desks" to describe this form. Like most of the writing tables and desks in Wye House, its survival is attributed to its serviceability and versatility, both of which transcended fashion in some instances. Today the writing desk is used as an occasional table.[60]

Figure 62 Chamber table, Baltimore, Maryland, ca. 1825. Mahogany with cedrella, white pine, and tulip poplar. H. 33", W. 26", D. 22". (Photo, Gavin Ashworth.)

Figure 63 Mantle clock, France, 1810–1820. Bronze, brass, steel, glass, enamel, and silk. H. 14½", W. 11", D. 4¾". (Photo, Gavin Ashworth.)

Like many of his contemporaries, Priestley furnished his clients with architectural components as well as furniture. In September 6, 1826, he billed Edward V $7.60 for two feet of planed mahogany, five unturned mahogany newels, three unturned poplar newels, and "30 feet Mahogany for a Hand Rail." Installed in the central passage at Wye House, Priestley's handrail (fig. 61) undoubtedly replaced an older one. Perhaps the old rail had candle arms that became redundant when Edward V purchased a "passage chandelier" from Baltimore merchant R. A. Campbell. Priestley's handrail is another Lloyd article that, given its proven service, has not required replacement.[61]

Like the shaving table ordered by Edward IV (fig. 31), the chamber table (fig. 62) valued at $15 in his son's private inventory probably survived because it remained useful. The sophisticated design, crisp turnings, and stylish cut glass pulls of the chamber table suggest that it is a Baltimore product but not necessarily by Priestley.[62]

Despite the quantity and significance of household furnishings associated with Edward V, the interior spaces of Wye House do not reflect his taste any more than that of other proprietors. The rooms are an eclectic assemblage of one family's prized and useful possessions. Family members saved, reproduced, and discarded items for a variety of reasons—some shifting from generation to generation. Fashion, sentiment, usefulness, historical importance, economics, and, more recently, the dictums of the colonial revival influenced which objects the Lloyd family saved and how these furnishings were arranged. Today, the rooms scrupulously combine objects of beauty and pride, such as the French mantle clock purchased by Edward V (fig. 63), with objects of comfort and utility, such as common chests of drawers (fig. 64). Like Edward III's silver, the ormolu clock is decorated with implements pertaining to wheat farming, signifying the source of the Lloyds' wealth. The clock has proudly graced the mantle of the small parlor or dining room since Edward V's proprietorship. Like

Figure 64 Chest of drawers, Baltimore, Maryland, 1795–1810. Mahogany with tulip poplar and white pine. H. 39¼", W. 39½", D. 21¼". (Photo, Gavin Ashworth.) This chest is one of four that remain in Wye House.

many French mantle clocks owned by American families, the Lloyd example was reputedly a gift from the Marquis de Lafayette. Although not documented, this history has some credibility since Edward V was the Marquis' official host when he visited Maryland in 1824.[63]

Upon the death of Edward V in 1834, his seven children received equal shares of his land, furnishings, and fortune. One incomplete inventory of Wye House taken before Edward VI moved in probably pertains only to the objects he inherited. Edward VI sold much less of his inheritance than the preceding proprietors. In November 1834, Captain William Powell paid him $228.62 for eighteen mahogany chairs, a sofa, a pair of pistols, an assortment of silver flatware, a silver siphon, bottles and canisters, a balance, a compass, and three cows. The latter's receipt is the only evidence that Edward VI sold household furnishings.[64]

Figure 65 Sideboard table and liquor case by Edward Priestley, Baltimore, Maryland, 1827. Sideboard table: Mahogany with tulip poplar and white pine; Pennsylvania clouded limestone. H. 42¾", W. 62", D. 26¾". Liquor case: Mahogany with tulip poplar and white pine. H. 20¼", W. 26½", D. 17½". (Photo, Gavin Ashworth.) Carved heads like those on the table are illustrated on plate 57 of Thomas Hope's *Household Furniture and Interior Decoration* (1807).

Edward VI: Fine Furnishings and Failing Finances
In 1824, Edward VI married Alicia McBlair (1806–1838) of Baltimore, and moved into Wye Heights, an old Lloyd plantation house specially redesigned for them. Three years later, "Edward Lloyd, Jr.," as he was called during his father's lifetime, purchased a "frame for a marble slab," a liquor case, a mahogany bedstead, a maple bedstead, and mattresses and ticking from Edward Priestley. The pier table and liquor case (fig. 65) became part of the furnishings of the north parlor in Wye House when Edward VI moved there after his father's death in 1834. The two pieces are listed consecutively in the former's 1861 inventory, and photographs indicate that they have remained together ever since:

2 Large Gilt frame Mirrors	20.00
2 Girandoles	5.00
2 Card tables	5.00
12 Arm chairs	12.00

1 Marble slab	5.00
1 Liquor case & bottles	2.00
5 Groups of ornaments	5.00
9 Mantle ornaments	3.00[65]

Edward VI bought most of his furniture from Baltimore cabinetmakers John (fl. 1810–1837) and James (fl. 1818–1848) Williams. He and Alicia paid the brothers nine dollars to make a cradle for their first child Edward VII (1825–1907) in 1825 and $45 for a wardrobe the following year. The wardrobe illustrated in figure 66 may be the one the couple commissioned.

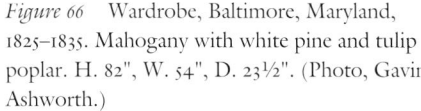

Figure 66 Wardrobe, Baltimore, Maryland, 1825–1835. Mahogany with white pine and tulip poplar. H. 82", W. 54", D. 23½". (Photo, Gavin Ashworth.)

Based on its late neoclassical cornice, thick reeded pilasters, and ring-and-ball turned feet, it appears to date from the mid-1820s. The decorative turned "capitals" are similar to the corner blocks on the window and door surrounds at Wye Heights. This motif is also common on mirror and picture frames, which tend to be highly architectonic.[66]

Five of eight wardrobes remain from those purchased during Edward VI's proprietorship, but existing receipts do not provide enough information to identify them or their makers. Baltimore cabinetmaker Henry Dukehart charged Edward VI $20 for a wardrobe in 1834 and $32 for a comparable example the following year. Two years later Edward VI paid John and James Williams $24 for a maple wardrobe and $50 for a mahogany one. The Lloyds' storage needs must have been considerable. In 1844, he commissioned the Williams brothers to make two more mahogany wardrobes for $45 each.

Figure 67 Wardrobe, Baltimore, Maryland, ca. 1825. Mahogany with white pine and tulip poplar. H. 80", W. 80", D. 20". (Photo, Gavin Ashworth.)

Figure 68 Wardrobe, Baltimore, Maryland, 1835–1845. Mahogany and rosewood inlay with white pine and tulip poplar. H. 86¾", W. 57", D. 21½". (Photo, Gavin Ashworth.)

An Egyptian-inspired winged wardrobe (fig. 67) is the most complex late neoclassical example in Wye House. It consists of three separately dovetailed cases set in a base. The center section has three drawers surmounted by two doors concealing linen trays and a pediment. Flanking this section are wings with tall doors, each having matching veneers in their vertical and horizontal panels. The maker also used the same flitch of veneer for the doors of the center section.[67]

Two later wardrobes are well developed examples of the form and style popularized by Baltimore architect John Hall in *The Cabinetmaker's Assistant* (1840), but one (fig. 68) is far superior to the other (fig. 69). The wardrobe illustrated in figure 68 is solidly built and has high quality mahogany veneers, whereas its gothic counterpart is poorly constructed and has minimally figured wood. The gothic example does have its original finish and is significant in having been part of a bedroom suite, the remainder of which was discarded in the mid-twentieth century.

The most extraordinary wardrobe (fig. 70) remaining in Wye House hails from New Orleans. Beginning in 1837, Edward VI embarked on a speculative venture to cultivate cotton in Louisiana, Arkansas, and Missis-

Figure 69 Wardrobe, Baltimore, Maryland, 1835–1845. Mahogany with white pine, tulip poplar, and white cedar. H. 84½", W. 66¼", D. 21". (Photo, Gavin Ashworth.)

Figure 70 Armoire, probably New Orleans, Louisiana, ca. 1825. Mahogany with cypress, tulip poplar, and white pine. H. 90½", W. 56½", D. 21¾". (Photo, Gavin Ashworth.)

Figure 71 Side chair, possibly by Tweed & Bonnell, New York, 1835–1840. Mahogany. H. 34", W. 18½", D. 18½". (Photo, Gavin Ashworth.)

sippi. He committed his strongest slaves to this enterprise and oversaw their work there until the early 1840s. While in the deep South, Edward VI acquired this early armoire which was among the "Domestics" returned to him from Madison County, Mississippi, by Jonathan H. Duvall Shipping of Baltimore in 1849. Although the armoire is the only object surviving from Edward VI's sojourn, a low post bedstead marked "Edward Lloyd Jr Esq." probably accompanied him during his travels. During the late 1820s and 1830s, he ordered several bedsteads from Baltimore cabinetmakers William Cook, Edwin S. Tarr, and John and James Williams.[68]

When compared with other furniture forms at Wye House, wardrobes survive in a disproportionately large number. The numerous sets of chairs acquired by Edward VI help put this in perspective. Between 1835 and 1840, he purchased 100 cane seat chairs from Richard "Boss" Tweed, a New York City chair maker who had a summer home near Wye House called "The Villa," and his partner Hezekiah W. Bonnell (fig. 71). Only three examples from this order survive and most are in bad condition. Similarly, John and James Williams of Baltimore sold Edward VI twelve mahogany chairs in 1832, of which only two survive. The other furniture he

Figure 72   Sideboard table, Baltimore, Maryland, 1825–1835. Mahogany with tulip poplar, oak, and white pine; marble. H. 40", W. 56", D. 24¾". (Photo, Gavin Ashworth.)

Figure 73   Rocking chair, probably Talbot County, Maryland, 1830–1840. Maple with oak. H. 46", W. 28½", D. 33". (Photo, Gavin Ashworth.)

ordered—center tables, sofas, occasional tables, bedsteads, washstands, window benches, rocking chairs, music chairs, and butler trays—is evident only through bills, receipts, and late nineteenth- and twentieth-century photographs.[69]

The Lloyd proprietors of the colonial revival era chose to keep wardrobes over other furniture forms for several reasons. First, the family continued to require more storage space than the house provided and wardrobes were costly to replace. These massive, durable forms were used in private spaces, thus they were less susceptible to changing tastes than the furnishings of public rooms. In contrast, seating forms and tables were more fragile and more movable; they could easily be divided among siblings or shifted from room to room as needs and fashions changed. The choice to save the wardrobes and discard other furniture from the same period was based largely on pragmatism, a powerful sentiment in molding the interiors of Wye House as they survive today.

The sideboard table illustrated in figure 72 was not included in the 1834 inventories of Wye House, but it was listed in the passage in 1861. While cabinetmakers working in other urban centers often applied gilt stencilled ornament and ormolu mounts to contemporary pier tables, Edward V and VI evidently preferred examples with bold turnings, figured veneers, and restrained carving as did many of their Maryland peers. During the late nineteenth century, the Lloyd table resided in the passage, but by the early twentieth century, it had a less charitable home—the screened-in north porch. In 1997, the current proprietress had the table conserved and moved into the narrow hallway leading to the plantation office.[70]

Like his father who owned numerous mahogany and hickory rocking chairs, Edward VI embraced the nineteenth-century rage for this seating form. In 1833, he bought an expensive upholstered rocking chair from

Figure 74   View of the north side of Wye House. (Photo, Gavin Ashworth.)

Figure 75   Detail of the left arm of the rocking chair illustrated in fig. 73.

Figure 76   Detail of the right arm of the rocking chair illustrated in fig. 73.

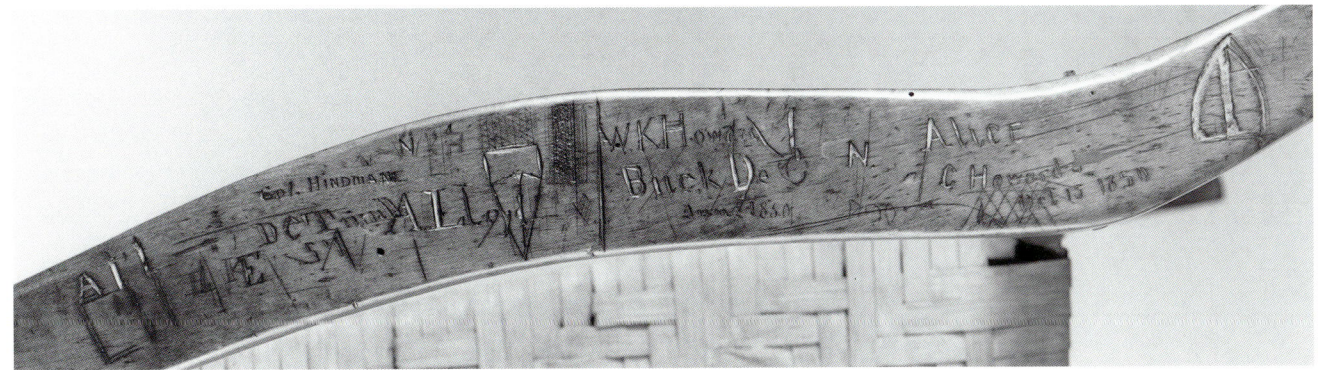

J. Hancock & Co. of Philadelphia. Regrettably, it is not among the furnishings remaining in Wye House. Edward VI purchased a set of at least fifteen rocking chairs (see fig. 73), presumably for use under the north portico (fig. 74), where they appear in late nineteenth-century photographs of Wye House. Most likely the products of a local turner or chair maker, these objects have flat arms carved with dates and the names and initials of at least two generations of Lloyd children (see figs. 75, 76). In the eyes of later family members, this grafitti elevated the chairs from the mundane to the sacred.[71]

43   LLOYD FAMILY'S FURNITURE LEGACY

Figure 77 Bedroom suite, Hart, Ware & Co., probably Baltimore, ca. 1855. (Photo, Gavin Ashworth.) Hart, Ware & Co. maintained warehouses in Philadelphia from 1852 to 1854 and in Baltimore from 1855 to 1859. The suite has painted decoration in imitation of mother-of-pearl.

Because the plantation economy that funded the Lloyd family's lifestyle began to decline during the 1830s, Edward VI spent less money acquiring new furnishings and devoted more attention to repairing old household items. Slaves were no longer utilized, as they had been before, to maintain the furniture and move it as seasons and the number of people living at Wye House changed. From 1834 to 1844, Sally Lloyd hired a handyman named William Ross to put up and take down beds, blinds, and carpets; mend blinds and windows; and repair and polish furniture.[72]

Edward Lloyd VI was powerless over the fact that the extravagant lifestyle to which his family had become accustomed over the past 200 years was slowly coming to close. When he died on the eve of the Civil War, his son made little effort to redecorate Wye House. Only a few objects associated with his proprietorship survive, including a blue painted bedroom suite (fig. 77) that Edward VII purchased when he married Mary Lloyd Howard (1831–1923) in 1851. Mary was still alive when her son Charles Howard Lloyd began refurbishing Wye House in the 1910s and 1920s. By the early twentieth century, her marriage furniture and the room it decorated—known since her marriage as the "blue room"—had acquired a fond aura of bygone years that no Lloyd family member would dare disrupt.[73]

Sparked by the Centennial in 1876, the Lloyds gained renewed appreciation for the history of their nation, state, and family. Rather than acquire new furnishings, Charles Howard Lloyd and his daughter Elizabeth Lloyd Schiller worked throughout the twentieth century to re-fashion Wye House in a style that honored their family. Respect for the Lloyds' historical legacy is equally apparent among family members today. As this article attests, the current proprietress and her children have supported research on the buildings and furnishings at Wye and are devoted to their conservation and preservation.

In the eyes of many, the surname Lloyd in an object's provenance does not immediately evoke prestige. If it does, it usually fails to register like that of Edward IV's brother-in-law John Cadwalader. The fact that John and Elizabeth received only one-third of her father's estate puts Edward III's vast wealth into perspective. Moreover, the silver, bureau bookcase, and pier glasses surviving from his proprietorship eclipse most objects owned by contemporary members of the colonial elite.

The reminiscences of Frederick Douglass (b. 1818, Frederick Augustus Washington Bailey, d. 1895), who belonged to the Lloyds' schooner captain Aaron Anthony and lived at Wye during the proprietorship of Edward V, provide a glimpse, albeit somewhat romantic, of the Lloyd estate during the mid-nineteenth century. Late in life, Douglass visited Wye House as the guest of Charles Howard Lloyd. The former slave described Edward V as "a gentleman of the olden time, elegant in his apparel, dignified in his deportment, a man of few words and weighty presence, and I can easily conceive that no governor of the State of Maryland ever commanded a larger measure of respect." Douglass also described the natural and man-made landscape at Wye in detail:

> There were barns, stables, store-houses and tobacco houses; blacksmiths' shops, wheelwrights' shops and coopers' shops, . . . but above all there stood the grandest building my eyes had ever beheld, called, by every one on the plantation, the "Great House" . . . The great house was surrounded by numerous and variously shaped out-buildings. There were kitchens, wash-houses, dairies, summer-houses, green-houses, hen-houses, turkey-houses, pigeon-houses, and arbors, of many sizes and devices, all neatly painted, and altogether interspersed with grand old trees, ornamental and primitive, which afforded shade in the summer, and imparted to the scene a high degree of stately beauty. The great house itself was a large, white, wooden building, with wings on three sides of it. In front, a large portico, extending the entire length of the building, and supported by a long range of columns, gave to the whole establishment an air of solemn grandeur. It was a treat to my young and gradually opening mind, to behold this elaborate exhibition of wealth, power, and vanity. The carriage entrance to the house was a large gate, more than a quarter of a mile distant from it; the intermediate space was a beautiful lawn, very neatly trimmed, and watched with the greatest care. It was dotted thickly with delightful trees, shrubbery, and flowers. The road, or lane, from the gate to the great house, was richly paved with white pebbles from the beach, and, in its course, formed a complete circle around the beautiful lawn. Carriages going in and retiring from the great house, made the circuit of the lawn, and their passengers were permitted to be-hold a scene of Eden-like beauty. Outside this select inclosure, were parks, where—as about the residences of English nobility—rabbits, deer, and other wild game, might be seen, peering and playing about, with none to molest them or make them afraid. The tops of the stately poplars were often covered with red-winged blackbirds, making all nature vocal with the joyous life and beauty of their wild, warbling notes. These all belonged to me, as well as to Colonel Lloyd, and for a time I greatly enjoyed them.[74]

Although few of the buildings that Douglass recalled still stand, the house, furnishings, and greenhouse provide a window into nearly three centuries of the Lloyd family's past. All of the objects that survive are the result of choices made over and over by individuals with different tastes, aspirations, and attitudes about historical value and family identity. As such, they are more informative and intimate than comparable objects in institutional collections, which are typically associated with an original owner, shop, region, or stylistic period. Like the great country houses of Britain, Wye House and its contents are a rare and valuable resource for present and future scholars.

ACKNOWLEDGMENTS For assistance with this article, the author thanks Gavin Ashworth, Luke Beckerdite, Dennis A. Carr, Joanna Lloyd Garbisch, Roger D. Kirtley, Marion Smith, Joanna Lloyd Tilghman, John A. S. Tilghman, and Beverly W. and Richard C. Tilghman. For her constant encouragement, inspiration, and assistance in the study of the Lloyd family objects, and her devotion to their preservation, the author gives special thanks to Mary Donnell Tilghman.

1. As quoted on <www.newguineaart.com>.

2. Much of the research contained in this article came from Alexandra A. Alevizatos, "'Procured of the best and most Fashionable Materials': The Furniture and Furnishings of the Lloyd Family, 1750–1850" (master's thesis, University of Delaware, 1999). Detailed construction and condition notes for most of the furniture illustrated in this article is in appendix d. Edward Lloyd I was born around 1610, perhaps in Wales or Elizabeth City. He matriculated at Magdalen College, Oxford University on March 16, 1626. His father was also a graduate of Magdalen. Edward I was in Virginia by 1637 and was elected a burgess for Lower Norfolk in 1644. He worked with his brother Cornelius (d. 1654) to establish viable trade routes to serve London merchants and also sought religious freedom as a Quaker. Edward I was excommunicated from the Colony of Virginia for refusing to recite the Apostles' Creed and the Nicene Creed and moved to Maryland in 1648. He founded Provincetown, south of Annapolis, on the Severn River, which he named after the Severn River in Wales. Edward I rose to immediate political, economic, and social prominence, thus initiating what would become a patrimony of Lloyd-dominated politics, economics, and society. The Lloyds quickly abandoned Edward I's Quaker beliefs in favor of the Anglican faith. For more information on Edward I, see <www.ancestry.com>; J. Henry Lea and J. R. Hutchinson, *English Origins of American Colonists* (New York: New York Genealogical and Biographical Record, 1903–1916), p. 10; and George Henry MacKenzie, *Colonial Families of the United States of America*, 7 vols. (Bowie, Md.: Heritage Books, 1912), 2: 454.

3. For more on Edward IV, see <www.ancestry.com>. Edward Lloyd VII to Charles and Mary Lloyd, April 23, 1906, Talbot County, Maryland, Deed of Property Transfer, Land Records, Liber TGW, no. 147, fl. 78. Plumbing was added inside the house in 1917. Confronted with a daunting preservation effort, Elizabeth and Joanna Lloyd toyed with the idea of donating Wye House to the National Trust for Historic Preservation. Instead, Elizabeth and her husband Morgan B. Schiller decided to use the money required to endow Wye House as a National Trust property to make it their permanent home. They added electricity and heat to Wye House in 1949.

4. The author thanks Mary Donnell Tilghman for recounting the oral tradition concerning Charles, Mary, and Elizabeth giving away objects and having reproductions made.

5. For more on Cadwalader, see Nicholas B. Wainwright, *Colonial Grandeur in Philadelphia: The House and Furniture of General John Cadwalader* (Philadelphia: Historical Society of Pennsylvania, 1964).

6. For unexplained reasons but likely as a result of the argument over his estate, the ledgers, purchase orders, and accounts books that would have provided the details about Edward III's business transactions and purchases of furnishings do not survive. The missing ledger of Edward III is referenced in the Lloyd Papers (Maryland Historical Society, hereafter cited MHS) and the Cadwalader Papers (Historical Society of Pennsylvania, hereafter cited HSP)

as "Ledger A." For biographical information on Edward III, see Edward C. Papenfuse, Alan F. Day, David W. Jordan, and Gregory A. Stiverson, *Biographical Dictionary of the Maryland Legislature, 1635–1789* (Baltimore: Johns Hopkins University Press, 1985), p. 535. Will of Edward Lloyd III, signed March 6, 1750 and probated March 26, 1770, ms. 2001, box 14, vol. 5 or reel 25, MHS. The inventories for Edward III, 1770; IV, July 21, 1796; V, after June 1834 (this will be referred to as Edward V's inventory, but it is actually "A List of Articles Left in Wye House Novr 1834"); VI, April 16, 1862; and Elizabeth Tayloe Lloyd, March 29, 1825 (this is actually "A List of Articles belonging to Edward Lloyd [V] Esquire in his House in Annapolis"), ms 2001, reel 40, MHS. Edward III's estate consisted of 43,000 contiguous acres of land in five Maryland counties, 174 slaves, 5 schooners, £10,961.3.7 in household furnishings, £11,462 in bills owed to the estate, and £8,200 in cash (Inventory of the estate of Edward Lloyd III). An entry in the estate ledger notes "By 1 large Blank Book purchased of Mr. Wallace & Co. for his own but afterwards made use of containing Receipts to prevent future claims from Mr. Cadwallader & Capt Lloyd on the Administrator" [Edward Lloyd IV] (Cash Book for the Estate of Edward Lloyd III, August 1776, ms. 2001, box 15, vol. 9, MHS). Despite always suspecting that Edward IV was taking more money from the estate than John Cadwalader felt he was due, the latter enjoyed a close and brotherly relationship with Edward IV, visited him often in Annapolis, and entertained Edward IV and his wife Elizabeth (Tayloe) in Philadelphia. The problems in the division of Edward III's estate persisted beyond the death of John Cadwalader, whose sons by his second marriage continued to claim rights to the Lloyd money (Receipt of Money Paid to Thos. Cadwalader [$137], 1815, ms. 2001, box 57, MHS). Inventory of the Estate of Edward Lloyd III.

7. Inventory of the Estate of Edward Lloyd III.

8. Ibid.

9. Ibid.

10. Ibid. Inventory of the Estate of Edward Lloyd IV. For more on upholstered armchairs, see John T. Kirk, *American Furniture and the British Tradition to 1830* (New York: Alfred A. Knopf, 1982), figs. 1142–46; and Robert F. Trent's entry for catalogue no. 91 in *Portsmouth Furniture: Masterworks from the New Hampshire Seacoast*, edited by Brock Jobe (Hanover, N. H.: University Press of New England for the Society for the Preservation of New England Antiquities, 1993), pp. 335–37.

11. Inventory of the Estate of Edward Lloyd III.

12. Ibid.

13. N. Hudson Moore, *The Old Clock Book* (New York: Frederick A. Stokes, Co., 1911), pp. 227, 259. Inventory of the Estate of Edward Lloyd IV. Photographs at Wye House.

14. Several objects listed in the probate inventory are not in the private inventory; for example, a nine-drawer chest. For the Philadelphia sale, see Edward Lloyd III Estate Ledger, ms. 2001, box 14, vol. 5, MHS. For the Annapolis sale, see Edward Lloyd III Estate Daybook, 1770–1774, box 15, vol. 6, MHS.

15. Inventory of the Estate of Edward Lloyd III. Affleck's bill is reproduced in Wainwright, *Colonial Grandeur*, p. 44. The bill totaled £119.8. The carvers' bills were tallied in a separate column and do not appear to have been included in Affleck's total. John J. McCusker, *How Much Is That in Real Money* (Worcester, Mass.: American Antiquarian Society, 2001), p. 70, table b1.

16. Inventory of the Estate of Edward Lloyd III. The inventories list nearly every silver form imaginable—castors, salts and shovels, wine funnels, dish crosses, teapots, coffeepots, chocolate pots, cups, candlesticks, salvers, tankards, canns, goblets, plates, knives, forks, spoons, and toothpicks. Silver tankards, candlesticks, taper sticks, and candle arms also survive from Edward Lloyd III's proprietorship. When Elizabeth Lloyd married John Cadwalader in 1768, Edward and Anne gave them a five-piece tea set made in London in 1763 (Philadelphia Museum of Art). "Savalls" are pans on candlesticks to save the candle ends. The branch candlesticks probably had the Lloyd coat of arms engraved on them as well. The candle arms do not appear in any inventory of the Cadwalader's townhouse (Wainwright, *Colonial Grandeur*, pp. 52–57, 72–73).

17. Wye Plantation Inventory, 1770, ms. 2001, reel 40, MHS. The tobacco leaf service does not appear on Edward III's private inventory. The term "tobacco leaf" was used in the eighteenth century to refer to this pattern, but it was not used in inventories of the Lloyds until the twentieth century. Charles Howard Lloyd kept two hundred pieces of the tobacco leaf service for himself and dispersed the remainder among his seven siblings in 1907.

18. Edward Lloyd V had a sixty-ton boat with cannons that made a "thunderous report" (Richard Parkinson, *A Tour in America in 1789, 1799, and 1800*, 2 vols. [London, 1805], 1: 230). Admiral Buchanan was the first superintendent of the United States Naval Academy. The Lloyd family donated the land for the Academy to the United States Government in the 1840s. During the Civil War, Admiral Buchanan sided with the Confederacy and captained the USS *Merrimack* in 1861 (Elihu S. Riley, *"The Ancient City": A History of Annapolis in Maryland, 1649–1887* [Annapolis, 1887], pp. 266–67).

19. Richard Bennett Lloyd moved to England in 1773 to purchase a commission in the Cold Stream Guards. In the enlistment book, he was identified as "Gent." He entered as an ensign in 1774 and was painted as the Officer of the Day in the antiquated uniform of 1773 by Benjamin West (fig. 4). As war with America loomed, he resigned his commission in February 1776, having achieved the rank of captain. Richard then began a family with his new wife Joanna Leigh Lloyd, a woman of noted beauty from the Isle of Wight. In fulfillment of his marriage contract, Richard and Joanna moved to France (from 1777 to 1780), where Richard acted as Edward IV's agent and sent them the latest French goods. He and Joanna set up home in Maryland by 1782, but by the time he died in 1787, his estranged wife had returned to England with their four children (Dennis A. Carr, "Carving out a Colonial Identity: The Revolutionary Era Portrait Commissions of Richard Bennett Lloyd," unpublished manuscript submitted for the Yale University History of Art Ph.D. program, spring 2002.). Because of Richard Lloyd's youth and peripatetic nature, most of the silver he inherited was described in Edward III's inventory as "on loan" to Elizabeth and John Cadwalader (Inventory of the Estate of Edward Lloyd III). The furnishings listed in Richard Bennett Lloyd's estate inventory appear to be those he inherited from his father, suggesting that his household goods were stored until he returned to claim them. (Inventory of the Estate of Richard Bennett Lloyd, January 12, 1788, ms. 2001, reel 16 and ms. 721, MHS.) For more on Shrewsbury Farm, see Wainwright, *Colonial Grandeur*, pp. 61, 62, 66–68, 71, 76, 126, 155. Shrewsbury Farm burned in 1812. After Elizabeth died in 1776, John Cadwalader, his second wife, and then a cousin raised Elizabeth's three daughters. Although the daughters' birth right to the furnishings inherited and purchased by John and Elizabeth is noted in the Cadwalader and Lloyd papers, no manuscripts documenting the sisters' receipt of furnishings is known. For more on the wall colors, upholstery and curtain fabrics, and carpets in the Cadwaladers' townhouse, see Wainwright, *Colonial Grandeur*, pp. 30, 31, 40–43, 50–52, 69; and Luke Beckerdite and Leroy Graves, "New Insights on John Cadwalader's Commode-Seat Side Chairs," in *American Furniture,* edited by Luke Beckerdite (Hanover, N. H.: University Press of New England for the Chipstone Foundation, 2000), pp. 160–68, nt 10. For the latest research on the chair illustrated in fig. 15, see Beckerdite and Graves, "New Insights," pp. 152–68.

20. Edward IV's library contained the following architectural design books: Abraham Swan's *A Collection of Designs in Architecture* (1757), Isaac Ware's translation of Andrea Palladio's *The Four Books of Architecture* (1738), a collection of Palladio's designs titled *Architecture, Revised, Designed, and Published by Giacomo Leoni* (1742), and James Gibbs' *Rules for Drawing the Several Parts of Architecture* (1738) (Edwin Wolf II, "The Library of Edward Lloyd IV of Wye House," *Winterthur Portfolio* 5, [1969]: 87–122). All of these books are in the library at Wye along with Edward IV's sterling silver surveying instruments made by E. Nairne of London. The instruments are in their original shagreen case lined with embossed paper and velvet. Ledger of Edward Lloyd IV, 1770-1791, ms. 2001, box 15, vol. 7, MHS.

21. Memoranda Book of Edward Lloyd IV, ms. 2001, box 15, vol. 10, MHS. Inventory of the Estate of Edward Lloyd IV. The information on Gardiner and Eaton is from Ledger of Edward Lloyd IV.

22. List of Goods Sent from Arthur Bryan to Edward Lloyd IV, March 1788, ms. 2001, reel 21, MHS. The pier glasses were valued at £30. Only the mahogany bed, silk bed curtains, window curtains, and six chairs with silk bottoms together added up to more than the pier glasses (Inventory of the Estate of Edward Lloyd III).

23. Microscopy performed by conservator Richard Wolbers in March 1999 revealed that the pier glasses were gilded twice. The earliest strata—gesso followed by bole and gold leaf—are consistent with the water gilding processes commonly used during the eighteenth century. The leaf and areas of the gesso were worn and soiled, obviously from exposure. The later strata—oil, litharge followed by gesso, a yellow, oil-bound layer, gold leaf, and a thin film of oil—are consistent with oil gilding. The author thanks Richard Wolbers for his continual assistance in analyzing materials from Wye House. For comparable designs, see Batty and Thomas Langley, *The Builder's*

Jewell, or Youth's Instructor (1741), pl. 78; and William Jones, *The Gentleman or Builder's Companion* (1739), pls. 43, 45, 47. John Fleming and Hugh Honour, *The Penguin Dictionary of Decorative Arts* (New York: Viking, 1989), p. 375.

24. The author thanks Mary Donnell Tilghman for information on room designations. Receipt from George Dudley documenting major repairs in Wye House and re-hanging the pier glasses, December 6, 1823, ms. 2001, reel 26, MHS.

25. Inventory of the Estate of Edward Lloyd V. Edward V ordered three "pairs" of girandoles from London merchants Thomas Eden, Christopher Court & Co. in 1810, but the firm sent six. Edward V clearly intended for each of his girandoles to have two branches, but the agent understood "pair" to mean two individual girandoles. A nine-year battle ensued during which Edward refused to pay the merchants £800 for the unwanted girandoles. In 1818, Edward V sold three of the six girandoles to Robert Oliver, a prominent merchant of Baltimore, for the dollar equivalent of £1053 (£800 plus £253 in interest) (Debit entry dated September 15, 1818, Account Book of Edward Lloyd V, 1803–1820, facsimile at Wye House). The third girandole survives and matches the two in front of the pier glasses. A note in a box of girandole prisms recently retrieved from the basement stated that the third girandole stood in front of the third pier glass in the large dining room. (The names of the rooms at Wye House varied during different periods of proprietorship and cultural fashion. The large north parlor was occasionally referred to as the "dining room.") In one of the four partial inventories taken after Edward V's death in 1834, "Three large looking Glasses, Gilt Frames" are listed in the large north parlor. The third looking glass does not appear in Edward VI's inventory.

26. Inventory of the Estate of Edward Lloyd III. Ledger of Edward Lloyd IV. The author thanks Mary Donnell Tilghman for the information on Charles and Mary Lloyd selling beds and Elizabeth Schiller rescuing beds.

27. Inventory of the Estate of Edward Lloyd IV.

28. Elizabeth met Edward IV through her father John Tayloe. Both men imported racehorses from the same broker in London (Papenfuse et al., *Biographical Dictionary of the Maryland Legislature,* p. 536). The quote is from a letter written by William Eddis on August 9, 1771 (William Eddis, *Letters from America,* edited by Aubrey C. Land [Cambridge, Mass.: Belknap Press, 1969], p. 57). Edward IV owned a copy of Eddis' *Letters* (Inventory of the Estate of Edward Lloyd IV). Marcia M. Miller, "The Chase-Lloyd House" (master's thesis, George Washington University, 1993). Buckland trained in London and came to Virginia in 1755. He designed Gunston Hall for George Mason and interior woodwork for Mount Airy, the house of John (1721–1779) and Rebecca (1731–1787) Tayloe in Richmond County, Virginia. Edward IV and Elizabeth convinced Buckland to come Annapolis in 1771. For more on Buckland and his Virginia commissions, see Luke Beckerdite, "William Buckland and William Bernard Sears: The Designer and the Carver," *Journal of Early Southern Decorative Arts* 8, no. 2 (November 1982): 6–41. Between the winter of 1771 and his death in 1774, Buckland designed the Lloyd House and the Mathias Hammond House. Buckland's principal carver in Annapolis was Thomas Hall. On December 16, 1773, the *Maryland Gazette* reported: "RAN away from [William Buckland] . . . a servant man named Thomas Hall, a carver by trade . . . . The indenture he signed in London was given up to him and a discharge, after which he executed another indenture by which he was to be allowed in consideration of his former service, wages after the rate of ten shillings per week till the time of his expiration, which would have been in September next." This suggests that Hall signed an indenture with Edward IV to pay for his passage. For more on Buckland and his Maryland workforce, see Luke Beckerdite, "William Buckland Reconsidered: Architectural Carving in Chesapeake, Maryland, 1771–1774," *Journal of Early Southern Decorative Arts* 8, no. 2 (November 1982): 45. Letter to Charles Carroll, Barrister, as transcribed in "A Lost Copy-Book of Charles Carroll of Carrollton," *Maryland Historical Magazine* 32, no. 3 (September 1937): 200.

29. Although Buckland designed furniture sympathetic with the woodwork in Gunston Hall and Mount Airy, there is no evidence that he provided furnishings for the Lloyds. For more on the work of Buckland and carver William Bernard Sears, see Luke Beckerdite, "Architect-Designed Furniture in Eighteenth-Century Virginia: The Work of William Buckland and William Bernard Sears," in *American Furniture,* edited by Luke Beckerdite (Hanover, N. H.: University Press of New England for the Chipstone Foundation, 1994), pp. 28–48. See Inventory of Elizabeth Tayloe Lloyd.

30. French chairs are illustrated in several British design books including Thomas Chippendale's *The Gentleman and Cabinet-Maker's Director* (1754, 1755, 1762), William Ince and John

Mayhew's *The Universal System of Houshold Furniture* (1762), Robert Manwaring's *The Cabinet and Chair Maker's Real Friend and Companion* (1762), The Society of Upholsterers' *Genteel Houshold Furniture in the Present Taste* (ca. 1765), and Robert Manwaring's *The Chair Maker's Guide* (1766). The Lloyd chairs (fig. 23) are listed in the inventories of Edward IV, Elizabeth Tayloe Lloyd, and Edward VI. They retain evidence of painted and gilded decoration underneath the upholstery. As with all of the furniture for the Annapolis townhouse, the order for the chairs and settee does not exist. The armchairs were definitely not part of the furnishings of Edward III's Wye House. Receipt for settee from J. and J. Williams, 1844, ms. 2001, box 14, vol. 7, MHS.

31. The bureau bookcase has details similar to those on several plates in Chippendale's *Director*. There is no evidence that the bookcase had an integral central ornament or bust. For more on the carving in the Lloyd's townhouse, see Beckerdite, "William Buckland Reconsidered," pp. 43–51.

32. Ledger entries, letters, notes, receipts for hauling, and miscellaneous documents in the Lloyd papers indicate that furniture moved back and forth from Annapolis to Wye. The desk-and-bookcase had a prospect drawer with a label by John Shaw dated 1797 when it was sent out for conservation in the 1970s. The piece returned without the label.

33. For more on John Shaw, see William Voss Elder III and Lou Bartlett, *John Shaw: Cabinetmaker of Annapolis* (Baltimore: Baltimore Museum of Art, 1983). Possibly owing to his frequent use of labels, Shaw became an icon of Maryland cabinetmaking at an early date. The desk-and-bookcase is consistently referred to as "The Shaw desk-and-bookcase" in twentieth-century inventories of Wye House.

34. Beckerdite, "William Buckland Reconsidered," p. 52.

35. Inventory of the Estate of Edward Lloyd IV. Inventory of the Estate of Elizabeth Tayloe Lloyd.

36. Related desks with blocked interiors appear to have been made in the southern area of eastern Maryland and on the Eastern Shore. A desk very similar to the Lloyd example is in a private collection in New York (the author thanks Sumpter Priddy III for this information). For related work from Virginia's Eastern Shore, see Ronald L. Hurst and Jonathan Prown, *Southern Furniture, 1680–1830, The Colonial Williamsburg Collection* (Williamsburg: Harry N. Abrams, Inc. for the Colonial Williamsburg Foundation, 1997), pp. 429–32.

37. For the orders, see ms. 2001, reel 21, MHS.

38. Several Baltimore chairs have splats similar to those of the English chairs furnished by Thomas Eden (fig. 34), but the American examples do not have overlapping leaves on the stiles. For similar designs, see Thomas Sheraton's *The Cabinetmaker and Upholsterer's Drawing Book* (1793), pl. 36; and George Hepplewhite's *The Cabinet-Maker and Upholsterer's Guide* (1794), pl. 1. The author thanks Mary Donnell Tilghman for the information on Charles Lloyd purchasing the Potthast chairs. For a comprehensive study of the Potthasts, see Catherine Rogers Arthur, "'The True Antiques of Tomorrow:' Furniture by the Potthast Bros. of Baltimore, 1892–1975," in *American Furniture*, edited by Luke Beckerdite (Hanover, N.H.: University Press of New England for the Chipstone Foundation, 2000), pp. 31–58.

39. Photographic inventory dated 1948, Wye House.

40. "Inventory for Goods to be Shipped by Messrs. Oxley, Hancock & Co Merchants London for the use of Edward Lloyd, Wye in Maryland," January 17, 1792, ms. 2001, reel 21, MHS. For unknown reasons, Edward IV sent a duplicate order to Thomas Eden & Co. on the same day. In a letter accompanying the order to Oxley Hancock & Co., Edward IV requested that the proprietors:

> Call [their] . . . attention to the ornaments for a Chimney Piece and particularly to the Ornamental decorations for a dining Table by which is Meant a Glass Mirror with Images . . . which I beg may be exceedingly elegant and by no means Paultry ~ The Price stated in the Invoice is Presumed to be equal to the Order but should it require a farther advance of a few Guineas you are at Liberty to do it - The setting of the Picture answers fully our expectations and it is thought by all that have Seen it very elegant and approve your Caution as to the Price which is equal to what was intended by my Letter- Your taste in this instance has Pleased us so much as to induce an allocation in an order.

Inventory of the Estate of Edward Lloyd IV.

41. Inventory for Goods to be Shipped by Messrs. Oxley, Hancock & Co. *Pictorial History of English Furniture Designs,* compiled by Elizabeth White (Suffolk, Eng.: Antique Collector's

Club, 1990), pp. 249–58. Dressing tables illustrated by Sheraton and Hepplewhite typically have fitted top compartments above a case of drawers on tapered legs. One design for a dressing table shown on plate 53 in Sheraton's *Drawing Book* has a case of drawers above a low skirt on splayed feet like the Lloyd example. Inventory of the Estate of Edward Lloyd IV. "Inventory for Goods to be Shipped by Messrs. Oxley, Hancock & Co."

42. The order for the pianoforte is documented in a letter from Edward Lloyd IV to Messrs. Thomas Eden & Co., April 11, 1792, ms. 2001, reel. 21, MHS. Inventory of Edward Lloyd IV. Receipt from J. & J. Boydell, May 7, 1802, ms. 2001, reel 21, MHS. Edward V apparently ordered more prints than the documents show. In 1804, the Boydells gave him a silver medal for his patronage. The photographs are in the collection at Wye House.

43. Inventory of the Estate of Edward Lloyd IV. Letter from Edward Lloyd IV to Thomas Eden & Co., June 7, 1792, ms. 2001, reel 21, MHS.

44. Henrietta Maria Neale Bennett Lloyd (d. 1697), the wife of the second proprietor Philemon Lloyd (1646–1685), is credited with introducing greenhouses to Wye and to the colonies in general. The central block of the present greenhouse dates from the 1740s, but that structure was not the first greenhouse at Wye. Ledger of Edward Lloyd IV, July 4, 1786, MHS.

45. Account Book of Edward Lloyd V, 1799–1803, facsimile copy at Wye House. The room where the billiard table stood has a considerable amount of base molding, a chair rail, and a chimney surround with carved egg-and-tongue molding. The author thanks Mary McGinn, Thomas Heller, Joseph Kindig, III, and Jenifer Kindig for their thoughts on the woodwork in this room. Account Book of Edward Lloyd V.

46. As quoted in Dickson J. Preston, *Talbot County: A History* (Centerville, Md.: Tidewater Publishers, 1983), p. 86. Ledger of Edward Lloyd V.

47. Inventory of the Estate of Edward Lloyd IV. The construction of the billiard table's playing surface has been characterized as unique among surviving examples, but John Shaw clearly based his design on the "universal table" illustrated on pl. 25 in Sheraton's *Drawing Book*. Winterthur Museum accession file 1958.58. Contrary to recent publications, Charles Willson Peale was a Maryland painter. He did not travel from Philadelphia to Maryland to paint Edward IV's family; rather, he was in Maryland and living at Wye when he executed the work shown in figure 3. He traveled from Maryland to Philadelphia to paint the Cadwaladers (see fig. 5) in 1776. Peale set up a painting room in Philadelphia in 1775 and moved there permanently in 1789. See Edgar B. Richardson, Brooke Hindle, and Lillian B. Miller, *Charles Willson Peale and His World* (New York: Harry N. Abrams, Inc., 1983), p. 50.

48. Alevizatos, "Procured of the best and most Fashionable Materials," pp. 17–21. For information on the objects Edward VI continued to use, see lists at Wye House and lists in ms. 2001, reel 40, MHS.

49. Inventory of the Estate of Edward Lloyd V.

50. Oswald Tilghman, *A History of Talbot County, Maryland, 1661–1861*, 2 vols. (Baltimore: Williams and Wilkins Co., 1925), 2:184–228.

51. See Kirk, *American Furniture and the British Tradition*, p. 181, fig. 496 for a British secretary similar to the Lloyd example.

52. Estate Account with Arthur Bryan, Edward Lloyd IV Estate Accounts, 1797, ms. 2001, reel 21, MHS. Estate Account with James Martin, Edward Lloyd Estate Accounts, ms. 2001, reel 26, MHS. All of the presses and wardrobes listed on Edward IV's inventory are pine or painted. The mahogany press draws primarily on designs for "wardrobes" illustrated on plate 87 in Hepplewhite's *Guide*.

53. Inventory of the Estate of Edward Lloyd IV. The shape of the square table with elliptical front is not commonly associated with Baltimore, but the table has several construction features associated with work from that city: laminated curved front rails, oak rear rails, flush rear leg construction, and a medial brace. An earlier table with an elliptical front is illustrated and discussed in Sumpter Priddy III, J. Michael Flanigan, and Gregory R. Weidman, "The Genesis of Neoclassical Style in Baltimore Furniture" in *American Furniture*, edited by Luke Beckerdite (Hanover, N. H.: University Press of New England for the Chipstone Foundation, 2000), p. 91, fig. 52. For more on American card tables, see Benjamin Hewitt, Patricia E. Kane, and Gerald W. R. Ward, *The Work of Many Hands: Card Tables in Federal America* (New Haven: Yale University Art Gallery, 1982).

54. Hurst and Prown, *Southern Furniture*, pp.121–23. On May 18, 1790, the *Maryland Gazette* reported that Singleton and his partner William McFaddon had just arrived in Baltimore: "from the experience [Singleton] . . . has had in Europe, and different parts of this Continent"

they would be pleased to complete work at their new business on Gay Street." The partnership dissolved in 1795, but Singleton's business thrived. The paterae with green copper-dyed accents may be the type Singleton purchased from Baltimore inlay maker Thomas Barrett, whom Singleton owed money for inlay work when Barrett died in 1800. In his advertisements, Singleton claimed he satisfied orders for making chairs, card tables, fire screens, and chests of drawers, and especially noted his desire to fill orders for those gentry who lived outside of Baltimore. When he died in 1803, Singleton owned a cabinetmaker's book of furniture designs and a subscription to the Baltimore Circulating Library (Inventory of William Singleton, September 28, 1803, pp. 54–57, copy m-1I, Joseph Downs Library, Winterthur Museum, original in Maryland State Archives, Annapolis.) A pair of chairs attributed to Singleton are illustrated and discussed in *Treasures of State: Fine and Decorative Arts in the Diplomatic Reception Rooms of the U.S. Department of State,* edited by Clement C. Conger and Alexandra Rollins (New York: Harry N. Abrams, Inc., 1991), pp. 196-98, no. 108. See also Susan Stuart, "Gillows of Lancaster and London as a Design Source for American Chairs", *Antiques* 155, no. 6 (June 1999): 866–75.

55. Alexandra Alevizatos Kirtley, "New Discoveries in Baltimore Painted Furniture," *The Catalogue of Antiques and Fine Art* 3, no. 2 (Spring 2002): 204–9. Payments to the Finlays are in the following documents: April 20, 1808 ($228.17), Ledger, 1803–1820, Wye House; November 4, 1809 ($10), Ledger, 1803–1820, Wye House; February 7, 1812 ($114.86), Ledger, 1803–1820, Wye House; March 21, 1815 ($24), Ledger, 1803–1820, Wye House; April 3, 1828 ($14.75), receipt, ms. 2001, reel 29, MHS; August 16, 1833 ($10.25), receipt, ms. 2001 reel 30, MHS, and August 9, 1834 ($3.75), Ledger, 1803–1820, Wye House. The table was probably in the order placed by Edward V's mother in 1808 or one of his orders in 1809, 1812, or 1815. The ledger entries for those four dates only record the amounts paid, whereas the entry for 1828 notes that Edward V paid Hugh Finlay $7 for each cornice.

56. See Alexandra Alevizatos Kirtley, "A New Suspect: Baltimore Cabinetmaker Edward Priestley (1778–1837)," in *American Furniture,* edited by Luke Beckerdite (Hanover, N. H.: University Press of New England for the Chipstone Foundation, 2000), pp. 101, 109, 113, 129(n10), 129 (n13), 131(n26), and 131(n34). For more on Priestley's work, see pp. 100–151.

57. Ibid., pp. 113–16.

58. Ibid., pp. 115–17.

59. Ibid., pp. 116–18. Receipt from Robert Ritherdon, July 24, 1798, ms. 2001, reel 21, MHS. See Sheraton, *Drawing Book,* pl. 24.

60. Kirtley, "A New Suspect," pp. 117–18.

61. Ibid., p. 119. The handrail is supported by balusters and newel posts made by William Roney (active 1810–1826), a Baltimore turner who frequently collaborated with Priestley and billed Edward V directly.

62. Inventory of the Estate of Edward Lloyd VII. The Lloyd marble-topped chamber table possesses hallmarks of Baltimore classical furniture, such as wide reeding and the globular turned legs. A table with similarly turned legs (Research file S-15437, Museum of Early Southern Decorative Arts, Winston-Salem, North Carolina) bears the label of John Needles, but because many cabinetmakers purchased legs and other components from turners, it is impossible to attribute the chamber table to him.

63. See J. Thomas Scharf, *The Chronicles of Baltimore* (Baltimore: Turnbull Brothers, 1874), p. 409.

64. Inventory of the Estate of Edward Lloyd V. An inventory of Wye Heights taken before Edward VI moved from there is distinguishable from the Wye House inventory. A third list tabulates those objects that Edward VI purchased from the estate. Receipt, November 1834, ms. 2001, reel 15, MHS.

65. Baltimore architect Robert Cary Long (1800–1849) measured Wye Heights, and Baltimore carpenter Jeremiah L. Boyd (active 1814–1844) transformed it from a derelict old farmhouse to a Greek Revival monument. For documentation of the building of Wye Heights, see Bill of Jeremiah Boyd, July 24, 1827, ms. 2001, reel 27, MHS. Bill from Edward Priestley to Edward Lloyd VI, June 24, 1827, ms. 2001, reel 27, MHS. See also, Kirtley, "A New Suspect," pp. 100, 119–22. Inventory of the Estate of Edward Lloyd VI. During the late 1820s and 1830s, Priestley repaired furniture for Edward V and made a secretary for his daughter Mary, who married William Tilghman Goldsborough.

66. Receipts dated October 7, 1825, and February 23, 1826, ms. 2001, reel 32, MHS. A Baltimore sideboard is incised "J. Williams," possibly for John Williams (Decorative Arts Photographic Collection [hereafter cited DAPC], Winterthur Museum Library, 82.817). John A.

Williams was apprenticed to Baltimore cabinetmaker John Denmead (active 1800–1810) in 1802 and purchased Denmead's shop at 66 South Street in 1810. His brother James became a partner in 1818. Their firm was extremely successful and endured until 1878 despite John's death in 1837 and James' retirement in 1848 (John Henry Hill, "The Furniture Craftsmen of Baltimore, 1783–1823" [master's thesis, University of Delaware, 1967], p. 166.) A table from their shop has a label in Spanish, which suggests they participated in the furniture export trade (DAPC, 84.872). The Ridgely family of Hampton House, Baltimore County, also ordered furniture from the Williams brothers in the late 1830s and 1840s (Hill, "The Furniture Craftsmen of Baltimore," p. 166). Receipt from John and James Williams, September 30, 1837, ms. 2007, box 63, MHS. The wardrobe is related to one illustrated in Edgar G. Miller, Jr., *American Antique Furniture*, 2 vols. (Baltimore: Lord Baltimore Press, 1937), 2: 857; and another labeled by Baltimore cabinetmaker John Needles (active 1814–1852) at the Historical Society of Talbot County. Edward VI did acquire a "bureau and looking glass" from Needles in 1835, but the pervasiveness of such broad styles in the 1830s and the number of itinerant craftsmen working in a shop the size of Needles' limits our ability to attribute the Lloyd wardrobe to him.

67. The design incorporates Egyptian-inspired motifs first published by English furniture designers in Thomas Sheraton's *Cabinet Dictionary* (1803) and Thomas Hope's *Household Furniture and Interior Decoration* (1807). The closest published parallel to the Lloyd press is shown on plate 33 of George Smith, *The Cabinetmaker and Upholsterer's Guide* (1826).

68. Receipt, 1849, ms. 2001, reel 34, MHS. Between 1837 and 1846, Edward VI traveled to and from his lands in the deep South on several occasions. The properties in Louisiana, Arkansas, and Mississippi were advertised for sale in 1852, but he still owned some slaves and land in those states in 1858. Land and Slave Inventories, ms. 2001, reels 15 and 24, MHS. The armoire is part of a group that share creolized French and Spanish features. The elongated reeded legs date this armoire to the early 1820s. For more on Edward VI's venture, see Tilghman, *History of Talbot County*, 2: 210–21.

69. Receipt from Tweed and Bonnell, undated, ms. 2001, box 28, MHS. Receipt from John and James Williams, October 5, 1832, ms. 2001, reel 30, MHS.

70. Partial Inventory of the Estate of Edward Lloyd V. Inventory of Edward Lloyd VI.

71. Ms. 2001, reel 30, MHS. Photographs at Wye House.

72. See miscellaneous receipts from William Ross between 1834 and 1844 and J. B. Mills between 1843 and 1844 in ms. 2001, reels 30–34, MHS.

73. Lloyd family tradition maintains that the blue suite was purchased in Baltimore from Hart Ware & Co., a firm with a wareroom there and in Philadelphia.

74. Frederick Douglass, *My Bondage, My Freedom* (1855; reprint, New York: Arno Press, 1968), pp. 66–68.

Figure 1 Detail of the Milwaukee Art Museum exhibition, *Furniture Fakes from the Chipstone Collection,* February 15, 2002–June 9, 2002. (Photo, Gavin Ashworth). The objects in this vignette are from left to right: Tea table, American, ca. 1958. Mahogany. H. 26½", W. 32¾", D. 22¾"; Tea table, Newport, Rhode Island, 1765–1785. Mahogany. H. 27", W. 23", D. 32" (private collection); Bureau table, Newport, Rhode Island, 1765–1780. Mahogany with white pine, chestnut, and tulip poplar. H. 32½", W. 37", D. 20¾". The tea table on the left is a complete fake inspired by authentic examples like the one in the center. The bureau table is a period example with replaced feet and foot blocks that have been distressed and colored to make them appear original. Both of the fakes were sold as authentic with no major repairs or replacements.

Luke Beckerdite and Alan Miller

Furniture Fakes from the Chipstone Collection

▼ NEARLY EVERY major collection of American furniture assembled during the last century has included objects that were intended to deceive. These pieces run the gamut from authentic furniture forms with carefully masked repairs, replacements, or embellishments to complete fakes. Although the subject of fraudulent objects can be a touchy one, everyone involved in collecting antique furniture has made mistakes. Reluctance among museums, dealers, and private collectors to discuss, let alone publish and exhibit fakes, contributes to their continued production and presence in the marketplace (fig. 1).

The prevalence and persistence of fakery are intimately linked to the demands and expectations in the marketplace. Few pieces of early American furniture survive in perfect condition, and even less are perceived as having the added qualities of artistic merit and/or historical significance. Although each of these considerations is important in assessing an object's monetary value, museums, collectors, and individuals in the American furniture trade have traditionally placed an unreasonably high premium on condition. Fakers or individuals who knowingly sell fraudulent objects often attempt to make pieces with condition problems appear perfect in order to reap the benefits of this perspective.

Because scholarship has always been tied to the marketplace, unrealistic expectations regarding condition have distorted American furniture history. Mass-produced or poorly made objects in excellent condition often command higher prices and more attention than important pieces with replaced parts. This is even true of replacements that are minimally conjectural. Fakes also distort furniture history by promulgating the notion of non-existent forms or by making extremely rare forms appear relatively commonplace. Scholarship is always tainted when it is based on forged source material.

The Chipstone Collection
All of the fraudulent objects in this article are from the collection of Stanley and Polly Stone of Fox Point, Wisconsin. The Stones began collecting American furniture in 1946, when they purchased a Salem, Massachusetts, secretary from Israel Sack. Within four years, they had acquired twenty-eight additional pieces ranging in quality from simple stands to monumental case pieces. The Stones' first opportunity to purchase a major piece of American furniture came in 1949 when New York antique dealers Benjamin Ginsburg and Bernard Levy offered them an eighteenth-century

Figure 2 Chest-on-chest, Providence, Rhode Island, 1765–1780. Mahogany with chestnut, cherry, and white pine. H. 82½", W. 42", D. 21½". (Chipstone Foundation; photo, Gavin Ashworth.)

Rhode Island chest-on-chest (fig. 2). Like many beginning collectors, the Stones agonized over their decision for months but eventually decided to purchase the chest-on-chest because it had carved shells, a blocked façade, and a history of ownership by a prominent individual—Providence merchant Jabez Bowen. They felt that it would be economical to acquire a single object with all of these attributes because they would complete their Rhode Island collection in "one fell swoop." The Stones' reasoning began to unravel almost immediately. Four years later they purchased a Newport chest of drawers (fig. 3) with carved shells, blocked drawers, and a history of ownership by Rhode Island governor Joseph Wanton.[1]

Figure 3 Chest of drawers, Newport, Rhode Island, 1765–1780. Mahogany with chestnut and white pine. H. 32", W. 37½", D. 22". (Chipstone Foundation; photo, Gavin Ashworth.)

In a newspaper interview, the Stones described themselves as "poor deluded victims" who failed to realize that they had been stricken with "virus antiquarium." Their "affliction" prompted them to commission Boston architect Andrew Hepburn to design a house to display their rapidly growing collection. Chipstone was completed in 1950, and like several of Hepburn's residential projects, it has details inspired by eighteenth-century buildings from the Chesapeake region of Maryland and Virginia.[2]

Figure 4 View of the living room at Chipstone, Milwaukee, Wisconsin, ca. 1975. (Chipstone Foundation.)

Figure 5 View of the living room at Chipstone, Milwaukee, Wisconsin, ca. 1975. (Chipstone Foundation.)

Figure 6 Upholstered armchair, American, ca. 1965. Mahogany with maple and pine. H. 43¾", W. 31½", D. 31½". (Chipstone Foundation; photo, Gavin Ashworth.)

Figure 7 Lolling chair, Portsmouth, New Hampshire, 1800–1810. Mahogany and satinwood with birch and white pine. H. 45¾", W. 25½", D. 30". (Courtesy, Milwaukee Art Museum; gift of Mr. and Mrs. Robert Stenger.)

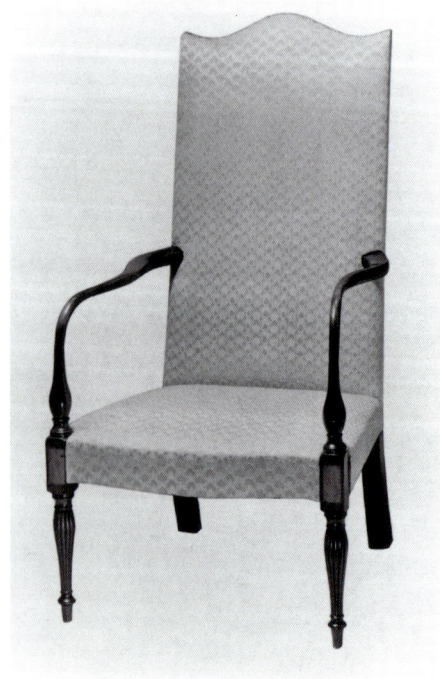

Although the Stones also collected early English pottery and American historical prints, they were primarily interested in furniture from the northeastern urban centers. During their collecting career, they acquired major works from Portsmouth, Boston, Newport, New York, and Philadelphia. Like nearly every major collector of their generation, they also purchased objects that were intended to deceive. In fact, nearly half of the furniture visible in figures 4 and 5 is fraudulent. These objects and other spurious pieces in the collection shed light on the techniques of a small group of fakers working from the 1940s to the 1980s.

A Rogue's Gallery

Upholstered armchairs are one of the most commonly faked types of seating furniture. Two examples in the Chipstone collection (see fig. 6) have frame components salvaged from neoclassical lolling chairs (see fig. 7), which probably had legs that were cut off or severely damaged. The dealer who sold the Stones the chair illustrated in figure 6 attributed it to Boston and described it as "one of the finest . . . of this type we have seen." Dozens

Figure 8 Upholstered armchair, Boston or Salem, Massachusetts, 1760–1770. Mahogany with maple. H. 35", W. 27¼", D. 25¼". (Chipstone Foundation; photo, Gavin Ashworth.) With its low back and serpentine crest, this armchair is a Boston version of a "French chair." In the second edition of *The Gentleman and Cabinet-Maker's Director* (1755), Thomas Chippendale noted that the carving on such chairs "may be lessened by an ingenious workman without detriment."

of similar fakes, most with tall backs and either claw-and-ball or pad feet, have appeared on the market during the past eighty years, and many have found their way into important public and private collections. The Chipstone chair is one of the least sophisticated because it has incompatible design features such as Boston-style legs and stretchers and Delaware Valley–style arms. During the eighteenth century, Boston chair makers typically followed British precedent in the design and construction of upholstered seating forms (see fig. 8).[3]

Evidence of wear on this chair is inconsistent with normal use. The undersides of the stretchers have the same dents, scuffs, and abrasion marks as the exposed surfaces, and all of the damage occurred at once rather than incrementally. In contrast, period objects typically have worn surfaces that reflect different patterns of use over many years. The faker used an object with an irregular surface to distress the arms, legs, and stretchers, then he applied a dark stain (fig. 9). The torn fibers absorbed the stain more than the undamaged surfaces; therefore, the dark color remained localized during the application of the finish coat.

Figure 9 Detail of the artificial distressing on the surface of a leg of the armchair illustrated in fig. 6.

The most compelling evidence that this chair is a fake is an old upholstery line for the neoclassical frame that extends *under* the present knee blocks (fig. 10). Some clever fakers used patches to remove this type of evidence. Because authentic chairs often have patches where repeated nailing has eroded the frame, care must be taken in evaluating such evidence. In some instances, it is necessary to plot all of the nail patterns to determine authenticity, especially in the case of complex fakes comprised of parts from more than one chair.[4]

To expedite and simplify their work, most fakers adapt parts from period objects. The individual who produced the fraudulent easy chair illustrated in figure 11 simply discarded the presumably damaged legs and stretchers on a mid-eighteenth-century Massachusetts easy chair (see fig. 12) and

Figure 10 Detail of nail holes under a knee block of the armchair shown in fig. 6.

Figure 11 Easy chair, American, ca. 1955. Mahogany with maple and pine. H. 49", W. 35¼", D. 29". (Chipstone Foundation; photo, Gavin Ashworth.)

Figure 12 Easy chair, Boston, Massachusetts, 1745–1765. H. 46 ½", W. 34⅝", D. 21⅜". Walnut and maple with white pine, birch, and maple. (Courtesy, Milwaukee Art Museum.)

Figure 13 Detail of the right front leg of the easy chair illustrated in fig. 11.

Figure 14 Detail of the left quarter-round tenon of the easy chair illustrated in fig. 11.

Figure 15 Detail of a ca. 1730 Boston backstool with quarter-round tenons similar to those of the easy chair illustrated in fig. 12. The tenon has a color and burnished appearance that differs markedly from the one shown in fig. 14.

added new legs in the Newport style. The front legs show no evidence of wear or damage, even along the lower upholstery line where the surface typically has scars from nail heads, knife cuts, or hammer impacts inflicted during repeated applications of fabric (fig. 13). The faces of the knee blocks are equally pristine, and their undersides are finished with a coarse file. Although the faker soaked the quarter-round tenons in stain to make them appear old (fig. 14), their color and character differ significantly from those on period examples (see figs. 12, 15). More importantly, the wood surface and undersides of the front legs match those of the rear legs, which are obvious replacements. The original rear legs on this chair were probably extensions of the back posts like those on the chair shown in figure 12.

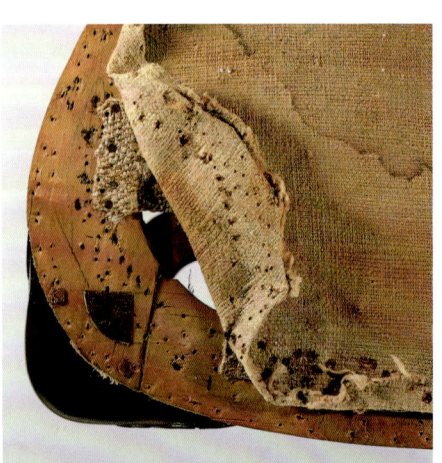

Figure 16 Detail of the right rear leg of the easy chair illustrated in fig. 11, showing the spliced joint.

Figure 17   High chest illustrated in Ralph Carpenter's *The Arts and Crafts of Newport* (Courtesy, Yale University Art Gallery, Mabel Brady Garvan Collection).

Figure 18   Detail of the leg of the high chest shown in fig. 17. (Courtesy, Yale University Art Gallery, Mabel Brady Garvan Collection.)

There is no way these spliced joints (see fig. 16) could be interpreted as original construction, even though the Stones received assurances that there were no major replacements or restorations.

Fakers often incorporate details from authentic published objects to make their work more believable. At first glance, the fake Newport easy chair (fig. 11) appears to be related to a Rhode Island high chest in the Yale University Art Gallery (fig. 17). Both pieces have knees with cut-card scrolls and husks and claw-and-ball feet with exaggerated knuckles and long talons (figs. 13, 18). The Stones would have recognized these features because the high chest appeared in Ralph Carpenter's *The Arts and Crafts of Newport* a year before they were offered the chair. The individual who sold the Stones this chair knew that they were avid collectors and students of Rhode Island furniture and close personal friends of Mr. Carpenter.[5]

Figure 19 Easy chair, American, ca. 1958. Mahogany with tulip poplar, pine, and oak. H. 48½", W. 33½", D. 32½". (Chipstone Foundation; photo, Gavin Ashworth.)

Figure 20 John Walton advertisement, *Antiques* 101, no. 4 (April 1971): 568. (Courtesy, *Antiques*.) The knee acanthus and feet of this chair are by the same hand that carved a dressing table and side chair that descended in the Gratz family. The latter examples are in the Winterthur Museum.

In assessing furniture, most collectors of the Stones' generation focused more on style, form, and ornament than on construction. Fakers often exploited this perspective by producing objects that were ostensibly from well-known suites or groups. The easy chair illustrated in figure 19 is one of three virtually identical fakes based on a period example commissioned by Michael and Miriam Gratz, probably just after their wedding in 1769. Antique dealer John Walton owned the original twice—once during the early 1950s and again in 1971 (fig. 20). The individual who sold the Stones their chair described it as a "mahogany claw-and-ball foot upholstered easy chair with fine carving similar to that on the Gratz Wing chair which was attributed to Thomas Affleck, the Gratz family cabinetmaker. This chair can reasonably be given the same attribution." The dealer knew that this history would appeal to the Stones because they had purchased a tea table with the same history in 1953 and were undoubtedly familiar with the Gratz high chest and dressing table at the Winterthur Museum.[6]

Figure 21 Detail of the knee carving on the easy chair illustrated in fig. 19.

Figure 22 Detail of the right front leg and side rail of the easy chair illustrated in fig. 19.

Each of the fake Gratz chairs has poorly executed carving that, aside from its basic design, has almost nothing in common with period workmanship (fig. 21). The sharp spines separating the leaves and divergent veining have no precedent in Philadelphia carving, and the work is contrived and overwrought. The seat rails provide conclusive evidence that the legs are modern replacements. Holes for wooden pins are present on the tenons, but absent on the corresponding faces of the front legs (fig. 22). This indicates that the seat rails are salvaged components from another chair that had pinned joints.[7]

Some of the most difficult fakes to identify tend to be period objects with carefully disguised restorations or replacements. The armchair illustrated in figure 23 is attributed to a member of the Gaines family of Portsmouth, New Hampshire, but it has a replaced crest rail (fig. 24) carved by the same faker who made the fraudulent Gratz easy chair (figs. 19, 21). Like many period chairs, the Gaines example sustained damage when it fell over—probably with the user sitting or standing in it—thus breaking the crest rail and upper portion of the stiles.[8]

The dealer who sold the Stones this armchair described it as "one of only three or four...known," and noted that an example in the Winterthur Museum had nearly identical carved details. The Stones probably recognized these similarities since they supported that museum and received information on new acquisitions. Winterthur published the authentic chair (figs. 25, 26) in a report titled *Accessions, 1960,* four years before the Stones purchased their example.[9]

Figure 23 Armchair attributed to a member of the Gaines family, vicinity of Portsmouth, New Hampshire, 1730–1745, with a crest rail dating ca. 1964. Maple with pine. H. 42½", W. 26½", D. 23¾". (Chipstone Foundation; photo, Gavin Ashworth.)

Figure 24 Detail of the crest rail of the armchair illustrated in fig. 23.

Figure 25 Armchair attributed to a member of the Gaines family, vicinity of Portsmouth, New Hampshire, 1730–1745. H. 43", W. 29¼", D. 21⅜". Maple and cherry. (Courtesy, Winterthur Museum.)

Figure 26 Detail of the crest rail of the armchair illustrated in fig. 25.

Figure 27 Armchair, American, ca. 1962. Mahogany with pine and tulip poplar. H. 43½", W. 33", D. 24½". (Chipstone Foundation; photo, Gavin Ashworth.)

Unlike the preceding fakes, which have component parts salvaged from period seating, the armchair illustrated in figure 27 is entirely new. Its basic design and carved details were derived from a well-known set of side chairs (see fig. 28) reputedly used by George Washington in the presidential house in Philadelphia. The Washington chairs date about 1755, and are part of a large group of Philadelphia furniture with carving attributed to Nicholas Bernard.[10]

The carving (fig. 29) is by the same hand that produced the fake Gratz easy chair and the crest rail on the Gaines armchair (figs. 19, 21, 23, 24). Although the design of the ornament on the two pieces is different, the leaves on both examples have excessively deep flutes and shading cuts that intersect at the tips of the leaves in an unconventional manner. The fraudulent nature of this work becomes even more apparent when compared with the period carving that inspired it (fig. 30). The leaves on the knees of the Washington chair have precisely cut edges, carefully regulated convex and concave surfaces, and crisp shading cuts. Bernard's style was fully developed; his designs, tools, and techniques were perfectly integrated; and he worked intuitively, efficiently, and quickly. In contrast, the carving

Figure 28 Side chair with carving attributed to Nicholas Bernard, Philadelphia, 1750–1755. H. 39 1/8", W. 23 1/4", D. 21 1/2". (Courtesy, Milwaukee Art Museum.)

Figure 29 Detail of the knee carving on the armchair illustrated in fig. 27.

Figure 30 Detail of the knee carving on the chair illustrated in fig. 28.

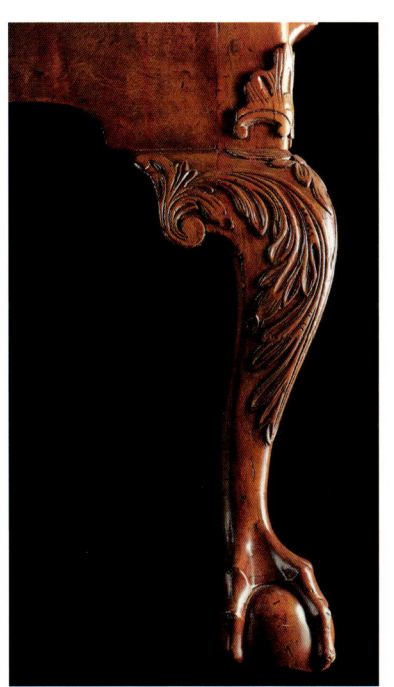

Figure 31 Card table, American, ca. 1959. Mahogany with white pine. H. 29", W. 32", D. 15¼". (Chipstone Foundation; photo, Gavin Ashworth.)

Figure 32 Card table illustrated in the catalogue of the *Loan Exhibition of Eighteenth and Nineteenth Century Furniture and Glass… for the Benefit of the National Council of Girl Scouts* (New York: American Art Galleries, 1929), no. 627.

Figure 33 Detail of the underside of the card table illustrated in fig. 31. The undersides of the front and side rails have been colored with black stain.

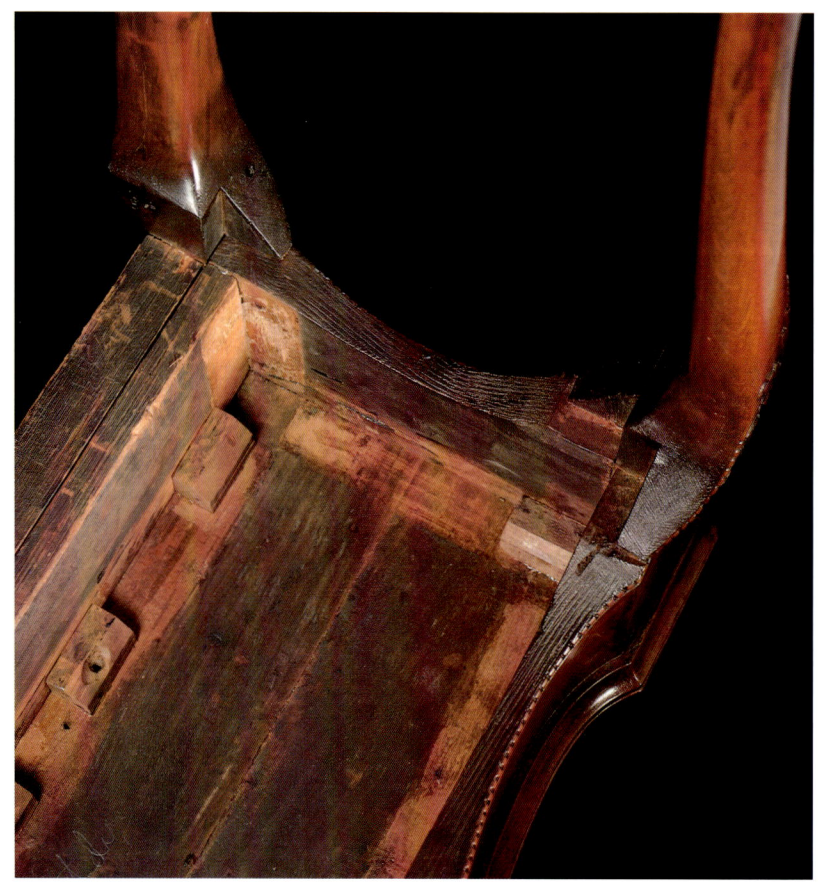

Figure 34 Detail of the underside of a Newport card table dating 1765–1775. (Chipstone Foundation; photo, Gavin Ashworth.) The secondary surfaces of this card table are very different from those of the fake illustrated in fig. 33. All of the components are the same color because they have been exposed to the same atmospheric conditions and level of light. The fine file marks on the undersides of the rail and knee blocks are typical of eighteenth-century Newport work.

on the Chipstone chair has a tedious quality, indicating that the faker struggled to mimic period work. His curled leaves are stiff and truncated, whereas those on the Washington chair have a more naturalistic flow and appearance.

As the fraudulent Philadelphia armchair suggests, the most convincing whole cloth fakes are made from old wood. Armchairs, side chairs, bedsteads, stands, and tea tables are the preferred forms for this type of chicanery because they have a minimal amount of secondary wood. Conifers and other softwoods are very difficult to color and age without the use of oxidants and stains, which are red flags to most collectors. To overcome this problem, fakers frequently use parts from damaged or undervalued period pieces, often of the same form as the object they intend to produce.

The faker responsible for the card table illustrated in figure 31 based his design on an example illustrated in the 1929 catalogue of the *Girl Scouts Loan Exhibition* (fig. 32) and incorporated a rear rail and fly rail from a period card table. The undersides of the front and side rails have deep striations produced by a rasp, a tool rarely used in the eighteenth century (fig. 33). Period tables with shaped rails occasionally have file marks in similar contexts, but the striations are invariably finer, more intermittent, and concentrated in areas where the maker had to remove saw kerfs or undercut his work (see fig. 34). The maker of this fake used glue blocks to conceal discontinuous surfaces and fresh saw cuts like those at each end of the shortened rear rail.[11]

Another fake card table in the Chipstone collection (fig. 35) also has a rear rail and fly rail from a period example. Like the preceding table, its design is based on a published form. Winterthur curator Joseph Downs illustrated the prototype in 1952 (fig. 36), eight years before the Stones

Figure 35 Card table, American, ca. 1958. Mahogany with oak and tulip poplar. H. 26½", W. 33½", D. 16½". (Chipstone Foundation; photo, Gavin Ashworth.)

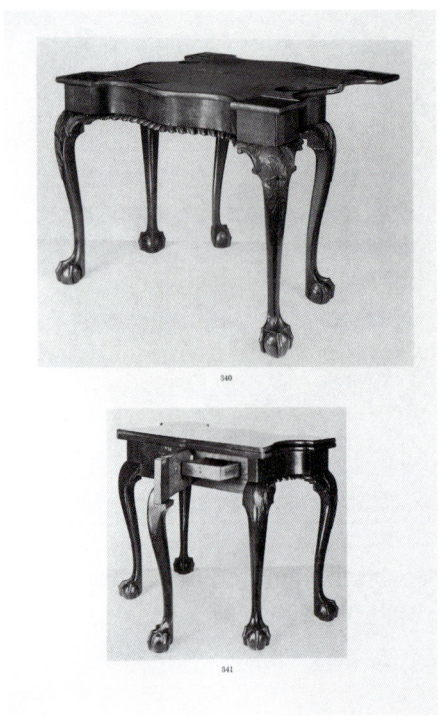

Figure 36 Illustration of a New York card table in Joseph Downs, *American Furniture: Queen Anne and Chippendale Periods in the Henry Francis du Pont Winterthur Museum* (New York: MacMillan Co., 1952), nos. 340–41.

acquired their fake. The text and views shown in his catalogue *American Furniture: Queen Anne and Chippendale Periods* provided basic information about the size, woods, and construction of the rear rail and drawer. The faker knew that a potential buyer would probably consult this publication and tailored his work accordingly.[12]

The knee acanthus (fig. 37) is by the same modern carver responsible for most of the fraudulent pieces in the Chipstone collection. The design of this individual's work varies a great deal, but his techniques and lack of skill remained relatively consistent. In contrast, the acanthus on the period table that inspired the fake is competent and relates to a large group of New York carving from the 1760s and 1770s.

The construction of the Chipstone table provides several clues that it is fraudulent. The pins on the fake table are perfectly round and flush with the surface (fig. 38) because the holes for the pins were drilled with a twist bit rotating at a very high speed and the maker used modern, kiln dried lumber. In contrast, the pins on authentic examples are slightly out-of-round and often protrude just above the surface (fig. 39). Most eighteenth-century cabinetmakers drilled their pin-holes with a spoon bit, a U-shaped tool that typically damaged the end-grain in the upper right or lower left corners if the bit rotated clockwise or in the opposite corners if it rotated

  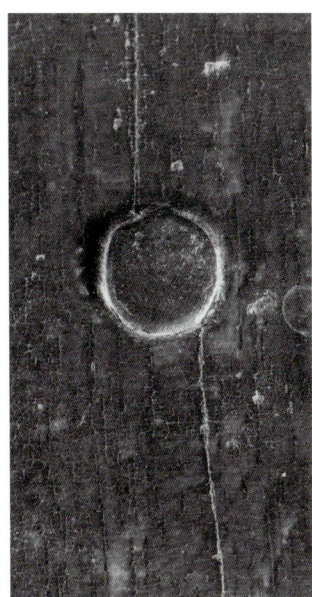

Figure 37 Detail of the knee carving on the card table illustrated in fig. 35.

Figure 38 Detail of a pin securing a mortise-and-tenon joint on the card table illustrated in fig. 35.

Figure 39 Detail of a pin securing a mortise-and-tenon joint on a New York card table with carving attributed to Henry Hardcastle (active 1750–1755). All of the pins securing the mortise-and-tenon joints are slightly distorted, and they protrude just above the surface of the leg stiles. The fractures extending from the corners indicate that the maker drilled his holes with a spoon-bit.

Figure 40 Details of the underside of the card table illustrated in fig. 35 showing (from left to right) the drawer inserted and the drawer withdrawn. The drawer may have come from the interior of a desk or bookcase.

counter-clockwise. The disturbances became more pronounced as the maker rotated his brace and bit to ream the mouth of the hole and provide a wedged fit for the tapered pin. Although the process of driving in the pins often created fractures emanating from the damaged end-grain, the pin distorted the hole much less than the shape of the hole distorted the pin.

To make the interior surfaces of the card table appear more convincing, the faker used old boards for the top and the side and front rails (fig. 40). He stained the areas sawn out in the process of forming the serpentine curves and used a drawer and drawer supports salvaged from one or more period pieces. Fortunately, the faker did not expend much effort integrating the old and new components. For example, there is no shift in the color of the top above the drawer. Given the fact that the table is supposed to be nearly 250 years old, one would expect a discernible difference.[13]

Although most of the spurious objects in the Chipstone collection date between 1950 and 1970, the practice of faking American furniture was well established by the early twentieth century. Small folding-leaf tables like the one shown in figure 41 are among the most commonly faked forms, owing to their rarity and long-standing popularity with collectors. Most are assembled from parts of larger tables.

Figure 41 Oval table, American, ca. 1961. Walnut with maple and pine. H. 26", W. 26", D. 26". (Chipstone Foundation; photo, Gavin Ashworth.)

Figure 42 Detail of the top of the table illustrated in fig. 41.

Figure 43 Detail of the inner frame of the table illustrated in fig. 41.

The top of this piece (fig. 42) is made from boards with different histories. There is almost no wear from rotation of the swing legs, and the rule joints between the top leaves were cut with a modern table saw. The color of the undersides of the leaves and center section of the top is very different when it should be similar, and the surface under a supposedly ancient wrought iron bracket is identical to that surrounding it when it should be different.

The ends of the inner rails have fresh saw kerfs indicating that they were cut from older boards (fig. 43). The dealer who owned this table also sold the Colonial Williamsburg Foundation a similar example during the 1950s. Although no correspondence concerning the Chipstone table survives, the Stones probably knew of the Williamsburg table and felt fortunate to acquire a comparable object.[14]

Of all the fake forms in the Chipstone collection, candlestands are the most numerous. The dealer who sold the Stones the stand illustrated in figure 44 noted that only three or four Philadelphia examples with "carving as rich" were known and assured them that the object was authentic and in good condition. In reality, nearly all of its components are new, and the knee acanthus (fig. 45) and feet are by the same carver responsible for many of the aforementioned fakes (see figs. 19, 23, 27, 31). Several stands

Figure 44 Candlestand, American, ca. 1959. Mahogany. H. 27⅜", Diam. of top: 22¼". (Chipstone Foundation; photo, Gavin Ashworth.)

Figure 45 Detail of the knee carving on the candlestand illustrated in fig. 44.

Figure 46 Candlestand, Philadelphia, Pennsylvania, 1765–1775. Mahogany. Dimensions not recorded. (Private collection; photo, Gavin Ashworth.)

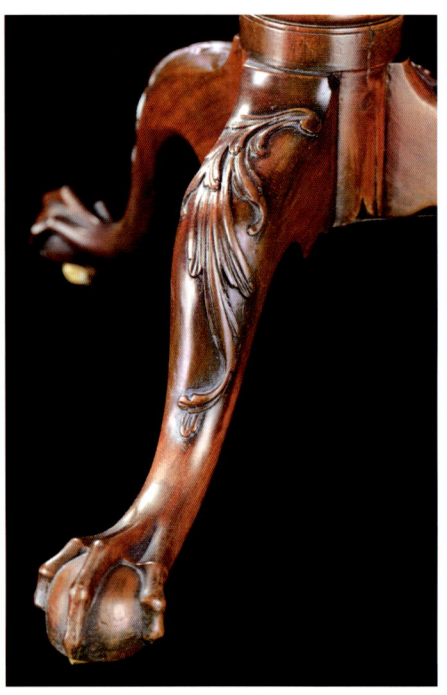

Figure 47 Detail of the knee carving on the candlestand illustrated in fig. 46.

and tea tables by this individual are known, most of which have unconventional and poorly regulated compressed ball turnings, badly designed and ineptly carved leaves, and exaggerated claw-and-ball feet. This work differs significantly from period Philadelphia carving like that on the candlestand illustrated in figures 46 and 47.[15]

The faker knew that collectors often checked circular tops to verify that they had shrunk across the grain, so he cut the top of the stand slightly out of round (fig. 48). Because this prevented him from turning the top, he used a router and edge tools to produce the molded rim. To fabricate period turning evidence, the faker drilled and plugged holes in the back of the top (fig. 49). He clearly understood that Philadelphia "dish" tops were usually turned on a lathe faceplate or turner's cross—an outboard set-up for turning objects with diameters too large to be shaped over the bed of the lathe. What he failed to understand, however, is that the edge moldings on any object turned in this manner are both regular and congruent. Because these moldings are produced in a single axis of rotation, they cannot wander in or out of their proscribed arcs; the individual elements cannot deviate in distance from the center or from each other nor can they vary in depth from each other (figs. 48, 50). The edge of a turned top will distort if the top shrinks, cracks, or warps, but the moldings and the relationship of one element to another remains constant.

Figure 48 Detail of the top of the candlestand illustrated in fig. 44.

Figure 49 Detail of a plugged hole on the underside of the top of the candlestand illustrated in fig. 44.

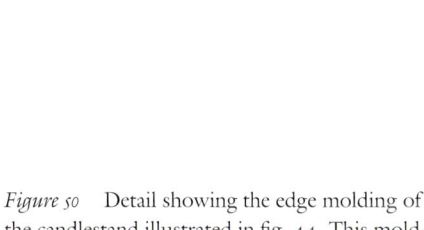

Figure 50 Detail showing the edge molding of the candlestand illustrated in fig. 44. This molding was cut with a router and edge tools rather than being turned on a lathe.

A late eighteenth-century Philadelphia candlestand (fig. 51) in the Chipstone collection exemplifies period design and workmanship. It demonstrates how the moving parts of such forms imprint evidence of rotation and bearing wear over time. The inner surfaces of the battens have rotation marks around the pentil holes. This wear occurred as the upper board of the birdcage rubbed against the battens when the top was raised and low-

Figure 51   Candlestand, Philadelphia, 1780–1800. Mahogany. H. 27¼", Diam. of top: 27⅞". (Private collection; photo, Gavin Ashworth.)

Figure 52   Detail of the underside of the top, birdcage, and battens (removed) of the candlestand illustrated in fig. 51. The bearing surfaces on stands and tea tables of this form are: the underside of the top bearing on the top board of the birdcage; the uppermost tip of the pillar on the hole in the underside of the top board of the birdcage; the shoulder of the tip on the underside of the top board of the birdcage; the collar on the upper side of the bottom board of the birdcage; and the underside of the bottom board of the birdcage on the large shoulder below. The wear on all of these surfaces should be consistent if all of the components are original.

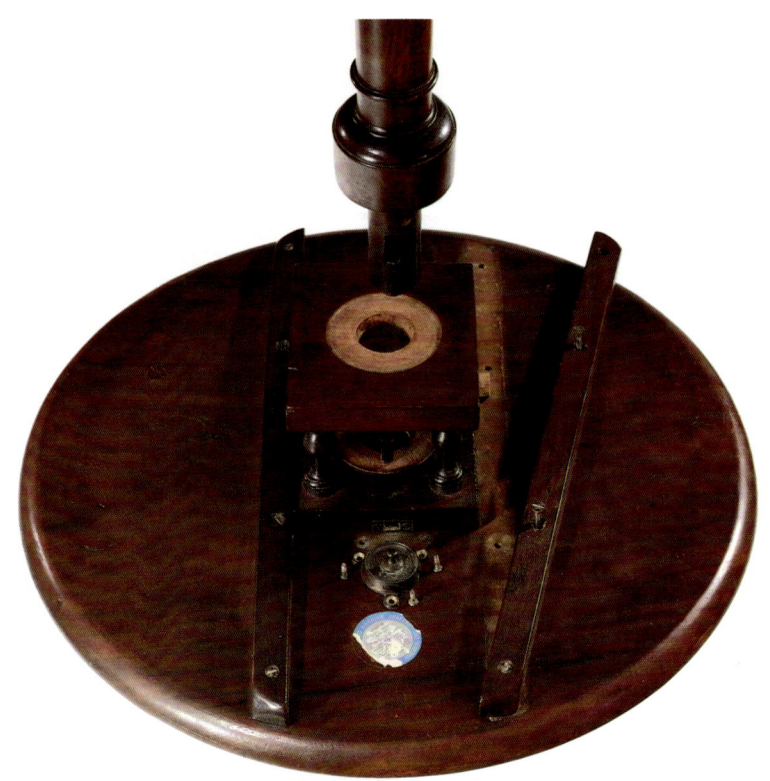

Figure 53   Candlestand, American, ca. 1961. Mahogany. H. 27", Diam. of top: 22". (Chipstone Foundation; photo, Gavin Ashworth.)

ered. The underside of the top also has a clear imprint from bearing on the birdcage, and the birdcage has predictable wear from bearing and revolving on the pillar (fig. 52).

The plugged holes on the back of the top and congruent moldings on the face indicate that the maker turned the top on a lathe. The top shrank about three-eighths of an inch, requiring the owner to reset the screws securing the battens (fig. 52). Obviously the amount of shrinkage and adjustment of the screws should be proportional. Most period tops have shrunk since their manufacture, although the amount can be minimal on those produced during the driest months.

The same individual who sold the Stones the preceding fake stand offered them the example illustrated in figure 53 three years later. He clearly understood the appeal of having two similar stands from the same city, one with a dish top and carving and another with plain knees and a scalloped top. The turning evidence on the pillars of both objects is at odds with period work. Eighteenth-century turners shaped their stock on relatively slow moving lathes using shearing cuts that removed wood in much the same manner as peeling an apple. Although woodworkers had access to rudimentary sandpapers and other abrasives, they rarely used them to finish turnings. By contrast, the pillars on the fake stands were turned and finished on a modern high-speed lathe. Both have fine concentric abrasion marks perpendicular to the axis of their pillars.[16]

Figure 54 Dressing table, American, ca. 1957. Mahogany with tulip poplar and yellow pine. H. 30¾", W. 34", D. 22". (Chipstone Foundation; photo, Gavin Ashworth.)

As one might expect, the most complex fakes in the Chipstone collection are case pieces. At first glance, the dressing table illustrated in figure 54 appears to be contemporary with one that descended in the Biddle family of Philadelphia (fig. 55). Both pieces have a molded top with shaped front corners, broad fluted chamfers, a deep skirt, and a long drawer over three smaller ones—details common on Philadelphia dressing tables made between 1730 and 1760.

The carving on the authentic dressing table (figs. 56, 57) is attributed to Nicholas Bernard. Unlike many Philadelphia carvers, Bernard was a locally trained artisan. He probably apprenticed or worked as a journeyman with Samuel Harding whose shop provided most of the architectural carving for the Pennsylvania State House, known today as Independence Hall. The maker of the Chipstone dressing table attempted to mimic Bernard's naturalistic style (figs. 58, 59), but was not up to the task. His acanthus appliqués consist of awkward clusters of deeply hollowed leaves similar to those on other fakes discussed here. The fake knee carving, for example, is virtually identical to that on the fraudulent armchair shown in figures 27 and 29.[17]

The construction details and materials used to fabricate this dressing table also identify it as a fake. All of the lower drawers are assembled from drawer parts from another case piece. Two appear to have been cut down from the upper drawers of a high chest, which typically have pulls placed near the top of the front. In contrast, the brasses on corresponding drawers of period Philadelphia dressing tables are usually centered. The faker pieced out the drawer sides and stained the bottoms (fig. 60) to hide reworked

Figure 55 Dressing table attributed to the shop of Henry Clifton and Thomas Carteret, Philadelphia, Pennsylvania, 1750–1755. Mahogany with pine and white cedar. H. 30¾", W. 34", D. 21". (Private collection; photo, Gavin Ashworth.) This dressing table is a superb example of Philadelphia case furniture from the early 1750s. Its construction is nearly identical to that of a dressing table and matching high chest made by Clifton and Carteret in 1753 (Colonial Williamsburg Foundation). Like those objects and other comparable forms documented and attributed to their shop, this dressing table has dustboards below the lower drawers.

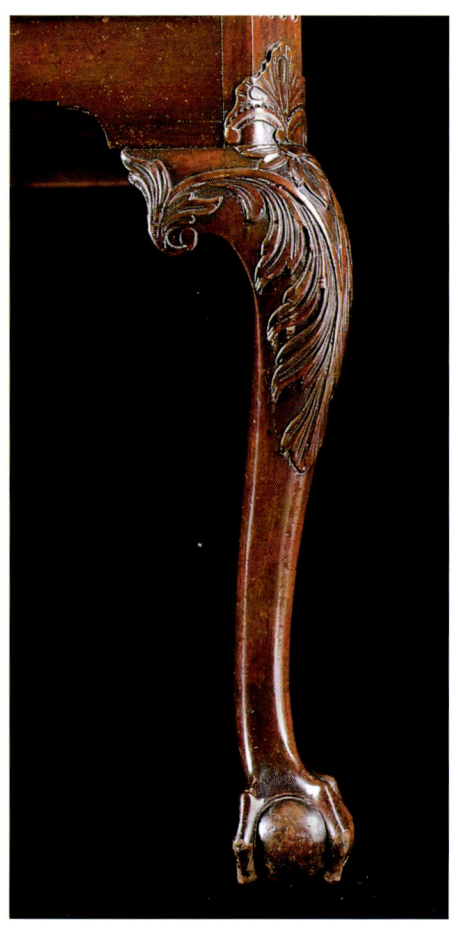

Figure 56 Detail of the carving on the lower center drawer of the dressing table illustrated in fig. 55.

Figure 57 Detail of the knee carving on the dressing table illustrated in fig. 55.

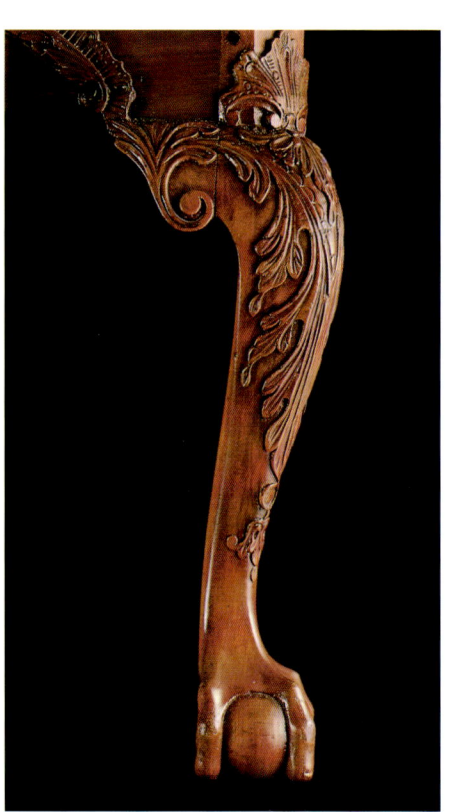

Figure 58 Detail of the carving on the lower center drawer of the dressing table illustrated in fig. 54.

Figure 59 Detail of the knee carving on the dressing table illustrated in fig. 54.

Figure 60   Detail of the bottoms of two lower drawers from the dressing table illustrated in fig. 54.

Figure 61   Detail of the underside of the top of the dressing table illustrated in fig. 54.

surfaces and color discrepancies resulting from the use and alteration of period components. Similarly, he used stain to obscure the newly scalloped lower edge of the backboard. The leaf of a dining table provided a reasonably convincing board for the top of the dressing table. Fortunately, the faker neglected to remove the scribe line (fig. 61) that originally denoted the position of the hinge joints.

A fake Newport dressing table (fig. 62) purchased by the Stones one year after they acquired the fraudulent Philadelphia example is related in being made of old boards, salvaged drawer parts, and a table top. The dealer's

Figure 62   Dressing table, American, ca. 1958. Mahogany with maple, chestnut, and tulip poplar. H. 33¼", W. 35⅛", D. 20½". (Chipstone Foundation; photo, Gavin Ashworth.)

Figure 63 Detail showing the interior case construction of the dressing table illustrated in fig. 62. The undersides of the rails were finished with a rasp rather than a file as was common in eighteenth-century Newport shops.

Figure 64 Detail showing the interior case construction of the dressing table illustrated in fig. 62.

invoice described the piece as a "lowboy made by the Goddard-Townsends" and noted that its "legs are the typical Newport removable type." He also called attention to other features characteristic of that town's production including the carved shell on the skirt and the object's chestnut and tulip poplar secondary woods.[18]

Given their interest in Newport furniture, the Stones would have recognized these features. Although they undoubtedly realized that dressing tables from that town with claw-and-ball feet were extremely rare, they would have been familiar with the authentic example exhibited at the 1950 loan exhibition of Rhode Island furniture. Ralph Carpenter illustrated the period dressing table four years later in *Arts and Crafts of Newport*.[19]

The faker responsible for the fraudulent dressing table knew that it had to satisfy certain expectations about design, construction, and materials, but he was not concerned that his fabrication would be carefully scrutinized or partially disassembled because standards for authentication were minimal at the time. Rather than distressing and staining new lumber, he assembled a variety of old boards to make the top, case sides, front skirt, and drawer fronts. The large front board of the top appears to have come from the top of a drop-leaf table. Its underside has marks from a water-powered saw, but the corresponding surface of the other top board does not. To create a visual link between these disparate surfaces, the faker painted the undersides with a grey wash. He used an electric rotary router to produce the edge molding, which has irregularities from the tool's vibration. To discourage removal of the top, the faker secured the boards with thirteen cut nails, two modern screws, and sixteen glue blocks. Many of the glue blocks vary considerably in age, color, and shape, but collectively they helped conceal the juncture and different surfaces of the case frame and top (fig. 63). After attaching the top, the faker painted the underside with a grey wash to make the surface uniform.

In a similar manner, the faker stained the underside of the modern chestnut drawer divider to make it appear that the center section was exposed to more light than the flanking areas above the drawers and had darkened over time (fig. 63). He also painted a dark wash on the back of the front rail but allowed the stain to bleed under the area covered by the lapped edges of each drawer guide. Surprisingly, the faker used glue and modern cut nails rather than forged ones to secure each joint.

The joinery of the case also provides indisputable evidence that it is fraudulent. Between the two boards of the back rail, the faker inserted thin strips of wood to make it appear that they had shrunk over time (fig. 64). However, the frame is essentially a dovetailed box with nothing to restrict the movement of the back or sides for that matter. The boards and their dovetail joints are at different heights and would not align without the strips, although they were ostensibly added after construction. Furthermore, the faker chopped the mortises for the drawer dividers *after* the strips of wood were in place.

Realizing that chestnut was a common secondary wood in eighteenth-century Newport furniture, the faker used it for the back of the case. Although the section below the shrinkage strips appears to be a single board with a crack, it is actually two pieces. The faker undoubtedly had a chestnut board with nail or screw holes that may have caused a potential buyer concern, so he removed the troublesome holes by sawing out a half-inch section with a band saw then glued the remaining sections together. He employed the same technique to remove marks on the chestnut boards used for the drawer bottoms.

Figure 65 Detail showing the drawer fronts, skirt, and carved shell of the dressing table illustrated in fig. 62. The convex and concave lobes of the shell are poorly regulated, and the central palmette is clumsy and overwrought. The faker responsible for this object was simply not up to the task of replicating eighteenth-century carving, even that as simple as the ornament commonly found on Newport furniture.

Figure 66 Detail showing the interior case construction of the dressing table illustrated in fig. 62. The drawer guides, drawer supports, and glue blocks are salvaged parts from other furniture.

The reuse of period parts created several problems for the faker (see figs. 63-66). The top drawer has little figure and witness marks for two different escutcheon plates (the current escutcheon is a converted pull plate) whereas the lower drawer fronts are clearly modern, have stripe figure, and were only recently fitted with brasses, which may have been salvaged from the piece of furniture that provided the upper drawer front. The faker used a lip patch on the lower left drawer to make it appear as though it was dam-

Figure 67 Detail of the right front foot of the dressing table illustrated in fig. 62.

aged through use. Other attempts to misdirect a potential buyer are evident in the intentional "repairs" to the toes of the claw-and-ball feet and "replaced" knee blocks, all of which are part of the original fabric of the fake.

The feet of the dressing table provide one of the strongest visual and stylistic clues that it is fraudulent (see fig. 67). They appear to be an amalgam of two types of Newport feet, although neither of the period varieties have flat, concave passages in the ankles. The feet on the dressing table do, however, resemble those on several other fakes including the easy chair illustrated in figure 11. The faker's inability to simulate the passage of time by modulating color and wear are evident on the feet of both objects. The finish is one-dimensional and does not vary even on the undersides and edges of the toes. Similarly, the only wear is a series of small, unconvincing dents all done at the same time.

The bombé desk-and-bookcase illustrated in figure 68 differs from the dressing tables in being a period object with significant repairs, all of which were intended to deceive. In his introduction to Oswaldo Rodriguez Roque's, *American Furniture at Chipstone,* Mr. Stone wrote:

> In March 1956, we went to Europe, and when we returned we dropped into [a dealer's shop] and there we saw a truly outstanding Massachusetts bombé secretary of great quality. Coincidentally, Maxim Karolick came in while we were there [and] rapsodized about the secretary until any doubts that we might have had about it, and I hasten to say they were minor, vanished.

When the Stones and Karolick examined this piece, it probably appeared more convincing than it does today. The modern door panels, fallboard, and feet would not have had their current greenish cast that has resulted from the use of a fugitive red dye.[20]

The doors were clearly constructed for mirrors rather than panels (figs. 69, 70). Scalloped, fielded panels are almost always trapped in grooves in the door stiles and rails, and the inner edges of the stiles and rails have the same outline as the panels. The doors on this example have

Figure 68 Desk-and-bookcase, Boston, Massachusetts, 1760–1770, with disguised repairs dati ca. 1956. Mahogany with white pine. H. 96", W. 41", D. 20¼". (Chipstone Foundation; photo, Gavin Ashworth.)

Figure 69   Detail of the left door of the desk-and-bookcase illustrated in fig. 68.

Figure 70   Detail of the inner surface of the left door of the desk-and-bookcase illustrated in fig. 68.

Figure 71   Detail of the foot and base construction of the desk-and-bookcase illustrated in fig. 68.

Figure 72   Detail of the back of the pediment of the desk-and-bookcase illustrated in fig. 68.

rectangular rabbeted openings, indicating that they were made for either mirrors or flat panels. Remnants of glue blocks on the edges of the rabbets suggest the former.

Damage to the lower edge of the base molding provides the first clue that the feet are replaced. Although the current feet are reasonably accurate interpretations of contemporary Boston examples, their stained inner edges, braces, and glue blocks identify them as modern replacements (fig. 71). The maker evidently used some old glue blocks from another case piece, but had to modify and color them to match the height, width, and shape of the feet.

The boards used to make the tympanum are from very different grades of stock, and the section behind the scrolls has end-grain laminations that deviate radically from eighteenth-century cabinetmaking practices (fig. 72). In a misguided attempt to create a period tool history, the faker used a rasp and a quarter-round gouge to shape the upper edge of the scroll board; however, he neglected to remove the modern mill marks on the pediment braces and glue blocks. To disguise new and inconsistent secondary surfaces, the faker used black paint and dark stain. All of the backboards, for example, are painted to match the exposed areas of the pediment.

The faker expended little effort on the fallboard of the desk, other than using an old mahogany board. Unlike many of his peers, he did not attempt to duplicate the water and ink stains on the floor of the writing compartment or the number and position of screw holes in the original hinge mortises. Most clever fakers either match the screw evidence or remove it by inserting patches that make it appear as though the floor of the writing compartment and fallboard have honest conforming repairs.

Figure 73 Desk-and-bookcase with carving attributed to John Welch, Boston, Massachusetts, ca. 1750. Mahogany with white pine. H. 97", W. 40½", D. 23". The turned feet and finials, tromp l'oeil decoration inside the bookcase, and carving are the work of independent specialists contracted by the shop master. (Chipstone Foundation; photo, Gavin Ashworth.)

An authentic Boston desk-and-bookcase purchased by the Chipstone Foundation in 1991 stands in sharp contrast with the fake (fig. 73). The former is part of a large group of furniture made in Boston between 1735 and 1755. The most elaborate examples have blocked or bombé desk sections, three or four engaged pilasters or columns, applied and relief carving, and tromp l'oeil decoration. Although the master of this shop has not been identified, he appears to have been the first American cabinetmaker to produce blockfront and bombé forms. He was clearly familiar with a broad range of stylistic details, some of which were fashionable during the late seventeenth century. The gadrooned ball feet on the desk-and-bookcase, for example, are similar to those shown in engravings by Huguenot designer Daniel Marot.[21]

As this desk-and-bookcase suggests, the many important pieces of American furniture collected by the Stones greatly overshadow the small number of fraudulent objects illustrated here. Much of the credit for rebuilding the collection must be given to Mrs. Stone, who insisted that the fakes be used for educational purposes and that pieces of comparable quality and historical significance be added to those that she and Mr. Stone assembled. Mrs. Stone acted bravely and responsibly in not allowing their mistakes to become someone else's mistakes, which could have occurred had these fakes re-entered the marketplace. She understood that fakes must be exposed and published to insure that American furniture scholars have reliable source material to study and interpret.

ACKNOWLEDGMENTS For assistance with this article the authors thank the staff of the Chipstone Foundation and the collectors who allowed them to illustrate authentic objects from their collections.

1. Stanley Stone, "Life Begins at Fifty," in Oswaldo Rodriguez Roque, *American Furniture at Chipstone* (Madison, Wis.: University of Wisconsin Press, 1984), vii, viii. Stanley Stone lecture notes, Chipstone Foundation, Milwaukee, Wis.

2. *Milwaukee Journal*, undated clipping, Chipstone Foundation. The Chesapeake details reflect Perry, Shaw, and Hepburn's experiences with the restoration and reconstruction of Colonial Williamsburg.

3. Invoice, April 22, 1964, accession files, Chipstone Foundation. All subsequent references to invoices are from these files.

4. Eighteenth-century designs for chairs with upholstered backs and open arms are shown in *Pictorial History of British Eighteenth-Century Design*, compiled by Elizabeth White (Suffolk, Eng.: Antique Collector's Club, Ltd., 1990), pp. 100–104. The earliest manifestations of this form have their origins in seventeenth-century seating commissioned for the courts of Paris and Versailles. Made with tall, upholstered backs and open arms, these *fauteuils* subsequently attained a measure of popularity in Britain where they were referred to by various names including "grand chairs" and "elbow stools." Daniel Marot illustrated the archetypal late seventeenth- and early eighteenth-century French model in *Second Livre d'Apartements* and *Nouveaux Livres di Licts de differentes penseez* (ca. 1703 and 1713), pls. 5, 7 (p. 98). These chairs and their later variants often had accompanying seating forms referred to today as "backstools." Gaetano Brunetti's *Sixty Different Sorts of Ornament* (1736) illustrates two upholstered armchairs and two similar backstools. The armchairs are essentially baroque forms with Italianate undercarriages and nascent rococo details (p. 99). These are the only published British designs for high-back upholstered chairs with open arms and cabriole legs known to the authors, and surviving examples of this form are extremely rare. Most eighteenth-century upholstered chairs with open arms and cabriole legs had low backs. British architect William Kent designed several types in his distinctive Palladian style, examples of which are shown in

J. Vardy, *Some Designs of Mr. Inigo Jones & William Kent* (1744), pl. 43 (p. 99). Although rococo versions probably became fashionable in Britain by the late 1740s, they were not represented in design books prior to the publication of Thomas Chippendale's *The Gentleman and Cabinet-Maker's Director* (1754). Chippendale called this form a "French chair" (pp. 100-101). Related seating forms described as "French chairs" and "French Back Stools" are also illustrated in William Ince and John Mayhew, *The Universal System of Houshold Furniture* (1762), pls. 55, 56, 58, 59 (p. 103); the Society of Upholsterers, *Genteel Houshold Furniture in the Present Taste* (1765), pls. 26–28 (p. 102); and Robert Manwaring, *The Cabinet and Chair-Maker's Real Friend and Companion* (1765), pls. 16, 17, 21–23 (p. 104). Plate 10 of George Hepplewhite's *The Cabinet-Maker and Upholsterer's Guide* (1794) illustrates designs for "cabriole chairs," which have upholstered backs, open arms, and a gap between the seat and back (p. 105). His designs for "state chairs" are similar but they do not show a gap in the back (p. 106).

The earliest publication showing an American chair with an upholstered back, open arms, and cabriole legs is Luke Vincent Lockwood's *Colonial Furniture in America*, 2 vols. (New York: Charles Scribners Sons, 1921), 2:109, no. 582. Although not examined by the authors, this chair appears to be a period example. It has extremely upright rear post/legs that extend almost straight down below the seat rails and small knee blocks that relate to corresponding elements on an authentic Rhode Island easy chair in a private collection (David Conradson, *Useful Beauty: Early American Decorative Arts From St. Louis Collections* [St. Louis, Mo.: St. Louis Art Museum, 1999], pp. 42–43). The absence of other illustrated examples in the major furniture compendiums of the 1920s and 1930s (i.e. Francis Clary Morse, *Furniture of the Olden Time* [1902; reprint, New York: MacMillan Co., 1917]; Esther Singleton, *Furniture of Our Forefathers* [New York: Doubleday, 1913]; Wallace Nutting, *Furniture Treasury*, 3 vols. [Framingham, Mass.: Old America Co., 1928]; Edgar G. Miller, *American Antique Furniture*, 2 vols. [1937; reprint, New York: Dover, 1966]) suggests that the form was extremely rare. Two chairs of this general form, but with turned stretchers and arms attached to the face of the side seat rails, are shown in *Loan Exhibition of Eighteenth and Nineteenth Century Furniture and Glass...for the Benefit of the National Council of Girl Scouts* (New York: American Art Galleries, 1929), nos. 577, 605. Following that publication, similar chairs began to appear in the advertisements of dealers. Most of the chairs of this type that have appeared in the marketplace are fakes. Like the example in the Chipstone collection, they tend to include parts salvaged from neoclassical lolling chairs and details that are either overstated or incorrectly adapted. These chairs represent a genre of fakes that continue to be bought by collectors, exhibited by museums, and published by furniture historians.

5. Ralph E. Carpenter, Jr., *The Arts and Crafts of Newport, Rhode Island, 1640–1820* (Newport, R.I.: Preservation Society of Newport County, 1954), p. 68. For more on the high chest, see Gerald W. R. Ward, *American Case Furniture in the Mabel Brady Garvan and Other Collections at Yale University* (New Haven, Conn.: Yale University Art Gallery, 1988), pp. 268–70, no. 141. The feet of this high chest are very unusual and resemble those on Irish furniture more than Newport work. The authors have not examined this chest. The easy chair shown in fig. 11 illustrates one avenue through which fakers exploited flaws in scholarship. During the middle of the twentieth century, regionalism was a major theme in the American furniture field, and many scholars and collectors ascribed to the theory that all major urban centers produced a similar range of case, table, and seating forms. Often overlooking channels of trade and commerce, this perspective tended to maintain that furniture used or found in a given region was made there. Recent scholarship has refuted this approach in many areas. Leigh Keno, Alan Miller, and Joan Barzilay Freund have demonstrated that Boston chair makers and merchant upholsterers dominated the market for seating furniture in New England and parts of the middle colonies prior to the Revolution (Leigh Keno, Alan Miller, and Joan Barzilay Freund, "The Very Pink of the Mode: Boston Georgian Chairs, Their Export, and Their Influence," in *American Furniture,* edited by Luke Beckerdite [Hanover, N. H.: University Press of New England for the Chipstone Foundation, 1996], pp. 266–306). Because of this dominance, few Newport easy chairs were made. The authors know of only three authentic examples: one illustrated in Conradson, *Useful Beauty,* pp. 42–43; one in the Rhode Island Historical Society (Carpenter, *Arts and Crafts of Newport,* p. 54); and one illustrated in Christie's *Important American Furniture, Silver, Prints, Folk Art, and Decorative Arts,* New York, January 18–19, 2001, lot 59.

6. Michael and Miriam Gratz were prominent members of Philadelphia's Jewish community. Michael was born in Lagersdorf, Silesia. In 1759, he emigrated from London to Philadelphia, where he joined his brother Bernard in the mercantile business. A decade later, Michael

married Miriam Simon. Her father, Joseph, was a Lancaster, Pennsylvania, merchant and business associate of Michael and Bernard (Roque, *American Furniture at Chipstone*, p. 208.) The couple may have purchased the original easy chair, a set of side chairs, and a dressing table shortly after their wedding in 1769. All of these objects were intended to match an elaborate high chest that Michael may have purchased soon after arriving in Philadelphia.

7. Philadelphia easy chairs with cabriole legs and arms shaped like those of a sofa rather than the more common double c-scroll variety are rare. Like the fake Gratz chairs, most fraudulent forms are built around the frames of straight-leg chairs. A few authentic Philadelphia easy chairs with sofa-form arms survive including one commissioned by John and Elizabeth Cadwalader (private collection on loan to the Philadelphia Museum of Art); one in the Winterthur Museum; one in a private collection in Milwaukee, Wis.; and one formerly in the Robb Collection (Israel Sack, Inc., *American Antiques from Israel Sack Collection*, 10 vols. [Alexandria, Va.: Highland House, 1974], 5: 1208–9).

8. For more on chairs attributed to members of the Gaines family, see *Portsmouth Furniture: Masterworks of the New Hampshire Seacoast*, edited by Brock Jobe (Boston: Society for the Preservation of New England Antiquities, 1993), pp. 295–300, nos. 77, 78; and Nancy E. Richards and Nancy Goyne Evans, *New England Furniture at Winterthur: Queen Anne and Chippendale Periods* (Hanover, N.H.: University Press of New England for the Winterthur Museum, 1997), pp. 31–36, nos. 17–19.

9. Invoice, February 14, 1964. Richards and Evans, *New England Furniture*, p. 35.

10. The attribution to Bernard is based on unpublished research by the authors. See J. Michael Flanigan, *American Furniture from the Kaufman Collection* (Washington, D. C.: National Gallery of Art, 1986), pp. 26, 27 for one of the chairs reputedly used by Washington.

11. *Loan Exhibition of Eighteenth and Nineteenth Century Furniture and Glass…for the Benefit of the National Council of Girl Scouts*, no. 627. Although the authors have not examined the table from the Girl Scouts Loan Exhibition, it too may be a fake. The shaped beaded skirt is similar to those on many straight-leg Newport card tables. It is possible that an early faker married thin, Boston-style legs to a Newport frame. If so, this would not be the first instance when one fake inspired another. Few eighteenth-century cabinetmakers had rasps, which were difficult and time-consuming to make. First-cut files produced most of the coarse striations found on the interior surfaces of early American furniture. Cabinetmakers typically owned several files ranging from coarse to fine.

12. Joseph Downs, *American Furniture: Queen Anne and Chippendale Periods at the Henry Francis du Pont Winterthur Museum* (New York: MacMillan Co., 1952), nos. 340, 341.

13. The histories of wear and use manifest on reused components are often inconsistent with their position and use on fakes. Visible discrepancies of this type are useful in identifying fakes.

14. Barry A. Greenlaw, *New England Furniture at Williamsburg* (Charlottesville: University Press of Virginia for the Colonial Williamsburg Foundation, 1974), p. 152, no. 132.

15. Invoice, April 15, 1959.

16. For a description of the traditional "peeling" technique of spindle turning, see F. Pain, *The Practical Woodturner* (1956; reprint, New York: Drake Publishers, 1974). Modern turning on a high-speed lathe is more akin to scraping than peeling.

17. For more on Harding, see Luke Beckerdite, "An Identity Crisis: Philadelphia and Baltimore Furniture Styles of the Mid-Eighteenth Century," in *Shaping a National Culture: The Philadelphia Experience, 1750–1800*, edited by Catherine E. Hutchins (Chicago: University of Chicago Press for the Winterthur Museum, 1995), pp. 243–81.

18. Invoice, November 25, 1958.

19. Carpenter, *Arts and Crafts of Newport*, p. 88, no. 60.

20. Stone, "Life Begins at Fifty," ix.

21. For more on this shop, see Alan Miller, "Roman Gusto in New England: An Eighteenth-Century Designer and His Shop," in *American Furniture*, edited by Luke Beckerdite (Hanover, N. H.: University Press of New England for the Chipstone Foundation, 1993), pp. 160–211.

Figure 1 Sideboard table with carving attributed to the shop of James Reynolds, Philadelphia, Pennsylvania, 1766–1776. Mahogany with yellow pine and walnut; clouded limestone. H. 33¼", W. 33", D. 21½". (Courtesy, Winterthur Museum.)

Figure 2 Map of the Philadelphia region showing quarries, churchyards, and towns. Quarries: (a) Henderson, (b) Brooks/Reeseville, (c) Wilkinson/Fritz/Potts, (d) Traquair/Cedar Grove, (e) Marble Hall, (f) Lentz. Churchyards: (1) Saint Peter's, (2) Great Valley Presbyterian, (3) Great Valley Baptist, (4) Trappe Lutheran, (5) Gloria Dei. Towns: (C) Conshohocken, (M) Malvern, (N) Norristown, (W) Whitemarsh.

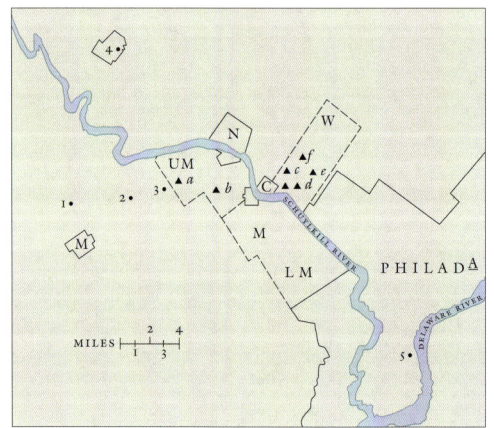

R. Curt Chinnici

Pennsylvania Clouded Limestone: Its Quarrying, Processing, and Use in the Stone Cutting, Furniture, and Architectural Trades

▼ THIS PROVINCE YIELDS *many kinds of marble, especially a white one with pale-gray, bluish spots, that is found in a quarry at the distance of a few miles from Philadelphia. They make many tombstones and tables, enclose chimneys and doors, floors of marble flags in the rooms, and the like of this kind of marble. A quantity of this commodity is shipped to different parts of America.*

Peter Kalm, September 20, 1748

Various stones quarried in the environs of Philadelphia—limestones, sandstones, and schists—have contributed significantly to the architecture and decorative arts of that city. This has led to much speculation regarding the source and geological composition of these stones, particularly those referred to generically as "marbles." The color and figure of limestone from southeastern Pennsylvania is varied, ranging from pure white to variegated blue and white to dark blue. Much of it was used for mantles and other architectural details, but some of the most beautiful and interesting examples of this stone are on furniture (see fig. 1). An analysis of the stone industry in Philadelphia and market distinctions made by eighteenth- and nineteenth-century craftsmen illuminates the uses and limitations of what is now known as "King of Prussia marble."[1]

Limestone from the Philadelphia Region
The pseudo-marble from southeastern Pennsylvania has garnered many names based on its supposed origin. "King of Prussia marble," "Conshohocken blue," and "Schuylkill gray" all derive from locations of quarries within the limestone belt crossing three counties that surround the city of Philadelphia. This extensive limestone deposit begins in Montgomery County, which is just north of the city, and crosses the Schuylkill River to the southwest extending through Chester and Lancaster counties. The length of the limestone belt is fifty-eight miles, and the widest section is three miles (fig. 2). The most productive quarries were only a few miles outside the city limits, and the names of towns near them became associated with the stone. Conshohocken and King of Prussia, for example, are situated along the Schuylkill River, which flows past the western edge of Philadelphia.[2]

The geological history of the limestone belt explains the beautiful color and durability of this material. Pennsylvania clouded limestone began its life as a sedimentary rock that underwent relatively light geologic pressure

Figure 3   Samples of European marble owned by James Logan (1674–1751). (Courtesy, Fairmont Park Commission.) Logan probably received these samples from colleagues in London. Similar marble appears on furniture used in Philadelphia during the eighteenth century.

to reach its current state during the Cambrian period. Often it is found under brownstone laid down in the Triassic period. The term "marble" is a marketing fiction on the part of merchants who wanted to get good prices for the stone, which could be polished like imported marbles (see fig. 3). True marbles are completely metamorphosed limestone and dolomite that have been subjected to extreme high pressure. One of its characteristics is its saccharoidal crystaline structure. Marble is made up of calcite ($CaCO_3$) or crystalline calcium carbonate. When magnesium ions replace calcium ions, as is the case with the Pennsylvania clouded limestone, the result is dolomitic marble $(MgCa)CO_3$. By contrast, limestone is made up of calcium carbonate and dolomite. The color of the metamorphosed limestone varies greatly. Gray was the most prevalent color quarried in Pennsylvania. Varying amounts of magnesia create equivalent variations of color throughout the limestone belt. The location of where this limestone metamorphosed determines its hue and the type of patterns found in it. Extraneous minerals cause color variations and affect the physical characteristics of the stone; some of these inclusions are quartz, iron, graphite, and several types of mica. Therefore, the colors and patterns of this dolomitic marble vary from quarry to quarry, and certain areas in the Philadelphia region became known for the visual attributes of the stone they produced.[3]

Traces of minerals such as magnesium give Pennsylvania clouded limestone a blue color, whereas graphite produces gray tones. In 1874, a leading geologist wrote:

> The bluish-white streaked marble which adorns the door steps and windows sills of the greater part of our houses comes from the limestone valley which, on either side of the Schuylkill, lies immediately north of the city. Originally formed by the accumulation of minute organic remains under deep sea water, subsequent changes have obliterated all traces of animal life, the streaks of carbonaceous material and the occasional specks of graphite alone remaining as witnesses. These same changes have altered certain strata of the limestone to the crystalline state known as marble.[4]

The most metamorphosed stone lies in the eastern portion of the limestone belt and gradually changes as it reaches the western edge in Lancaster County. Material not suitable for use as a marble was burned in kilns to produce lime for mortar, tanning, and agricultural purposes. The intense heat removed carbonic acid from the limestone leaving valuable calcium oxide, or quicklime, behind. During the eighteenth and nineteenth cen-

Figure 4 Lime kilns on Germantown Avenue in Plymouth Township, Pennsylvania. (Photo, Gavin Ashworth.) Plymouth Township is approximately twenty miles northwest of Philadelphia. These kilns were loaded from the top with limestone blocks then burned for days.

turies, hundreds of kilns flourished in this region, and those from the Philadelphia area were renowned in America and abroad (fig. 4). Lime production slowed dramatically with the invention of Portland cement at the end of the nineteenth century. Although this had an adverse impact on local quarries, surviving accounts document their earlier output and describe the stone they produced.[5]

Geological Surveys

Two geological surveys from the nineteenth century are important in identifying deposits of Pennsylvania clouded limestone. The earliest survey was conducted by Dr. Gerhard Troost who published a short report on deposits and quarries of various types of rock that he discovered in the Philadelphia region in 1826. A hand-colored map accompanying his report depicts deposits of serpentine, limestone, gneiss, clayslate, and the eurite and transition formations (fig. 5). Troost described the limestone valley as one composed of "granular limestone, through which different strata of marble run, which is quarried in various places for building purposes, con-

Figure 5 Detail of a geological map of Philadelphia illustrated on page 10 of Dr. Gerhard Troost's *Geological Survey of the Environs of Philadelphia performed by the order of the Philadelphia Society for promoting Agriculture* (Philadelphia: H. S. Tanner, 1826). (Courtesy, Ewell Sale Library, Academy of Natural Sciences of Pennsylvania.)

Figure 6 Elevation of the Pennsylvania State House shown on Matther A. Lotter, *A PLAN of the City and Environs of PHILADELPHIA, Pennsylvania, 1777*. This image shows the north façade which has figured limestone panels between the first and second floor windows and soapstone quoins. (Courtesy, Winterthur Museum.)

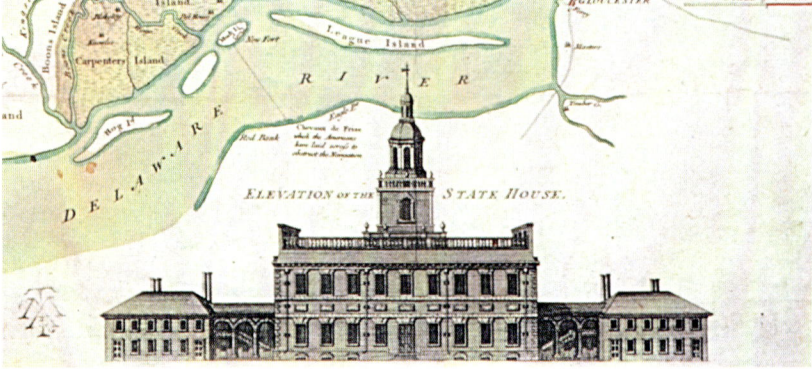

taining veins of cipolin (a granular limestone . . . containing veins of micaceous green talc), which characterize the marble used in Philadelphia." The only quarry mentioned by name is "Anderson's." Troost also described a variety of soapstone that is probably the same material that forms the quoins of the Pennsylvania State House (Independence Hall) in Philadelphia (fig. 6). The panels on the north façade are limestone (fig. 7).[6]

Figure 7 Detail showing a panel and a keystone on the Pennsylvania State House. This fielded panel is one of nine placed between the first and second floor windows of the north façade.

Dr. Henry Darwin Rogers (1804–1866)—the first official state geologist of Pennsylvania—catalogued several varieties of limestone quarried in the Philadelphia area. Appointed by the legislature in the 1830s, he spent decades taking samples of indigenous minerals and promoting his theories on ancient mountain formations of Appalachia. The initial purpose of this survey was to publicize the vast deposits of money-producing iron ore and coal in the eastern part of the state, but it documented the presence of other minerals including pseudo-marbles. In his *Geological Survey of Pennsylvania* (1858), Rogers noted that "marble of Potts Quarry" tended to be "clouded" or white. This descriptive term was also prevalent among marble dealers and architects who used "cloudy" to characterize the shadowy veining that ran through the stone. Rogers also noted that the "marble" outside of Philadelphia was "a highly metamorphic variety of . . . ordinary Magnesian limestone, crystallised and changed in tint by igneous action from within the earth." His use of the term "marble" to refer to metamorphosed limestone undoubtedly reflects his knowledge of its commercial applications.[7]

Dr. Rogers spent twenty years surveying Pennsylvania with the help of several assistants who took mineral samples from all over the state. These samples were labeled, numbered, and put into a collection in the 1850s. This collection was later broken up and replaced with another assembled by the authors of the *Second Geological Survey* between 1870 and 1880. According to Dr. Robert Sullivan, Curator of Paleontology and Geology at the State Museum of Pennsylvania, the collection from the second survey is incomplete and in poor condition, but several numbered samples listed in the "catalogue of specimens" survive. This catalogue refers to the clouded limestone as "bastard marble," indicating that its incomplete state of metamorphosis approaches true marble but falls short of the real thing.[8]

These samples were in storage for many years at the Academy of Natural Sciences in Philadelphia and were moved several years ago to the State Museum in Harrisburg, Pennsylvania. One sample is a "bluish limestone with bands of white limestone, and small flecks of mica" (fig. 8). The surveyors collected it at C. Earnest's quarry, on the eastern side of the Schuylkill

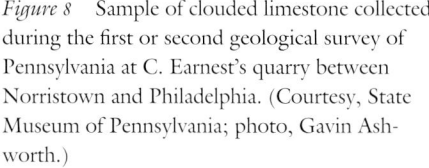

Figure 8 Sample of clouded limestone collected during the first or second geological survey of Pennsylvania at C. Earnest's quarry between Norristown and Philadelphia. (Courtesy, State Museum of Pennsylvania; photo, Gavin Ashworth.)

River between Norristown and Philadelphia. With its dark blue color, bright white veins, and passages of gray, this sample resembles the slabs on several opulent tables made in Philadelphia during the eighteenth and nineteenth centuries (see figs. 30, 31). A similar sample came from a quarry near Upper Merion Township below the village of King of Prussia on the western side of the river (fig. 9). The catalogue of specimens describes this piece as "white and blue marble with hydro-mica and pyrite." Other samples are referred to as "bastard marble," "limestone," "(compact) limestone,"

Figure 9 Sample of clouded limestone collected during the first or second geological survey of Pennsylvania at a quarry near Upper Merion Township. (Courtesy, State Museum of Pennsylvania; photo, Gavin Ashworth.) The brown diagonal line across the top of the sample is iron, and the large blue areas are deposits of magnesium within the matrix of calcium carbonate.

and "slaty limestone." These varied descriptions reflect different stages of metamorphosis, with "marble" being the hardest, and "limestone" the softest. The geologists also noted the variety of colors and color combinations that were available to the marble trade.[9]

The specimens assembled during the second geological survey are a benchmark for the study of Pennsylvania clouded limestone. Although the samples are very small, they document the colors and inclusions of stones that the surveyors considered representative of each quarry or area. By correlating the physical attributes of these samples with period descriptions of each quarry's output, it is possible to pinpoint the source of stone used in some Pennsylvania furniture and architecture.

Ecclesiastical Monuments and Gravestones

Tombstones, grave markers, and monuments are another important resource for identifying the location and production methods of early limestone quarries in southeastern Pennsylvania. Many of the churchyards in outlying areas are near quarries. In addition to revealing possible sources for specific types of marble, the tombstones in these yards show what types of stone were available and fashionable at a given date. The latter is also true of churchyards in Philadelphia, although the stones in urban burial grounds probably reflect more diverse sources.

Founded by Welsh settlers in 1711, the Great Valley Baptist Church in Upper Merion Township has a churchyard with several early, ornate tombstones. These are important because the church is near the site of the Henderson quarries not far from Bridgeport in Montgomery County. Another nearby quarry is the Brooks quarry in King of Prussia; however, the earliest record of its existence is 1815. Two of the oldest tombstones (see figs. 10, 11) are made of dark clouded limestone similar to the geological sample illustrated in figure 9. One has a baroque crest with carved scrolls (fig. 10), whereas the other has an arched crest and cyma-shaped elements on each side (fig. 11). The backs of both tombstones are quite rough (see fig. 12). This may be evidence of quarrying with wedges, wherein slabs were split from larger rock masses before trimming.[10]

Figure 10 Tombstone for David James, Great Valley Baptist Church, Upper Merion Township, Pennsylvania, dated 1730. (Photo, R. Curt Chinnici.) This is one of the earliest Pennsylvania tombstones made of clouded limestone.

Figure 11 Tombstone with an eroded inscription, Great Valley Baptist Church, Upper Merion Township, Pennsylvania, dated 1733. (Photo, Gavin Ashworth.)

Figure 12 Detail showing the back of the tombstone illustrated in fig. 11.

Figure 13   Tombstone for James David, Saint Peter's Church, Chester County, Pennsylvania, dated July 24, 1746. (Photo, Gavin Ashworth.)

Figure 14   Detail of the back of a tombstone for P. Lloyd, Great Valley Presbyterian Church, Chester County, Pennsylvania, dated April 1802. (Photo, Gavin Ashworth.)

Another old burial ground further west is adjacent to Saint Peter's Church, built in 1744 by Welsh congregants in the Great Valley in Chester County. There were several quarries in Chester County at Henderson Station, on Whitford Road, and near Downingtown, but there are no records of when they began excavating limestone. Early "quarrying" may have been done by farmers who sold off exposed stone for lime burning and architectural elements. At Saint Peter's, thirty-seven burial sites are eighteenth century, and the earliest is that of James David, who died in 1746 (fig. 13). His memorial is made of highly figured local limestone with blue-gray veining and has crossbones on the crest.

Other significant burial stones from Chester County quarries are in the churchyard of the Great Valley Presbyterian Church. Many exhibit a variety of tool marks indicative of their date. Most of the eighteenth-century stones are clouded limestone and relatively small. Some have backs with irregular facets left by flat chisels, whereas others have backs with small toothed marks in broad sweeping patterns (see fig. 14). Stone cutters used toothed chisels of various sizes to produce this "corrugated" surface. The later burial stones are larger and lighter in color. Most of those dated between 1795 and 1819 have backs with parallel grooves that cross from left to right (see fig. 15). These marks indicate that the stones were cut with

Figure 15   Detail showing the saw kerfs on the back of a tombstone for Major Ezekiel Howell, Great Valley Presbyterian Church, Chester County, Pennsylvania, dated October 4, 1812. (Photo, Gavin Ashworth.)

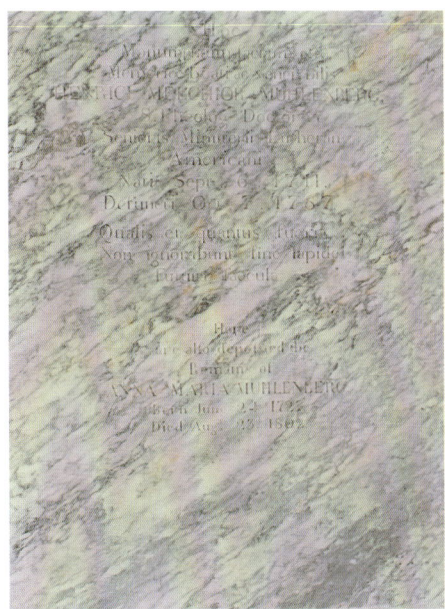

Figure 16   Altar tomb for Henry and Anna Marie Muhlenberg, Augustus Lutheran Church, Trappe, Pennsylvania, dated October 7, 1787, and August 23, 1802. The stone for the tomb was probably cut in 1787. (Photo, Gavin Ashworth.)

abrasives and a sash-hung wire powered by water. The toothed saws used later in the nineteenth century performed the same function. This process became even more efficient with the advent of steam power in the 1820s.[11]

Several late eighteenth- and early nineteenth-century tombstones in the burial ground of the Augustus Lutheran Church in Trappe, Pennsylvania, have backs with uniform marks from a sash-hung wire or toothed saw blade. The color and figure of these stones varies, but most are white with gray and blue-gray patterns. Two of the most dramatic memorials are a massive altar tomb with a slab measuring four by six feet (fig. 16) and a tombstone with German script (fig. 17). Both are highly figured limestone with a deep blue and white pattern.

Limestone quarried outside Philadelphia made its way into the city during the early eighteenth century. Gloria Dei, or Old Swedes Episcopal Church, in Philadelphia has several important tombstones from the mid-eighteenth century. Built in 1698, Gloria Dei was a Swedish Lutheran church until 1845 when it became an Episcopal church. Three exquisite markers commemorating the interments of pastors are installed on the floor. The two earliest examples are gray and white with a very distinctive pattern (figs. 18, 19). Both have carved cherubim in the upper corners and brief biographies below. The marker for Andrew Ridman is dated 1708; however, it appears to have been produced at the same time and by the same stone cutter who made the marker for John Dylander in 1741. The third marker for Olamus Parlin is dated 1757. His stone is very dark and has a black field with dark blue veining. All of these markers are important in documenting the use of certain types of limestone at specific dates and for the prestige accorded this otherwise humble material. Although none of the stones in the churchyard are comparable, an eighteenth-century baptismal bowl with a nineteenth-century stand (fig. 20) appears to be made from the same limestone as the three early markers.

Figure 17 Tombstone with old German script, Augustus Lutheran Church, Trappe, Pennsylvania, dated 1751. (Photo, Gavin Ashworth.)

Figure 18 Grave marker for Rev. Andrew Ridman, Old Swedes Episcopal Church, Philadelphia, Pennsylvania, dated 1708. (Photo, Gavin Ashworth.)

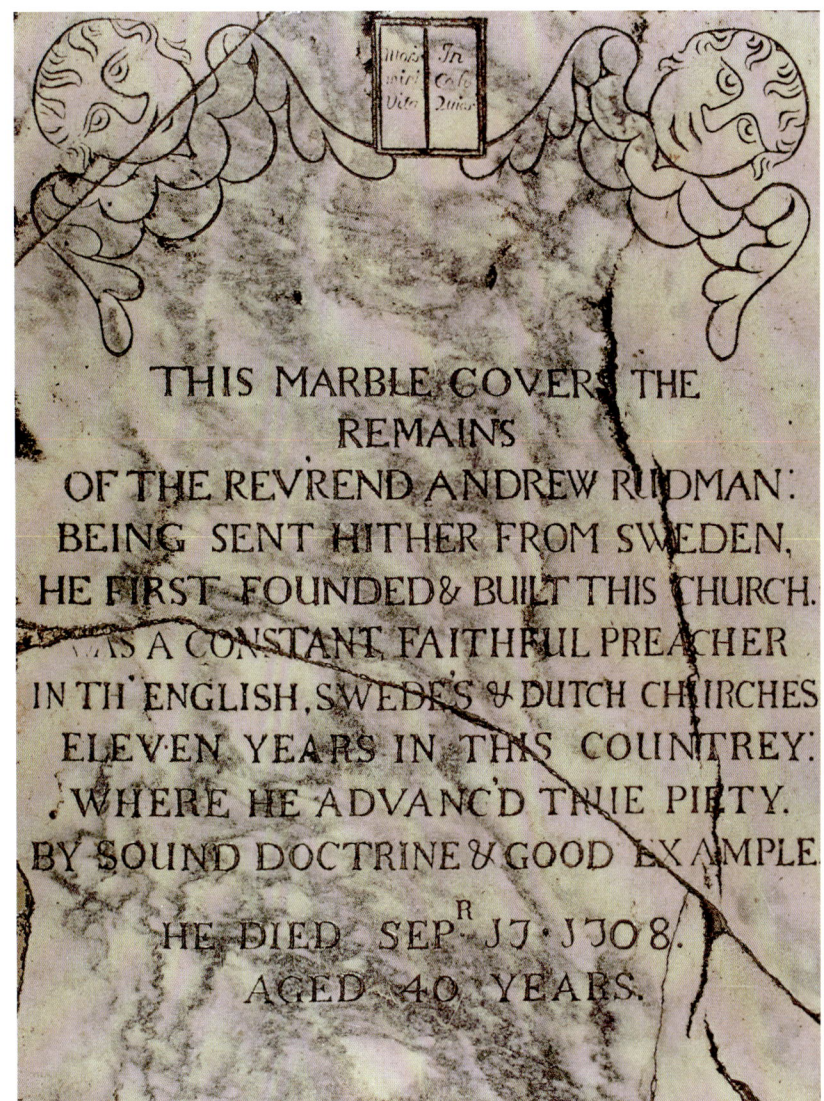

Figure 19 Grave marker for Rev. John Dylander, Old Swedes Episcopal Church, Philadelphia, Pennsylvania, dated 1741. (Photo, Gavin Ashworth.)

Figure 20 Baptismal bowl, Old Swedes Episcopal Church, Philadelphia, Pennsylvania, eighteenth century. (Photo, Gavin Ashworth.)

Processing Marble for Architectural Components and Furniture

As the aforementioned burial stones and monuments reveal, early marble slabs often have tool marks made by quarry laborers, mills, and stone cutters. Since technology changed over time, these marks can provide evidence of a stone's processing date and, in the case of a furniture slab, its use on a given object. The originality of a table slab or other component that is easily removable can be difficult to ascertain. A stone's exposure to light and other environmental factors as well as compression marks and wear on the frame are equally important considerations.

During the eighteenth century, quarries sent stone cutters and marble dealers rough slabs that had been cleaved from the rock. Later, saw mills associated with quarries produced smooth slabs that stone cutters sawed

Figure 21 Detail of the back of the tombstone illustrated in figs. 11, 12.

Figure 22 Detail of the underside of the top of the sideboard table illustrated in fig. 30.

and finished to their patrons' specifications. Like the backs of early tombstones (see figs. 12, 21), the undersides of marble tops for tables often have uneven surfaces where the slabs broke away from the quarry wall (see fig. 22). Most early stone cutters did not grind the surface down far enough to make the slab perfectly flat. Later slabs typically do not have irregularities or tool marks on their undersides owing to the use of steam-operated saws. Regardless of their date or intended function, marble slabs were generally cut in the same direction in which they were quarried.

Often specific tools can be associated with the marks on eighteenth-century table slabs. *The Marble Worker's Manual, Designed for the Use of Marble Workers, Builders, and Owners of Houses* (1865) illustrates a variety of tools and implements used by stone cutters and describes their function (fig. 23). Most stone cutters followed the same basic procedures to process their slabs; they cut the stock into shape (fig. 23, nos. 61–62), hewed it with chisels and a mallet (fig. 23, nos. 2, 4, 19, 20, 64, and fig. 24a), dressed or "boasted" it with edge tools (fig. 23, nos. 8, 9, 27, 28, and fig. 24b), and finished it with chisels, rasps, and burin (fig. 23, nos. 13–16, 22–31, and fig. 24c). After performing these tasks, the stone cutter used pieces of sandstone to planish the exposed surfaces and a pumice stone and cushion to

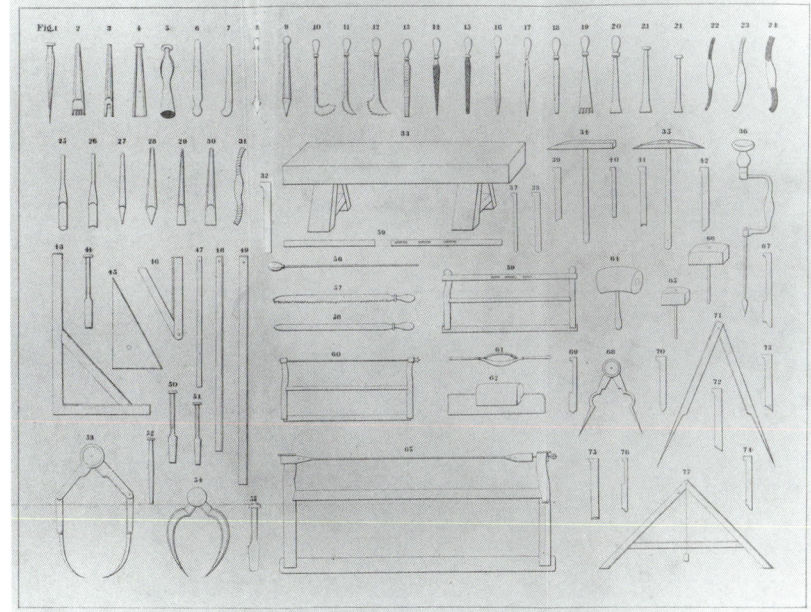

Figure 23 Illustration showing stone cutters' tools illustrated in *The Marble Worker's Manual*. No. 1 — square etching needle; nos. 2, 4, 19, 20, 64 — marteline chisels used for etching and with a mallet or sledge hammer, no. 5 — puncheons; nos. 8, 9, 27, 28 — partly flattened, very sharp etching needles called houguettes; no. 10 — hooks for sinking and leveling cavities; no. 11 — round-nosed chisels for sinking and leveling cavities; no. 12 — sharp edged and notched scrapers for fluting; no. 19 — scrapers for fluting; no. 31 — parting tools bent round and steeled at each end to smooth areas difficult to reach; no. 34 — martelines (iron mallets pointed at one end, and diamond shaped at the other) used to pierce and shell off the marble without splintering; no. 61 — sebillas, or wooden bowls for holding the sand and water that would be thrown under the saw; no. 56 — wooden or metal ladles used with the sebillas; no. 62 — handsaws without teeth, used to cut stone or marble with the aid of sand or water. "A skillful workman often confines himself to making a deep groove in the Marble or stone, and then by a quick blow, separates the two pieces." (Courtesy, Winterthur Museum Library: Printed Book and Periodical Collection.)

polish them. Eighteenth-century stone cutters usually tabled their slabs on the edges of the bottom surface so they would rest level on a furniture frame, but they did not make them flat like many of their nineteenth-century counterparts. On early slab tables, gaps between the stone and top of the frame are usually present. Most stonecutters did not planish the underside of such tops.[12]

Figure 24 Details showing (from left to right): an etching needle and mallet being used to chip away small pieces of stone, a flat marteline chisel being used to level the surface, and a chisel and mallet being used to table the edges of a slab. (Photo, R. Curt Chinnici.) The marteline chisel performs the same function as an etching needle, but it leaves parallel tooth marks.

Eighteenth-Century Quarries and Marble Dealers

Although many objects made of Pennsylvania clouded limestone survive, information on eighteenth-century quarries is scarce. Since records of lime burning exist from early in that century, it is probable that marble was a commodity at about the same time. The earliest quarries were in Whitemarsh Township and Harmanville, both in Montgomery County, Pennsylvania. Several quarries near Harmanville are mentioned in a 1714 deed wherein David Henry sold Thomas Coldee 150 acres of land east of Conshohocken Pike and south of Ridge Road. Philadelphia carver Anthony Wilkinson purchased this tract between 1720 and 1731.[13]

Bills and advertisements indicate that Wilkinson carved ship figureheads and sold marble pieces such as hearths. He may also have been the first entrepreneur to own a quarry and a marble shop in the city. In the Novem-

Figure 25 Sideboard table with carving attributed to the shop of Samuel Harding, Philadelphia, Pennsylvania, 1740–1755. Mahogany with yellow pine and white cedar; Italian marble. H. 29", W. 42", D. 22". (Courtesy, Diplomatic Reception Rooms, U. S. Department of State; photo, Will Brown.) The top appears to be the third one used on this frame. Screw pockets on the inner faces of the rails indicate that the table had a wooden top at one point, but its original was probably clouded limestone or marble.

ber 2, 1727, issue of the *American Weekly Mercury,* Wilkinson offered a reward of forty shillings for a runaway servant named "Richard Peckford, a stone cutter by trade." Wilkinson's dual business evidently flourished since he continued to advertise carving and stone work during the 1730s and 1740s. When London-trained mason William Holland left Philadelphia for an extended trip to New York in 1739, he advised his customers to purchase marble from Wilkinson. Holland's production included "Marble Chimney Pieces, Grave Stones, Mortars, Tables, Monuments and Steps, Pavements of All Kinds, [and] Hearths." Two years later, the *Pennsylvania Gazette* reported: "MASON work done by Anthony Wilkinson, Ship Carver, in Water Street, just above the street commonly call'd Arch Street, and to be done of the best marble, in the quarry, he having lately found a vein of much better than has been formerly us'd."[14]

It is conceivable that Wilkinson provided marble slabs and carved ornaments for local cabinetmakers. No documented example of his work survives, but the sideboard table illustrated in figure 25 is representative of the era in which Wilkinson worked. This example is from a large cabinet shop that produced several dressing tables, cabriole leg high chests, and other case and table forms (see fig. 26), most of which have details associated with Irish furniture. The shell and leaf ornament on the front rail is closely related to carving in the Pennsylvania State House. One of the carvers who

Figure 26 Sideboard table, Philadelphia, Pennsylvania, 1735–1745. Mahogany with tulip poplar; clouded limestone. H. 30", W. 44¾", D. 21½". (Courtesy, Baltimore Museum of Art, bequest of J. Gilman D'Arcy Paul; photo, Gavin Ashworth.)

Figure 27 Detail of the edge molding on the top of the sideboard table illustrated in fig. 26.

Figure 28 Detail of the underside of the top of the sideboard table illustrated in fig. 26.

Figure 29 Detail of the saw kerfs on the back edge of the top of the sideboard table illustrated in fig. 26.

submitted bills for this architectural work was Brian Wilkinson, Anthony's son. The other carver, Samuel Harding, was one of the principal specialists employed by this cabinet shop.[15]

Although the marble top on the aforementioned table is replaced, the original slab may have resembled the one on an earlier frame (fig. 26). Made of deep blue and white clouded limestone, the top has an unusually complex molding on the front and sides (fig. 27). Its underside is planished, although rough impressions indicate that the stone was broken from the wall or floor of the quarry with a mallet and wedges (fig. 28). The back edge of the top has deep saw kerfs (fig. 29). Like the frame with the replaced top (fig. 25), the example illustrated in figure 26 has an unmistakable Irish aspect. The bulbous slipper feet and distinctive rail scalloping have parallels in other Irish-influenced forms from Philadelphia as well as the Rappahannock River Valley of Virginia. Based on its design, this slab table could date from the late 1730s.[16]

Figure 30 Sideboard table attributed to the shop of Henry Cliffton and Thomas Carteret, Philadelphia, Pennsylvania, ca. 1755. Mahogany; clouded limestone. H. 29¼", W. 36½", D. 22¼". (Private collection; photo, Gavin Ashworth.)

One of the earliest references to this table form in Philadelphia is the 1734 inventory of John Bryant who had "a Slab in a frame for a table." Unfortunately, it is impossible to determine whether the top was imported or made in the region. Six years later, stone cutter Anthony Engelbreckt advertised marble "Chimney Pieces, Tables, Tea Boards, Coats of Arms, Tomb Stones, &c. made in the newest Italian and French fashion; and in the neatest and best Manner." Although not conclusive, his reference to tables and tea boards suggests the production of furniture slabs. In 1738, the *Philadelphia Gazette* reported that cabinetmaker Joseph Claypoole made sideboards, a term used interchangeably for frames with marble slabs or wooden tops. Judging from advertisements placed by his son, Joseph almost certainly made frames for slabs. In the March 22, 1740, issue of the *South Carolina Gazette,* Josiah Claypoole reported that he had recently moved "from Philadelphia" and advertised "all sorts of Joyner's and Cabinet-Maker's Work" including "Frames for Marble Tables." Less than two

years before moving to Charleston, Josiah had inherited his father's cabinetmaking business, stock, and "Implements of Trade."[17]

Most of the surviving slab frames made by Philadelphia cabinetmakers before the mid-1760s have flat rails, occasionally ornamented with scalloping, moldings, or, more rarely, carving. To support the weight of the marble, these artisans relied on thick materials and sturdy mortise-and-tenon joints, the latter occasionally reinforced with vertical glue blocks. Crossbraces and corner braces also occur on some eighteenth-century examples.[18]

An elegant sideboard table attributed to the shop of Henry Clifton and Thomas Carteret (fig. 30) displays an unusual method of indexing the top (figs. 22, 32). In the center of each rear leg is a round hole, presumably for a now missing metal pin that engaged a hole in the underside of the top. The stonecutter responsible for this slab probably used a bow-drill and "piercer" (a U-shaped bit) to hollow out the holes in the limestone. A few other eighteenth-century American slab frames have evidence for metal indexing pins, but most cabinetmakers relied on the tabled edges and the weight of the stone to register the top and prevent it from moving.[19]

The stone on the sideboard table shown in figures 30 and 31 appears by its color and complex figure to be from a quarry on the eastern side of the Schuylkill River, possibly one from the vicinity of Whitemarsh Township.

Figure 31 Top of the sideboard table illustrated in fig. 30.

During the eighteenth century, several proprietors including David Henry, Thomas Coldee, and Anthony Wilkinson managed these quarries. The slab on this table was cut from the rock with wedges and mallet, and both sides were roughly smoothed with chisels followed by a burin tool. To remove the burin marks on the upper surface, the stonecutter used sandstone or a similar abrasive. He also used crushed sandstone or sand worked with iron or wooden mullers and a coarse file to shape the edge. Then, he rubbed the stone with a succession of grinding materials that gradually became finer in consistency. Often polishers began by rubbing the stone with pieces of fired clay followed by pumice stone, lead filings with emery mud, English rouge, and for a brilliant effect, a linen cushion moistened with water and calcined tin.[20]

Figure 32 Detail of the underside of the top of the sideboard table illustrated in fig. 30, showing a hole for a metal indexing pin.

The stone cutter used toothed chisels to shape and smooth the bottom edges of the slab to make it sit level, but he did not remove the quarrying marks from the area inside the frame since it would not be visible. The section that drops into the frame is carefully sculpted to clear the inner edges of the rails and glue blocks (figs. 22, 32). This keys the stone to the frame so that it rests safely and securely.

By the middle of the eighteenth century, Philadelphia cabinetmakers had established a relatively standard vocabulary for sideboard table frames. A manuscript titled "Prices of Cabinet & Chair Work/ Benjamin Lehman January 1786" lists the options for standard cabriole leg forms that were fashionable from the 1740s to the 1780s as well as straight leg examples that became popular by the late 1760s. Columns list from left to right prices for mahogany and walnut and the rates paid journeymen:

Frames for Marble Slabs

Frame for Marble slab Marlborough feet with out Bases or Brackets about 4 feet long	2.10.0	1.10.0	0.12.0
Do. with Bases and Brackets Commode Rails	3.10.0		0.17.0
Do. with plain Knees & Claw feet	4.10.0		1.0.0
Do. with Leaves on the Knees & Carved Mouldings	5.0.0		1.0.0
Do. 5 feet with 6 legs	6.10.0[21]		

As the term "frame for a slab" implies, furniture makers typically made table bases to accommodate marble slabs. This was especially true of tables with elaborately shaped and/or molded tops, which were more difficult and more expensive to cut. The slab on the table illustrated in figure 33 is made of highly figured limestone with dark blue inclusions. To complement its complex shape, the owner commissioned a conforming frame with a drawer, a feature rarely encountered on eighteenth-century sideboard tables from the middle Atlantic region. With its lavish knee carving, gadrooned molding, and powerful claw-and-ball feet, this table is one of the finest Philadelphia examples in the rococo style.

The carving on the table is attributed to Nicholas Bernard and Martin Jugiez who first advertised in the November 25, 1762, issue of the *Pennsylvania Gazette*. Their firm received commissions for architectural carving from several prominent Philadelphians including Chief Justice Benjamin Chew, John Cadwalader, and Samuel Powell, and they worked for the city's leading cabinetmakers including Benjamin Randolph, Thomas Affleck, and William Wayne. They also advertised "Carving in Wood or Stone and gilding done in the neatest Manner." No stone carving can be attributed to Bernard and Jugiez, but their references to such work during the 1760s and 1770s imply that there was demand. Presumably their stone carving was sculptural rather than utilitarian. Like most of their competitors, they probably purchased marble slabs from local stone cutters.[22]

During the eighteenth century, several Philadelphia masons and stone cutters placed advertisements in Philadelphia newspapers. In addition to those mentioned earlier, these tradesmen included William Peters (1752), John Stanaland (1752), Brian Wilkinson and Son (1774), David Chambers (1780), William Stiles (1785), and William Payne (1798). At least one of these men employed slave labor. On July 16, 1752, the *Pennsylvania Gazette* reported: "A Likely young Negroe man, who has been employed for some years in the stone cutting business, country born, and has had the small pox, to be sold, or hired out by WILLIAM PETERS." Peters' advertised products, which included chimney pieces, slabs, tomb and head stones, and "other pieces of wrought marble," suggest that his slave artisan possessed a great deal of skill.[23]

Nineteenth-Century Quarries
Many of the limestone quarries active during the nineteenth century were established much earlier. Philadelphia marble dealer James Traquair purchased one of Anthony Wilkinson's. The former employed Italian sculptor Guiseppa Jardella and boasted that he had the "best quarry in this State [and produced] . . . twelve different kinds of beautiful clouded marble, which takes as high a polish as any of the Italian." He also advertised "tombs, headstones, chimney pieces, side and currying tables [and] . . . monuments in the ancient or modern style."[24]

Jardella and Christopher Hocker continued Traquair's business until the middle of the nineteenth century, when Peter Dager and his son Daniel assumed ownership of the quarry. The business subsequently passed into the Potts family through marriage. Robert T. Potts and E. Channing Potts managed the quarry with great success until 1880, when the business became known as the Cedar Grove Marble Works. The quarry's output

Figure 33 Sideboard table with carving attributed to the shop of Nicholas Bernard and Martin Jugiez, Philadelphia, Pennsylvania, 1760–1770. Mahogany with yellow poplar; clouded limestone. H. 29⅞", W. 42⅝", D. 21". (Courtesy, Museum of Fine Arts, Boston; M. and M. Karolik Collection.)

Figure 34 Detail of a chimneypiece and fireplace surround in Graeme Park, Montgomery County, Pennsylvania, 1750–1760. (Courtesy, Winterthur Museum Library: Printed Book and Periodical Collection.) This is the earliest fireplace surround made of highly variegated Pennsylvania limestone in its original location. The horizontal stone is 64" wide and 9⅞" high. The two supporting side panels are 44" high and 7" wide. The inner edge of the stone has a ⅜" bead on three sides. The bead stops 10" from the floor, which is the same height as the baseboard. On the left panel, a horizontal, scored line indicates the baseboard level. The hearth stones are original, but they have been reset. Similar tiles and limestone surrounds are in later Philadelphia residences including the Physick House.

Figure 35 Detail of a chimneypiece and fireplace surround in Andalusia, Bucks County, Pennsylvania, 1833–1835. (Courtesy, Andalusia Foundation; photo, Gavin Ashworth.)

was 12,000 cubic feet per year in 1858, and its most esteemed varieties of marble were "blue" and "mottled-white-and-blue." Many houses near the quarry and in Philadelphia have surrounds made of marble similar to that from the Cedar Grove Quarry and nearby Fritz Quarry (see figs. 34, 35).[25]

Wilkinson's other quarries passed through several hands before Peter Fritz acquired them by 1830. Fritz was a prolific manufacturer of limestone mantles, monuments, and furniture slabs. An 1832 engraving of his marble

Figure 36 View of *Race Street between 6th & 7th, Philadelphia*, 1834. (Photo, R. Curt Chinnici.) This image from a newspaper fragment shows the Franklin Marble Mantel Manufactory and funeral statuary owned by Peter Fritz.

yard on Race Street in Philadelphia shows large slabs leaning against his office and showroom (fig. 36). These slabs could be cut down and the edges finished to the patron's specifications. As the illustration indicates, Fritz kept a large variety of stones and designs on hand. The limestone from his quarry was a very fine white and blue variegated type described during the period as "Pennsylvania clouded."[26]

The Pennsylvania Land and Marble Company purchased the Fritz quarry together with a neighboring quarry in 1854. The company attempted to generate interest in the quarries by selling stock to investors and announcing plans to build a new railroad line to transport the stone and ore to the river where it would be loaded onto barges and shipped to the city. A stockholders' report published in 1854 described the physical attributes of the land as well as its deposits of marble, limestone, and iron ore:

> On account of the beauty of the location, and its springs of pure water, this place is visited by thousands of our citizens during the year. There is not a more fashionable place of resort for Pic-Nics, Sunday Schools, and other respectable associations in the vicinity of Philadelphia, than Spring Mills. There cannot be a doubt that these beautifully located lands will be surrounded with a dense and intelligent population; these lands will be worth more after the marble limestone and iron ore are taken off, than they cost this company, with their rich mineral deposits included at the time of their purchase.

The Pennsylvania Land and Marble Company quarried "five specimens of Marble . . . in demand by the trade in all cities of the Union." These included a "dark colored variegated chimney marble," a "light colored variegated marble," a "light clouded marble, used for all the purposes of building," a "light clouded marble with white veins interspersed through it, a beautiful article," and a "grey marble used for house and store fronts, columns, &c." According to the stockholders' report, local marble was selling for ten cents per square foot in 1854, whereas imported marble cost between two dollars and four dollars a square foot. Pennsylvania white marble was selling for one dollar per cubic foot, and one variety of blue and black marble was available for forty cents per cubic foot. The report also listed marble masons who would attest to the fine quality of the stone from the company's quarries: J. Eckstein, Jr., Edwin Greble, Thomas Hargrave,

Figure 37 Girard College, designed by Thomas Ustick Walter (1804–1887), Philadelphia, Pennsylvania, 1833–1847.(Courtesy, Girard College; photo, Gavin Ashworth.)

Robert Harvey, J. E. & B. Shell, Oliver Ottinger, Henry S. Tarr, Adam Steinmetz, Lewis Thompson, J. Struthers and Son, S. F. Jacoby and Co., School & Faurest, and John Baird. Ultimately, the Pennsylvania Land and Marble Company failed. The old Fritz Quarry appears to have been nearly depleted when Dr. Henry Rogers conducted his geological survey in 1858.[27]

Like the Fritz Quarry, Marble Hall grew out of quarries established in the eighteenth century, most notably those founded by Thomas Moore in Whitemarsh Township by 1785. Marble Hall actually consisted of several quarries, "two stores, a marble mill, wheelwright, blacksmith shop and 42 houses." Moore's son Daniel Hitner expanded operations in 1813, and by the middle of the century, his sons Daniel O. Hitner and Henry S. Hitner added iron ore quarries and steam marble sawing mills. The largest quarry was 400 feet long, 60 feet wide, and 265 feet deep. Most of Marble Hall's limestone was white or white with gray clouded veins. Many Philadelphia townhouses are fitted out in this white stone, probably because of its similarity to Italian Cararra marble. Marble Hall ceased to operate in 1870. By that date the extreme depth of the quarry made further excavation impractical and expensive.[28]

John Henderson's quarry, established in Upper Merion Township in 1795, was esteemed for its white and blue limestone, often found in alternating layers. According to architect Thomas U. Walter (1804–1887), Girard College bought marble from Henderson Quarry in 1833 for the eastern flank of the cell, its portico, platform, and steps at a cost of one dollar per cubic foot (fig. 37). He specified "the whole to be of light blue marble similar to that used on the United States Mint and the Philadelphia Merchants' Exchange" (fig. 38). The Second Bank of the United States was also constructed using stone from the Henderson Quarry (fig. 39).[29]

Figure 38 Merchant's Exchange Building, designed by William Strickland (1788–1854), South Third and Walnut Streets, Philadelphia, Pennsylvania, 1832–1834. (Photo, Gavin Ashworth.)

Figure 39 Second Bank of the United States, designed by William Strickland, Chestnut Street, Philadelphia, Pennsylvania, 1818. (Photo, Gavin Ashworth.)

The nearby Brooks Quarry in King of Prussia was renowned for its light blue limestone, which appears on the north side of Girard College. This quarry also produced one of the largest slabs excavated in the Philadelphia region. This monumental stone was exhibited at the Chicago World Fair in 1898 and measured sixteen feet, two inches by six feet, nine inches.[30]

The Oakland Quarry in Chester County was opened for the sole purpose of supplying limestone for Girard College. Architect Samuel Sloan wrote "the Corinthian capitals and their sculptured work were from the Oakland quarries, their marble being well adapted to the purpose, on account of the compactness of its crystallization, thus enabling the artist to cut it into any desired form, and closely resembling in that respect, the Italian statuary marble."[31]

Figure 40   Pier table, Philadelphia, Pennsylvania, 1820–1830. Mahogany and mahogany veneer with pine; imported white Italian marble. H. 43$^{15}/_{16}$", W. 50$^{1}/_{8}$", D. 23$^{15}/_{16}$". (Courtesy, Winterthur Museum.)

Figure 41   Corner table, Baltimore, Maryland, 1795–1805. Mahogany and satinwood with white pine; clouded limestone. H. 37", W. 27$^{1}/_{2}$", D. 20$^{7}/_{8}$". (Courtesy, Winterthur Museum.)

Architects and builders also used locally quarried marble for residential projects. Numerous marble yards supplied them with stone for steps, water tables, lintels, fireplace surrounds, and other architectural components. An account book from the firm of Foust and Weaver (1854–1861) lists hundreds of orders for building details as well as tops for furniture: "one Italian slab for counter top $13.64," a "wash stand top $6.50," an "Italian wash stand top $22.00," and a "second hand table top $6.00." The reference to a "second hand table top" suggests that patrons often reused valuable marble parts, either with or without alteration. Anthony Quervelle paid Foust and Weaver $130 for "one white front, heads and sills" for his house on "Pine St. East of Sixth," although he used imported marble for most of his furniture (see fig. 40). The white stone ordered by Quervelle for his residence was less expensive than the blue variety.[32]

New Tastes for Old Stone

Just as furniture styles changed from the eighteenth to the nineteenth century, so did tastes for stone components for decorative objects. Although clouded limestone occasionally appears on neoclassical furniture (see figs. 41, 42), its use diminished significantly owing to the popularity of Italian marble. White Carrara marble with slight veins of gray was considered ideal, but local stone of similar coloring was readily available and less expensive. The taste for exotic marbles increased throughout the nineteenth century, and local marble dealers maintained varied stocks. In 1853, James and Michael Baird advertised, "Carrara Statuary, Carrara Ordinary, Carrara Veined, Egyptian, or Black and Gold; Sienna, Levant, Brocatelle, Pyrenees, Bardilla and Lisbon." This firm's marble showrooms featured "130 patterns of mantels, slabs for the trade for tables, bureaus and workstands," and their workshops had the latest steam-powered saws and abrasive

Figure 42 Center table, Philadelphia, Pennsylvania, 1825–1835. Maple and maple veneer with white pine; clouded limestone. H. 27", Diam. of top: 43⅝". (Courtesy, Andalusia Foundation; photo, Gavin Ashworth.) This table is part of the furniture brought to Andalusia by Nicholas Biddle when he moved from Philadelphia to this country house on a permanent basis.

Figure 43 Illustration titled the "Sawing-Rooms of J. & M. Baird's Steam Marble Works," from *Godey's Lady's Book* (1853). (Photo, R. Curt Chinnici.)

devices to cut and polish their stone (fig. 43). The Bairds owned the largest marble yard in Philadelphia in the nineteenth century, but they received brisk competition from smaller firms, many located at Thirteenth Street and the terminus of Ridge Pike. Massive blocks of local stone arrived at Ridge Pike transported by large teams of horses. The Bairds and other major firms had equipment to cut blocks of stone into workable slabs, whereas smaller shops cut slabs into shapes and did edge work.[33]

The Decline of the Marble Business in Southeast Pennsylvania
By the middle of the nineteenth century, quarries in the Philadelphia region began to close. Many sites had become depleted or were so deep that the cost of quarrying the stone made them unprofitable. Some quarries, like

Figure 44 Washstand, Philadelphia, Pennsylvania, 1830–1845. Mahogany veneer on white pine; clouded limestone. H. 28", W. 28", D. 22¾". (Private collection; photo, Gavin Ashworth.) Unlike most nineteenth-century slabs, the top on this stand is rough on the underside and tabled to fit the frame. The tableing actually impedes a towel bar that pulls out on one side. A similar washstand with three drawers has a stenciled label of Anthony Quervelle.

those at Marble Hall, had steam- and water-powered lifts, but they eventually became impractical as well. Pennsylvania limestone also went out of fashion among furniture makers and consumers during the 1840s. Very few Philadelphia pieces from the Victorian era have locally quarried slabs (see fig. 44), no doubt a result of the growing popularity and availability of foreign and exotic marbles.

Pennsylvania clouded limestone continued to be used by the building trades until regional quarries ceased production. Some quarries were re-opened for special projects, like refurbishing the mantles at Independence Hall at the beginning of the twentieth century, but the business was essentially dead by the end of the nineteenth century. However, the adaptive reuse of architectural components made of Pennsylvania limestone today attests to the beauty, durability, and connotations of wealth and permanence associated with this important regional commodity.

ACKNOWLEDGMENTS For assistance with this article, the author thanks Jeffery Adams, the staff of the Andalusia Foundation, Mark Anderson, Gavin Ashworth, Luke Beckerdite, Wendy Cooper, the staff of the Montgomery County Historical Society, the staff of the Historical Society of Pennsylvania, Susan Newton, Jeanne Soletsky, Earle Spamer, Dr. Robert Sulivan, Angelo Tartaglini, Charles Tonnetti, H. Mack Truax, and Brenda Wetzel. The author is especially grateful to Robert F. Trent for his insights, scholarship, and encouragement.

1. From the *Travels of Peter Kalm* as quoted in Edwin J. Hipkiss, *Eighteenth-Century American Arts: The M. and M. Karolik Collection* (Cambridge, Mass.: Harvard University Press, 1941), p. 96.

2. Unpublished manuscript, "Ores, Minerals and Geology of Montgomery County," Montgomery County Historical Society (hereafter cited, MCHS), Norristown, Pennsylvania, p. 25.

3. Curt Chinnici interview with Earle Spamer, Geologist and Archivist for the Academy of Natural Sciences, Philadelphia, Pa., August 30, 2001. For a detailed analysis of Pennsylvania limestone, see Jocelyn Kimmel, "Characterization and Consolidation of Pennsylvania Blue Marble with a Case Study of the Second Bank of the United States, Philadelphia, Pennsylvania" (master's thesis, University of Pennsylvania, 1996).

4. The quote is taken from a lecture given by Professor Henry Carvill Lewis (1853–1888) at the Franklin Institute and published as *The Surface Geology of Philadelphia and Vicinity* (Philadelphia, c. 1881). The lecture was "Read before the Mineralogical and Geological Section of the Academy of Natural Sciences of Philadelphia, November 25th, 1878."

5. According to John Oldmixon's *British Empire in America* (1708), the first North American limestone was quarried at Letitia Penn's manor, Mount Joy. This quarry was probably in the vicinity of Port Kennedy. William J. Buck, *History of Montgomery County Within the Schuylkill Valley* (Norristown, Pa.: E. L. Acker, 1859), p. 37: "The census of 1840 shows the lime then manufactured in Montgomery County at about one third of that produced in the entire country." For more on the lime burning industry, see Heinz J. Heinemann, *The Lime Industry at Hope Lodge* (Fort Washington, Pa.: privately printed, 1990).

6. Gerhard Troost, *Geological Survey of the Environs of Philadelphia Performed by the Order of the Philadelphia Society for Promoting Agriculture* (Philadelphia: H. S. Tanner, 1826), pp. 9, 10.

7. Ibid.

8. Sean Patrick Adams, *Partners in Geology, Brothers in Frustration: The Antebellum Geological Surveys of Virginia and Pennsylvania* (Baltimore, Md.: Genealogical Publishing Co., 1998). This book describes in depth the political and scientific worlds that coexisted when the Rogers brothers were working as state geologists during the mid-nineteenth century. Henry Darwin Rogers, *Geological Survey of Pennsylvania* (Philadelphia: J. B. Lippincott, 1858), p. 215.

9. Charles E. Hall, *Catalog of Specimens, Second Geological Survey of Pennsylvania* (Harrisburg, Pa.: Board of Commissioners for the Second Geological Survey, 1883), pp. 135, 139.

10. Several other tombstones and altar tombs in the churchyard are made of highly figured

limestone, and their colors are typically dark gray and bluish gray. Altar tombs, which were common in the eighteenth century, consist of a large inscribed slab raised on four piers of stone or brick. Occasionally the sides are enclosed, but those in this churchyard are open.

11. Edwin Troxell Fredley, *Philadelphia and Its Manufactures* (Philadelphia: E. Young, 1867), p. 362: "Less than twenty-five years ago, all Marble was sawed by the friction of a saw without teeth, aided by sharp sand, pushed backward and forward by manual force. Now, Marble is sawed, rubbed and polished by steam power; and a block of Italian Marble has been converted into four hundred superficial feet of slabs in twelve hours."

12. *The Marble Worker's Manual, Designed for the Use of Marble Workers, Builders, and Owners of Houses,* translated by M. L. Booth (Philadelphia: Henry Carey Barid, 1865). "Planishing [is] . . . the process of giving a smooth finish to metal surfaces by a rapid series of overlapping, light hammerlike blows, or by rolling in a planishing mill" (*Academic Press Dictionary of Science and Technology,* <www.harcourt.com/dictionary>).

13. Unpublished manuscript, "Pennsylvania Marble Quarries Chronology c. 1714–1997," MCHS. Excerpts from this paper appeared in articles by Edward Hocker in the *Norristown Times Herald* in 1930.

14. In July 1730, Anthony Wilkinson charged Captain Bignell (or Bicknell) £4.4 for a six-foot lion figurehead for the ship *Tryall*. The vessel was jointly owned by Samuel Powel, Jr. and Clement Plumstead (Powel Family Business Papers, Joseph Downs Library, Winterthur Museum.) Philadelphia joiner John Head credited Wilkinson £1.11.16 for a "marvel harth" on March 8, 1734 (Jay Robert Stiefel, "Philadelphia Cabinetmaking and Commerce, 1718-1753: The Account Book of John Head, Joiner" [Philadelphia: American Philosophical Society, 2001]). On November 22, 1739, the *Pennsylvania Gazette* reported: "MASONRY in all its Branches, is performed by WILLIAM HOLLAND, Mason, lately from London, viz. Marble Chimney Pieces, Grave Stones, Mortars, Tables, Monuments and Steps, Pavements of all Kinds, Hearths, &c. to be had at his Shop in Water Street, next Door to Mr. Stephen Beezley's, Philadelphia. N. B. The above mentioned W. Holland is now at New York, fixing some Works for a Gentleman of that City, wherefore this is to desire all Gentlemen and others, to apply to Mr. Anthony Wilkinson, Ship Carver in Philadelphia, until he return, which will be in 14 Days from the Date of this Paper (if God permit)" (as cited on <www.accessible.com>). Unless otherwise noted, all eighteenth- and early nineteenth-century newspaper advertisements cited in the footnotes are from this database. *South Carolina Gazette,* March 22, 1740, as cited in *The Arts and Crafts in Philadelphia, Maryland, and South Carolina,* 2 vols., compiled by Alfred Coxe Prime (1929; reprint, New York: Da Capo Press, 1969), 1:163. *Pennsylvania Gazette,* May 21, 1741, as cited in Prime, comp., *Arts and Crafts,* 1:163.

15. For more on this Philadelphia cabinet shop, see Luke Beckerdite, "An Identity Crisis: Philadelphia and Baltimore Furniture Styles of the Mid-Eighteenth Century," in *Shaping a National Culture: The Philadelphia Experience, 1750–1800,* edited by Catherine E. Hutchins (Winterthur, Del.: Winterthur Museum, 1994), pp. 254–81, figs. 9–15, 22–30, 33, 37–39. Brian Wilkinson also advertised marble and stonecutting, although the date when he began this business is not known. In the December 19, 1774, *Pennsylvania Gazette,* Brian Wilkinson and Son offered "chimney pieces of all kinds" and "Marble Stone cutting . . . in all its branches" (as cited in Prime, comp., *Arts and Crafts,* 1: 311).

16. For Irish influences on Virginia furniture, see Ronald L. Hurst and Jonathan Prown, *Southern Furniture, 1680–1830: The Colonial Williamsburg Collection* (New York: Harry N. Abrams, Inc. for the Colonial Williamsburg Foundation, 1997), pp. 305–8; and Ronald L. Hurst, "Irish Influences on Cabinetmaking in Virginia's Rappahannock River Basin," in *American Furniture,* edited by Luke Beckerdite (Hanover, N. H.: University Press of New England for the Chipstone Foundation, 1997), pp. 170–95.

17. William MacPherson Hornor, Jr., *Blue Book: Philadelphia Furniture* (Philadelphia: privately printed, 1935), p. 61. *Pennsylvania Gazette,* January 4, 1739. On May 18, 1738, the *Pennsylvania Gazette* reported: "This is to Certify that Mr. Joseph Claypoole, Joyner, has left off his Trade; and has given his Stock and Implements . . . to his son [Josiah] . . . who has Removed . . . to the Joyners-Arms in Second-Street . . . where all Persons may be supplied with all Sorts of . . . Desks, . . . Chests of Drawers, . . . Dining Tables, Chamber Tables, . . . Tea Tables and Sideboards; he having the largest and oldest Stock of Timber in the Province, some of which have been in Piles near 25 years, . . . and a fine Sortment of the newest fashioned Brass Work Furniture, lately imported from London (as cited in Prime, comp., *Arts and Crafts,* 1:162, 163).

18. An early sideboard table formerly in the collection of Mrs. Lamont du Pont Copeland and another example with a history of descent in the Waln and Ryerss families (see Hornor, *Blue Book,* pl. 131) have cyma-shaped rails (the shaped sections are attached to flat inner rails). The latter table also has an applied skirt with relief carving.

19. The end rails of this table are similar to those on a high chest signed by Henry Cliffton and Thomas Carteret and dated 1753 (Colonial Williamsburg Foundation). Furniture historian Alan Miller was the first scholar to suggest that this table was a product of their shop.

20. *The Marble Worker's Manual,* pp. 52–54.

21. As cited in Hornor, *Blue Book,* p. 146.

22. For more on Nicholas Bernard and Martin Jugiez, see Luke Beckerdite, "Philadelphia Carving Shops, Part II: Bernard and Jugiez," *Antiques* 128, no. 3 (September 1985): 498–513.

23. *Pennsylvania Gazette,* July 16, 1752 (Peters); *Pennsylvania Gazette,* May 15, 1755 (Stanaland); *Pennsylvania Packett,* December 19, 1774 (Brian Wilkinson and Son) (from Prime, comp., *Arts and Crafts,* 1:311); *Pennsylvania Gazette,* May 10, 1780 (Chambers); *Pennsylvania Gazette,* April 6, 1785 (Stiles); *Porcupine's Gazette,* August 22, 1798 (Payne). David and William Chambers provided stone work for the Philadelphia townhouse renovated by John Cadwalader and his wife Elizabeth (Lloyd):

A marble Chimney Piece and Hearth for front Parlor	16⅓ feet @ 12/	0.9.16
1 do. for back do.	17½ feet @12/	0.10.7
1 do. for small do.	13¼ fo @ 12/	0.7.19
1 do. for large front chamber	20½ feet @12/	0.12.6
1 do. for small do.	15½ feet @12/	0.9.11
do. for back do.	21¼ feet @ 12/	0.12.15
setting 6 chimney pieces	@ 15/	0.4.10
10 iron clamps	@ 4	0.3.4
lime		0.3.9
by 42½ feet of old Marble	@ 5/6	11.12.10
by cash		0.15.0
		£26,12,10
Balance		£408.2

Receipt for stone work for John Cadwalader, 1770, Cadwalader Collection, series 2 box 2, ch-cl, Winterthur Museum Library, Joseph Downs Manuscript Collection. William Payne reported that he was a marble mason from London and the "ORIGINAL INVENTOR and PATENTEE of the much improved SOAP-STONE STOVES." He informed "his Friends and the Public, that they may be supplied with the above stoves, either plain or embellished with American or Italian Marble. Those stoves can be adapted to any size chimney, or attached to the most elegant chimney-pieces without interfering with the design, and are allowed to be an ornament to the handsomest drawing room. . . . Likewise on hand, for sale, several new and secondhand American and Italian marble chimney-pieces ornamented and plain—Where also may be had, monuments, head and foot-stones, press . . . stones for printers, &c." (*Porcupine's Gazette,* August 22, 1798).

24. The information on James Traquair is derived from an article on him in the September 26, 1798, issue of *Porcupine's Gazette,* as cited in "Pennsylvania Marble Quarries Chronology" and excerpts from that chronology published by Edward Hocker in the *Norristown Times Herald* (Edward Hocker, *Collection of Norristown Times Herald Articles* [MCHS, 1947], pp. 4, 5).

25. Ibid.

26. John Cole apparently took over the day-to-day management of Wilkinson's stone cutting business following the latter's death in 1765. In the April 4, 1765, issue of the *Pennsylvania Gazette,* Cole advertised "the marble cutting Business . . . in all its several Branches, at the Shop late occupied by Mr ANTHONY WILKINSON, deceased; where all Persons that please to favour me with their Custom, may depend on having their Orders obeyed, with care and Dispatch." Peter Fritz acquired quarries formerly owned by Wilkinson before 1832. For more on Fritz and his business, see Edwin T. Freedley, *Philadelphia and Its Manufacturers* (Philadelphia: Edward Young, 1859), pp. 360–66.

27. Freedley, *Philadelphia and Its Manufactures,* pp. 360–66: "The Fritz Quarry, recently purchased by the Pennsylvania Land and Marble Company, is an old quarry, and has produced a

very fine white and blue variegated marble, known as the 'Pennsylvania Clouded,' formerly much used for mantels and chimney-pieces in old Pennsylvania houses of the better kind." The *Charter and By-Laws of the Pennsylvania Land and Marble Company* (1854) reported:

> Large importations of different varieties of Marble, but principally veined Italian, are annually made from Leghorn, and sold on arrival at public auction, at prices varying from $2 to $4 per cubic foot. One establishment, that of Mr. John Baird, consumes annually over 15,000 cubic feet of Italian Marble. The quarries of JK and M Freedley, at West Stockbridge, Mass., supply a good quality of ordinary building Marble, which is extensively used in Philadelphia; and the Vermont quarries, particularly those at Rutland, from which the finest varieties of American Marble are obtained. It is not an unusual circumstance for quarry operators in New England to consign a cargo of Marble to this city on a venture; and as ventures do not always arrive exactly at the time of demand, the jobbers and dealers in Philadelphia can frequently purchase on terms so favorable, that they can in turn supply customers in the South and West with Marble in slabs cheaper that either could purchase it in block at the quarries. The wholesale dealers in this city, however, are generally owners of quarries—Mr. SF Prince is the only jobber who has no interest in any quarry.

As quoted in Freedley, *Philadelphia and Its Manufactures*, p. 362. An original copy of this document is in the Historical Society of Pennsylvania. The white marble was wrought from the Hitner quarries of Marble Hall near Barren Hill, and the less expensive black and blue marble was from the Lentz Quarry. Rogers, *Geological Survey of Pennsylvania*, p. 21.

28. William J. Buck, *History of Montgomery County Within the Schuylkill Valley* (Norristown, Pa.: E. L. Acker, 1859), pp. 63, 64.

29. See "Pennsylvania Marble Quarries Chronology," p. 8. Thomas U. Walter, "Girard College Contracts and Diary, 1833–1836," unpublished manuscript, Philadelphia Athenaeum, series 3.

30. "Pennsylvania Marble Quarries Chronology," p. 8.

31. Samuel Sloan, *Sloan's Architectural Review and Builder's Journal,* July–December 1868 (Philadelphia: Claxton, Remsen & Haffelfinger, 1868–1870).

32. Foust and Weaver Account Book 1854–1861, account book n, 339, Historical Society of Pennsylvania.

33. See Freedley, *Philadelphia and Its Manufactures,* pp. 363, 364.

Peter Follansbee

Manuscripts, Marks, and Material Culture: Sources for Understanding the Joiner's Trade in Seventeenth-Century America

▼ LIKE MOST DISCIPLINES, furniture scholarship is profoundly influenced by prevailing social and cultural attitudes. During the late nineteenth and early twentieth centuries, Americans threatened by the rapid pace of modernization and growing population of European immigrants looked to the past for remedies to perceived social ills. The nostalgic and often fictional histories crafted to reinforce traditional American values have parallels in decorative arts literature from the 1920s and 1930s. Wallace Nutting's romantic depiction of the makers, patrons, and context of "Pilgrim Century" furniture is typical. In 1924, he wrote:

> There is an interesting variation in these [seventeenth-century Connecticut "sunflower"] chests . . . which clearly indicates that they were made to order, and that the feeling of the cabinet maker and his patron coincided in the thought of giving individuality to each piece. Thus we observe that the carving, the ornaments, the size and many other particulars are varied slightly. A chest, especially when designed as a gift, was regarded properly as appropriately marked by some peculiarity. It is this variety, so natural to a good workman, and so fine a stimulus in all artistic production, that the seventeenth century had and we have not. It is this feature which must be introduced again into American life. It is one thing to standardize the mechanism of automobiles. That may be possible and is certainly desirable. But we ought to distinguish between mechanics and artisanship. Unless we are to revive individuality in our characters as well as in our surroundings, true progress will be at an end. There is no stimulus in thinking, and no character development, if every household is to be furnished with standard articles.

Several of the attitudes expressed by Nutting and his contemporaries remain current today. Although many early furniture makers were ingenious, proficient artisans, most were concerned more with satisfying the demands of their patrons than self-fulfillment in a personal creative process. Indeed, the notion of "making art for art's sake" is a modern construct with little relevance to the historic trades. A significant percentage of early artisans abandoned their trades as soon as it was financially viable, having experienced the numbing repetition of cutting thousands of mortise-and-tenon joints and countless feet of molding.[1]

In *American Seating Furniture 1630–1730*, Benno Forman asked the question: "Did . . . [a] craftsman really contemplate the beauty his work might result in and strive for it, or did he long for his twelve-hour day to end?" Salem, North Carolina, silversmith John Vogler's diary entry stating that "my hands could always do what my mind dictated" certainly suggests that he was proud of his accomplishments, whereas the notebooks of London turner Nehemiah Wallington (1598–1658) paint a more dismal picture of his trade. On one occasion Wallington confessed: "At night after examination how I have spent the day, after a chapter read I went to prayer with my family; then I went into my shop to my employment more out of conscience to God's commands than of any love I had unto it." Regardless of their attitudes toward their work, all historic tradesmen shared one reality—they had to put a roof over their heads, clothes on their backs, and food on their tables. Achieving this goal required quick, efficient work methods and the ability to respond to local tastes.[2]

In "Eighteenth-Century Cabinet Shops and the Furniture-Making Trades in Newport, Rhode Island," furniture scholar Mack Headley discusses problems inherent in elucidating procedures and shop arrangements for workmen of that period. Although less documentary evidence pertaining to seventeenth-century New England joiners and turners survives, a great deal of information can be extrapolated from court records, period artwork, and treatises such as Joseph Moxon's *Mechanick Exercises; or the Doctrine of Handy-works* (1677) and Randle Holme's *Academie or Store-House of Armory and Blazon* (1688). Using these sources, physical evidence on surviving furniture, and information gleaned from the use of period tools in reproduction work, this article will attempt to describe the activities and environment of seventeenth-century American furniture makers.[3]

Tools and Materials

Probate records are one of the best sources for determining a person's trade, although some documents are more specific than others. One perplexing inventory is that of Martha Harding of Plymouth, Massachusetts. She died in 1633 leaving "Joyners tooles wth other things" valued at thirteen shillings, as well as "a servts time" worth six pounds. The name and trade of her husband and servant are not known, but it is likely that the former was a joiner. The 1651 inventory of Henry Birdsall of Salem, Massachusetts, lists "tooles for his trade" valued at two pounds, which suggests that his estate appraisers and the local community knew which trade he practiced. Typically, inventories that itemize tools and materials are the most useful in determining a person's profession. Salem joiner John Symonds' 1671 inventory listed "Joyners Tools benches and lare [lathe]" valued at £5.5.6, "2 Bedsteds almost finished" valued at three pounds, "Timber, planke & board" valued at £5.12, "part of a chest" appraised with other items, "a [pair] . . . of Jemmils" valued at five shillings, "Timber in the Woods" valued at £1.2 and "an apprentice of 17 years old who hath 3 year and 9 moneths and 2 weekes to serve." Used primarily for chests and boxes, "jimmals" are hinges comprised of two linked rings spread apart like a cotter-pin. A 1630 English broadside lists "gimmals for chests" along with other types of ironware that would be useful for prospective New England settlers.[4]

Most seventeenth-century joiners had more than one piece underway at any given time. Although it is obvious that Symonds was working on two bedsteads, and possibly a chest, prior to his death, some inventories group unfinished work under a single entry. In those instances, values often provide a clue as to whether the work consisted of one or more objects. The £10.3 value placed on "New joynery worke unfinnished" in the 1672 inventory of Thomas Little, Sr., of Marshfield was sufficient for several pieces of furniture.[5]

Like tools and unfinished work, materials can also provide clues to an individual's trade. Symonds' inventory listed "timber, planke & board"—terms referring to wood in various stages of processing. "Timber" refers to wood in log form, "board" to thin, sawn stock, usually one inch thick, and "planke" to thicker sawn material, often two inches or more. The term "bolt" is less specific and can refer to joiners' stock as well as carpenters' clapboards and coopers' staves. Manchester, Massachusetts, carpenter John Pickworth owned "a p[a]rcell of bowlts" in 1663, and Braintree, Massachusetts, joiner William Savell, Sr.'s inventory listed "joiners stuff and ceder boults" in 1669. Materials cited in the 1655 inventory of Salem turner Thomas Wickes include "flags" for chair seats, "timber" (presumably riven wood), boards, and planks: "one dwelling house with a shopp & barn & ground £35 in flagges £2/10 in working timber £1/10 in made ware as green Chayres, wheeles & Reemes £5 in plank & boards £1 in tooles £6."[6]

Although inventories and treatises pertaining to the joiners' and turners' trades provide a wealth of information on tools, jigs, lathes, and other implements, the best depiction of a seventeenth-century woodworking shop is the carved panel illustrated in figure 1. Thought to date from the

Figure 1 Carved panel depicting the interior of a woodworking shop, probably England, 1590–1620. Oak. 14½" x 28½". (By permission of John Stent of Shere.)

early-to-mid-seventeenth century, this panel depicts a joiner and turner at work—the joiner leaning into a stroke with his plane and the turner working on a large pillar at a pole lathe. Behind each man hang tools in racks on the wall. Tool historian W. L. Goodman suggested that the panel could be English, based on the type of handsaw between the benches. The placement of the saw, hatchet, and low bench in the center was intentional, since both trades use them. The joiner's tools consist of planes (probably molding planes), chisels, a compass, a hammer, a bench hook, and a holdfast,

Figure 2 Cabinet attributed to the Symonds shops, Salem, Massachusetts, 1679. Red oak, black walnut, and maple with white pine. H. 16⅜", W. 17", D. 9½". (Courtesy, Peabody Essex Museum; photo, Gavin Ashworth.)

whereas the turner's consist of long gouges, chisels, and a large compass. The lathe is a slab with "stake" feet, and its top has a slot to accommodate the upright "poppets" that hold the workpiece. A wooden bracket in the ceiling supports the pole, which has a cord that runs around the workpiece and extends to the foot treadle under the lathe.[7]

    The importance of this panel resides in its having been made by a seventeenth-century tradesman who worked in a similar shop rather than being an artist's interpretation. All of the tools depicted in the carving are described in detail in Moxon's *Mechanick Exercises* and appear in early New England

Figure 3 Detail of the back of a drawer from the cabinet illustrated in fig. 2. Tears from riving are present along the lower edge of the back.

Figure 4 Chest, Boston, Massachusetts, 1660–1690. Oak, cedrella, and walnut with oak and white pine. H. 30½", W. 45", D. 20½". (Chipstone Foundation; photo, Gavin Ashworth.)

Figure 5 Detail of the upper rear rail of the chest illustrated in fig. 4.

inventories. More importantly, marks left by similar tools are present on the interior and exterior surfaces of surviving furniture, including cabinets and other joined case forms attributed to the Symonds shops of Salem.

The cabinet illustrated in figure 2 is in remarkably good condition having lost only one interior drawer, two small pieces of the molding forming the octagon on the door, and one of the triglyphs below. In typical New England joined fashion, all of its oak components were riven from a log. Although most of the stock has been planed smooth, some parts display tears from this splitting process (see figs. 3, 31). Evidence of riving is usually found on surfaces not intended to be seen such as the undersides of table tops, cupboard shelves, chest and box lids, and the backs of case pieces (see figs. 4, 5). Seventeenth-century inventories often list tools associated with riving—beetles, wedges, froes, and mallets— which was practiced by many different trades. Moxon's treatise does not mention the froe (fig. 6), but Randle Holme referred to one in his discussion of cooper's tools:

> A Lath Axe [or froe], is an Iron Instrument like a Knife Blade, with a round thick back, having an Eye, into which a thick strong Handle is put, the edge standing outwards: With this, great Timber after it is cloven with the Maul and Wedges into small pieces, it afterwards cleaves them into Laths, Barrel Boards, and Pannels.[8]

Although inventory references to chisels, saws, and axes are also of little use in determining an individual's trade, an entry for a workbench in conjunction with certain woodworking tools suggests that the deceased made furniture. Joinery required a bench, but carpentry did not. Regrettably, workbenches are rarely listed in probate documents, probably because most appraisers considered them a fixture in the shop rather than a "moveable." The benches listed in John Symonds' inventory are an exception, as are the "workeing benches" valued at five shillings in the inventory of

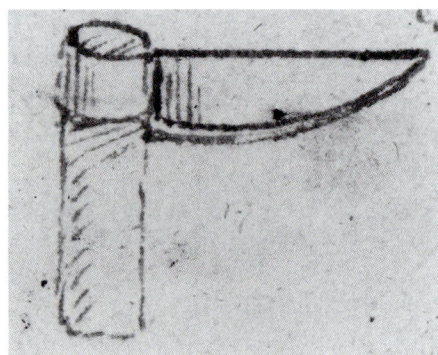

Figure 6 Randle Holme, drawing of a "lath axe" (froe), England, ca. 1688. (Courtesy, British Library.)

Joseph Carpenter of Rehoboth, Massachusetts. Both Moxon and Holme illustrate a workbench, but neither describe it. Instead, their discussions focus on the use of the bench, its various appurtenances, and the process of joiner's work (fig. 7).[9]

Certain implements can document an individual's ownership of a workbench even if it is not listed in that person's inventory. Moxon's illustration (fig. 7) and the early pictorial panel (fig. 1) show two tools that are useless without a bench—the holdfast and bench hook. Therefore, the "broken holdfast & a bench hooke" valued at 1 shilling in the 1633 inventory of Plymouth, Massachusetts, carpenter Francis Eaton suggests that he owned a workbench and, by extension, made furniture.[10]

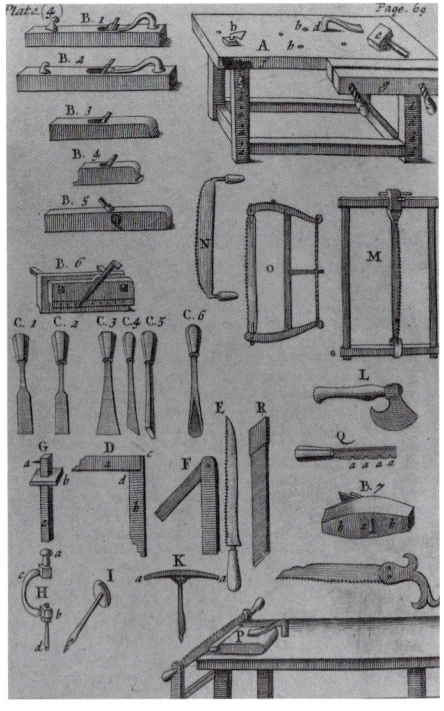

Figure 7 Workbench and tools illustrated on page 69 in the third edition of Joseph Moxon, *Mechanick Excercises; or the Doctrine of Handyworks* (1703). (Courtesy, Winterthur Museum Library: Printed Book and Periodical Collection.)

Figure 8 Holdfasts and bench hook being used to position a board for planing. (Photo, Gavin Ashworth.)

Holme described the holdfast (fig. 8) as "an Instrument of Iron, which being put into a loose hole of a Joyners Bench, and the Beak set upon any piece of Timber, with the Knock of an Hammer or Mallet upon the head of it, will cause the Work to ly fast upon the Bench, till the Work-man either Saw, Tennant, Mortess, or Plain it." Used primarily for holding stock for planing, bench hooks are small iron implements with a toothed surface on one end and a wooden block at the other (figs. 9, 10). The block drops into the bench, leaving the teeth raised just above the top. The end of the workpiece is shoved against the teeth, which function as a stop for the planing action. Although most joiners worked with stock that was slightly oversized so they could trim away the indentations left by the teeth

Figure 9   Bench hook being used to hold stock for planing. (Photo, Gavin Ashworth.)

Figure 10   Detail of the bench hook marks on a seventeenth-century English box.

on the end grain, some period pieces have evidence documenting the use of a bench hook. The toothed marks (fig. 10) on a seventeenth-century English box, for example, are clear enough to indicate the size and shape of the hook used by its maker.[11]

John Thorp's 1633 inventory is the first in Plymouth Colony that lists planes, one of the main tools that help determine if a tradesman was strictly a carpenter or if he also did joinery. Although carpenters used planes, joiners required a greater variety of sizes, shapes, and types. Thorp's tools included "inboring planes," a "joynter plane," a "foreplane," a "smoothing plane," a "halferound plane," a holdfast, three "broade chisels," two "gowges & 2 narrow chisels," three "Augers Inch & 1/2," a "great auger," an adze, a "felling Axe," a handsaw, and "1 short 2 handsaw." His appraisers also noted that "Will Palmer the [elder] . . . owes for a servt £2 . . . pt of a fframe of an howse that is neere Wellingsly £2."[12]

Thorp used the fore plane, smoothing plane, and jointer (fig. 7, b1, b4, and b2 respectively) to flatten rough boards, a critical step in furniture making. Moxon noted that the fore plane is used:

> before you come to work either with the Smooth Plane, or with the Joynter. The edge of its Iron is not ground upon the straight, as the Smooth Plane, and the Joynter are, but rises with a Convex Arch in the middle of it; for its Office being to prepare the Stuff for either the Smoothing Plane, or the Joynter, Workmen set the edge of it Ranker than the edge either of the Smoothing Plane or the Joynter.

As this reference suggests, the iron on a fore plane was typically set to take a thick shaving and remove stock quickly. Marks left by this tool are common on the backs, bottoms, and interior surfaces of period furniture (see figs. 11, 12). "The *Smoothing-Plane*," Moxon wrote, "must have its *Iron set*

Figure 11 Cupboard, Boston, Massachusetts, 1675–1690. Oak, walnut, maple, chestnut and cedar with oak and white pine. H. 55⅝", W. 49½", D. 21¾". (Chipstone Foundation; photo, Gavin Ashworth.)

Figure 12 Back of the cupboard illustrated in fig. 11. The smoothing plane marks appear as concave undulations on the back panels.

very *fine*, because its Office is to smoothen the work from those Irregularities the *Fore-plane* made." Different styles of each plane were available during the seventeenth century. The "little short Plain" described and illustrated by Randle Holme (fig. 13) resembles Netherlandish *gerfschaff* and differs significantly from the smoothing plane shown in *Mechanick Exercises* (fig. 7, b4). Defined as "a plane for superficial planing," *gerfschaff* were present in New England at an early date. John Ward (1652–1732) of Salem, Massachusetts, owned the example illustrated in figure 14.[13]

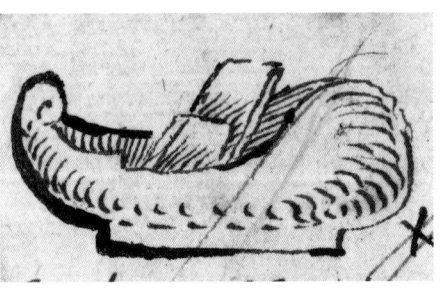

Figure 13 Randle Holme, drawing of a smoothing plane, England, ca. 1688. (Courtesy, British Library.)

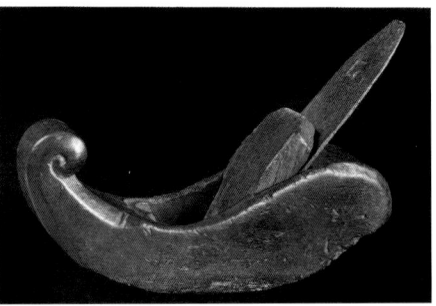

Figure 14 Smoothing plane, possibly New England, 1630–1700. Fruitwood and iron. L. 6⅞". (Courtesy, Peabody Essex Museum.)

The jointer plane (see fig. 7, b2) is "made somewhat longer than the Fore-plane, and hath its Sole perfectly straight from end to end." Moxon noted that its "office is to follow the Fore-plane, and to shoot an edge perfectly straight, and not only an edge, but also a Board of any thickness." Holme described this tool similarly, but added "all the difference is in the Tote or Handle, which every Workman maketh according to his own Fancy, all other parts in the stock agreeing." This supports the widely held theory that most tradesmen made the bodies, or stocks, of their planes. Merchants' inventories and shipping records often list plane irons, but not "planes." Making tools and parts integral to them was part of most apprentices' training. Indentures often stipulated that the apprentice would receive a set of tools upon completion of his term. Although individual tools are rarely mentioned in period indentures, John Sparke of Bristol, England, agreed to give Humphrey Bryne "a Rule, a compass, a hatchet, a hansawe, a fore plane, a joynter, a smothen plane, two moulden planes, a groven plane, a paren chysell, a mortisse chesell, a wymble, a Rabbet plane, . . . six graven Tooles, and a Strykinge plane" when the latter signed his indenture in 1594.[14]

Molding planes, like the "inboring" and "halferound" examples noted in John Thorp's inventory, are often listed in the inventories of seventeenth-century joiners who typically produced a greater range of moldings than carpenters. Holme stated that the terms "round" and "half-round" refer to the same plane. In period documents, round planes typically appear in conjunction with "hollow" planes. When used in tandem, these tools can generate a variety of moldings and architectural details (see figs. 15, 16).[15]

Of all the planes listed in New England probate inventories, the plow (fig. 7, b6)—also referred to as a "joiner's plow," "wainscot plow," or "grooving plane"—is most indicative of the joiner's trade. The 1659 inventory of

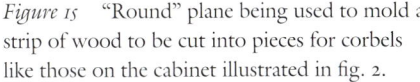

Figure 15 "Round" plane being used to mold a strip of wood to be cut into pieces for corbels like those on the cabinet illustrated in fig. 2.

Figure 16 Detail of the right corbel and side of the cabinet illustrated in fig. 2. (Photo, Gavin Ashworth.)

Figure 17 Plow plane being used to cut a groove in a framing member.

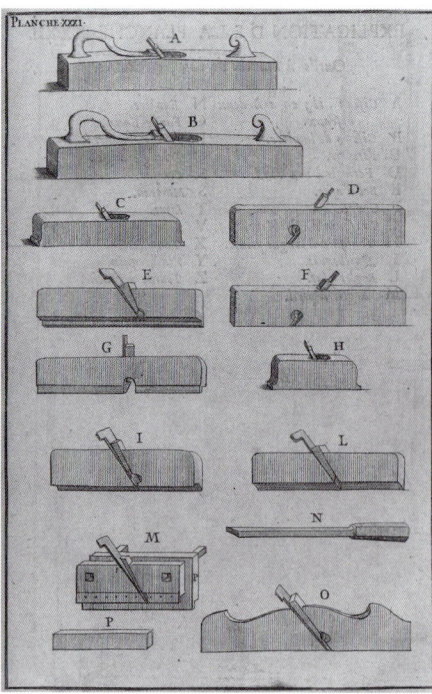

Figure 18 Planes and mortise chisel illustrated on plate 21 of Andres Felibien's *Des Principes de l'Architecture* (Paris, 1676). (Courtesy, Winterthur Museum Library: Printed Book and Periodical Collection.) The plow plane is designated "M".

Figure 19 Detail of the door of the cabinet illustrated in fig. 2 showing the plowed groove.

Plymouth, Massachusetts, joiner William Carpenter, Sr. lists "three Joynters," "3 hand plaines," and "one fore plain" valued at ten shillings and "Rabbeting plaines, . . . hollowing plaines, and one plow" valued at one pound. Plow planes (fig. 17) are used only for cutting grooves to receive panels and are absolutely necessary for performing joinery. They are fitted with a fence that guides the tool along a board as the narrow blade "plows" a groove in the edge of the stock. Moxon illustrated a plow plane in *Mechanick Exercises*, but the fence is shown on the wrong side of the tool. The engraver responsible for this image copied a plane depicted in Andres Felibien's *Des Principes de l'Architecture* (Paris, 1676) but reversed the image (fig. 18). Most of the planes in Moxon's plate of joiner's tools are copied from this important French work.[16]

The door of the cabinet illustrated in figure 2 has grooves plowed through the tops of the stiles (fig. 19). This feature was a direct result of the plow plane's design. The distance from the "toe," or front, of the plane dictated that the joiner extend each stroke beyond the mortise in order to produce a full-depth groove to accept a panel. The exposed grooves on some period case pieces have been patched, but this invariably represents incorrect restoration.

As the indenture between Sparke and Bryne suggests, the "hansawe," "mortisse chesell," and "paren chysell" were principal tools of early joiners. Before cutting their mortises and tenons, most joiners used a marking gauge to inscribe layout lines on the edges of the framing parts. After determining the appropriate size of the joints, the tradesman set the gauge to match the width of his mortise chisel. Moxon described this process and noted that the joiner needed a "piercer," or brace and bit (see fig. 20), to bore the holes for the pins that secure the joint. "Its Office is so well

Figure 20 Detail of *Annunciation Tryptich* by Robert Campin and an assistant (possibly Roger van der Weyden), Netherlands, 1406–1444. Oil on panel. Braces like the one shown here are still used today.(Courtesy, Metropolitan Museum of Art.)

Figure 21 Randle Holme, drawing of a brace and bit, England, ca. 1688. (Courtesy, British Library.)

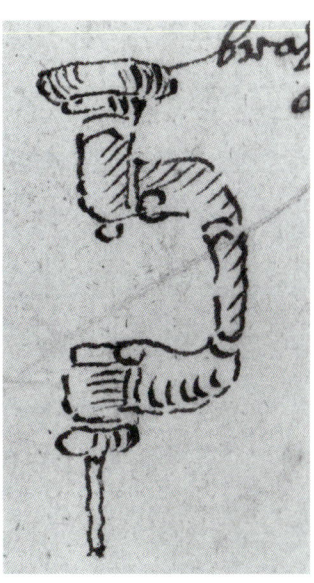

Figure 22 Detail showing the cross-section of a pair of the half-columns on the cabinet illustrated in fig. 2.

known, that I need say little to it. Only, you must take care to keep the Bitt straight to the hole you pierce, lest you deform the hole, or break the Bitt." Moxon also recommended that the joiner have several bits of various sizes. Holme's description of the brace and bit (fig. 21) is similar, but he gives additional names for the tool: "for of some it is termed a Brace, others a Wimble, others a Wimble-Brace, and a Vambrace; in *London* it is generally termed a Piercer. It is used in Boring of Holes to drive Wooden Pins through Mortesses and Tennants in Joyners work." In New England inventories, the term "wimble" appears more regularly than the other names for this tool.[17]

Although treatises like those written by Moxon and Holme are invaluable sources of information, they fail to mention many processes and techniques employed by period tradesmen. Consequently, this information must be surmised from evidence on surviving artifacts. The half-columns on the cabinet illustrated in figure 2 have subtle chisel marks indicating that a turner produced them on a pole lathe. Each of these appliqués is less than half-round (see fig. 22), which suggests that the turner formed them from

Figure 23   Turning blank for half-columns and completed workpiece.

Figure 24   Chest attributed to John Thurston, Dedham or Medfield, Massachusetts, 1640–1650. Oak with pine. H. 31 3/8", W. 47 3/4", D. 21". (Courtesy, Museum of Fine Arts, Boston; Otis Norcross Fund.)

Figure 25   Detail of a carved panel on the chest illustrated in fig. 24.

two equal size pieces of stock glued together with a thin strip of wood between them (see fig. 23). After turning the workpiece, he separated the pieces and discarded the strip. Turners probably developed this process to reduce the chance of damaging the workpiece on the lathe. The center core provided material to engage the points of the lathe—the screw and pin—and protect the primary components of the turning blank.[18]

Evidence of the tools and techniques used for carving also survives on many pieces of seventeenth-century furniture. A joined chest attributed to Dedham and Medfield, Massachusetts, joiner John Thurston has foliate panels that retain many of the original layout lines (figs. 24, 25). Generated

Figure 26   Side of a cabinet being carved. The workpiece is nailed to a board secured to the bench with holdfasts. The carving design duplicates that on the side of the cabinet illustrated in fig. 2.

Figure 27 Detail of the left pillar of the cupboard illustrated in fig. 11.

Figure 28 Fragment of a cupboard attributed to the Savell shop, Braintree, Massachusetts, 1640–1670. (Courtesy, Winterthur Museum; photo, Gavin Ashworth.)

Figure 29 Detail of the door frame of the cupboard illustrated in fig. 28, showing the offset of the draw-bored holes.

with a compass and awl, these marks established the basic pattern for Thurston's design. The radius of his gouges and width of his chisels determined the precise shapes of each element. Some tradesmen used V-shaped parting tools for outlining, but chisels and gouges were faster and easier to control. Few shops used templates; joiners achieved symmetry through basic geometry and sheer repetition. Most of the carving on seventeenth-century American furniture is in relief rather than applied. Some relief-carved panels (see fig. 25) have small square holes on the perimeter (these are usually visible on the outermost edges of panels that have shrunk). Presumably these are from nails used to attach the panel to the bench or to a board secured with a holdfast (see fig. 26).

In *Sylva, or a Discourse of Forest-Trees, and the Propagation of Timber in His Majesties Dominions* (1664), John Evelyn wrote, "the greenest Timber is sometimes desirable for such as Carve and Turn." Wood with a relatively high moisture content is softer and, in the case of some varieties, easier to cut than drier stuff. The use of green wood in seventeenth-century construction is most apparent in turned work like chair parts, table legs, cupboard pillars (see fig. 27), "ball" feet, and other components that have shrunk from round to oval in cross-section.[19]

Joiners also used green timber for structural components. The framing members on many period objects display minor distortion from moisture loss, and the pins securing mortise-and-tenon joints often extend just above the surface. Presumably, joiners trimmed the pins flush originally. As the stiles and rails seasoned and shrank in thickness, the length of the pins remained constant. The resiliency of green wood also facilitated the use of draw-bored, mortise-and-tenon joints—a standard feature in seventeenth-century joinery. Most joiners drove the pegs through holes that were intentionally offset (the hole in the tenon is closer to the shoulder than the hole in the mortise) which made the joints draw together tightly (see figs. 28, 29). Moxon recommended a difference "about the thickness of a shilling."[20]

During the seventeenth century, nailed or "boarded" construction was a relatively inexpensive alternative, and occasionally an accompaniment, to joinery. The artisan who made the cabinet illustrated in figure 2 used nails to secure the bottom, top, and back boards to the sides and fasten the interior dividers in place. All of the nails driven through the top, bottom, and sides into the dividers are visible, and in some instances they disrupt the carving design on the sides (see fig. 30). The interior nails securing the dividers are countersunk, so they do not interfere with the drawers as they are opened and closed.

The joiner had to be careful in nailing the partitions, because oak tends to split easily especially when the stock is thin. Many joiners pre-bored nail holes with a tool Holme described as a "Sprig Bitt, . . . a thing like an Awl;

Figure 30   Detail of the cabinet illustrated in fig. 2, showing a nail driven through the side into an interior partition.

having a four square Blade, with which holes are made in thin and narrow Stuff, to drive in small and slender . . . sprigs, Nails without heads." The maker of the cabinet illustrated in figure 2 pre-bored the holes for all the large nails as well as the headless sprigs used to make the drawers (see figs. 3, 31). Nevertheless, he split the side when nailing the hinges in place. Each leaf of the "dovetail" hinges was made for four nails, but the upper side leaf only has three nails even though the joiner bored a hole for a fourth

Figure 31   Detail showing the nails used to construct the drawers in the cabinet illustrated in fig. 2.

Figure 32   Detail showing the nail used to reinforce a split in the right side of the cabinet illustrated in fig. 2.

138   PETER FOLLANSBEE

(fig. 16). He evidently realized that the side was beginning to split—either from one of the three nails or from a nail driven through the top into the side—and chose not to use a fourth nail to secure the leaf. Instead, the joiner drove a nail into the front edge to repair the split (fig. 32.)[21]

The Patron and the Maker
Like many examples of New England joinery, the cabinets attributed to the Symonds shop (see fig. 2) are commissioned objects that reflect the tastes of their owners as much as the style of their makers. Contracts for joiners' work are rare, and most of the entries in surviving daybooks and other period documents are vague. An invoice from Wethersfield, Connecticut, joiner Peter Blin to Peter Bulkeley is typical. In 1681, Blin charged his patron three shillings for "a leaf of a table," ten shillings for a chest, and two shillings for twenty-four trenchers. Ironically, one of the most detailed contracts is from the South, a region with very little furniture surviving from the seventeenth-century. On June 6, 1668, Accomack County, Virginia, joiner John Rickards agreed to make Anne Boote fifty-four pieces of furniture.

> These presents bindeth mee John Rickards . . . to pay or cause to be paid unto Mrs. Anne Boote . . . These followinge works, Eight bedsteads, Nine tables & ten formes, five close Cupboards, five Courth Cupboards, one Courth Cupboard very handsome according to Mrs. Boote her directions, one close Cupboard also, Six Spinne wheels, five chaire Tables, four chests this worke is to bee done by me Jno. Rickards . . . or else to forfeit one thousand lb. of Tobacco.

As furniture historian Robert Leath suggests, Mrs. Boote probably intended to sell most of the objects, but the "very handsome" court cupboard and "close" cupboard made to her specifications were almost certainly for personal use. The phrase "according to Mrs. Boote" implies that she contributed to the design of both objects.[22]

A 1681 suit involving Lynn, Massachusetts, joiner John Davis and John Tawley of Salem implies how their arrangement was intended to work. According to the court records, Tawley showed Davis a chest at the former's house and asked him to make "two or three as good . . . for 25*s*." A witness reported that Tawley said he "would rather Davis have his money than anyone else" and gave him five shillings as a deposit. Another deponent testified that he delivered four chests reputedly worth thirty shillings each from Davis' shop to Tawley's house. The transaction evidently had a somewhat violent ending, for Davis subsequently went to Tawley's house, called him a "cheating knave," and challenged him to a fight. Davis won the suit even though testimony showed that he took "hold of a wainscot chest in the room" and threw it "up and down . . . breaking several pieces of the font."[23]

Several aspects of this suit shed light on the oral contract between the joiner and his client. Tawley made a conscious choice in patronizing Davis even though excellent joiners like Symonds were active in his home town at the same date. The fact that Tawley showed Davis a chest and requested two or three "as good" suggests that the former provided guidelines about the basic design and construction and the latter agreed to respond to his specifications. If the phrase "breaking several pieces *of* the front" means breaking several pieces *off* the front," Davis' chest probably had applied moldings and turnings similar to those on the cabinet illustrated in figure 2. Given the location of Tawley's home, it is possible that Davis agreed to make chests more like those from Salem than from northern Essex County.[24]

Order of Work

Once the patron and joiner reached an agreement, the joiner began procuring materials. Although some joiners maintained a stock of logs and boards that could be reduced into parts, others obtained timber as need arose. The town of Ipswich, Massachusetts, granted certain tradesmen access to timber from the commons. In 1670, Freegrace Norton felled "3 trees for joynary worke." Most towns restricted timbering to protect local resources.[25]

Descriptions of the most rudimentary aspects of seventeenth-century joinery—planing stock, framing, and executing decorative work—are absent in the written record. Similarly, no document specifies the amount of time required to perform any of these tasks, although it is obvious that joiners had to be efficient, or "workmanlike," to survive in their trade. The repetitive nature of joinery, which revolves around frame and panel construction, and the use of unseasoned wood allowed most artisans to work at a relatively quick pace.

There are numerous records pertaining to the daily wages joiners charged their patrons. A 1640 court record from New Haven, Connecticut, outlines restrictions imposed on several trades:

> In callings wch require skill and strength, as carpenters, joyners, plasterers, bricklayers, shipcarpenters, coopers and the like [master] . . . workemen not to take above 2s6d a day in sumr, in wch men may worke 12 howers, butt lesse than 10 howers dilligently improved in worke cannot be accounted nor may be admitted for a full dayes worke, nor in winter above 2s a day, in wch at least 8 howers to be dilligently improved in worke. . . . Butt all workemen in the former and like trades, who are not as yet allowed to passe under the names of [master] . . . workemen, not to take above 2s a day in sumr and 20d a day in winter as above expressed.

In November 1633, Massachusetts Bay governor John Winthrop complained that, "the scarcetye of workmen had caused [tradesmen] . . . to rayse their wages to an exessive rate, so as a Carpenter would have 3s the daye a labourer 2s6d &c." After receiving complaints about "ill disposed [persons] . . . takeing excessive wages for worke, or unreasonable prizes for . . . necessary merchandizes or othr commodytyes," the Massachusetts Bay court passed a law that would punish anyone caught overcharging for labor or goods. At the same time, Winthrop remained concerned that excessive regulations would cause workmen to "remove to other places . . . or live by planting and other employments."[26]

Regrettably, none of these references indicate how much time it took joiners to make a specific object or how they priced their wares. The 1674 inventory of John Legg of Marblehead listed "one new Chest" valued at twelve shillings, and "one new Box" at five shillings. Using the aforementioned wages, one might conclude that Legg's chest required six days of labor and his box two. However, the cost of materials and ironwork, not to mention the fact that pay varied significantly depending on an individual workman's skill, local demand, and myriad other factors, makes such calculations highly problematic.[27]

The number of tradesmen and distribution of labor in a given shop undoubtedly influenced the pace of work. In most instances, large shops probably turned out work faster than smaller ones, especially those of yeomen-artisans who devoted limited time to their trade. Nevertheless, it is possible to speculate on the time required to make certain objects by reproducing them using period tools and techniques. The author required approximately seventy-five hours to make a joined and carved chest similar to those attributed to the Savell shops of Braintree, Massachusetts (see fig. 33). Preparing the framing stock required about two days; performing

Figure 33 Chest attributed to the Savell shop, Braintree, Massachusetts, 1660–1680. Oak with white pine. H. 24 9/16", W. 51 1/2", D. 20 1/2". (Private collection; photo, Dan Gair.)

the joinery—cutting the tenons, chopping the mortises, plowing grooves for the panels, and boring pin—required approximately one day; and executing the carving required about six hours. Most of the materials and processes used to make this chest are described in detail in John D. Alexander and the author's article, "Seventeenth-Century Joinery from Braintree, Massachusetts: The Savell Shop Tradition," in the 1996 volume of *American Furniture*. Although both authors have spent a good deal of their lives making furniture using only period tools and methods, it is doubtful that they, or any of their modern contemporaries, are capable of working as quickly as seventeenth-century joiners.[28]

Figure 34 Chair table, southeastern Massachusetts, 1650–1700. Oak with pine and maple. Dimensions not recorded. (Private collection.)

Figure 35 Detail showing a mortising mistake on the chair table illustrated in fig. 34.

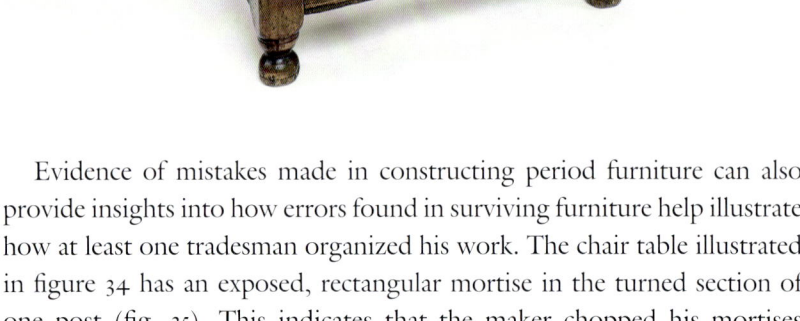

Evidence of mistakes made in constructing period furniture can also provide insights into how errors found in surviving furniture help illustrate how at least one tradesman organized his work. The chair table illustrated in figure 34 has an exposed, rectangular mortise in the turned section of one post (fig. 35). This indicates that the maker chopped his mortises

Figure 36 Chest attributed to John Norman, Sr., or Jr., Marblehead, Massachusetts, 1630–1680. Oak and pine. H. 27¾", W. 44¾", D. 20⅜". (Chipstone Foundation; photo, Gavin Ashworth.)

Figure 37 Detail showing a mortising mistake on the chest illustrated in fig. 36.

before turning the posts. It would have been virtually impossible to make this error once the posts were turned, but the joiner could have oriented the post improperly while it was square in section and chopped the mortise in the wrong place.

A chest attributed to John Norman, Sr., or Jr., from Marblehead, Massachusetts, has evidence of a similar error (fig. 36). The upper rail has a mortise and two plugged pin holes to the right of the muntin separating the left and center panels (fig. 37). This indicates that the joiner chopped the mortise and bored the pin-holes before realizing that he was working on the wrong side of the layout line. He probably bored the pin-holes after chopping each mortise, or after chopping all the mortises in a given piece of stock. In the latter scenario, boring the pin-holes may have marked the piece "finished." Most likely, the joiner discovered his mistake during a test assembly of the façade, cut a new mortise, and plugged the offending extra holes.[29]

As the documents and objects discussed in this article reveal, joinery was a complex trade requiring both proficiency and creativity. Some tradesmen prospered and established family dynasties that flourished for generations, whereas others enjoyed moderate success. Less fortunate artisans often moved from town to town in search of work or failed entirely. This is not to say that most early artisans suffered a miserable existence or that they despised working in their trade, but that their lives were far more challenging than we imagine today.

ACKNOWLEDGMENTS For assistance with this article the author thanks John Alexander, Gavin Ashworth, Mark Atchison, Luke Beckerdite, Stuart Bolton, Victor Chinnery, Robert F. Trent, and the museums and individuals who provided photographs and access to their collections.

1. Wallace Nutting, *Furniture of the Pilgrim Century* (Boston, Mass.: Marshall Jones, 1924), pp. 53, 54, no. 18. Irving P. Lyon described Ipswich, Massachusetts, joiner Thomas Dennis as a "really great artisan" and suggested that the artisan's forebears were joiners and "craftsmen of distinction . . . to judge by the standard of our Thomas." Lyon also speculated about a theoretical ancestor of Thomas Dennis "plying his trade with integrity and skill." Irving P. Lyon, "The Oak Furniture of Ipswich, Massachusetts, Part 1, Florid Type," *Antiques* 32, no. 5 (November 1937): 230–37; "The Oak Furniture of Ipswich, Massachusetts, Part 2, Florid Type, Miscellaneous Examples," *Antiques* 32, no. 6 (December 1937): 298–301; "The Oak Furniture of Ipswich, Massachusetts, Part 3, Florid Type, Scroll Detail," *Antiques* 33, no. 2 (February 1938): 73–75; "The Oak Furniture of Ipswich, Massachusetts, Part 4, The Small-Panel Type," *Antiques* 33, no. 4 (April 1938): 198–203; "The Oak Furniture of Ipswich, Massachusetts, Part 5, Small-Panel-Type Affiliates," *Antiques* 33, no. 6 (June 1938): 322–25; "The Oak Furniture of Ipswich, Massachusetts, Part 6, Other Affiliates: A Group Characterized by Geometrical Panels," *Antiques* 34, no. 2 (February 1939): 79–81. All of Lyon's *Antiques* articles are reprinted in *Pilgrim Century Furniture: An Historical Survey*, edited by Robert F. Trent (New York: Main Street/Universe Books, 1976), pp. 55–78. Dennis' birthplace and the name of his master are still unknown.

2. Benno M. Forman, *American Seating Furniture 1630–1730: An Interpretive Catalogue* (New York: W. W. Norton, 1988), p. 60. Forman's chapter titled "Seventeenth-Century Woodworking Craftsmen and their Crafts" concerns many of the themes contained in this article. Frank L. Horton, founder of the Museum of Early Southern Decorative Arts, reported a phone conversation with a direct descendant of John Vogler who claimed to have the diary and who read Horton the aforementioned entry. Although the diary has never surfaced, Horton was convinced that it existed (Luke Beckerdite to Peter Follansbee, February 2000). As

quoted in Paul S. Seaver, *Wallington's World, A Puritan Artisan in Seventeenth-Century London* (Stanford, Ca.: Stanford University Press, 1985), p. 113. Nehemiah Wallington's comments help dispel romantic notions about period tradesmen "painstakingly" laboring over their work in an effort to satisfy an artistic impulse, but his case was extreme. His father, John, Sr., was a warden of the Turner's Company of London. Recognizing that his son and apprentice was depressed and suicidal, the elder Wallington paid the Turner's Company to accept Nehemiah as a master after only two years of training.

3. This article was inspired by Mack Headley, "Eighteenth-Century Cabinet Shops and the Furniture-Making Trades in Newport, Rhode Island" in *American Furniture*, edited by Luke Beckerdite (Hanover, N.H.: University Press of New England for the Chipstone Foundation, 1999), pp. 17–37. On page 17, Headley notes that "modern perceptions about historic trades often conjure up images of infinitely patient craftsmen working to the highest standards with no thought given to the time invested." Joseph Moxon, *Mechanick Exercises; or the Doctrine of Handy-works Applied to the Arts of Smithing, Joinery, Carpentry, Turning, Bricklaying* (3d ed., London, 1703; reprint, Mendham, N.J.: Astragal Press, 1994). The first edition of Moxon's work appeared in 1677. For more on Moxon and his publishing efforts, see *Mechanick Excercises: on the Whole Art of Printing*, edited by Herbert Davis and Harry Carter (2d ed., London; reprint, New York: Dover, 1978). Randle Holme, *Academie or Store-House of Armory & Blazon* (London, 1688; reprint, Menston, Eng.: Scolar Press, 1972). Holme's work is available as a CD-Rom (*Living and Working in the Seventeenth Century: an Encyclopedia of Drawings and Descriptions from Randle Holme's original manuscripts for the Academy of Armory*, edited by N. W. Alcock and Nancy Cox), and all subsequent citations are from the digital version. Holme's work is divided into chapters, which are described as books. Subsequent references will give the book number followed by the page number. Alcock and Cox's excellent introduction identifies many of Holme's sources. Tool historians have traditionally focused more on Moxon than on Holme. See James M. Gaynor, *Eighteenth-Century Woodworking Tools* (Williamsburg, Va.: Colonial Williamsburg Foundation, 1997), pp. 99–116.

4. For the Harding inventory, see *Plymouth Colony Records Volume 1: Wills and Inventories 1633–1669*, edited by C. H. Simmons (Camden, Me.: Picton Press, 1996), pp. 24, 25. Robert Charles Anderson, *The Great Migration Begins: Immigrants to New England, 1620–1633*, 3 vols. (Boston, Mass.: New England Historic Genealogical Society, 1995), 2: 854, 855. For the Birdsall and Symonds references, see *Probate Records of Essex County, Massachusetts, 1635–1681*, edited by George Francis Dow, 3 vols. (Salem, Mass.: Essex Institute, 1916–1920), 1: 143, 144 and 2: 247–50 respectively. The *Oxford English Dictionary* defines "lare" as a turner's lathe, citing a 1611 reference from Randle Cotgrave, *A dictionarie of the French and English tongues*: "*Tournoir*, a Turne, turning wheele, or Turners wheele, called a Lathe or Lare." The broadsheet is discussed in David Cressy, *Coming Over: Migration and Communication Between England and New England in the Seventeenth Century* (Cambridge, Mass.: Cambridge University Press, 1987), pp. 112–14.

5. For more on the Symonds shops, see Martha H. Willoughby, "Patronage in Early Salem: The Symonds Shops and Their Customers," in *American Furniture*, edited by Luke Beckerdite (Hanover, N. H.: University Press of New England for the Chipstone Foundation, 2000), pp. 169–84; Robert F. Trent's catalogue entry in *The Joseph and Bathsheba Pope Valuables Cabinet*, Christie's, New York, January 21, 2000, pp. 18–21; and Robert F. Trent, "The Symonds Shops of Essex County Massachusetts," in *The American Craftsman and the European Tradition 1620–1820*, edited by Francis J. Puig and Michael Conforti (Minneapolis, Minn.: Minneapolis Institute of Arts, 1989), pp. 23–41. Little's inventory is dated April 4, 1672. Plymouth Colony Probate Records 3: 46, 47. Anderson, *The Great Migration Begins*, 2: 1189–92.

6. For the Symonds, Pickworth and Wickes inventories, see Dow, ed., *Probate Records of Essex County*, 2: 247–50; 1: 428, 429 and 1:241–43. Peter Follansbee and John Alexander, "Seventeenth-Century Joinery from Braintree, Massachusetts: the Savell Shop Tradition," in *American Furniture*, edited by Luke Beckerdite (Hanover, N.H.: University Press of New England for the Chipstone Foundation, 1996), pp. 81–104.

7. W. L. Goodman, *The History of Woodworking Tools* (London: G. Bell and Sons, 1964), pp. 147–48. On page 45 of *American Seating Furniture*, Forman argues that the panel does not depict a London shop because the joiner's and turner's trades were separated by regulation. The "slab" type lathe seen in this panel is not unusual, though Moxon depicts a framed construction for his lathes.

8. Holme, *Academie of Armory & Blazon*, 3:317. Holme mentions but does not illustrate an "Iron Frower," which was used to cleave laths and wood. He considered this tool "necessary

for a good farm or dairy." In his section on joiner's terms, Holme defines panels as "little cleft boards, about 2 foot high, and 16 or 20 inches broad, of these Wainscot is made."

9. For more on the duality of the carpenter's and joiner's trades, see Robert F. Trent, Peter Follansbee, and Alan Miller, "First Flowers in the Wilderness: Mannerist Furniture from a Northern Essex County, Massachusetts, Shop" in *American Furniture*, edited by Luke Beckerdite (Hanover, N. H.: University Press of New England for the Chipstone Foundation, 2001), pp. 3, 4. In the present article, the term "joiner" is used to describe an artisan who made joined furniture while acknowledging that carpenters occasionally produced such goods. Simmons, ed., *Plymouth Colony Wills and Inventories*, 2: 349.

10. For the Francis Eaton inventory, see Simmons, ed., *Plymouth Colony Wills and Inventories*, 1: 41–44.

11. Holme, *Academie of Armory & Blazon*, 3:368.

12. Simmons, ed., *Plymouth Colony Wills and Inventories*, 1: 37–40. Thorp and his servant are mentioned twice in the colony's records:

> Jan 20 1632   Robt Barker servt of John Thorp, complayned of his mr for want of clothes. The complaint being found to be just, it was ordered, that Thorp should either foorthwith apparell him or else make over his time to some other that was able to provide for him.
>
> Aug 15 1633   Whereas Robt Barker had bound himselfe an apprentise to John Thorp in the trade of carpentry, the said Thorp being dead, Alice , his wife, hath turned over his time, wch will be exspired the first of April 1637 to William Palmer, nayler, of Plymouth, by free consent of the said Robert, the said William promising to instruct & teach him his said trade of nayling & at the end of his time to give him onely two sutes of apparell.

Records of the Colony of New Plymouth in New England, edited by Nathaniel Shurtleff and David Pulsifer, 12 vols. (Boston, Mass., Press of William White, 1855–1861), 1: 7, 16.

13. Moxon, *Mechanick Exercises*; p. 71. Gerrit van der Sterre, *Four Centuries of Dutch Plane Making* (Leiden, Netherlands: Primavera Press, 2001). Van der Sterre's definition of the *gerfschaff* indicates a fore plane rather than a smoothing plane, putting Randle Holme at odds with some modern tool historians. Holme includes a second version of the tool, one with a convex sole, which he calls a "round" smoothing plane. On pp. 51–53, van der Sterre cites surviving "traditional" examples of these planes with many different sole shapes: "The sole can be straight, hollow, or rounded in cross-section, as well as straight or curved lengthways." *New England Begins: The Seventeenth-Century,* edited by Jonathan L. Fairbanks and Robert F. Trent, 3 vols. (Boston, Mass.: Museum of Fine Arts, 1982), 3: 542–43. The sole of this plane is curved along its length, with a short flat section where the iron fits through the mouth. Holme, *Academie of Armory & Blazon*, 3: 367.

14. Moxon, *Mechanick Exercises*, pp. 69–70. Holme, *Academie of Armory & Blazon*, 3: 352. W. L. Goodman, "Woodworking Apprentices and their Tools in Bristol, Norwich, Great Yarmouth, and Southampton, 1535–1650" in *Industrial Archaeology* 9, no. 4 (November 1972), 376–411. Research by W. L. Goodman (see *British Planemakers from 1700*, 3d ed. [Mendham, N.J.: Astragal Press, 1993], pp. 13–16) and Donald and Anne Wing supports Holme's claim that woodworking craftsmen often made their own plane bodies. Wing and Wing cite Francis Purdew (active 1704–1722) and Thomas Granford (active 1687–1715) as the earliest plane makers on record (Donald Wing and Anne Wing, *The Case for Francis Purdew* [Marion, Mass.: Privately printed, n.d.], pp. 9–22).

15. Simmons, ed., *Plymouth Colony Wills and Inventories,* pp. 37–40. Holme, *Academie of Armory & Blazon*, 3: 369.

16. For the February 21, 1685, inventory of William Carpenter, Sr. of Rehoboth, Massachusetts, see Simmons, ed., *Plymouth Colony Wills and Inventories*, pp. 361–67. Moxon, *Mechanick Exercises,* pp. 71–73. Moxon borrowed heavily from the French work of Andres Felibien (see Benno M. Forman's introduction in *Joseph Moxon's Mechanick Exercises: or the Doctrine of Handy Works,* edited by Charles F. Montgomery [New York: Praeger Publishers, 1970], pp. ix–xxvi). Felibien's discussion of wainscotting differs from that of Moxon and Holme: "The strongest are those which are set into a furrow."

17. Goodman, "Woodworking Apprentices," pp. 376–411. Moxon, *Mechanick Exercises*, p. 94. Holme, *Academie of Armory & Blazon*, 3: 368.

18. Modern turners often use brown paper to help separate the glue line when breaking the finished turning apart. Animal hide glues like those used by period tradesmen are easily

soluble with warm water or steam unlike modern yellow glues, which can be quite tenacious.

19. John Evelyn's *Sylva, or a Discourse of Forest-Trees, and the Propagation of Timber in His Majesties Dominions, &c.* (1664). The reference cited here is from the text by Guy de la Bédoyère (1995) and cited with permission (<www.british-trees.com/bibliography/silv.html>).

20. Moxon, *Mechanick Exercises*, p. 88.

21. Holme, *Academie of Armory & Blazon*, 3: 368.

22. For the Blin reference, see Patricia E. Kane, "The Joiners of Seventeenth-Century Hartford County," *Connecticut Historical Society Bulletin* 35, no. 3 (July 1970): 65–85. Bond of John Rickards to Anne Boote, June 6, 1668, Accomack County, Va., Orders, Wills &c. 1671–1673, fol. 231, as cited in Robert A. Leath, "Dutch Trade and Its Influence on Seventeenth-Century Chesapeake Furniture," in *American Furniture,* edited by Luke Beckerdite (Hanover, N. H.: University Press of New England for the Chipstone Foundation, 1997), pp. 35–36.

23. *Records and Files of the Quarterly Court Essex County, Massachusetts,* edited by George Francis Dow, 8 vols. (Salem, Mass.: Essex Institute, 1911–1921), 8: 123, 124.

24. Ibid. Some tradesmen kept account books, as indicated by Ipswich, Massachusetts, wheelwright Richard Kimball, Sr.'s 1675 inventory listing £15.11 "due by Booke," but none are known today. Kimball's inventory is in Dow, ed., *Probate Records of Essex County*, 3: 16–19.

25. Photocopy in author's possession with title page reading "Records of the Town of Ipswich volume 1, 1634–1674, copied by the Order of the Town of Ipswich, by Nathaniel Farley, 1890."

26. *Records of the Colony and Plantation of New Haven, from 1638 to 1649,* edited by Charles J. Hoadly (Hartford, Conn.: Case, Tiffany and Co., 1857) pp. 36, 44. *The Journal of John Winthrop 1630–1649,* edited by Richard S. Dunn, James Savage, and Laetitia Yeandle (Cambridge, Mass.: Belknap Press of Harvard University Press, 1996), p. 102. Part of Winthrop's concern was that "the evills . . . were . . . many spent muche tyme idlely &c: because they could gett as muche in four dayes as would keepe them a weeke . . . they spent muche in Tobacco & strong waters." *Records of the Governor and Company of the Massachusetts Bay in New England,* edited by Nathaniell B. Shurtleff (Boston: Press of William White, 1853), 1: 160. Dunn et al., eds., *Journal of John Winthrop 1630–1649*, p. 345.

27. In a 1682 court case, Thomas Dennis reported that "Grace Stout bought a carved box with a drawer in it of him in 1679 and it had two locks." For this, Dennis was paid 2 shillings 6 pence. Although this may have represented one day's labor, the value of the locks makes any calculation problematic (Lyon, "The Oak Furniture of Ipswich Massacusetts," in Trent, ed., *Pilgrim Century Furniture*, p. 56).

28. Follansbee and Alexander, "Seventeenth-Century Joinery from Braintree," pp. 81–104.

29. For more on Norman, see Robert F. Trent, "The Marblehead Pews," in *New England Meeting House and Church*, edited by Peter Benes as volume 4 of the Annual Proceedings of the Dublin Seminar for New England Folklife (Boston: Boston University, 1980), pp. 101–11.

Andrew Brunk

The Claypoole Family Joiners of Philadelphia: Their Legacy and the Context of Their Work

▼ DESPITE ONGOING research, recent museum exhibitions, and market demand, only a few Philadelphia case pieces in the late baroque, or "Queen Anne," style can be confidently attributed to a specific cabinetmaker or shop tradition. Similarly, the scarcity of dated case pieces has prevented scholars from developing a chronology of forms and stylistic conventions for Philadelphia furniture made during the second quarter of the eighteenth century. To begin redressing this problem, this article will examine the formal attributes and historical context of a small group of furniture associated with members of the three generations of Claypoole family joiners whose working dates collectively encompassed most of the eighteenth century. Distinctive or idiosyncratic stylistic and structural details provide a benchmark for beginning to attribute other work to these individuals, whereas more generic features document prevailing tastes and establish a rough chronology for shifts in form and ornament.

Among the constellation of immigrants who participated in William Penn's great experiment in the New World, James Claypoole (1634–1687) must have been among the most colorful. The progenitor of the Philadelphia branch of his family, James was one of fourteen children born to John and Mary (Angell) Claypoole—prosperous Puritan landowners who resided at the Manor of Northborough in Northampton Shire (fig. 1). After serving an apprenticeship in Bremen, Germany, James achieved success as a merchant in London. He was a member of the Church of England

Figure 1 Northborough Manor, County of Cambridgeshire, England, built beginning ca. 1333. James Claypoole (1532/34–1599), grandfather of James Claypoole, (1634–1687) who came to Philadelphia in 1683, purchased the manor in 1572. The younger James was born in this house in 1634. (Photo, Brian Davies.)

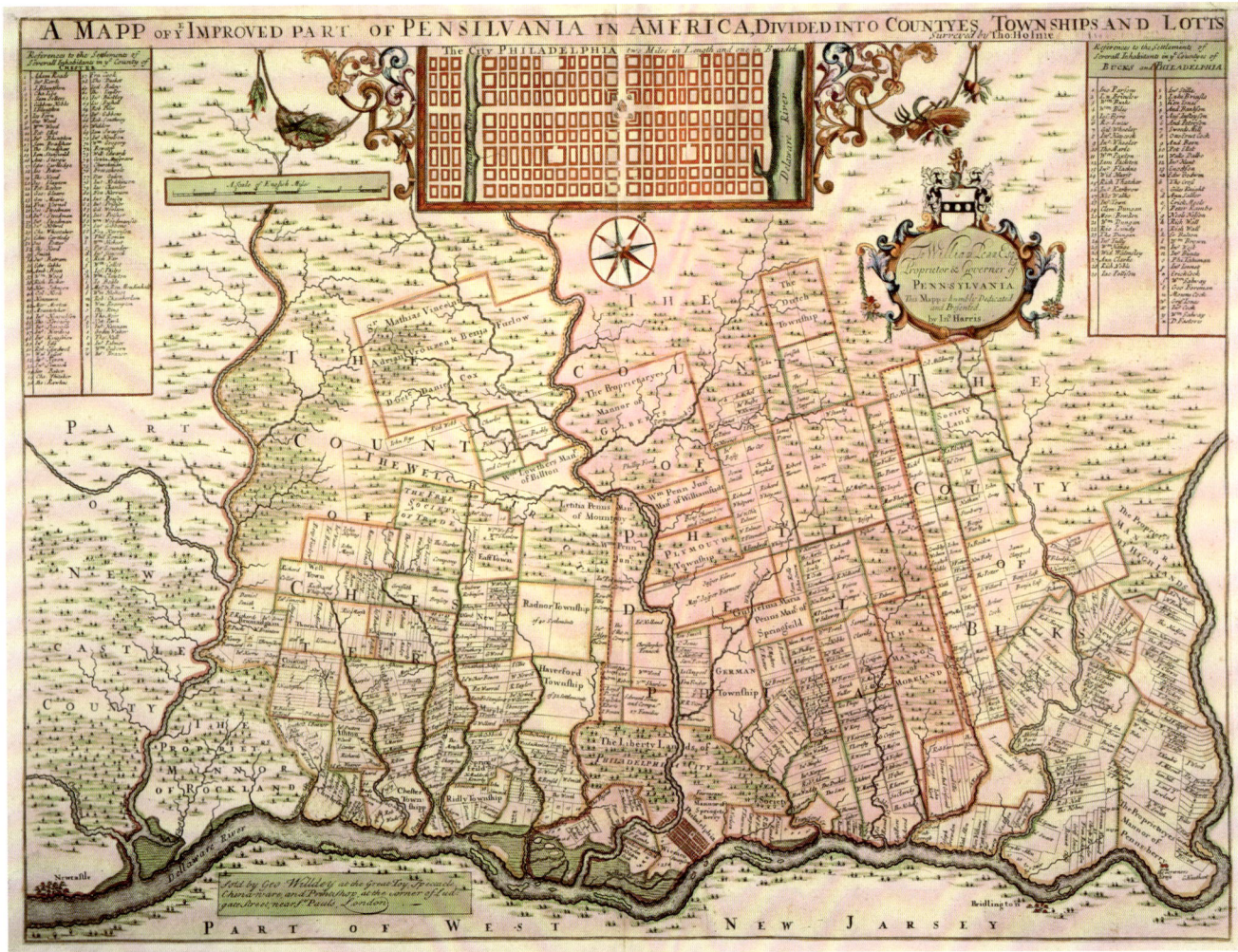

Figure 2 Thomas Holme (1624–1695), *A Mapp of Ye Improved Part of Pensilvania in America*, London, ca. 1700. Hand colored engraving. 12 1/8" x 18". (Private collection; photo, Lynne Rosenthal.) James Claypoole's land appears on this early map to the left of the tract designated "German Township." His eldest son John, who worked as an assistant to Thomas Holme, likely played a part in its creation. The engraving is by George Willdey.

and enjoyed a limited brush with fame after his oldest brother married Oliver Cromwell's daughter. Shortly after Cromwell's fall, James converted to Quakerism. He became a close friend of William Penn, and frequently entertained George Fox, George Whitehead, and other prominent members of the Society of Friends. Like many Quakers, Claypoole was persecuted for his faith. When authorities locked the doors of the Gracechurch Street Meeting on April 8, 1682, Claypoole responded by preaching to the congregation in the street. He was summarily arrested, fined, and imprisoned for seventeen days. Similar, and often harsher punishments, compelled many English Quakers, like Claypoole, to find a more tolerant and welcoming home.[1]

James purchased 5000 acres of land in Pennsylvania in 1681 and another 5000 acres in 1683 (see fig. 2). After his initial purchase, he sent servants to plant a garden, buy livestock, and build a house on the town lot he received for being one of the original participants in Penn's new experiment. "In a few years," he wrote, "we hope to have corn and wine and cattle." Like many of his fellow Quakers, Claypoole was optimistic about his future in the New World: "I hope to carry 10 or 12 servants from hence, and many people that love us well are inclined to go when we go. William

Penn himself and family goes this Summer, and probably about 1000 people. He is so much my friend that I can have anything in reason I desire of him." After several delays, James set sail on July 24, 1683, with his wife, their seven children, and four servants.[2]

When they arrived the following October, the Claypooles received a warm welcome from William Penn, their Quaker friends, and the servants who had recently built him "a house like a barn without a chimney." Measuring forty feet by twenty feet, James' residence had a dry cellar and "proved an extraordinary conveniency for securing our goods and lodging [his] . . . family." The following spring, he built a proper house, reputedly the first brick one in Philadelphia. "It was a double two-story brick house, had four leaden-framed windows in front, and the same in the rear . . . with a beautiful south exposure, down a descending green into the pleasant Dock Creek" (see fig. 3).[3]

Notwithstanding his resources and social connections, Claypoole struggled to prosper in his new environment. His wealth and image within the Quaker community suffered because of his involvement with the Free Society of Traders. As a founding member, treasurer, and major investor, Claypoole had to defend his actions in court when the society failed. These proceedings as well as Claypoole's aggressive pursuit of public positions embarrassed his peers. However, he eventually served as a judge of the Provincial Court and Register General and was poised to be one of five governors of the colony when he died in 1687. Although numerous debtors defaulted on loans (including his brothers John and Norton), Claypoole's appraisers valued his estate at £481.10.3 not counting several thousand acres of land.[4]

Despite their friendship, William Penn referred to Claypoole as a "sly spirit—inclinable to be to inferiors insolent, to superiors creeping—he is the man of all the province that . . . is least well spoken of." Accusations of bribery and Claypoole's ownership of slaves did little to improve his status within the Quaker community. Other members of the family had similar problems. In 1687, James' eldest son John got into trouble in Barbados and had to flee to Pennsylvania where he worked as an assistant to Thomas Holme, the surveyor general. John later became sheriff of Philadelphia, but he was dismissed for "lameness and misbehaveor" after releasing pirates and allowing them to walk the streets on hot summer days.[5]

James Claypoole's youngest son Joseph (1677–1744) arrived in Philadelphia at about age six. With four older brothers, the younger Claypoole was not destined to inherit a large share of his father's estate. Consequently, Joseph elected to enter the joiner's trade. Joiners were in great demand during this period, as indicated by James' frequent letters asking London acquaintances to encourage carpenters and joiners to immigrate. In 1683, he wrote: "I desire thee, if thou canst hear of a carpenter, or joiner that will go over as a servant, let me know of it. Such may have as good terms from me as any." Another letter written eight years later implies that only one cabinetmaker and one joiner were active in Philadelphia in 1691, although documentary evidence indicates that at least eleven men capable of making

Figure 3 *Samuel Carpenter's Mansion*, attributed to George Strickland, Philadelphia, Pennsylvania, 1825–1845. Ink wash on card. 5⅝" x 7⅛". (Private collection; photo, Schwarz Gallery, Philadelphia.) During his second trip to Pennsylvania, William Penn resided in Carpenter's home (built ca. 1687–1699). Carpenter's house was located near James Claypoole's residence on Second Street, but the former did not begin construction until shortly after the latter's death.

furniture worked in the Delaware Valley region. Such skilled labor remained in high demand well into the eighteenth century.[6]

According to furniture historian William MacPherson Hornor, Joseph Claypoole "learned his trade [in Philadelphia] . . . probably with Charles Plumley; and [was] in business for himself by July 1708." Although Hornor's statements cannot be verified, Claypoole was undoubtedly working as a joiner by 1710 when he received cash from merchant John Moore for an order on joiner Edward Evans' account. This indicates that the two joiners were acquainted and suggests that Claypoole may have worked as a journeyman in Evans' shop (see fig. 4). The latter joiner is documented in Philadelphia in 1702, but he may have been working there earlier. If so, he is another possible candidate for Joseph's master. Claypoole probably began serving a seven-year apprenticeship at age fourteen, thus completing

Figure 4 Fall-front desk signed by Edward Evans, Philadelphia, Pennsylvania, 1707. Walnut with white cedar and white pine. H. 66½", W. 44½", D. 19⅞". (Courtesy, Colonial Williamsburg Foundation.) This desk is the earliest signed and dated piece of furniture from Pennsylvania.

Figure 5 Oval table, Philadelphia, Pennsylvania, 1700–1730. Walnut with tulip poplar and white cedar. H. 29", W. 43¼" (open). (Courtesy, National Society of the Colonial Dames of America in the Commonwealth of Pennsylvania at Stenton.) James Logan also purchased oval tables from Edward Evans (1714/15), John Widdowfield (1717), and Thomas Staplefoot (1717). This example, which reputedly belonged to Logan, may represent the work of Joseph Claypoole or one of the aforementioned artisans.

his term about 1697. Plumley's inventory, taken in 1708 by joiner John Jones and Joseph Shippen, lists two indentured servants or apprentices—David and Isaac—who had not completed their terms, but it does not mention Claypoole. At any rate, Claypoole was one of the earliest joiners trained in the city.[7]

During his career, Claypoole received commissions from several prominent clients. He made "packing chests" and an "oval table" (see fig. 5) for James Logan between 1712 and 1714, did unspecified work for Isaac Norris in 1713, and billed James Bonsall £18.4.3 for "joinery" in 1725. Like many joiners and cabinetmakers, Claypoole also made coffins. He received £5.5 for a "Mahogany Coffin of ye Best fashion" from merchant Richard Hill's estate in 1729 and charged Nathaniel Allen, executor of his father's estate, £3.5 for a coffin on August 28, 1736.[8]

Joseph Claypoole was approximately sixty when he signed his will in 1738. His inventory taken six years later lists a variety of furniture forms—some undoubtedly made by him—including two chamber tables, two tea tables, a maple cabinet, two large cedar chests, two oval tables (one large and one small), a black walnut desk, eighteen chairs, a spicebox, and a walnut book frame. He left his daughter Edith (1723–1800) a "black walnut Drawers case upon case and ye largest cedar chest" and his son James (1720–1796) "a maple cabbenet and black walnut writing desk." Joseph's son George (1706–1793) received a parcel of land and his other son Josiah (1716/17–1757) inherited his tools, wood, and hardware. On May 18, 1738, the *Philadelphia Gazette* reported:

> Mr. Joseph Claypoole, Joyner, has left off his Trade; and has given his Stock and Implements . . . to his son [Josiah] . . . who has removed from his shop in Walnut Street to the Joyner-Arms in Second Street . . . where all Persons may be supplied with all Sorts of Furniture of the best Fashion; as Desks, . . . Chests of Drawers, . . . Dining Tables, Chamber Tables, Tea Tables and Sideboards; he having the largest and oldest Stock of Timber, of the Produce of this country and the West-Indies, of any in this Province, some of which having been in Piles near 25 Years; he has likewise a Parcel of choice curl'd Maple; and a large Parcel of choice Wood for bedsteads, and a fine Sortment of the best and newest fashioned brass Work Furniture, lately imported from London.

In placing this advertisement, Josiah hoped to capitalize on his father's reputation and retain his patrons and business contacts. At the time of Joseph's retirement, Josiah was only twenty-one, having married Sarah Jackson at Christ Church a year earlier. Presumably both Josiah and his brother George apprenticed with their father, and Joseph's retirement seems to coincide with the completion of Josiah's apprenticeship. The fact that Joseph left his tools and materials to Josiah suggests that George was established in his trade. Despite the elder Claypoole's best efforts, Josiah's career went awry, and he fled to Charleston, South Carolina, accused of theft.[9]

Although no information pertaining to Josiah's alleged crime survives, he faced prison, public whipping, or banishment if convicted. While it is possible that he was banished after a trial, it is more likely that he moved to avoid prosecution. He probably chose Charleston as his new home because it was the birthplace of his father's first wife Rebecca Jennings (d. 1715), and he probably had relatives living there. Josiah never returned to Philadelphia, and his name appears occasionally in Charleston newspapers and documents until his death in 1757. In his first Charleston advertisement, Josiah gave notice that:

> Persons may be supplied with all sorts of Joyner's and Cabinet-Maker's Work, as Desk and Book Cases, with arch'd, Peidiment or OG heads, common Desks of all sorts, Chests of Drawers of all Fashions, fluted or plain; all sorts of Tea Tables, Side-Boards and Waiters, Rule joint Skeleton Tables, Frames for Marble Tables, all after the newest and best fashions, and with the greatest Neatness and Accuracy by Josiah Claypool from Philadelphia, who may be spoke with at Capt. Crosthwatte's in King-street, or at his shop next door to Mr. Lorimer's near the market square, he has Coffin Furniture of all sorts, either flour'd, silver'd or plain. . . . He will warrant his work for 7 years, . . . The ill Usage of careless Servants only excepted.

Like his father, Josiah appears to have been capable of producing a wide range of stylish, structurally complex furniture. The products of Josiah's shop at "the sign of the Cabinet and Coffin" were clearly well received, and his business seems to have gotten off to a strong start. In the April 9, 1741, issue of the *Charleston Gazette*, he advertised "Coffins of any sort, made cheaper and better than any ever made in this Town" and apologized if "a constant Hurry of Cabinet Work" had caused him to disappoint "several good Customers." To remedy the situation, Josiah promised to employ "two good Workmen from London" so he would have the "Capacity to suit any Person who shall favour me with their Employ." One of his "good workmen" ran away almost immediately. On August 9, 1742, Claypoole offered a £25 reward for "an indented servant from London, named Robert Allen, by Trade a Carpenter, but can work at the cabinet maker's Business." Claypoole was still in business in February 1744/45, but his later advertisements imply financial duress. By April 18, 1748, he was involved in bankruptcy proceedings precipitated by a suit by William Greenland.[10]

Claypoole's only documented commission occurred a year before his death, when the vestry of St. Johns Parish in Colleton County agreed to pay him £192 and £100 board for the "Speedy Repairing of the Parish Church." The vestry minutes describe him as a "carpenter," but there is no reason to assume that Josiah had given up the cabinetmaking trade. He was "in custody" by February 6, 1757, when the vestry "advanced to Mr. Claypole as pr Receipt £15 / To do. paid his Suit when in custody 103." Perhaps the suit filed by Greenland caught up with Josiah, and the church endeavored to get him out of jail so he could undertake the repairs. Claypoole died that same year, possibly while still in prison.[11]

Josiah's personal life was equally troubled. An undated entry in the Register of St. Andrew's Parish documents the birth of his and Sarah's son John. The child was baptized on September 15, 1756, and, sadly, died the following month. Sarah suffered the "melancholy necessity" of procuring two more coffins during the following year: "Thomas son of Josiah Claypoole Decsd. and Sarah his wife buried Octr. 23rd 1757 Interd without a minister." Sarah's fate after this date is unknown, but the Claypoole line in Charleston evidently came to an end in 1757.[12]

Josiah's brother George continued the family's trade in Philadelphia, and was apparently very successful. In 1783, the latter paid $200 in occupational taxes, an amount surpassed only by Thomas Affleck ($250), and matched only by Benjamin Randolph and William Cox. Bills of sale document a wide range of objects produced in George Claypoole's shop. He made Quaker merchant John Reynals (Reynell, Reynolds) two bedsteads, a square dining table, and a chamber table in 1738 and a square mahogany tea table the following year. Reynals must have been pleased with George's work, since his transactions with the cabinetmaker continued for another twenty-four years. During this period Reynals paid Claypoole for rudimentary tasks, such as "wheting and setting a saw" and "mending a tea table & new mouldin," and commissioned costly pieces of furniture. In 1754/55, Claypoole billed the merchant for a "large double desk & leather to coverit," a "mahogany clockcase of ye best fashion," and a "Large pillar and claw table with casters." The cabinetmaker also made mahogany coffins for four of Reynals' children. Other Quaker clients included Edward Shippen, Jr., who paid Claypoole £14 for a "walnut double chest of drawers with archt head" in 1754.[13]

George Claypoole's status within the cabinetmaking community is confirmed by his 1772 bill to Samuel Meredith (1741–1817) listing an extensive array of furniture valued at £130.2.7. Meredith was a signer of the Non-Importation Agreements, a general in the Continental Army, a delegate to the Continental Congress, and the first treasurer of the United States. His order coincided with his marriage to Margaret Cadwalader (b. 1753), whose brother John was furnishing his Philadelphia townhouse about the same time. Claypoole's bill listed eighteen mahogany chairs, two dining tables, two card tables, a breakfast table, a walnut clothes press, a walnut chest of drawers, a mahogany bedstead and cornice, a mahogany sofa, a mahogany easy chair, and a frame for a marble slab. Although none of these objects can be identified today, the cost of several pieces was quite high. The card tables were six pounds each and the sofa was £10.14.6. By comparison, the pair of "commode card tables" and a large commode sofa that Cadwalader purchased from Thomas Affleck in 1771 cost five pounds each and ten pounds respectively, although that valuation may not have included the carving. Similarly, Meredith's mahogany chairs cost three pounds each (totaling fifty-four pounds), an amount sufficient for an elaborate set. Like Affleck, Claypoole may have subcontracted carving to specialists.[14]

Although no furniture signed by George or Josiah is known, the former's bills and the latter's advertisements offer some insight into their and their father's work. Josiah's reference to "Desk and Book Cases, with arch'd, Peidment or O G Heads" two years after moving to Charleston suggests that he learned to make similar furniture in Joseph's shop. Joseph probably began making double-case forms with complex pediments, along with "all sorts of tea tables and sideboards," by the 1730s. During the preceding decade, most double case forms had flat tops, and tea tables and sideboards were not in common usage. The elder Claypoole probably used the term "sideboard" to refer to tables with either wooden or marble tops, whereas his son was more specific. Josiah advertised "frames for marble" (see fig. 6) and apparently used the term "sideboard" to refer to a frame

Figure 6 Sideboard table, Philadelphia, Pennsylvania, 1735–1745. Mahogany with tulip poplar; clouded limestone. H. 30", W. 44¾", D. 21½". (Courtesy, Baltimore Museum of Art, bequest of J. Gilman D'Arcy Paul; photo, Gavin Ashworth.) This example probably resembles the "sideboards" and "frames for marble" that Josiah Claypoole advertised between 1738 and 1740. Presumably, he learned to make such tables in Joseph's shop.

Figure 7 High chest signed by Joseph Claypoole, Philadelphia, Pennsylvania, 1743. Mahogany with maple, tulip poplar, white cedar, and yellow pine. H. 84⅛", W. 44⅛", D. 23¼". (Courtesy, Philadelphia Museum of Art, gift of Martin A. Battestin.) This is a unique example of an ogee head on a high chest of drawers.

Figure 8 Drawing showing the molding profiles of the high chest illustrated in fig. 7.

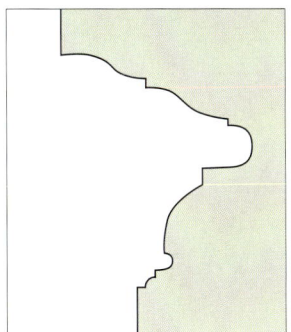

with a wooden top. The "arched," "pediment," or "ogee heads" probably referred to examples like those on the case pieces illustrated in figures 15, 19, and 7 respectively. Presumably Josiah learned to make all of these variants in Philadelphia.[15]

The high chest signed by Joseph Claypoole in 1743 (figs. 7-9) confirms that his shop was producing such complex pediments, and indicates that he and, probably, his sons made case furniture and tables with pad feet and

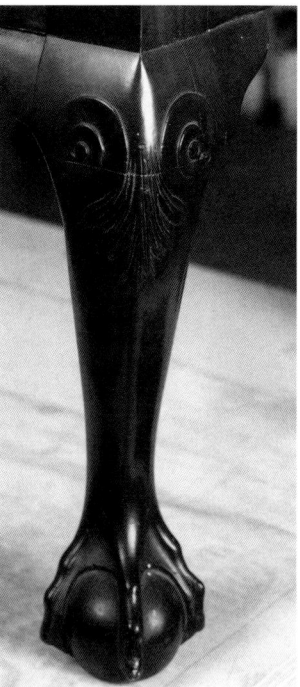

Figure 9 Detail of the left front leg and foot of the high chest illustrated in fig. 7. The naturalistic design and assured carving suggests that Joseph Claypoole's shop produced claw-and-ball feet before 1743.

claw-and-ball feet. Although the chest is the earliest dated Philadelphia piece with the latter foot form, claw-and-ball feet were undoubtedly popular in the city before 1743. Such feet were popular in London by the 1730s, and the regular trade between the two cities supports the hypothesis that this design element was in use well before Joseph fashioned this high chest. More importantly, the design and modeling of the feet on the chest (fig. 9) suggest that Joseph, or a specialist he contracted, had carved similar examples many times before.[16]

The signature, initials, and date on the chest are somewhat puzzling given the fact that Joseph Claypoole announced his retirement in 1738. When Josiah fled Philadelphia to avoid incarceration, he probably left behind tools and most of the materials he had received from his father. It is conceivable that Joseph resumed his trade, or that he made the chest to fulfill one of his son's obligations. The elder Claypoole's name and the date are written in large script on the inside bottom boards of the upper case, and his initials are in several places. Although this may reflect pride that Joseph took in the object's completion, there is no evidence that he made it for himself. He died in early 1744, and no high chest is listed in his inventory.[17]

All of the drawer fronts of Claypoole's chest have curly maple cores, thick (three-eighths inch) mahogany veneer, and applied cockbeading. The small drawers have poplar frames and yellow pine bottoms nailed to the sides and back. Although the large drawers are composed of the same woods, their bottoms have thin strips of wood glued to each side and a beveled front edge that engages a groove in the front. Oak blocks attached to the drawer fronts function as stops, and strips of wood nailed to the case sides support them.

The most distinctive feature of the chest is its ogee head, which Joseph attached using two sliding dovetails (now missing). Ornamented with two concave shells, the basic design of the pediment has precedents in both English and Philadelphia case furniture from the 1730s, but it is unique among high chests. Shells on desk-and-bookcases may have inspired those on the Claypoole chest, although the former are usually concealed as components of the bookcase interior. The carving on the knees of the chest is also unusual. Rendered in shallow relief, the shells resemble those on Newport, Rhode Island, furniture more than those on contemporary Philadelphia examples.

The high chest's ogee head ties it to three Philadelphia desk-and-bookcases (figs. 10–12). Two of these desk-and-bookcases (figs. 10, 11) are from the

Figure 10 Desk-and-bookcase, Philadelphia, Pennsylvania, 1730–1745. Mahogany with cedar, oak, and tulip poplar. H. 98", W. 38¾", D. 22¾". (Courtesy, Wyck Association; photo, Eric Mitchell.) This desk has a history of descent in the Wistar family. Probable candidates for its maker are Joseph Claypoole or George Claypoole, Sr.

Figure 11 Desk-and-bookcase, Philadelphia, Pennsylvania, 1730–1745. Mahogany with maple, oak, pine, and tulip poplar. H. 96", W. 40", D. 24¼". (Courtesy, Tryon Palace Historic Sites and Gardens, New Bern, North Carolina.)

same shop and share enough details with the chest to warrant a tentative attribution to one of the Claypooles, most likely Joseph or his son George. The desk-and-bookcase illustrated in figure 10 reputedly descended in the Wistar family of Philadelphia and is the only one with original finials. Its lower drawer is branded "WA," but the initials do not match those of any known member of the Wistar family or any Philadelphia cabinetmaker active during the period. Oral tradition maintains that James Logan purchased the third desk-and-bookcase (fig. 12) from Phila-

Figure 12 Desk-and-bookcase attributed to Stephen Armitt, Philadelphia, Pennsylvania, 1725–1740. Mahogany and exotic hardwoods with cedar, oak, and tulip poplar. H. 94", W. 34¾", D. 22". (Courtesy, National Society of the Colonial Dames of America in the Commonwealth of Pennsylvania at Stenton.)

Figure 13 Stenton, Germantown, Pennsylvania, built 1727–1730. (Courtesy, National Society of the Colonial Dames of America in the Commonwealth of Pennsylvania at Stenton.)

Figure 14 Detail of the interior of the desk-and-bookcase illustrated in fig. 12.

delphia joiner Stephen Armitt (1705–1751). Logan's son James married Armitt's daughter Sarah, and the desk-and-bookcase descended through the Armitt family to Mrs. John F. Doremus, who donated it to Stenton (fig. 13), the elder Logan's home just outside Philadelphia. James Sr. probably commissioned the piece just before or after building his residence, which was under construction from about 1725 to 1730. With its mirrored doors and exotic hardwoods (fig. 14), the Logan desk-and-bookcase was clearly the most expensive of the three related examples. Like the house in which it stood, it reflected its owner's wealth, education, and taste.[18]

The desk-and-bookcases illustrated in figures 10–12 are among the most elaborate case forms made in Philadelphia during the 1720s and 1730s. As early advertisements and bills indicate, cabinetmakers offered a wide range of structural and decorative options for this furniture form. Arched pediments occur on several contemporary desk-and-bookcases, some of which have carved ornaments, mirrored doors, and other expensive features (see fig. 15). By the mid-1740s, Philadelphia cabinetmakers had abandoned ogee and arched heads for scrolled pediments like the one on the chest-on-chest illustrated in figure 17.

Although a Philadelphia desk-and-bookcase similar to the Logan and Wistar examples may have inspired the pediment of the Claypoole high chest, virtually identical ogee heads occur on British furniture from the 1710s and 1720s. A desk-and-bookcase similar to Logan's bears the signature of London joiner Peter Miller and the date 1724, and another example signed by William Palleday appears to be contemporary with both pieces. English case furniture of this caliber was undoubtedly present in the colonies during the 1720s and 1730s. Sir Danvers Osborn (d. 1753), who served as Royal Governor of New York in 1753, owned the japanned desk-

Figure 15 Desk-and-bookcase, Philadelphia, Pennsylvania, 1730–1745. Mahogany with yellow pine and tulip poplar. H. 89", W. 41⅛", D. 24¾". (Private collection; photo, Philadelphia Museum of Art.)

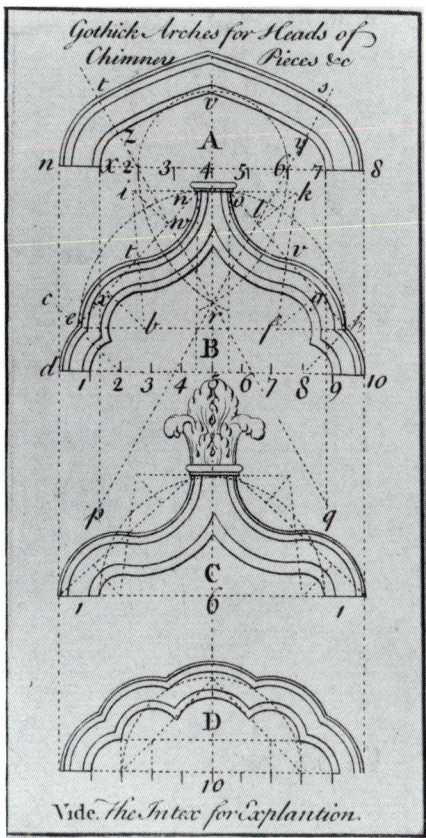

Figure 16 Pediment designs illustrated on p. 186 in Batty and Thomas Langley's *The Builder's Jewell, or Youth's Instructor* (1741). Architectural engravings may have inspired the pediment designs used by the Claypooles and their contemporaries.

Figure 17 Chest-on-chest, Philadelphia, Pennsylvania, 1730–1745. Mahogany with unrecorded secondary woods. H. 95", W. 44", D. 23½". (Private collection; photo, Christie's.)

Figure 18 Desk-and-bookcase, London, 1720–1730. Oak with pine; japanned decoration. (Courtesy, Metropolitan Museum of Art, gift of James DeLancey Verplanck and John Bayard Rodgers Verplanck.)

and-bookcase illustrated in figure 18. Architectural books depicting related pediments were available in Philadelphia (see fig. 16), but imported furniture was the most prevalent design source for joiners like Armitt and the Claypooles.[19]

A chest-on-chest (fig. 17) probably made by Joseph or his son George has an enclosed arched pediment and a molding surrounding the upper and lower ranks of drawers. This molding creates a visual effect reminiscent of the pseudo-pilasters flanking the drawers on the signed high chest (fig. 7). The former case piece differs from the latter in having an integral pediment rather than a removable one, but both objects have drawers with thick veneer and cockbeading. Ogee bracket feet were a relatively new option when the chest-on-chest was made. Such feet remained popular through the remainder of the colonial period, as did straight bracket feet on less expensive or more austere designs.

Like the ogee heads on Joseph Claypoole's high chest (fig. 7) and the aforementioned desk-and-bookcases (figs. 10–12), pitch pediments are rare on Philadelphia case pieces in the late baroque style. This is surprising given the fact that pitch pediments appear in many contexts in British architectural books; in local buildings such as Stenton, Graeme Park (built ca. 1722), and Hope Lodge (built ca. 1723, current interior installed ca. 1735); and on seventeenth- and eighteenth-century British case pieces. A pump cabinet made by John Harrison for the Library Company of Philadelphia in 1739 (fig. 19) is the earliest documented Philadelphia case piece with this detail, but Joseph Claypoole probably made furniture with "pediment heads" at the same date if not earlier.[20]

Given the years of Joseph's activity in the cabinet trade, he undoubtedly witnessed many changes in local and international furniture styles. The

Figure 19 Case for an air pump by John Harrison, Philadelphia, Pennsylvania, 1739. White pine; painted. H. 130½", W. 71¼", D. 20¼". (Courtesy, Library Company of Philadelphia.) Josiah Claypoole advertised desk-and-bookcases with "Peidment" heads in 1739/40.

Figure 20 Dressing table, Philadelphia, Pennsylvania, 1715–1725. Walnut with white cedar and yellow pine. H. 29¾", W. 33⅜", D. 20⅛". (Private collection; photo, Gavin Ashworth.)

Figure 21 Dressing table attributed to Joseph Claypoole or George Claypoole, Sr., Philadelphia, 1725–1740. Mahogany and maple with white cedar and yellow pine. H. 30", W. 34", D. 21¼". (Courtesy, Israel Sack, Inc.) The two over two drawer arrangement seen here was common during the 1730s.

turned legs of the baroque style (see fig. 20) were still popular in 1726, when Joseph's competitor John Head made a high chest and matching dressing table (Philadelphia Museum of Art) for Caspar Wistar. By the late 1720s, Philadelphia cabinetmakers were producing similar case forms with angular cabriole legs and plain or carved "Spanish" feet (see figs. 21, 22). Round cabriole legs with paneled (see fig. 23), slipper, and trifid feet became fashionable during the 1730s, and as Joseph Claypoole's signed high chest indicates, claw-and-ball feet were an option by 1743, if not earlier. Joseph must have been at the vanguard of Philadelphia cabinetmakers catering to the latest tastes, but both he and his sons had to respond to the demands of conservative patrons as well as more progressive ones (see fig. 24). Evidence suggests that Philadelphia cabinetmakers produced old-fashioned and avante garde forms simultaneously as did their counterparts in other colonial cities.[21]

The dressing table and high chests illustrated in figures 21–23 show how the Claypooles responded to changing tastes during the second quarter of the eighteenth century. Separating the work of Joseph and his sons is impossible at this time owing to the fact that he trained George Sr. and Josiah, and no documented work by them is known. It is unlikely, however, that any of the aforementioned objects are by Josiah given his early move to Charleston. Like the high chest signed by Joseph, the example illustrated in figure 23 has a lower rail with a distinctive "fish tail" pendant and unusual combination of cyma and astragal elements. The cornice and waist moldings of the two chests vary slightly, but they are much more alike than they are different. Although it is tempting to date the high chest and dressing table with "Spanish feet" (figs. 21, 22) earlier, it is possible that

Figure 22 High chest attributed to Joseph Claypoole or George Claypoole, Sr., Philadelphia, Pennsylvania, 1725–1740. Walnut with unrecorded secondary woods. H. 71½", W. 41", D. 21½". (Courtesy, Israel Sack, Inc.)

Figure 23 High chest attributed to Joseph Claypoole or George Claypoole, Sr., Philadelphia, Pennsylvania, 1730–1750. Mahogany with unrecorded secondary woods. H. 71½", W. 43½", D. 22⅞". (Courtesy, Israel Sack, Inc.)

Figure 24 Dressing table attributed to Joseph Claypoole or George Claypoole, Sr., Philadelphia, Pennsylvania, 1725–1740. H. 29", W. 34½", D. 20¼". (Private collection; photo, Christie's.)

Figure 25 High chest attributed to Joseph Claypoole or George Claypoole, Sr., Philadelphia, Pennsylvania, 1740–1750. H. 93", W. 42", D. 22¼". (Private collection; photo, Sotheby's.)

all of these objects were made only a few years apart. The drawer support system and partition construction of the dressing table, for example, is identical to that of the high chest with paneled feet (fig. 23). Similarly, the dressing table with turned legs probably dates from the late 1720s or 1730s since it has lip-molded drawers (fig. 24).[22]

Documentary evidence indicates that all of the Claypooles produced a standard range of case and table forms. On September 18, 1746, Thomas Penn wrote that if his mahogany parlor chairs had not "been burnt or destroyed Claypool might fit them up again, and with new seats they would be as good as ever." Presumably, the "Claypool" mentioned in this letter was George Sr., and if so, it is likely that Penn purchased furniture as well as services from the cabinetmaker. Despite William Penn's disparaging reference to James Claypoole, both families appear to have maintained ties throughout the eighteenth century.[23]

A high chest that reportedly descended in the Penn family (fig. 25) is one of the most fully developed case forms from the Claypoole shop tradition. Like the aforementioned pieces, it is probably by Joseph or George Sr. The cornice molding has the same sequence of ovolo and astragal elements as the cornice of the Joseph Claypoole high chest (fig. 7), and the lower rail has a pendant with bold cyma curves and an underscaled terminal. Moreover, the tympanum opening and position of the cornice relative to the lamb's tongue "capitals" of the side chamfers are similar to those on a chest-on-chest signed by George Claypoole, Sr.'s son and namesake (fig. 26). On both pieces the lamb's tongues are applied rather than worked from the solid.[24]

Figure 26 Chest-on-chest signed "Geo. Claypoole, Jr.," Philadelphia, Pennsylvania, ca. 1754. Walnut with yellow pine and white cedar. H. 97", W. 43¼", D. 22½". (Private collection; photo, Gavin Ashworth.) Presumably, George Jr. made this piece shortly after completing his apprenticeship.

Figure 27 Chest-on-chest, Philadelphia, Pennsylvania, 1740–1750. Walnut with tulip poplar and pine. H. 93", W. 42½", D. 23½". (Private collection; photo, Graydon Wood.)

Figure 28 Detail of the carved shell on the upper drawer of the chest-on-chest illustrated in fig. 26.

George Jr. probably trained with his father and completed his apprenticeship about 1754. Not surprisingly, the former's chest-on-chest reflects styles current during the 1740s. Like the early chest-on-chest illustrated in figure 27, the signed example has a tympanum drawer with a relief carved shell composed of broad convex and concave segments and no applied leaf carving (fig. 28).[25]

The stylistic and structural features of the signed chest-on-chest (fig. 26) may eventually assist scholars in identifying additional work by George Claypoole, Jr. as well as other members of his family. George Sr. clearly made similar forms as indicated by his 1754 bill to John Reynals for a "Mahogany Chest of Drawers & table of the best fashion . . . £24." Philadelphia patrons often ordered dressing tables to accompany both chest-on-chests and high chests. Chest-on-chests were clearly in the repertoire of all the Claypooles. Joseph left his daughter a "case of drawers case on case" valued at £4.10 in 1744; Josiah's first advertisement in Charleston mentioned "all sort[s] of chests fluted or plain"; and George Sr. made a chest-on-chest for Edward Shippen, Jr.

The foot and base molding profiles of the chest of drawers illustrated in figure 29 are nearly identical to those on the chest-on-chest signed by George Claypoole, Jr. Both pieces also have similar returns and chamfers with three flutes. Although it is not clear which George made the chest, it is obviously the precursor to examples made by the elder Claypoole's apprentice Jonathan Gostelowe (1744–1795) (fig. 30). Gostelowe served his term during the late 1750s and early 1760s. On July 12, 1762, Jonathan

Figure 29 Chest of drawers attributed to George Claypoole, Sr. or George Claypoole, Jr., Philadelphia, Pennsylvania, 1755–1770. Walnut with unrecorded secondary woods. H. 31¼", W. 36", D. 21". (Courtesy, Israel Sack, Inc.)

Figure 30 Chest of drawers bearing the label of Jonathan Gostelowe, Philadelphia, Pennsylvania, 1781–1793. Mahogany with tulip poplar, white cedar, and yellow pine. H. 37¼", W. 47¼", D. 25½". (Courtesy, Cliveden, a National Trust Historic Site.)

Gostelowe acknowledged his receipt of £2.19 "in full of all accounts for my master George Claypoole." Although typically updated with "commode" fronts, most chests attributed to Gostelowe have fluted chamfered corners and bold ogee feet—details associated with the Claypooles and several of their competitors. A labeled Gostelowe chest (fig. 30) also has a top drawer with partitions for dressing or writing implements like the chest illustrated in figure 29. Gostelowe may have made such chests as late as 1793, when he advertised the contents of his shop for sale.[26]

The furniture documented and attributed to the Claypooles presents a rather fragmented picture of one of Philadelphia's most important multi-generational shop traditions. Nevertheless, these objects and the documentary evidence surrounding them reveal how knowledge, tools, and customers were passed from father to son and from master to apprentice. The Claypooles' extended family and their varied religious affiliations, which covered both Quaker and Anglican congregations, helped them build a commercial network that undoubtedly contributed to their success. As additional documents and objects associated with the Claypooles and their competitors emerge, scholars will begin to understand the complex community of artisans and patrons that existed in Philadelphia during the first half of the eighteenth century.

ACKNOWLEDGMENTS   For assistance with this article, the author thanks Neal Alford, Luke Beckerdite, Dr. and Mrs. John Boor, Lauren Bresnan, H. L. Chalfant Antiques, Rachel Ciba, Brian Davies, David Demuzio, Bert Denker, Susan Detweiler, Susannah Doherty, Glynnis Doucette, Jeff Groff, Morrison Heckscher, Peter Kenny, Alexandra Kirtley, Bernard and S. Dean Levy, Jack Lindsey, Alan Miller, Rick Mones, William Nacey, Pook and Pook Auctions, C.L. Prickett Antiques, Nancy Richards, Martha Rowe, Albert Sack, Philip Seitz, Kelly Seltzer, Jeanne Solensky, and Laura Stutman.

1. For his support of Cromwell during the English Civil Wars, James' father John was created a baronet in 1657. By this date, however, James was apprenticed to a merchant in Bremen, Germany. In 1658 he was married by a Calvinist minister to Helen Mercer and soon returned to London to establish himself as a merchant. For more on the Claypoole family, see Evelyn Claypoole Bracken, *The Claypoole Family in America* (Indiana, Pa.: A. G. Halldin, 1971). Much of the Claypoole genealogy is also available online. See, for example, <http://freepages.genealogy.rootsweb.com/~heritagecrossroads/clayfam1.htm>.

2. William Penn's *A Letter From William Penn, Proprietary and Governour of Pennsylvania in America, to the Committee of the Free Society of Traders* (London: Andrew Sowle, 1683), p. 3, states that "the purchasers of 1000 acres and upwards are placed in the Front and High Streets and begin on Delaware Front at the South end at Number One to Proceed with the Front to the North End to No. 43." James Claypoole was no. 14 and Samuel Carpenter was no. 16. Although Claypoole and Carpenter were neighbors, they disagreed over a debt case against the Free Society of Traders which Claypoole fought vigorously.(James Claypoole to Edward Claypoole, February 20, 1682, cited in *James Claypoole's London Letter Book,* edited by Marion Balderston [San Marino, Ca.: Huntington Library, 1967], pp. 86–87, 109–10.)

3. Information on the house is derived from James Claypoole to Edward Claypoole, October 2, 1683, in Balderston, ed., *James Claypoole's London Letter Book,* pp. 20–21. John F. Watson, *Annals of Philadelphia,* 2 vols. (Philadelphia, 1857), 1: 558.

4. Claypoole discussed his appointment as treasurer of the society in his correspondence. See James Claypoole to Edward Claypoole, April 27, 1682, in Balderston, ed., *James Claypoole's London Letter Book,* p. 127. James Claypoole's will, dated December 5, 1686, is transcribed in Bracken, *Claypoole Family in America,* p. 14.

5. Although Penn recognized Claypoole's faults, he continued to support him and remained a loyal friend. Penn Mss, Domestic and Miscellaneous Letters, Historical Society of Pennsylvania (hereafter cited HSP), Philadelphia, as cited in Balderston, ed., *James Claypoole's London Letter Book,* pp. 8, 19.

6. James Claypoole's will left "Joseph, my youngest son, my plantation bordering on Lewis Creek in Sussex County which I bought from my brother, Norton Claypoole." (Bracken, *Claypoole Family in America,* p. 14). Norton had preceded James to the New World and settled in Delaware. William Penn and Thomas Lloyd were overseers of James' will, and his wife was executrix. See James Claypoole to William and Elizabeth Hard, February 14, 1683, in Balderston, ed., *James Claypoole's London Letter Book,* p. 208. This letter was meant to encourage new immigrants by suggesting the opportunities that awaited them. John Goodson to John and S. Dew, June 24, 1690, as quoted in "Letters from Pennsylvania, 1691," *Pennsylvania Magazine of History and Biography* 4, no. 2 (1880): 195. At least eleven joiners were working in the Delaware Valley by 1691 (Jack Lindsey, Richard S. Dunn, Edward C. Carter II, and Richard Saunders, *Worldly Goods: The Arts of Early Pennsylvania, 1680–1758* [Philadelphia, Pa.: Philadelphia Museum of Art, 1999], pp. 247–54).

7. William MacPherson Hornor, *Blue Book: Philadelphia Furniture* (Philadelphia, Pa.: privately printed, 1935), p. 3. Although Hornor's book does not contain footnotes or other citations, many of his statements have proved accurate. Joseph Claypoole was undoubtedly acquainted with Plumley. On April 17, 1711, Claypoole witnessed an exchange of property between Richard Heath and Rose Plumley, Charles' widow. Charles Morton Smith Papers, vol. 3, nos. 18, 19, HSP. John Moore Daybook, Sept. 2, 1710, and July 28, 1716, HSP, as cited in Cathryn McElroy, "Furniture of the Philadelphia Area: Forms and Craftsmen before 1730" (master's thesis, University of Delaware, 1970), pp. 170–72. See also Arthur Leibundguth, "The Furniture Making Crafts in Philadelphia, c. 1730–c. 1760" (master's thesis, University of Delaware, 1964), pp. 8–14. Both authors cite additional documents pertaining to the Claypoole family. Inventory of Charles Plumley, October 15, 1708, ms 111, Philadelphia City Hall.

8. Raymond V. Shepard, Jr., "James Logan's Stenton: Grand Simplicity in Quaker Philadelphia" (master's thesis, University of Delaware, 1968). Account Book of Isaac Norris (1709–1740), p. 104, HSP. James Bonsall Account Book, p. 93; and Richard Hill Estate, vol. 18, pp. 52–60 both HSP and both cited in McElroy, "Furniture of the Philadelphia Area," p. 171. Claypoole also charged Hill's estate three pounds for making 120 "pidgeon holes" for papers and other documents. In her thesis, McElroy suggests that John Willet apprenticed with Joseph Claypoole. However, Willet was born in New York and began training with joiner Aaron Goforth in 1728 (Indenture between John Willett and Aaron Goforth, April 11, 1728, Richard Hill Estate, Logan Papers, vol. 18, p. 25, HSP). In his will, Goforth left his "books, wearing apparel and working tools" to his son-in-laws Richard Hill and Thomas Campbell

(McElroy, "Furniture of the Philadelphia Area," p. 184). Account Book of Nathaniel Allen, p. 100, HSP, as cited in Leibundguth, "The Furniture Making Crafts in Philadelphia," p. 9.

9. Joseph Claypoole Will, Philadelphia Wills and Inventories, ms. 81, January 18, 1738. Joseph Claypoole Inventory as cited in McElroy, "Furniture of the Philadelphia Area," p. 170. No apprenticeship record for Josiah is known. This supports the theory that he apprenticed with his father, since formal agreements were not required for contracts between family members. In January 1738, Josiah appears in the account book of Nathaniel Allen. He paid part of his £18 debt in cash and the remainder with "9 Pickturs Sent to John Hawes of Antegua" and a "pr. of Chest of Drawers for Moley" (presumably a ship). He purchased paper and books from Benjamin Franklin, and was credited for framing 36 pictures. Account Book of Nathaniel Allen, p. 149, HSP, as cited in Leibundguth, "The Furniture Making Crafts in Philadelphia," p. 13. Josiah advertised in the *South Carolina Gazette* on March 22, 1739/40, April 16, 1741, August 9, 1741/42, and April 18, 1748, research files of the Museum of Early Southern Decorative Arts, Winston-Salem, North Carolina (hereafter cited MESDA). Claypoole's indictment is mentioned in Cathryn J. McElroy, "Furniture in Philadelphia: The First Fifty Years," *Winterthur Portfolio* 13 (1979): 80. November 10 and 21, 1739, Indictments, 1717–1790, Philadelphia County Court Papers, HSP. Despite extensive efforts, the HSP has been unable to locate these papers. For more on the punishments that thieves and other criminals faced, see Theodore Thayer, "Town into City 1746–1765," in *Philadelphia: A 300-Year History,* edited by Russell Weigley (New York: Barra Foundation, 1982), pp. 76–78.

10. Joseph married Rebecca Jennings on July 20, 1703. While there is some evidence that they married in Charleston, there is no evidence that Joseph ever worked in that city. The date and location of the marriage is referenced on <http://www.Flash.net/~wlemmon/HTML/d0002/g00000.93.htm>. *South Carolina Gazette,* March 22, 1739/40, August 9, 1741/42, February 4, 1744/45, April 18, 1748.

11. Vestry Minutes, St. John's Parish, Colleton, S. C. 1734–1817, pp. 43, 44, 89, South Carolina Historical Society, Charleston, S. C., typescript in MESDA research files.

12. Josiah Claypoole's first child was born just a few months after his marriage to Sarah Jackson. "Register of St. Andrew's Parish, Berkeley County, South Carolina," edited by Mabel L. Webber, *South Carolina Historical and Genealogical Magazine* 14, no. 3 (1913): 155–59, as cited in MESDA research files.

13. Horner, *Blue Book,* pp. 317–26. Bills from George Claypoole, Sr. to John Reynals, October 30, 1730–May 4, 1764, Coates-Reynell Papers, HSP, microfilm copy in the Joseph Downs Library (hereafter cited JDL), Winterthur Museum. Bill from George Claypoole, Sr. to Edward Shippen, dated paid on April 22, 1755, photocopy cataloged as ph1380, Col. 521, JDL. On October 27, 1783, George Claypoole, Sr. charged Greenberry Dorsy £10.1.1 for a mahogany chamber table (bill from George Claypoole to Greenberry Dorsey, October 27, 1783, ms. 55.528, JDL).

14. Bill from George Claypoole to Samuel Meredith, December 5, 1772. ms. 55.528, JDL. Samuel and Margaret were apparently married on May 21, 1772, <www.FamilySearch.org>. For a copy of Affleck's bill, see Nicholas Wainwright, *Colonial Grandeur in Philadelphia* (Philadelphia, Pa.: Historical Society of Pennsylvania, 1964), p. 44.

15. There are clear affinities between Charleston and Philadelphia furniture. Future research may clarify the role that Josiah played in introducing or perpetuating such attributes into Charleston's cabinet trade. Eighteenth-century terminology is not precise, and cabinetmakers occasionally used the same term to describe two different things. The term "ogee head," for example, could also refer to a "scroll pediment," or what modern collectors call a bonnet top.

16. Evidence suggests that Joseph or a carver in his shop executed the knee acanthus. The inside front of the upper middle drawer has a carved volute that appears to have been cut before the drawer was assembled. The upper right drawer also has an inscribed design showing the scalloping of the skirt. An Irish tea table with deeply webbed claw-and-ball feet that appears to predate the high chest was among the early furnishings of Graeme Park, built in 1721 or 1722 (Lindsey et al., *Worldly Goods,* p. 13, fig. 23).

17. Claypoole's signature is not complete, but reads "Jos Claypoole 1743." Since Josiah never returned to Philadelphia, this is almost certainly the signature of Joseph. Bracken, *Claypoole Family in America*, p. 48.

18. A related group of four Boston-area case pieces with ogee heads is discussed in Edward S. Cooke, Jr., "Boston Clothespresses of the Mid-Eighteenth Century," *Journal of the Museum of Fine Arts, Boston* 1 (1989): 75–95. For more on Armitt and the descent of the desk-and-

bookcase, see Stenton object file 72.4. Logan's household accounts do not mention the purchase of an "escritoire," as desk-and-bookcases like the one illustrated in fig. 12 were often called. A 1754 inventory of Stenton lists an "Escritoire with glass doors," which may be this example. (An inventory of the Personal Estate of Sarah Logan, Deceased, taken June 4, 1754, Smith Family Papers, vol. 4, p. 182, HSP.)

19. Sir Danvers Osborn was appointed governor in May 1753 and took office in July. A troubled man, he committed suicide in October of that year. Christopher Gilbert, *A Pictorial Dictionary of Marked London Furniture* (Suffolk, Eng.: Furniture History Society, 1996), pp. 331, 337. A desk-and-bookcase similar to the Osborn example is illustrated in Geoffrey Beard and Judith Goodison, *English Furniture 1500–1840* (Oxford, Eng.: Phaidon/Christie's, 1987), p. 50. Fielded mirrors also occur on case pieces with broken-arch, or "scrolled" cornices. See Herbert Cescinsky, *English Furniture From Gothic to Sheraton* (Grand Rapids, Mich.: Dean-Hicks Co., 1929), p. 203.

20. A desk-and-bookcase with a pitch pediment reputedly made for Charles Norris in 1756 is in the collection of Independence National Historic Park. A photograph of this object is in the Decorative Arts Photographic Collection, Winterthur Museum.

21. John Head recorded the high chest and dressing table in his account book on April 4, 1726 (John Head Account Book, Vaux Papers, American Philosophical Society, Philadelphia.) Both pieces are in the Philadelphia Museum of Art.

22. A dressing table similar to the example illustrated in fig. 21, but with a skirt shaped like the high chest shown in fig. 22, is illustrated in Wallace Nutting, *Furniture Treasury*, 2 vols. (Framingham, Mass.: Old America Co., 1928), 2: fig. 422. A spice cabinet that also appears to be by either Joseph Claypoole or George Claypoole, Sr. is shown in Lindsey et al., *Worldly Goods*, p. 140, no. 9.

23. "Letter of Thomas Penn to Richard Hockley, 1746–1748," *Pennsylvania Magazine of History and Biography* 40, no. 158 (April 1916): 226–27.

24. Sotheby's *Important Americana: Furniture, Folk Art, and Decorations*, New York, October 15, 1999, lot 93.

25. Other apprentices in George Sr.'s shop included Thomas Rutter, who began his term on September 9, 1746 (Thomas Rutter Indenture, Account of Servants and Apprentices Bound and Assigned before James Hamilton, Mayor of Philadelphia [1745–1746], HSP, as cited in Liebundguth, "Furniture Making Crafts in Philadelphia," p. 10). Further evidence that George Jr. trained in and continued to work in his father's shop is found in a transaction between the Claypooles and Joseph Shippen in 1766. Shippen purchased a coal box, a box for a gun, a lock and a "pine case for papers." The bill reads "Mr. Joseph Shippen to Geo. Claypoole" but is signed "received the above in full George Claypoole Junr" (bill from George Claypoole, Sr. to Joseph Shippen, January 28, 1766, Shippen Papers, vol. 10, pp. 73, 77, HSP). Either the bill was simply not specific in its initial reference to Claypoole, or it indicates that George Jr. continued to be active in his father's shop. In 1770 George Sr. drafted his will leaving his namesake "all . . . [the] half inch walnut now cut out and planed, and lying in the loft over . . . [his] shop." The elder George lived another 23 years, and he and his son died in the yellow fever epidemic of 1793 (Liebundguth, "The Furniture Making Crafts in Philadelphia," p. 10). The elder George and his wife Catherine were buried in St. Paul's Episcopal Churchyard; his wife's death date is noted on the gravestone as March 31, 1770, and his is marked October 3, 1793. Numerous sources note his death date as 1770, which is incorrect.

26. Deborah Federhen, "The Serpentine-Front Chests of Drawers of Jonathan Gostelowe and Thomas Jones" *Antiques* 133, no.5 (May 1988): 1174–83.

Figure 1 Side chair, Boston, Massachusetts, 1710–1720. Walnut. H. 44⅝", W. 20 1/16", D. 21⅜". (Courtesy, Wadsworth Atheneum; photo, Gavin Ashworth.)

Glenn Adamson

The Politics of the Caned Chair

▼ THE FAVORITE PUNCHING BAG of American furniture scholarship is elitism—the historical preference for objects made for the wealthy. Yet, scholars often focus on extraordinary pieces of furniture for a good reason: because they seem to have more to say. They may have more ornament to be identified or read symbolically or a more ambitious design that may reflect a surprising degree of cosmopolitanism. Similarly, the presence of an exotic wood, textile, or brass fitting can illuminate relationships between distant locations, cultures, and economies. Too often material culture scholars assume that all objects from the past have something interesting to say about the cultural context that created them; in fact, this is not always true. One reason that historians routinely focus on the belongings of the aristocracy is that they are frequently complex, ambitious objects that have a similarly complex content. This quality of "textuality" is evident without any reference to aesthetic superiority or lack thereof, which is properly the terrain of the collector and not the historian.

An object's value as a text can take many forms, however, and if the American furniture establishment is guilty of elitism, it is because scholars have not always searched for textual complexity in simple-looking objects. A likely subject for study in this regard is a group of approximately thirty middle-market caned chairs made in Boston in the early eighteenth century. All are related in having a mysterious punched and cross-serifed "I" mark (fig. 1). The most detailed study of these chairs is the chapter "Cane Chairs and Couches," in Benno Forman's *American Seating Furniture, 1630–1730*. Forman was the first to attempt a comprehensive analysis of the chairs and their features and the first to identify the "I" mark as that of a caner, rather than a chair maker or owner. This article will not challenge any of Forman's fundamental assumptions about the "I" chairs, even though several related examples have emerged since the publication of his book. Rather, it will attempt to read them as texts—that is, to place them and the style that they exemplify into a broader sociohistorical context than has previously been considered.

The Diffusion Model
The style of the "I" chairs is typically referred to as "William and Mary," or less commonly but more accurately, "Restoration." Both of these terms contain more than a hint of outdated assumptions about stylistic transmission. According to the diffusion model, furniture forms like the caned chair are invented for consumption among the aristocracy, only gradually

trickling down to the level of popular consumption. In the process, the form undergoes simplification, losing both aesthetic value and importance as a cultural text. In the case of the American caned chair, this mechanistic story of emulation and simplification is twofold, because the form was already an imitation when the English got hold of it; they were mimicking their commercial rivals, the Dutch and the French, who actually invented the design. This narrative has some truth to it, and it is also true that the caned chair experienced drastic formal reduction in its travels. Yet this information tells us little about the historical importance of caned chairs once they reached Boston, or London for that matter. Like most furniture, the "I" chairs are the end products of cosmopolitan stylistic invention and exchange; but what makes them distinctive is their reflection of late-seventeenth-century bourgeois values in a specific place. In general, unidirectional diffusion—either downward through the class hierarchy, or centripetally from center to periphery—tells us little about the motivations of the receiving group. In a diffusion model, those who produce and consume derivative versions of a form are seen as trying to keep up as best as they can; but as British architect Colin Campbell wrote, "imitative behavior is not necessarily emulative." The average middle-market caned chair is a good demonstration of this fact, because it embodies an intricate and specific set of class and economic concerns that are not simply imitative. It may have been derivative, but it was also the first middle-class furniture form par excellence, and thus an expression of a new way of thinking about economics and fashion.[1]

In the 1950s, British furniture historian Robert W. Symonds argued that caned chairs were first popular among the middle class who desired "cheap chairs of plain quality." He noted that "the improving quality and increasing ornateness of cane chairs enlarged their market, and they were bought for more fashionable homes." Symonds probably erred in arguing for a "reverse diffusion" from the middle class upwards—average and exceptional caned chairs seem to have been made side by side from the moment of the form's introduction—but his basic intuition was correct: the makers of middling caned chairs were truly innovative. They broke with precedent in their use of craft strategies that were easily adaptable to the subtle dynamics of a mass market. A novel system of piece-work, which included easily modulated, optional details such as decorative carving, provided bourgeois patrons with a means to express developing sensibilities of display. Likewise, in helping to establish their middle-class customers' position within a larger culture of exchange, chair makers engaged with new attitudes toward propriety, prosperity, and fashionability.[2]

The Theory and Practice of Mercantilism
First made in England in the mid-1660s, caned chairs were probably produced in vast numbers following the Great Fire of London in 1666, which created a demand unparalleled in the history of English furniture. The new form was a locus at which the various fashionable motifs of Restoration furniture converged: baroque carved decoration extrapolated from the

central motif of the c-scroll; fragile construction; a lightening and exaggeration of structural form; the use of new materials including imported cane; and the gradual introduction of curvilinear elements. These features all increased over time in both high-style and middling versions of English caned chairs, with the form gradually becoming more vertical in its orientation, more flimsy in its joinery details, and more codified in its ornament (figs. 2, 3). In comparison with the simple joined chairs, forms, and stools

Figure 2   Ruben Moulthrop, portrait of an unknown man, New England, 1770–1790. Oil on canvas. (Courtesy, Winterthur Museum.)

Figure 3   Armchair, England, 1660–1670. Beech. H. 53½", W. 25", D. 22½". (Private collection; photo, Gavin Ashworth.)

Figure 4   Side chair, England, 1690–1700. Beech. H. 50", W. 18⅛", D. 19¾". (Courtesy, Yale University Art Gallery.)

used previously in middle-class homes, the new turned and carved caned chairs were extroverted and demonstrative. They represented a dramatic increase in what might be called the "signification value" that was available to the average furniture buyer. In adopting the marks of wealth (such as ornamental carving and fragility), but translating them into an affordable form, caned chair makers produced furniture that was primarily about symbol instead of substance.[3]

Figure 5 Detail of the back of the side chair illustrated in fig. 4.

This is truer of bourgeois examples than of contemporary upper-class ones. Examination of a typical English caned chair shows the way that such middle-market work was executed in London (fig. 4). From the front, the chair looks to be respectably made. The carving is rudimentary, but attention is paid to the overall composition, as can be seen in the visual rhyme between the profile of the baluster turnings on the stiles and the c-shaped scrolls on the splat. A rear view of the chair tells a different story, however, with hastily scribed layout lines and rough edges attesting to the rapid execution of the job (fig. 5). For the makers of this chair, façade and display were clearly at a premium, even when this meant sacrificing quality in craftsmanship. This same pattern emerges in the case of most average caned chairs. They trade away the nuances of three-dimensional sculptural treatment in favor of a directed, one-point visual impact. They imply display, rather than comfort and durability, as their primary function. The question remains, though: if caned chairs were about signification, then what were they signifying?

It seems contradictory that the English would enthusiastically adopt a Dutch style of seating furniture during the 1670s at the very time they were engaged in a struggle with the Netherlands for supremacy in naval trade. (Maritime wars between the two countries [1662–1667 and 1672–1674] coincided precisely with the caned chair's rise to prominence.) Part of the answer may lie in the demographics of the craft industry. Large numbers of French Protestant craftsmen began immigrating to England in the 1660s, many having lived in the Netherlands where they gained an understanding of Dutch styles. Immigration was particularly heavy after the revocation of the Edict of Nantes by Louis XIV in 1685, but the Huguenot diaspora had begun much earlier due to repeated prosecution and religious wars. In addition, the Rebuilding Act of 1667, passed in the wake of the Great Fire, extended generous opportunities for immigrant artificers to settle and work in London. Just as earlier generations of religiously and economically motivated immigrants had done in the 1560s and the 1630s, a wave of foreigners in the 1670s and 1680s supplied skilled labor that enabled English manufacturers to improve finished goods industries, especially textile production. Huguenots also provided labor necessary to the operation of the caned chair industry. Like immigrant workers today, their presence both boosted production and engendered resentment. English craftsmen in the Joiners' and Carpenters' Company railed against this foreign presence in a petition to Parliament in 1687—a complaint that signals probable depression of wages owing to the increase of skilled workmen.[4]

Without the workmanship of the Huguenots, the phenomenon of the middle-class caned chair would probably not have occurred. But even if immigrant craftsmen facilitated the caned chair industry's expansion, they could not have been responsible for creating demand. The underlying reasons for the acceptance of the foreign-born caned chair were entirely domestic in nature and had to do with England's desire not to emulate the commercially successful Dutch, but rather to beat them at their own game. In this sense, the caned chair can best be described not as "William and

Figure 6 Benjamin Franklin, *The Colonies Reduced,* designed and engraved for *The Political Register,* December 1768. (Courtesy, Print Collection, Lewis Walpole Library, Yale University.) This satire of the Stamp Act attacks Britain's mercantilist strategy of preventing the colonies from trading among themselves.

Mary," or even as "Restoration," but rather as "mercantilist" in style. Mercantilism was a socioeconomic doctrine that guided trade and military policy roughly from the mid-sixteenth century to the early eighteenth century. The fundamental point that drove mercantilist thought was that economic wealth and power were inextricably linked, and that a nation's control of trade was therefore inseparable from its dominance in military and political affairs. It was English mercantilism that introduced the concept of the "balance of trade" to economics. Indeed, mercantile thinkers thought that balance of trade was the most important determinant in a nation's prosperity, because it was the only measure of a country's total control of the world's wealth. Unlike later *laissez faire* theorists such as Adam Smith, they believed that one state's gain in wealth necessarily meant the impoverishment of other competing states. Eli F. Heckscher, a Swedish economic historian who was the twentieth century's most influential commentator on mercantilism, has referred to this "static conception of the total economic resources in the world" as the "tragedy of mercantilism," because it motivated England, France, and other countries to engage in constant commercial warfare (fig. 6).[5]

Mercantilism's emphasis on the balance of trade arose from the attempt to explain the success of England's enemy, the Netherlands. The puzzle of Dutch prosperity was their control of commerce in finished goods despite their lack of raw materials. As one frustrated pamphleteer put it, "the exceeding Groves of Wood are in the East-Kingdomes [of Europe]: But the huge Piles of Wainscot, Clapboards, Fir-Deale, Masts, and Timber, . . . [are] in the Low-Countries . . . where none groweth." The first systematic attempt to understand this conundrum was made in the 1620s by Thomas Mun (1571–1641), an early governor of the nascent English East India Company. Mun's *England's Treasure by Forraign Trade* (written 1628, but not published until 1664 when Mun's son John printed it to lend theoretical support to the first Anglo-Dutch war) codified the precepts of early English mercantilism. Mun viewed the control of raw materials and currency as the main economic goal of government. He famously distin-

Figure 7 *Josiah Child,* attributed to John Riley, England, ca. 1680–1690. Oil on canvas. 40½" x 34⅝". (Courtesy, National Portrait Gallery.)

guished between "intrinsic" and "artificial" forms of wealth, the first consisting of natural resources such as land, timber, and iron, and the second of "manufactures and industrious trading with forraign commodities." Later English merchant-economists, such as Sir Josiah Child (fig. 7), another governor of the East India Company (1630–1699), and merchant Nicholas Barbon (d. 1698), preserved and refined Mun's distinction. Because raw materials were limited and static, they reasoned that it was only artificial wealth that could bring an increase in real prosperity. They gradually came to argue that domestic production should rest not only on the extraction of raw materials, but also on the way those materials were processed and circulated. It was this new tide in mercantilist thought that led to the infamous Navigation Acts passed by the English parliament in the 1660s. These measures were quintessential expressions of mercantilism in that they attempted to limit colonial production to the furnishing of raw materials rather than finished goods. On the domestic side, similarly, writers like Child and Barbon anxiously promoted the development of new processing industries that would add to the nation's sources of "artificial wealth."[6]

This focus on finished goods led quickly to the most radical and fiercely debated discoveries of late seventeenth-century economics: that middle-class novelty and fashion could be exploited as engines of commerce. The rapid overturn of production created by the vagaries of style was recognized as one of the secrets of Netherlandish wealth. Child wrote in the 1660s that the success of the Dutch was due in part to "their giving great incouragement and immunities to the Inventors of New Manufactures." During the 1670s and 1680s, English writers praised the salutary effects of domestic imitation of stylish imports. John Houghton noted in 1677 that French goods "have set us all a-gog, and have encreas'd among us many considerable trades," whereas Dalby Thomas wrote that imported luxuries were "true Spurs to Virtue, Valour and the Elevation of the Mind," and more importantly, grist for the fashion mill. It is important to distinguish, however, between three distinct types of import: the borrowing of styles, the immigration of craftsmen, and the actual importation of finished goods. Mercantilist ideas about the balance of trade still held enough sway to encourage the acceptance of foreign ideas and skilled workers but not commodities themselves. One writer argued that England's cause should be advanced "by our own Art and Industry, bringing in whatever Foreign Arts, Trades or Husbandries may be profitable to us." By supplying "ourselves within ourselves," he wrote, "we need few Foreign things, and make as many Commodities at home as possible." John Houghton, similarly, endorsed the immigration of workmen, such as the Huguenots who enhanced the furniture and textile trades. Although Houghton "could wish there would 20,000 [artificers] come in next year," he welcomed only the importation of unfinished goods such as Scandinavian timber. The fashion for the foreign could be seen positively only if other nations could be tapped for marketable ideas and able workers without threatening domestic manufactures.[7]

The Caned Chair as an Expression of Mercantilism

In this context, it is easy to understand how the English caned chair reflected prevailing ideas about production. Insofar as it was adapted from Dutch stylistic sources, the caned chair was an example of competition in action. If the English could make their own stylish chairs, they did not need to import any from the Netherlands. Furthermore, the caned chair's novelty, its emphasis on display, and its impermanence all made it both an example and a stylistic expression of "artificial wealth." Unlike previous middle-class seating furniture, the caned chair declared its status as a commodity. Its quick and expedient carving would have gratified contemporary preferences for finished goods without making the chairs unaffordable. Its fragile construction—a kind of seventeenth-century planned obsolescence—underscored the fact that it was a fashionable object, not just a serviceable one. In both its style and its method of construction, the caned chair was an appropriate expression of currents in mercantilist theory.

A parliamentary petition written by the Joiners' Company in 1688 suggests that caned chair makers thought of their products in precisely these terms. Discovered and published by R. W. Symonds in 1951, this document was written as a rebuttal of a petition from the textile manufacturers of the town of Bradford proposing the suppression of caned chair manufacture, which had brought about a rapid decline in the demand for upholstery. The textile merchants had complained:

> Since Cane chairs, stools and couches, which generally the frames are made of French Walnut, and the Seats of Indian Canes, are become so much in use; the Consumption of Wool is greatly decreased; and above 50,000 of his Majesties Subjects formerly employed in the Manufactury thereof, have lost their Employment, to the Ruine of them and . . . [their] numerous Families.[8]

There are several interesting aspects to the case of the Bradford textile merchants and the mercantilist precepts that motivated it. First, the foreign origin of the caned chair is emphasized, particularly that of its materials ("French walnut" and "Indian canes"). This was problematic from the perspective of mid-seventeenth-century economic theory, which held that the balance of trade in raw materials was the key to national prosperity. Second, the document explicitly recognizes the field of general consumption as a vital site of competition in its statement that caned chairs are "so much in use," or by inference, more popular than upholstered chairs. This amounted to a tacit awareness that fashions among the general populace could be economically significant. Third, the argument for the suppression of caning rests on the livelihood of people employed in the production of wool. As a non-crafted good, most wool workers were involved not with finishing the material but producing it. In this sense, the argument lodged against the Joiners' Company was that an industry that focused on raw material production was suffering at the hands of an industry that consisted entirely of processing.[9]

In responding to these charges, the Joiners' Company went beyond a simple refutation of the facts of the case, instead engaging the textile merchants within the terms of contemporary mercantilist theory. Their petition to Parliament argued that caned chairs in fact had come to make up a substantial part of the English economy:

> Before Cane-Chairs, Stools, Squobs and Couches were made in England, there was not (according to the largest Information that can be gathered) above One hundred and eighty Persons employed in Making and Turning of Chair-Frames to be covered in Turkey-work, Serge, Camblets, *Kidderminster,* and other Stuffs of Woolen Manufacture; there being but little work in the Making, less work in the Turning, and generally no carving at all in the Frames. . . . [caned furniture] gave so much Satisfaction to all the Nobility, Gentry, and Commonality of this Kingdom . . . that they came to be manufactured in *England,* and sent to all parts of the World; which occasioned the Chair-Frame Makers and Turners to take many Apprentices; and Cane-Chairs, &c. coming in time to be carved, many Carvers took Apprentices, and brought them up to the Carving of Cane-Chairs, Stools, Couches and Squobs only. And there were many Apprentices bound only to learn to split the Canes, and Cane those Chairs, &c. And as the Trade for Cane-Chairs, &c., increased, the People bread [*sic*] up in the several Trades depending upon them also increased, their Number being (upon a true Survey) found to be at this day many Thousands of People, many of whom pay very great Rents, and have long Leases of Houses, taken purposively to Make and Sell Cane-Chairs.

Interestingly, there is no mention of what is ostensibly the textile manufacturers' most damning argument: that chair makers' dependence on foreign materials is bad for the English populace. The Joiners' Company could, for example, have mentioned the common use of domestic English beech in caned chair manufacture.[10]

Instead, the Joiners' Company stressed the fact that England was able to gain what Mun would have called artificial wealth by sending chairs "to all parts of the World," thus helping achieve a favorable balance of trade. Furthermore, they directed attention toward the turning and carving that went into the furniture (unlike upholstered chairs which necessitated "little work in the Making") and the training of apprentices who provided the semi-skilled labor to cane the chairs. The Joiners' Company also pointed out that high demand for workmanship and rapid change translated into jobs for numerous skilled craftspeople. The caned chair was, according to this view, to be valued precisely for the employment provided by the process-intensive character of the industry—a textbook case of "artificial wealth" translating into general prosperity. Indeed, two years after the Joiners' Company's petition, mercantilist theorist Nicholas Barbon noted that fashionable products such as chairs helped to boost the economy:

> The Shoo-makers, Saddlers, Coach, and Chair-makers [provide] with abundance more for the Ease of Life. . . . Thus Busie Man is imployed, and it is for his own Benefit; for by Trade, the Natural Stock of the Country is improved; the Wool and Flax, are made into Cloth; the Skins, into Leather; and the Wood, Lead, Iron and Tin, into a thousand useful Things.[11]

The interest that the later mercantilists showed in the "ease of life" fostered by the luxury trade—an area of production that had once seemed marginal to the economy—was a turnabout from the policy and economic theory of the pre-Restoration era. As the seventeenth century progressed, it became increasingly clear that processing materials was often more profitable than producing them. Rural and urban manufacturing projects gained momentum, and the quality of English-made luxury goods began to rival that of foreign nations. The social freedoms of the Restoration era made the advantages of finishing goods even more apparent, as the sumptuary laws of the Elizabethan and Jacobean periods and the imposed restraint of the interregnum were overturned. Rural households increasingly bought finished goods instead of fashioning every necessity at home. Having seen these changes, economic theorists concluded that it was not only the rich whose consumption could be turned to advantage. As Dudley North wrote in 1691, "The main spur to Trade, or rather to Industry and Ingenuity, is the exorbitant Appetites of Men... for did Men content themselves with bare Necessities, we should have a poor World." Bernard Mandeville's comments in *The Grumbling Hive* (1705) were even more pointed. He wrote that "frugality... [is] an idle dreaming Virtue that employs no hands, and therefore very useless in a trading country, where there are vast Numbers that one way or another must all be set to Work." On the contrary, "Fickleness in Diet, Furniture and Dress, that strange ridic'lous Vice, was made the very Wheel that turn'd the Trade."[12]

Good Taste
The sanguine attitude with which economists first met the popularity of foreign styles and the pretensions of the bourgeoisie was not universally shared, however. As the 1690s progressed, protectionism and xenophobia reared their heads increasingly under the double pressures of crushing war debt and domestic currency shortages. In 1700, Daniel Defoe criticized such attitudes with typical wit: "Tis worth observing, that we ne'er complain'd of foreigners, nor of the Wealth they gain'd, till all their services were at an end." But by this time, few economists were inclined to agree. Commentary on the luxury trade acquired a tinge of moral repugnance, and extravagances welcomed by economists in the 1670s and 1680s became increasingly suspect. The economic benefits of "outvying" the middle classes were disregarded, and writers grew increasingly fearful of social misrepresentation and the unpredictable consequences of blurring "natural" class boundaries. Novelty itself came under assault in this elitist backlash. Protestant religious groups, who had long opposed luxury, took the lead in criticizing those who put on airs. Quaker reformer John Bellers, for example, characterized the unpredictability of the luxury trade as destructive to a rational, well-planned economy. The rapid turnover of styles, he argued, made it impossible to maintain consistent employment: "The uncertainty of fashions doth increase our Necessitous Poor... a Voluptuous Age may easily fall into excess, with dress and pleasure, by [that which is] Ornamental and Delightful."[13]

Moral indignation directed against the improper display of affluence went far beyond the convictions of religious sectarians. A distrust of showy luxury goods was widely held by the turn of the century, most famously

Figure 8 The Third Earl of Shaftesbury, engraving after a painting by John Closterman, London, ca. 1700. Ink on paper. Dimensions not recorded. (Courtesy, National Portrait Gallery.)

by the aesthetic philosopher, Anthony Ashley Cooper, the third Earl of Shaftesbury (1671–1713) (fig. 8). A pupil of John Locke, Shaftesbury became the foremost turn-of-the-century aesthetic philosopher in England and helped formulate a theory of taste that was antithetical to late seventeenth-century notions of middle-class fashionability. He argued that the appreciation of beauty transcended the realm of common sense and that taste was a learned faculty rather than an instinctive one. Consequently only an educated, polite gentleman could grasp proper aesthetic and ethical standards. Such "virtuosi," Shaftesbury claimed, were capable of the disinterest necessary for accurate aesthetic judgment. Nor was Shaftesbury alone in his opinions. The great essayist Joseph Addison explicitly compared aesthetic sensibility to the ownership of property by a gentleman: "A Man of a Polite Imagination is let into a great many Pleasures that the Vulgar are not capable of receiving. He can converse with a Picture, and find an agreeable Companion in a Statue.... It gives him, indeed, a kind of Property in every thing he sees, and makes the most rude uncultivated Parts of Nature administer to his Pleasures."[14]

The development of an aesthetic based on elitist concepts of taste had important consequences for the development of English luxury goods, including furniture. A sense of the rapid stylistic change can be gotten from a comparison of Shaftesbury's portrait (fig. 8) with that of his grandfather, the first Earl of Shaftesbury (fig. 9). The first earl (1621–1683) had been one

Figure 9 The First Earl of Shaftesbury, London, 1673. Ink on paper. Dimensions not recorded. (Courtesy, Print Collection, Lewis Walpole Library, Yale University.)

of the most convinced and effective mercantilist politicians in the early years of the Restoration and held the position of president of the Board of Trade during the 1670s. He was also involved in a variety of private commercial pursuits, including the Royal African Company and the Hudson Bay Company. A caned chair owned by the first earl (fig. 10) is typical of examples made during the 1660s or 1670s in having a short back, boxy proportions, and limited carving. It is unlikely that the third Earl of Shaftes-

Figure 10 Armchair, England, 1670–1680. Dimensions and woods not recorded. (Courtesy, Winterthur Museum Decorative Arts Photographic Collection, R. W. Symonds Collection.)

Figure 11 Side chair, England, 1710–1720. Walnut. H. 44⅝", W. 20¼", D. 21½". (Courtesy, Wadsworth Atheneum, Wallace Nutting Collection, Gift of J. P. Morgan; photo, Gavin Ashworth.) The front legs have been pieced below the break in the knee.

bury would have considered purchasing an example like this one given his aesthetic preferences. An up-to-date chair would have suited his taste much better, particularly during the later years of his life (see figs. 11–13). Indeed, one of Shaftesbury's lists of the properties of polite deportment could just as well apply to the differences between the two chair forms: "mobility rather than stiffness, informality over formality, openendedness rather than over-determination and dogmatism, conviviality rather than solemnity and gravity." One can see how Shaftesbury's aesthetic values directly challenged those of the previous generation. Chairs in the new Georgian

Figure 12 Detail of the crest of the chair illustrated in fig. 11.

Figure 13 Detail of the right front leg of the chair illustrated in fig. 11.

idiom featured fluid lines, a sculptural and "openended" composition, and a lower, more "informal" and "convivial" back height. All of these features were implicit rejections of the caned chair's rigid array of vertical elements. Shaftesbury would no doubt have found his grandfather's chair "stiff" and "dogmatic."[15]

The early Georgian chair carried more than a superficial relationship to Shaftebury's rhetoric of taste. No longer was there a vocabulary of display that could, as simply as an appliqué, be transported to chairs for any market level. Although caned chairs incorporate curvilinear elements, these details are isolated from each other so that legs, stretchers, and seats can be made separately through a system of piece-work. This seventeenth-century compartmentalization of workmanship allowed chairs to accommodate different levels of consumer investment without losing a basic sense of display. The early Georgian chair, by contrast, is an all or nothing proposition requiring subtle modeling to unify the shape so all of the curved surfaces resonate with each other and transition gracefully to the seat frame. Some of the piece-work systems that had been a mainstay of middle market Restoration design remained in place, but others disappeared or changed to meet the exigencies of the new taste. Furthermore, in the early Georgian style there is no variable equivalent to the differences in carving which distinguish different levels of the caned chair market. When carved decoration is added to the form, as in the first Georgian-style chairs made in Boston during the onset of the style in America, it feels disjunctive with the rest of the composition. In a caned chair, the carving on the crest (and often a matching front stretcher) is manifestly the point—the formal gesture for which the rest of the object is but an armature. In this regard it is a perfect middle-class form. The early Georgian chair, on the other hand, simply makes no sense when executed below a certain level of time, care, material investment, and skill. This is not to say that the onset of Georgian styles suddenly deprived the middle classes of furniture, since consumers at that level continued to purchase and use caned chairs and their derivatives. Rather, the new seating forms embraced by the gentry and the nobility were intentionally distinguished from those of the lower ranks by a barrier of taste and affordability.

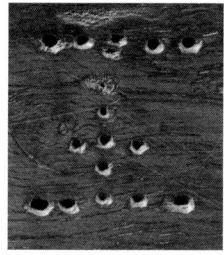 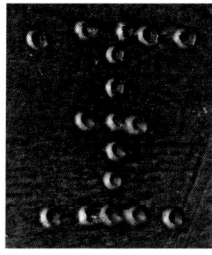 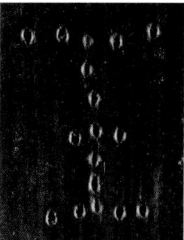 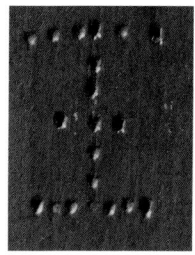 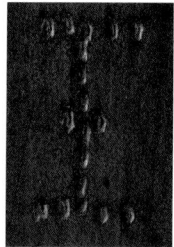 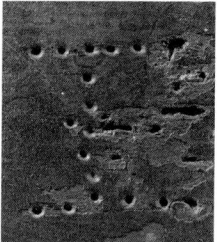

Figure 14 Detail of the "I" stamps on the chairs illustrated left to right in figs. 1, 23–25, 30, 35.

Figure 15 Side chair, England, 1685–1710. Beech. H. 51⅞", W. 18¼", D. 15¼". (Courtesy, Winterthur Museum.)

The Caned Chair in America

In England, the correlation between the early Georgian style and elite notions of politeness serves to mark the close of the caned chair's moment of cultural currency. But in America, the inception of the caned chair actually post-dated both the writings of Shaftesbury and the momentous turn-of-the-century shifts in furniture design. The results can be seen in the group of Boston chairs mentioned at the beginning of this article. Traditionally the central point of debate about these objects is the meaning of the punched "I" that they bear on their backs—some on the rear face of the left stile, and some on the left end of the lower stay rail of the back (see fig. 14). Benno Forman convincingly argued that this is a caner's or caning shop's mark for a variety of reasons, including the fact that there are no leather-upholstered chairs with the mark (as one would expect if this were the mark of a frame maker), and the impossibility of so many unmatched chairs belonging to a single family (which eliminates the possibility that this is an owner's mark, as Richard Randall had argued in 1965).[16]

Today it is possible to make an even stronger case for Forman's interpretation of the mark, because at least two of the chairs bearing it appear to be English. One was thought by Forman to be American on the basis of wood analysis conducted in the 1970s (fig. 15). Regrettably, the accuracy of these tests has been widely discredited since it is currently impossible to distinguish between American and English species of beech. In the absence of such evidence, there is no reason to believe that the chair illustrated in figure 15 is anything other than a standard, middle-market English example. In addition to the fact that this chair looks English, its stamped mark "IP" is similar to that on an English chair in the New Hampshire Historical Society (fig. 16). Furthermore, the chair shown in figure 15 has a virtual mate with a different mark and a history of having been imported from England in the mid-1680s by the Winthrop family. In all probability, the mark on the chair illustrated in figure 15 was made when the chair was re-caned some fifty years after it arrived in New England.[17]

The theory that the "I" refers to a caner or caning shop is also bolstered by the character of the marks, which do not have the professional quality one might expect from a joinery shop. Although the execution of the "I" marks varies, implying a number of different hands, all are punched rather than stamped or branded like most owners' marks on furniture of the period. Other caned chairs with punched letters or symbols are known, however (see figs. 17, 18). The shallow, round indentations comprising these marks may have been made with a common caning tool. Caners typ-

Figure 16 Side chair, England, 1685–1710. Beech with pine. H. 50½", W. 17½", D. 20". (Courtesy, New Hampshire Historical Society.)

Figure 17 Side chair, England, 1710–1720. Beech. H. 48", W. 17½", D. 14". (Courtesy Jeffrey Tillou; photo, Gavin Ashworth.)

ically used small metal styluses to push the cane through holes, particularly those with more than one strand running through them.[18]

Regardless of the meaning of the punched "I," the mark serves to group these chairs in time and space. All were either made or present in Boston between about 1710 and 1725. The Boston examples display a remarkable degree of stylistic conformity, most incorporating features derived from London caned chairs of the 1690s as well as early Georgian chairs of the 1710s. Although it is possible that many of these chairs are from the same shop, the structural shortcuts and piece-work systems that developed to support Boston's leather chair manufacturing and export business contributed to the standardization of design. Specialists such as carvers and turners sold similar components to different chair makers who produced assembled frames for local clients as well as merchants and upholsterers engaged in the coastal trade.

All of the Boston chairs have turned undercarriages with similar front, medial, and rear stretchers. The stretcher configuration on the chairs comes in two versions, one with the medial stretcher joined into the side stretchers at their midpoint, and the other with the medial stretcher shifted towards the front of the chair. Forman thought the latter configuration to be later because of its use in Boston Georgian seating, but this can be neither proved nor disproved. Most Boston caned chairs have turned front legs with "Spanish" or tassel feet, or square "unwrought" cabriole legs.

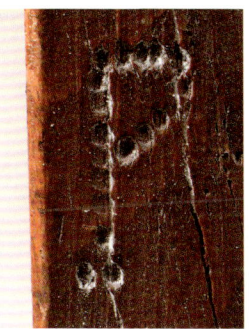

Figure 18 Detail of the stamp on the side chair illustrated in fig. 17.

Again, one would like to believe that the cabriole legs indicate a later date within the overall sequence of the group, but it could well be that this was simply an interchangeable feature. When turned, the legs conform to one of two patterns, distinguishable by the degree of elongation in the upper vase turning. Most if not all of the chairs had shaped aprons attached with nails (see fig. 1), though most have been lost. A few examples have similar aprons on the side rails, but this does not appear to have been a common feature. Most crucially, all of the "I" chairs have molded stiles that move fluidly into the crests, showing that the shop or shops that produced them had some awareness of early Georgian composition.

The crests of the "I" chairs display more variation than any other component, but a degree of uniformity is evident. All of the crests have shallow, carved leaves in the lower corners of the design, and all have carved edge beads that intersect the planed beads on the stiles (see fig. 19). These

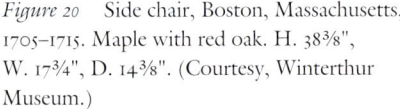

Figure 19   Detail of the crest of the side chair illustrated in fig. 1.

Figure 20   Side chair, Boston, Massachusetts, 1705–1715. Maple with red oak. H. 38 3/8", W. 17 3/4", D. 14 3/8". (Courtesy, Winterthur Museum.)

signature elements link all of the Boston chairs stylistically. The style and basic composition of the carving, which is similar to that on several unmarked, Boston caned chairs, has precedents in earlier low-backed, leather chairs (see fig. 20). Somewhat later, Philadelphia chair makers used similar motifs (see fig. 21), probably in an effort to compete with fashionable Boston imports.[19]

Apart from the leaf carving and edge moldings, the crest patterns are quite different from each other. The most common variant has a foliate spray that extends upwards from the middle of the crest (see figs. 1, 19). Often the points of intersection between this element and the other parts of the crest are small, leaving very little wood to hold the top of the chair together (see fig. 22). Perhaps owing to this fragile design, chair makers occasionally left a "bridge" of wood on the lower, rear edge of the crest. This feature provided additional support to resist the torque and stress of the caning process and subsequent use. Two of the three extant armchairs in the "I" group have foliate sprays and unusually short arms that rest on supports joined directly into the middle of the side seat rails (see fig. 23). As is the case with later Georgian armchairs, they are broader in seat width than the side chairs in the group.[20]

Figure 21   Side chair, Philadelphia, Pennsylvania, 1715–1725. Maple. H. 41", W. 18¾", D. 16". (Chipstone Foundation; photo, Gavin Ashworth.)

Figure 22   Detail showing the back of the crest of the chair illustrated in fig. 1.

Figure 23 Armchair, Boston, Massachusetts, 1710–1720. Maple. H. 50¾", W. 23⅜", D. 16⅜". (Private collection; photo, Gavin Ashworth.)

The second most common type of crest, which occurs on at least five of the "I" chairs, is clearly derived from late English caned chairs (see fig. 24). This design features a squared-off top that is connected to the stiles by sinuous molded serpentine shapes. Decorative carved volutes, either two or four in number, articulate the upper edge of these crests. Like the first crest pattern (see figs. 1, 12), this variant sometimes has a strengthening bridge in the back. It bears a strong visual relationship to both of the other crest designs, particularly the one with a central foliate spray, but in many examples it is carved in a summary fashion. The sloping planes of the front of the crest are often choppy, and the carved leaves are reduced to nearly illegible stubs. In these crests the rapidity of manufacture is obvious, and such chairs were no doubt produced in large numbers. There are versions of this same crest pattern on many Boston area chairs outside the "I" group.

Figure 24 Side chair, Boston, Massachusetts, 1710–1720. Soft maple with oak. H. 45¼", W. 18", D. 14¼". (Private collection; photo, Gavin Ashworth.)

Two caned chairs with squared-off crests have leaf elements that were outlined, modeled, and shaded more professionally than those on other chairs in the group. The example shown in figures 25 and 26 has two small leaf clusters with carefully regulated shading cuts. This work may be a precursor to the linear acanthus carving found on two of the earliest Boston Georgian chairs. The most ornately carved of the chairs related to the "I" group (fig. 27) is not caned at all, but it seems to represent the apotheosis

Figure 25 Side chair, Boston, Massachusetts, 1710–1720. Maple. H. 45½", W. 18", D. 14¼". (Private collection; photo, Gavin Ashworth.)

Figure 26 Detail of the crest of the chair illustrated in fig. 25.

Figure 27 Side chair, Boston or Ipswich, Massachusetts, 1715–1725. Maple. H. 42½", W. 18½", D. 15". (Courtesy, Ipswich Historical Society; photo, Gavin Ashworth.)

Figure 28 Detail of the right front foot of the chair illustrated in fig. 27.

Figure 29 Detail of the crest of the chair illustrated in fig. 27.

of the Boston style. The chair appears to have been made in that city or in nearby Ipswich, Massachusetts. With its shaped stretchers, collared cabriole legs (fig. 28), and Chinese banister, this object may be slightly later than the "I" chairs. It does, however, preserve the basic form of the "I" chair crests. The signature leaf carvings are present, but they are more naturalistic and complex than those on any "I" chair (fig. 29). If the chair illustrated in figure 27 is an Ipswich product, it may well be from the Gaines family shop, which frequently adapted and amplified designs from Boston-area products.[21]

The third crest found on the "I" chairs is the most complex, with molded cyma elements terminating in bold scroll volutes, multiple leaf elements outlined by piercings, and flat planes decorated with small carved panels and chip cuts (see figs. 30, 31). This is an extraordinarily fragile design, and like the two most common crest patterns, it is held together with a bridge of wood at the lower, back edge of the crest (fig. 32). In terms of the overall handling of the carving, this crest type stands apart in its contrast of strong graphic and fussy passages. The carving is also flatter and less refined than that seen on most of the other chairs. It is likely that these chairs represent the work of a different carver or even a different shop than the other "I" group chairs.

The fourth and fifth crest patterns are rare, one appearing on two chairs (see fig. 33) This yoke or saddled crest has no decoration other than simple leaf carving; however, this work is less perfunctory than that found on many "I" chairs. The final and most idiosyncratic crest occurs on a single

Figure 30 Side chair, Boston, Massachusetts, 1710–1720. Maple. H. 45", W. 17½", D. 14½". (Private collection; photo, Gavin Ashworth.)

Figure 31 Detail of the crest of the chair illustrated in fig. 30.

Figure 32 Detail of the back of the crest of the chair illustrated in fig. 30.

Figure 33 Armchair, Boston, Massachusetts, 1710–1720. Maple. H. 46⅜", W. 24½", D. 22". (Courtesy, Museum of Fine Arts, Houston; Bayou Bend Collection, gift of Miss Ima Hogg.)

Figure 34 Side chair, Boston, Massachusetts, 1710–1720. Maple. H. 43¼", W. 17½", D. 14⅝". (Courtesy, Museum of Fine Arts, Boston; gift of Mr. and Mrs. Herbert Edes.)

chair that descended in the Edes family of Boston (fig. 34). This design has the vestigial leaves of the other patterns and the intact "bridge" of wood in the back, but otherwise stands apart from the rest of the group.

The structural and stylistic features of the "I" group and its relatives indicate that Boston chair makers adopted the tricks of the middling London trade. At first one would think that the chairs are the confused products of makers who were operating with an imperfect understanding of the new Georgian style. With two exceptions, the stiles of the chairs are straight from seat rail to crest, so they could be made simply by preparing a straight piece of lumber and then running a molding down each side. One of the

Figure 35 Side chair, Boston area of Massachusetts, 1715–1725. Maple. H. 45¼", W. 18", D. 14½". (Private collection; photo, Gavin Ashworth.)

Figure 36 Detail of the back of the chair illustrated in fig. 35.

Figure 37 Detail of the front stretcher of the chair illustrated in fig. 35.

Figure 38 Side chair, Boston, Massachusetts, ca. 1740. Walnut and walnut veneer with maple and white pine. H. 38½", W. 20¾", D. 18½". (Chipstone Foundation; photo, Gavin Ashworth.)

"I" chairs that does have cyma-curved stiles also features a "crook'd," vasiform splat, and the other is made of walnut, suggesting a more mature awareness of Georgian design and perhaps a later date than the other chairs in the group (figs. 35–37). Even these two chairs lack the overall compositional unity that Shaftesbury and his generation prized; for that, Bostonians would have to wait a decade or more (see fig. 38). Yet it is not a coincidence that the early Georgian features that appear on the chairs—notably molded stiles and square cabriole legs—are neither time-consuming to execute, nor disruptive to an established tradition of piece-work manufacture. In this respect, the makers of the chairs should be seen, like English caned chair makers before them, as canny artisans who were able to adapt new stylistic features without disrupting their own profit margin and way of working.

Figure 39 Armchair, Boston, Massachusetts, 1700–1715. Maple. H. 50¾", W. 25¾", D. 27". (Chipstone Foundation; photo, Gavin Ashworth.)

The "I" chairs clearly occupy a complex position in furniture history. They are structurally simple objects, but extremely complicated texts. The chairs reflect some of the same cultural preoccupations that spurred the popularity of the caned chair in England in the 1670s even though the "signifying" crest is the only salient compositional feature surviving from the earlier forms. The "I" chairs also have little in common with the first generation of Boston caned chairs (see fig. 39), which, like most seminal seating forms produced in that city, were more direct transpositions of London models.

In many respects, the "I" chairs can be interpreted as descendants of early Boston leather chairs, which performed the same role for that city's trade that the caned chair had played in London. As historian Neil Kamil has shown, the leather chair was part of a conscious and ultimately successful attempt to right Boston's own balance of trade. Although New Englanders could not compete with the staple producing colonies to the south, they could produce furniture and other finished goods that would give them a favorable balance of trade with the Middle Atlantic. This strategy was obviously based on the more entrenched mercantile system of the mother country.[22]

Against this backdrop, it is possible to find in the "I" chairs more than an example of a shift toward Georgian style. Their part in this broad stylistic trend is undeniable, but it is also clear that the "I" chairs were perfect symbols of an even more large-scale attempt to transform the symbolic culture of the mercantile class. By combining the carved crests of the English caned chair and Boston leather chair with nascent Georgian features, the "I" chairs crystallized the mentality of Boston's upwardly mobile commercial elite. In this sense the chairs mark the transition between what might be called the "mercantilist style" and a new concept of taste and fashionability. Though culturally severed from the elitism of Shaftesbury and his contemporaries, they are nonetheless structurally consonant with that elitism. All of the examples with credible provenances descended in families of the upper class including the Hancocks, Holyokes, and Aldens. These seating forms mark the appropriation by such civic leaders of competitive tactics that had put Londoners at the center of that empire. And like the Georgian style in England, they mark the end of those tactics' efficacy. From the 1710s to the 1740s, Boston was the most important center of the American carrying trade, and its merchants grew wealthy through commerce with the West Indies. This elite identified strongly with the English monarchy and was instrumental in transforming New England into a class-conscious society. As in England, the government's role in the economy was reimagined, and the theocracy of the seventeenth century gave way to a more instrumental oligarchy that tried to foster the success of trade. Given the presence of this upwardly mobile clientele, it was only logical that Boston chair makers embraced the same strategy that guided their London counterparts thirty years before. It is ironic that so much scholarly effort has been expended on reading the inscrutable "I" marks on these chairs, when those marks were not intended to be highly legible. To read these chairs as texts, we need to pay the most attention to the areas where the makers invested the majority of their skill and labor—the crests, which were the site of greatest visual impact. After all, the chairs were not so much fashionable as representations of fashionability itself. In this respect, they bespeak conscious participation in the larger world of English mercantilism, in which membership in the middle class was more a matter of assertion than taste.[23]

ACKNOWLEDGMENTS   The author thanks Gavin Ashworth, Luke Beckerdite, Ann Bermingham, Edward S. Cooke, Jr., Tom Denenberg, Janet Deranian, Bert Denker, Eleanore Gadsden, Constance and Dudley Godfrey, Charles Hummel, Alan Miller, Jonathan Prown, Robert F. Trent, Maria Theresa and John Van Der Sande, Anne and Fred Vogel, and Alicia Volk.

1. For characteristics distinguishing Dutch chairs from English derivatives, see Adam Bowett, "Myths of Furniture History: Anglo-Dutch (Part II)," *Antique Collecting* 34, no. 8 (February 2000): 4–9. Colin Campbell, "Understanding Traditional and Modern Patterns of Consumption in Eighteenth-Century England: A Character-Action Approach," in Brewer and Porter, *Consumption and the World of Goods* (London: Routledge, 1993), p. 40. See also Lorna Weatherill, *Consumer Behaviour and Material Culture in Britain 1660–1760* (London: Routledge, 1988); Weatherill argues that "If social emulation were at work as a dynamic force behind people's motivation in owning goods, then we would expect higher proportions of the most highly regarded group to own many [items], and we would also expect them to be the first to own the new things. Yet... this was not the case, for a higher proportion of professionals and tradesmen owned the goods associated with front stage areas of the house" (p. 195). For a more general objection to diffusion models on theoretical grounds, see Dell Upton, "Towards A Performance Theory of Vernacular Architecture: Early Tidewater Virginia As a Case Study," *Folklore Forum* 12, no. 2/3 (1979). Benno M. Forman, *American Seating Furniture, 1630–1730: An Interpretive Catalogue* (New York: W.W. Norton for the Winterthur Museum, 1988), pp. 229–81.

2. R. W. Symonds, "English Cane Chairs: Part I," *Connoisseur* 27, no. 3 (March 1951): 8.

3. Symonds, "English Cane Chairs: Part I," p. 8. Since Symonds' analysis in the 1950s, Peter Earle has questioned the importance of the Great Fire in initiating cane chair manufacture. In his analysis of middle-class estate records, the form appears only rarely in the 1670s and does not become common until the 1680s. This may, however, simply reflect a time lag between the introduction of the form and its appearance in the inventories of decedents, who might have owned the chairs for some time before the furniture came to be recorded. See Peter Earle, *The Making of the English Middle Class* (London: Methuen, 1989), p. 294.

4. Irene Scouloudi, "The Stranger Community in the Metropolis, 1558–1640" in Scouloudi, *Huguenots in Britain and Their French Background* (Basingstoke, Eng.: Macmillan Press, 1987), pp. 48–49; Penelope Corfield, "A Provincial Capital in the Late Seventeenth Century: The Case of Norwich," in *Crisis and Order in English Towns*, edited by Peter Clark and P. Slack (London: Routledge and Kegan Paul, 1972), p. 282; Christopher Hartop, *The Huguenot Legacy: English Silver 1680–1760* (London: Thomas Heneage, 1996). Jonathan Israel, "England, the Dutch, and the Struggle for the Mastery of World Trade in the Age of the Glorious Revolution," in *The World of William and Mary*, edited by Dale Hoak and Mordechai Feingold (Stanford: Stanford University Press, 1996), p. 75. Bernard Cottret, *The Huguenots in England* (Cambridge: Cambridge University Press, 1985), p. 198.

5. Eli F. Heckscher, *Mercantilism*, 2 vols. (New York: Macmillan, 1955), 2: 25–26.

6. John Keymer, *A Clear and Evident Way* [1650], quoted in Joyce Appleby, *Economic Thought and Ideology in Seventeenth-Century England* (Princeton: Princeton University Press, 1978), p. 76. On Mun, see Kustaa Multamäki, *Towards Great Britain: Commerce and Conquest in the Thought of Algernon Sidney and Charles Davenant* (Helsinki: Finnish Academy of Arts and Letters, 1999), p. 83 ff.; Jules Lubbock, *The Tyranny of Taste* (New Haven, Conn.: Yale University Press, 1995), pp. 93–94; Michael Kammen, *Empire and Interest: The American Colonies and the Politics of Mercantilism* (Philadelphia: J. P. Lippincott, 1970), pp. 5–6; and Heckscher, *Mercantilism*, 2: 281–82. Thomas Mun, *England's Treasure by Forraign Trade* (London: Thomas Clark, 1664; written 1623), p. 15. On the effects of the Navigation Acts on the colonies, see Susan Previant Lee and Peter Passell, *A New Economic View of American History* (New York: W. W. Norton, 1979), chapter 2. For contemporary arguments about the importance of finished goods, see Dalby Thomas, *An Historical Account of the Rise and Growth of the West-India Colonies* (London: Joseph Hindemarsh, 1690), p. 5; Appleby, *Economic Thought and Ideology*, chapter 7, passim.

7. Sir Josiah Child, *A Discourse About Trade* (London: A. Sowle, 1690; written 1660s), p. 4. John Houghton, *England's Great Happiness, or, A Dialogue Between Contentment and Complaint* (London: Edward Croft, 1677), p. 5; Thomas, *An Historical Account of the Rise and Growth of the West-India Colonies*, p. 16. Carew Reynel, *The True English Interest* (London: Giles Widdowes, 1674), preface 4; p. 2. Houghton, *England's Great Happiness*, pp. 5, 10.

8. Quoted in Symonds, "English Cane Chairs: Part I," p. 12. For further discussion of this document, see Margaret Swain, "The Turkey-work Chairs of Holyroodhouse," in *Upholstery in America and Europe from the Seventeenth Century to World War I*, edited by Edward S. Cooke, Jr. (New York: W. W. Norton, 1987), pp. 54–55.

9. The rattan or cane used in such chairs might have come from a variety of sources, as the plant is native to China, India, Ceylon, and Malaysia. In all likelihood the canes used in

English shops were bought from Dutch or Portuguese middlemen. On cane, see Gertrude Z. Thomas, *Richer Than Spices* (New York: Alfred A. Knopf, 1965), chapter 5; and *Encyclopedie Methodique, Tome Quatrieme* (Paris: Chez Panckouche, 1785).

10. Symonds, "English Cane Chairs: Part I," pp. 13–14. The Joiners' Company's claim that "many thousands" of workers benefited seems dubious, but it is a figure substantiated by modern research. Peter Earle notes that "several thousand" people were employed in the furniture trade in London alone, concentrated in the area north of the Strand.

11. Earle, *The Making of the English Middle Class,* p. 23. Nicholas Barbon, *A Discourse of Trade* (London: Thomas Milbourn, 1690), pp. 34–35.

12. Joan Thirsk, *Economic Policy and Projects* (Oxford: Clarendon Press, 1978), pp. 107–9. Lubbock, *The Tyranny of Taste,* p. 76. On the embrace of luxury trades within mercantilism, see also Heckscher, *Mercantilism,* 2: 190. Carole Shammas, "The Domestic Environment in Early Modern England and America," *Journal of Social History* 14, no. 1 (1980): 18. Dudley North, *Discourses Upon Trade* (London: Thomas Basset, 1691), pp. 2, 14; Bernard Mandeville, "The Grumbling Hive, or Knaves Turn'd Honest" (1705), in *The Fable of the Bees,* edited by F. B. Kage (Oxford: Clarendon Press, 1924), pp. 102–5, 25. See also Herlitz Lars, "Conceptions of History and Society in Mercantilism, 1650–1730," in *Mercantilist Economics,* edited by Lars Magnussen (Boston: Kluwer Academic Publishers, 1993), p. 111.

13. Ralph Davis, *A Commercial Revolution* (London: Historical Associations Pamphlets, 1967), p. 4. On the currency shortage, see Appleby, *Economic Thought and Ideology,* p. 231. Daniel Defoe, *The True Born Englishman: A Satyr* (London: n.p., 1700), p. 57. Iain Pears, *The Discovery of Painting* (New Haven, Conn.: Yale University Press, 1988), esp. pp. 13–26. John Bellers, *Essays About the Poor, Manufactures, Trade, Plantations and Immorality* (London: T. Sowle, 1699), p. 11.

14. Robert Voitle, *The Third Earl of Shaftesbury 1671–1713* (Baton Rouge: Louisiana State University Press, 1984); Rex A. Barrell, *Anthony Ashley Cooper, Earl of Shaftesbury and 'Le Refuge Français'—Correspondence* (Lewiston/Lampeter/Queenstone, Eng.: Studies in British History, Volume 15, The Edwin Mellin Press, 1989). Lawrence Klein, *Shaftesbury and Culture of Politeness: Moral Discourse and Cultural Politics in Early Eighteenth-Century England* (Cambridge: Cambridge University Press, 1994); John A. Bernstein, "Shaftesbury's Identification of the Good and the Beautiful," *Eighteenth Century Studies* 10, no. 3 (spring 1977): 306–7; and John A. Bernstein, *Shaftesbury, Rousseau, and Kant* (London and Toronto: Associated University Press and Farleigh Dickinson University Press, 1980), p. 26. Joseph Addison, *The Spectator,* no. 411 (June 21, 1712).

15. Kammen, *Empire and Interest,* p. 38; Heckscher, *Mercantilism,* 2: 19. The first Earl died in exile in Holland, after being imprisoned in the Tower of London in 1673 for his opposition to the accession of James II to the throne. Shaftesbury is quoted in David Solkin, *Painting for Money* (New Haven, Conn.: Yale University Press, 1993), p. 12. See also Klein, *Shaftesbury and Culture of Politeness,* p. 5.

16. Benno Forman, *American Seating Furniture,* pp. 264–66; Richard Randall, *American Furniture in the Museum of Fine Arts, Boston* (Boston: Museum of Fine Arts, 1965), pp. 162–64.

17. For the Winthrop family chair, see Patricia E. Kane, "Furniture Owned by the Massachusetts Historical Society," *Antiques* 109, no. 5 (May 1976): 960–69.

18. For stamped and branded examples, see Roderic H. Blackburn, "Branded and Stamped New York Furniture," *Antiques* 119, no. 4 (May 1981): 1130–45.

19. See Forman, *American Seating Furniture,* cat. nos. 55, 63.

20. Colin Streeter thought that the motif on this crest type might be based upon the Chinese *ruyi,* an abstraction of a mushroom. Forman repeats this idea in *American Seating Furniture,* p. 267, footnote; see also Philip M. Johnston et al., *Courts and Colonies; The William and Mary Style in Holland, England, and America* (Seattle: University of Washington Press and Cooper-Hewitt Museum, 1988), p. 162. Johnson notes that if this is the case, then these chairs are the first instances of a Chinese motif appearing on American furniture.

21. For more on these early Boston Georgian chairs, see Joan Barzilay Freund and Leigh Keno, "The Making and Marketing of Boston Seating Furniture in the Late Baroque Style," in *American Furniture,* edited by Luke Beckerdite (Hanover, N. H.: University Press of New England for the Chipstone Foundation, 1997), pp. 14–16, figs. 20–24.

22. Neil D. Kamil, "Hidden in Plain Sight: Disappearance and Material Life in Colonial New York," in *American Furniture,* edited by Luke Beckerdite and William N. Hosley (Hanover, N. H.: University Press of New England for the Chipstone Foundation, 1995), pp. 191–249. Kamil notes that in one case, William Gooch of Virginia complained to Parlia-

ment that Boston's chair trade was in direct conflict with England's own mercantile interests, which was of course true (p. 193). For a lively riposte to Kamil's argument that New York chairs were made in competition with Boston imports, see Roger Gonzales and Daniel Putnam Brown, Jr., "Boston and New York Leather Chairs: A Reappraisal," in *American Furniture,* edited by Luke Beckerdite (Hanover, N. H.: University Press of New England for the Chipstone Foundation, 1996), pp. 175–94.

23. Freund and Keno, "The Making and Marketing of Boston Seating Furniture," pp. 1–40. Of the chairs in the group with a known provenance, one descended to the Hancock family (Winterthur Museum); one was owned by Edward Holyoke, president of Harvard University (Fogg Art Museum, Harvard); and one was acquired by the Pilgrim Society from Marcia Alden Welch in 1883 and has been ascribed an Alden family provenance. On Boston's mercantile class, see Bernard Bailyn, *The New England Merchants in the Seventeenth Century* (Cambridge: Harvard University Press, 1955); Jack P. Greene, *Pursuits of Happiness: The Social Development of Early Modern British Colonies and the Formation of American Culture* (Chapel Hill: University of North Carolina Press, 1988), pp. 67–76; Philip S. Haffenden, *New England in the English Nation, 1683–1713* (Oxford: Clarendon Press, 1974), p. 120; James Henretta, "Economic and Social Structure in Colonial Boston," *William and Mary Quarterly,* 3rd ser., 22 (1965): 75–92; reprint, Henretta, *The Origins of American Capitalism* (Boston: Northeastern University Press, 1991). Margaret E. Newell, "A Revolution in Economic Thought: Currency and Development in Eighteenth-Century Massachusetts," in *Entrepreneurs: The Boston Business Community, 1700–1850,* edited by Conrad Edick Wright and Katheryn P. Viens (Boston: Massachusetts Historical Society, 1997), pp. 1–21.

Jonathan Prown and
Katherine Hemple
Prown

The Quiet Canon:
Tradition and
Exclusion in
American Furniture
Scholarship

▼ THE HISTORY OF THE *cabinet-maker's art is the record of the unconscious struggle toward an ideal which, when finally attained, destroyed all further inspiration. This ideal persisted from one age to another, never retrograding, and each succeeding age saw it more clearly, until, at the close of the eighteenth century, it was found this limitation had been reached.*

Luke Vincent Lockwood, 1913

History has to be rewritten in every generation because, although the past does not change, the present does; each generation asks new questions of the past, and finds new areas of sympathy as it re-lives different aspects of the experiences of its predecessors.

Sir Christopher Hill, 1972

The symposium "American Art Worlds and Material Culture," held at the Winterthur Museum in November 2001, explored the scholarly intersections of art historical, decorative arts, and material culture studies. Participants were asked to focus on "the divisions that continue to limit inquiry and to celebrate the points of conjunction that hold the potential for expansive approaches to the universe of art, artifacts, and performance." This essay, which is drawn from comments presented at the Winterthur symposium, suggests the need for greater critical consideration of American furniture scholarship and the long-standing cultural, intellectual, and institutional forces that inform its character.

While American museums of all stripes have begun to experiment with innovative ways of interpreting and presenting the past in order to engage today's audiences, the display of early American furniture—and the scholarship on which it is based—remains largely dependent on a specialized interpretive model crafted over a century ago. Rooted in the efforts of nineteenth-century museum leaders to elevate and Americanize the working class and immigrant "masses" by teaching them good taste, this orthodoxy continues to promote standards of decoration associated with the most ornate or expensive artifacts owned by prominent early Americans—a narrow reading ultimately more about the retention of cultural authority than the exploration of educational and intellectual potential. The following essay examines the origins, ideological foundations, and limitations of conventional interpretive methods and is intended to spark thoughtful discussion about the ways in which early American scholarship and display may benefit from exploring interpretive strategies that may be more relevant and engaging to today's museum visitors.[1]

The 1924 opening of the American Wing at the Metropolitan Museum of Art stands as a defining moment in the historiography of American decorative arts interpretation. The event formally codified a wide range of post-Victorian historical, aesthetic, and cultural beliefs that would become central to the evolution of subsequent American furniture scholarship. Opened fifteen years after the pioneering Hudson-Fulton Celebration (fig. 1) and the gift of the Bolles collection, which for the first time brought

Figure 1 American furniture and decorative arts installation, Hudson-Fulton Celebration, Metropolitan Museum of Art, New York, 1909. (Courtesy, Metropolitan Museum of Art.)

the "domestic arts" into the Metropolitan, the American Wing presented the arts in North America over a two century span linking specific stylistic changes with the progressive civilizing of the people with whom the art was associated. The nineteenth-century "curiosities of the past" approach to decorative arts display—with its anthropological interest in relics and its more democratic aesthetic—was replaced by installations such as the colo-

Figure 2 Parlor from Marmion (Prince George County, Virginia) installed in the American Wing, Metropolitan Museum of Art, New York, photograph ca. 1925. (Courtesy, Metropolitan Museum of Art.)

nial Virginia parlor (fig. 2). In that vignette, artfully arranged high-style objects functioned as symbolic representations of the elevated tastes and values associated with the founding fathers and other elites. In short, the American Wing's storyline, crafted by R. T. H. Halsey and Charles Over Cornelius, celebrated the nation's historic inheritance, its craft ingenuity, and its "most beautiful" objects. In this way the Wing helped establish the self-sustaining aesthetic and ideological hierarchies that continue to inform decorative arts installations and publications today.²

On the most obvious level, the American Wing and other formative decorative arts installations sought to expose the public to the refined tastes

Figure 3 Gallery 283, Philadelphia Museum of Art, 1934. (Courtesy, Philadelphia Museum of Art.)

and lofty principles of colonial elites (fig. 3). But as a number of scholars have noted, beneath the surface lay a more complex agenda preoccupied with cultural literacy, ethnic identity, class distinctions, and changing ideas about race and gender. Early twentieth-century museum professionals and social and political leaders relied on the objects and apocryphal histories associated with the nation's past as a means to "civilize" the working classes and school immigrants in the ideals of American culture. Colonial era antiques were, according to Elizabeth Stillinger, understood as "appropriate vehicles for informing foreigners and less enlightened natives as to American traditions and values" and as "educational tools" that could encourage assimilation.³

Museum catalogues and auctions of several important collections also played a crucial role in promoting the evolution of this more select, elitist canon of American decorative arts objects. So too did the emergence of new publications aimed at the general public. Homer Eaton Keyes, the first editor of *The Magazine Antiques,* envisioned a journal devoted to "recording and interpreting those significant souvenirs of man's creative genius" and that could serve as the foundation upon which to build a "superstructure of steadily increasing beauty, power, and usefulness." *Antiques* provided a forum that effectively supported the mutually beneficial scholarly and financial agendas of influential collectors, dealers, and curators and reinforced the same lofty themes that underlay the formative decorative arts displays of the 1920s.[4]

Other pivotal events included the 1926 Philadelphia Sesquicentennial Fair, which initiated visitors to the colonial revival ethos at its most potent. The aptly named "High Street" exhibition celebrated the nation's political and cultural legacy and glorified the beauty, productivity, and domestic virtues embodied in early American shops and homes (fig. 4). As the authors of the 1929 Girl Scouts Loan Exhibition catalogue explained, the objects owned by early Americans revealed them as a people who were both "cultured and courageous," capable of creating an "atmosphere of comfort, of beauty, and of culture" in even the most humble of circumstances (fig. 5).[5]

Figure 4 High Street, Sesquicentennial of Independence, Philadelphia, 1926. (Courtesy, Library Company of Philadelphia.)

Figure 5 Chippendale Room, Girl Scouts Loan Exhibition, American Art Association Galleries, New York, 1929. (Courtesy, Girl Scouts of the U.S.A.; photo, Lawrence X. Champeau.)

Figure 6 Plan for reinstallation of the drawing room for the Samuel Powell House (ca. 1768–1772), Philadelphia, ca. 1927. (Courtesy, Philadelphia Museum of Art.)

The Girl Scouts Loan Exhibition and other shows and publications of the era helped codify what social historian Steven Conn refers to as an "emerging twentieth-century fantasy of what life was like in the eighteenth century"—a fantasy rooted equally in nostalgia and didacticism. Conn recounts the story of the opening of High Street, where a hostess at the Stephen Girard House told a reporter that the purpose of the exhibition was "to reveal the fine heritage of beauty and dignity in ordinary everyday life which our ancestors have passed on to us. It proves that our beginnings were not chaotic, lawless, cheap or tawdry, but essentially noble and dignified." Early decorative arts displays and publications created a vision of the past that offered the so-called cultured classes symbolic refuge from the intrusions of mass culture in all its vulgarity. At the same time, they provided immigrant and working classes with a model of the accessories and associated ideals that could help them achieve middle-class status and become literate in core American values.[6]

A similar agenda informed pioneering decorative arts installations at the Philadelphia Museum of Art (fig. 6), the Museum of Fine Arts in Boston, and Colonial Williamsburg—institutions whose ideological orientation echoed that of the celebrated 1893 World's Columbian Exposition, with its pointed division between the Midway Plaisance and the fittingly named White City. The former venue was exciting, crowded, and meant to entertain the masses; the latter sought to expose them to the most ennobling art and ideals of western culture. As historian Lawrence Levine suggests, the White City encouraged and helped maintain the division between "highbrow" and "lowbrow." American art museums, concert halls, and department stores likewise functioned to make public audiences more cognizant of the divide between high and low culture and, simultaneously, to render museum visitors more docile. Art gradually became a one-way process, with the artist and the curator giving and the museum audience receiving.[7]

One of the main messages early twentieth-century museum leaders promoted was the idea that America's artistic traditions, most fully expressed in the material culture of the elite, had descended directly from England. "To study artistic development in its relation to nationality," explained Charles Over Cornelius, "the opportunity for expression of personal taste must be sought in the homes of the rich or well-to-do," the segment of society most likely to display the "sophistication of taste" characteristic of a nation's best and most refined art, including furniture and other craft traditions. As the authors of the catalogue to the Hudson-Fulton Celebration explained, the "history of American furniture is comprehended in the history of English furniture," while the contributions of "Dutch, French, Spanish, and Swedish" and other ethnic groups were, at best, negligible. By the start of the twentieth century, scholars and curators of American decorative arts had forged an aesthetic whose ideological underpinnings were based on a yearning for the cultural stability and ethnic homogeneity of an imagined past, where Anglo-American craftsmen transformed utilitarian objects into art forms that were used by and expressed the values of an enlightened and educated clientele (fig. 7).[8]

Figure 7 American furniture and decorative arts installation, Hudson-Fulton Celebration, Metropolitan Museum of Art, New York, 1909. (Courtesy, Metropolitan Museum of Art.)

As ideas about ethnicity and race began to change in the decades that followed, American decorative arts scholars developed a more nuanced understanding of the role that non-English immigrants played in contributing to America's artistic heritage. In *Early American Furniture Makers* (1930), Thomas Ormsbee described a colonial America whose relatively diverse craft traditions reflected the contributions not just of the English but of the "Scotch, Welsh, Irish, Hollander, and French Huguenots" along with a "few Germans, Swiss, Swedes, and Spanish and Portugese Jews," whose presence added "cosmopolitan variety." Underlying the seemingly more democratic characterization of colonial America, however, was an increasingly polarized definition of race, as the "alien" ethnic identity of certain groups—such as Germans, Irish, and, to a lesser extent, Jews—was

Figure 8 "The New England Kitchen in the Old Log Cabin," Philadelphia Centennial, 1876. (Courtesy, Winterthur Museum.) This image appeared in *Frank Leslie's Illustrated Newspaper* on June 10, 1876.

Figure 9 American decorative arts installation, Yale University Art Gallery, New Haven, Connecticut, ca. 1928. (Courtesy, Yale University Art Gallery.)

gradually subsumed under a new racial identity defined as "white." This more expansive definition of Anglo-American identity and tradition coincided with and depended upon the deliberate erasure of blackness in American decorative arts scholarship and remains evident today in the conspicuous placement of African-American, Native American, and Latino craft traditions in the categories of "folk" and "outsider" art.[9]

The emerging construct of an American decorative arts tradition based in the primacy of white, Anglo-American culture depended not just on the erasure of the non-white but on the marginalization of the female as well. As historian Patricia West has documented, the rise of large metropolitan museums in the late nineteenth and early twentieth centuries was led by a class of professional men who implemented a new aesthetic based on a notion of connoisseurship defined in opposition to the "ladies auxiliary" aesthetic at work in the largely female-dominated house museums, fairs, and historic monuments (fig. 8). Newer, more rigidly ordered, and masculinized displays (fig. 9) promoted a "slick, professional exhibitry" that reinforced "a growing element of elitism and connoisseurship" in museums generally and resulted in diminished leadership roles for women.[10]

An emphasis on the implicitly masculine virtues of early American furniture was also exemplified in written histories through the transformation of the cabinetmaker into an iconic figure. "Where formerly the joiner had built not only furniture but also wainscoting and the great wood roofs of halls and rooms," noted Charles Over Cornelius in 1930, "his place was taken by the man who made furniture only." The result of this transformation was the emergence of a figure who was not only an artisan but an artist as well. The colonial cabinetmaker was increasingly depicted as a heroic figure who, like the founding fathers, embodied such masculine ideals as individualism, independence, self-determination, and creative ingenuity. In 1928, Edward Stratton Holloway wrote that early American furniture "was made not by machines but by *men*: and man when he works individually is invariably possessed by the itch to create, to develop his own idea, to express himself, and not literally to copy." Reflecting antimodernist concerns regarding the emasculating threat posed by the machine age, twentieth-century furniture scholars envisioned the cabinetmaker as a figure who embodied the manly "vigour" that lay at the heart of America's national character and its craft traditions.[11]

Today, too many displays of early American furniture continue to rely on interpretive approaches that were born out of the nineteenth century and shaped by the era's particular cultural concerns regarding gender, race, ethnicity, and class. Pioneering decorative arts exhibitions such as the American Wing can and should be celebrated for their contributions to preserving and understanding early American art and history. But there remains a pressing need for today's curators to recognize what cultural historian Paul Dimaggio terms "the cognitive and institutional barriers" that stifle the consideration of alternative modes of interpretation more attuned to contemporary sensibilities. In an essay on museum ethics, David Carr contends that the central failing in many institutions is their tendency to leave the visitor feeling powerless and disengaged. Too often decorative arts displays do just that by relying on a time-worn presentation of early American material culture that is communicated to the public via jargon-filled labels and presumed aesthetic hierarchies. Generally only the most discerning or highly trained viewer can distinguish one exhibition of early American chairs, tables, and chests from another (figs. 10–12). One promising strategy involves greater critical consideration of the exhibits themselves, "which may be artifacts of a higher order and which require important and serious analysis." This process necessarily involves a trans-disciplinary approach built on theoretical advancements in other areas of cultural studies.[12]

Early American furniture scholarship and display could benefit from incorporating advanced interpretive models in fields such as history and

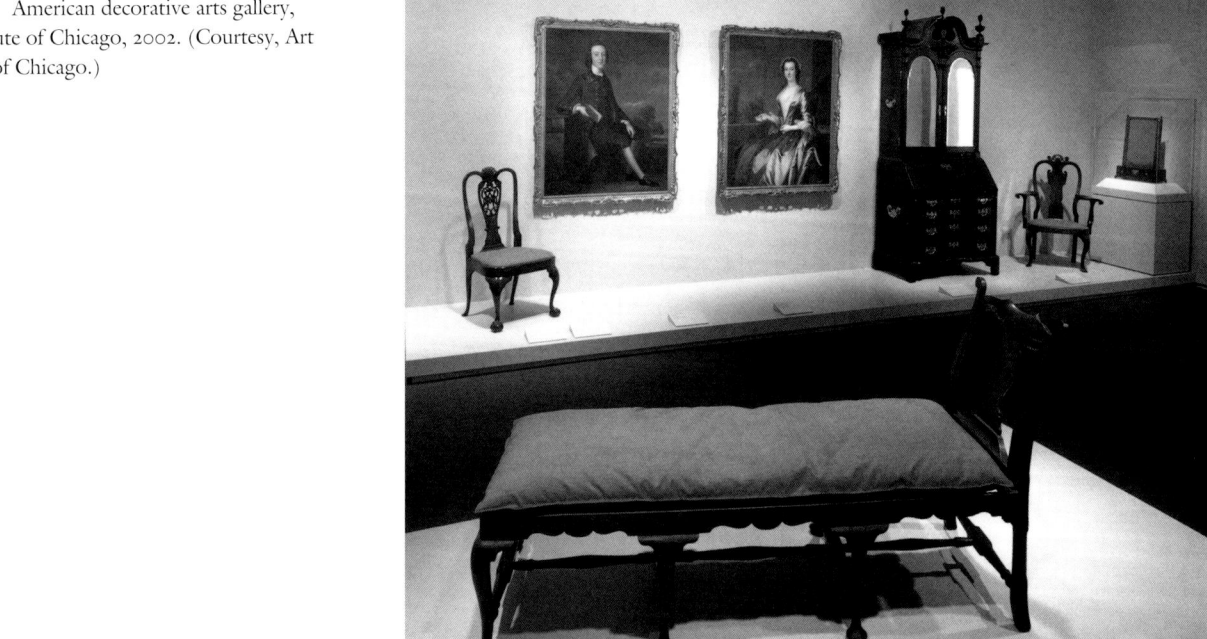

Figure 10 American decorative arts gallery, Art Institute of Chicago, 2002. (Courtesy, Art Institute of Chicago.)

Figure 11 American collections gallery, Milwaukee Art Museum, Milwaukee, Wisconsin, ca. 1999. (Courtesy, Milwaukee Art Museum.)

Figure 12 View of "An American Vision: Henry Francis du Pont's Winterthur Museum," National Gallery of Art, Washington D. C., May 5–October 6, 2002. (Courtesy, Winterthur Museum and the National Gallery of Art.)

art history. Literary studies, which like the study of decorative arts emerged as a formal academic discipline in the nineteenth century, offer another promising source. The intellectual and aesthetic preoccupations of both fields were shaped by the same early twentieth-century cultural anxieties, which were largely fueled by industrialization, urbanization, the rise of mass culture, the growing influence of the market, and other sweeping changes associated with modernization. As each discipline evolved into a profession practiced within institutional settings, literary and decorative arts scholars embraced formal analysis based on subjective evaluation and presumed aesthetic hierarchies. This interpretive strategy encouraged the development of a canon of objects and texts grounded in Anglo-American culture and largely produced by educated, affluent, native-born white men.

Literary and decorative arts scholarship continued to follow parallel paths until the mid-twentieth century, when female and minority scholars of literature, who had previously been underrepresented in the field, began to expand the study of what had traditionally been considered non-canonical works. Newer, student-centered pedagogies emerged that encouraged the teaching and interpretation of texts more broadly reflective of the diversity of American society and the growing diversity of its universities. Scholars gradually abandoned formalist aesthetic hierarchies in favor of a greater consideration of a wider range of interpretive strategies. The result of these changes was not, as some feared, the widespread rejection of such authors as Nathaniel Hawthorne, Herman Melville, or William Faulkner, but the emergence of spirited and less formulaic scholarship on canonical writers generally. At the same time, the newer interpretive approaches helped uncover the literary, cultural, and historical richness in the work of previously neglected authors such as Frederick Douglass, Harriet Beecher Stowe, and Zora Neale Hurston.[13]

The study and teaching of American history experienced a similar evolution, as the "great men" and "great events" paradigm was expanded to include the histories of women, minority and non-western cultures, and non-elites. Historians have largely accepted what historian Gary Nash terms the "pragmatic revolt in American history" and, like literary scholars, have recognized the ways in which embracing diversity, utilizing multiple interpretive strategies, and accepting the subjective nature of interpretation itself can only enrich scholarship in their field.[14]

By contrast, scholars of American furniture have yet to formally acknowledge the existence of a canon, let alone engage in critical discourse about its origins, contents, or functions. Decorative arts historian Edward S. Cooke argues that the canonization of a select group of American furniture makers, such as Benjamin Randolph and Duncan Phyfe, "permits little understanding of the individual's relation to other furniture makers or to his society." The canonization of specific regional designs and forms—Newport blockfront furniture, Boston bombé case pieces, and Philadelphia high chests, to cite just a few—similarly limits understanding of interrelationships among objects and results in a narrow interpretive model in which the discrete object is held above and apart from the cultural and historical contexts in which it was produced (fig. 13).[15]

Figure 13 American collections gallery, Milwaukee Art Museum, Milwaukee, Wisconsin, ca. 1976. (Courtesy, Milwaukee Art Museum.)

The quantity of publications and symposia in the field each year gives the impression that early American furniture scholarship is robust, but these forums often fail to reflect or incorporate creative theoretical models that have advanced scholarship in other fields within the humanities. Certainly

Figure 14 Albert Sack, *The Fine Points of Furniture, Early American: Good, Better, Best, Superior, Masterpiece* (New York: Crown Publishers, 1993), p. 185. (Courtesy, Israel Sack, Inc. and Crown Publishers, Inc.)

the best known new methodology in the area of artifact interpretation is material culture studies, which promotes the inclusion of a wide range of scholarship, encourages cooperation between academic and museum-based scholars, and allows for the merging of inductive and deductive modes of reasoning. Despite the potential of this innovative and inclusive approach, too many museum installations rely on the same interpretive strategies that informed the pioneering decorative arts displays and that are exemplified in the "good-better-best" formula (fig. 14) first articulated half a century ago in dealer Albert Sack's *Fine Points of Furniture, Early American*. In 1985, *Perspectives on American Furniture,* a published collection of papers presented at a Winterthur Museum conference, proclaimed a generational shift in furniture studies. The new approach promised to incorporate a specific "emphasis on furniture as a cultural index to human behavior and on the wide-ranging approach that takes in stride all manner of furniture regardless of aesthetic merit." While articles in *American Furniture* and other publications over the past decade suggest a wide range of topics, progress has been relatively slow. As Henry Glassie and others have noted, scholars in both museums and the academy have failed to fulfill material culture's potential as "a new transdisciplinary practice, at once scientific and humanistic." Decorative arts displays and publications continue to devote approximately ninety percent of their interpretation to "material" and only ten percent to "culture," which becomes all the more significant in light of the fact that more than ninety percent of the objects shown were owned by less than ten percent of early Americans.[16]

To be sure, contemporary curators bring to their analyses unprecedented object literacy, which has resulted in a better understanding of regional furniture making and individual shop traditions. But museum displays in particular have generally neglected to build on the work of innovative scholars and curators who have explored alternative modes of interpretation that forward, challenge, or even invert basic decorative arts assumptions. Laurel Thatcher Ulrich and Amanda Carson Banks have, for example, used theory on gender and material culture to develop new readings of familiar objects like the Hannah Barnard cupboard and to shed light on birth chairs and other previously neglected furniture forms. Museum installations could benefit from incorporating these and other innovative approaches, including decorative arts scholar Kenneth Ames' study of Victorian furniture titled *Death in the Dining Room*. Ames demonstrates the ways in which both the design and the thematic complexity of Victorian furniture reflect the larger social, moral, and economic complexities of late nineteenth-century America. Ambiguity and contradiction, Ames argues, lie at the heart of the material culture of the intensely materialistic Victorians and necessitate an artifactual interpretation that is "appropriately and consciously broad and general." For instance, he contextualizes the immense and ornate sideboards of the era (fig. 15) within the "iconography of dining." These monumental forms—covered with carved depictions of hunting paraphernalia, dead animals, and symbolic hunters—literally and figuratively brought death into Victorian dining rooms in a manner that today

Figure 15 Sideboard, American, ca. 1853. Walnut with tulip poplar and white pine; marble. H. 106", W. 69", D. 28". (Courtesy, Museum of Fine Arts, Houston; museum purchase with funds provided by Anaruth and Aron S. Gordon.)

seems disturbingly graphic and violent. Sideboards functioned as the ritualized products of an "undeniably romantic and self-conscious age" whose intensely realistic imagery suggests an acknowledgment of "the earthly origins" of food and "the relationship of humankind to the rest of the animal kingdom." Ames' interpretive model is highly adaptable and offers access to cultural concepts that conventional, more deductive forms of artifact analysis would necessarily overlook.[17]

Equally creative are the museum installations of exhibit curator and designer Fred Wilson, who deliberately subverts traditional decorative arts standards by taking the most celebrated museum pieces and juxtaposing or positioning them in unexpected ways. By focusing on the deeply entrenched cultural imbalances that influence much decorative arts scholarship, he challenges both the canon and the canonizers. "Mining the Museum," a 1992 exhibition at the Maryland Historical Society, featured expensive silver teapots and wrought-iron slave shackles side-by-side in a display of early American metals. Similarly he arranged high style chairs—seating associated with wealthy, educated elites—around a whipping post that he had "mined" from the museum's own storerooms (fig. 16). As Wilson explains,

Figure 16 Furniture installation from "Mining the Museum," Maryland Historical Society, April 1992–February 1993. (Courtesy, Maryland Historical Society.)

such juxtapositions "disrupt the standard way of looking at museums" by directly confronting the fiction that they are objective or removed from specific political, historical, or aesthetic points of view. Wilson's installation—what he terms an "intervention"—exposed a shameful historical practice. At the same time, it challenged the very character of the museum and, as Hilde S. Hein elaborates, in effect charged the institution "with a deception, witting or unwitting, that belies its dedication to authenticity."[18]

The exploration of cultural diversity and multiple scholarly perspectives—what Lawrence Levine calls the "opening of the American mind"—has become increasingly common throughout many American institutions,

Figure 17 Armchair attributed to Charles-Honore Lannuier, New York, ca. 1812. Mahogany and rosewood; brass inlay. H. 35". (Courtesy, Christie's.)

Figure 18 Armchair, possibly by John Hemings, Monticello joinery, Albemarle County, Virginia, 1790–1815. Cherry; original under-upholstery and leather cover. H. 34⅞", W. 23¼", D. 19¼". (Courtesy, Colonial Williamsburg Foundation.)

including schools and universities, government organizations, public museums, and libraries. Decorative arts scholarship and, in particular, the museum displays that draw from it can only benefit from a more widespread incorporation of interpretive possibilities that offer new ways of looking at old things. The conventional decorative arts paradigm, for example, would justify the inclusion of a French-influenced New York neoclassical armchair (fig. 17) in the canon of furniture on the basis of aesthetics alone, just as it would justify the exclusion of a Virginia, French style armchair on the same grounds (fig. 18). Indeed, only the fact that the latter chair was made for Thomas Jefferson might allow for a special exemption. But a more nuanced and ultimately more fruitful interpretive approach to these two chairs would also consider other forces that shaped their creation. The Virginia chair was made in the slave joinery shop at Monticello where Jefferson obsessively managed craft production by controlling the design of furniture produced there and by altering the design of furniture imported from other places. Jefferson had little use for the highly sculpted or carved colonial forms so valued by today's curators, collectors, and dealers. Instead, like many other affluent southerners, he preferred what was commonly known as "neat and plain" style, the only difference being that he favored furniture that spoke with a French rather than an English accent. Like so many other pieces at Monticello, the chair reflects Jefferson's regionally influenced and somewhat idiosyncratic aesthetic sensibilities and speaks as well to issues concerning race, slavery, and the canonization process. An interpretive approach more fully grounded in contemporary cultural studies might, for example, explore the relationship between the non-canonical status of this chair and its maker—most likely John Hemings, who as a slave could never embody the qualities of self-determination, independence, individualism and artistic freedom associated with the iconic figure of the American craftsman. Viewed through the lens of traditional decorative arts interpretation, the New York chair stands as a fine example of sophisticated, early American design. But viewed from a transdisciplinary perspective more fully grounded in cultural studies, the Jefferson chair arguably tells a more complex and, for many modern viewers, a more meaningful and distinctly American story.[19]

These kinds of interdisciplinary, culturally grounded modes of artifact analysis—as well as an interest in the novel methods of interpretation and presentation found in other kinds of museums—are explored in the recent reinstallation of the decorative arts galleries at the Milwaukee Art Museum, which merges the museum's collection with those of the Chipstone Foundation and the Layton Art Collection. Created by a team of curators with diverse scholarly interests, the Milwaukee galleries largely abandon the specialized categories of art historical difference that are the essence of conventional decorative arts interpretation—the time-honored strategy of teaching the distinctive stylistic, structural, and regional features that distinguish one piece or group of early American furniture from another. Instead, the aim is to more broadly consider ideological and stylistic continuities, an interpretive strategy that characterizes much of the newer scholarship in other fields. The value of an interpretive method grounded in "continuities rather than ruptures," argues literary critic Jane Tompkins, lies in the potential it offers for "tapping into a storehouse of commonly held assumptions" not typically found in the more exceptional or canonical works. By employing an interpretive method that looks for value not in difference but in a text or object's "embrace of what is most widely shared," it becomes possible to find much of scholarly interest in the non-canonical as well as to find new ways of understanding the canonical (fig. 19).[20]

Figure 19 "Reinventing the Past," American collections gallery, Milwaukee Art Museum, Milwaukee, Wisconsin, 2001. (Courtesy, Milwaukee Art Museum; photo, Gavin Ashworth.)

The Milwaukee exhibitions ask new questions of the canonical objects that comprise the majority of the three collections, an approach that in turn reveals alternative interpretive strategies. The focus on cultural and stylistic continuities, for example, shows how a "William and Mary" *kast,* a "Vic-

Figure 20   "Classical Chaos," American collections gallery, Milwaukee Art Museum, Milwaukee, Wisconsin, 2001. (Courtesy, Milwaukee Art Museum; photo, Gavin Ashworth.)

Figure 21   "Sign Language," American collections gallery, Milwaukee Art Museum, Milwaukee, Wisconsin, 2001. (Courtesy, Milwaukee Art Museum; photo, Gavin Ashworth.)

torian" parlor chair, and a "Chippendale" desk-and-bookcase all share a fundamental allegiance to the precepts of classical order and geometry, or how a Philadelphia rococo side chair and Eero Saarinan's contemporary "Womb Chair" both are linked to decidedly more chaotic themes found in classical literature and art (fig. 20). This interpretive process also leads to an expanded understanding of the complex symbolic interactions between

Figure 22 "Of the Maker, By the Maker, and For the Maker," American collections gallery, Milwaukee Art Museum, Milwaukee, Wisconsin, 2001. (Courtesy, Milwaukee Art Museum; photo, Gavin Ashworth.)

people and artifacts and the ways in which, for instance, signatures on furniture may simultaneously reflect and shape the identities of owners and makers alike (fig. 21).

In considering other issues, such as to what extent early American furniture was genuinely "American," the curatorial team drew from the work of a range of scholars to look beyond the traditional decorative arts aesthetic. Edward S. Cooke's methodological analysis of chair making in rural New England, particularly his emphasis on the distinctive web of relations "that inseparably linked the furniture maker's craft decisions to the unique social and economic contexts in which they were made," offered a useful interpretive model. For example, the earliest furniture makers, including immigrant joiners such as Ralph Mason and Henry Messinger, were able to replicate familiar British furniture designs for use in relatively insulated cultural settings. Later American furniture makers—including members of the famed Townsend and Goddard families of Newport—faced ever more complex social economies in which uneven access to cosmopolitan fashion systems and varying degrees of artifact and artisan movement led to the increased diversity of American furniture designs (fig. 22). According to traditional decorative arts standards, a Colchester high chest (fig. 23) is eccentric, "rural," and stylistically derivative of forms produced in urban centers such as Boston or Salem (fig. 24). Understood as the product of a specific social economy, however, the piece emerges as a distinctively American object whose meaning and form were shaped by a "web of relations and activities" unique to its locale. Milwaukee's decorative arts galleries seek to move beyond a presentation of the evolution of form, style, and construction—as is the decorative arts norm—and set aside the rigid cultural hierarchies and specialized art historical jargon found in so many museum displays. Rather, these spaces explore alternative interpretive possibilities that may

Figure 23 High chest of drawers, Colchester, Connecticut, ca. 1785. Cherry with white pine. H. 82½", W. 41¾", D. 21½". (Chipstone Foundation; photo, Sumpter Priddy, III.)

Figure 24 High chest of drawers, Boston or Salem, Massachusetts, 1755–1775. Mahogany with white pine. H. 85½", W. 40½", D. 20¾". (Courtesy, Milwaukee Art Museum.)

more effectively engage contemporary museum visitors, especially those who may arrive thinking that, beyond stylistic evolution, "a chair is a chair is a chair."[21]

Ultimately, museums that exhibit and, in the process, interpret American decorative arts need to more critically assess traditional modes of artifact analysis and to draw more directly from scholarship in other areas of cultural studies and exhibition innovations in other museums. "Themed" displays, which invariably claim to offer a new perspective, need to do more than just re-order or re-describe conventional interpretive paradigms. In a process literary critic Henry Louis Gates, Jr., terms the "reconstruction of instruction," the American furniture canon—like the literary canon—must either be expanded, dismissed altogether, or thoughtfully reconfigured into entirely new canons that reflect a perspective markedly different from the received tradition. Just as the pioneering museum displays were distinctive expressions of late nineteenth-century America, contemporary decorative arts installations need to reflect the issues and concerns relevant to early twenty-first century America.[22]

ACKNOWLEDGMENTS   The authors thank Glenn Adamson, Luke Beckerdite, Edward S. Cooke, and Gerald W. R. Ward for their critical comments on this work and Robert F. Trent for his research on the formative American furniture histories and installations.

1. Scholars and curators of decorative arts have long debated the value of aesthetic evaluation and cultural hierarchies. Michael J. Ettema, "Forum—History, Nostalgia, and American Furniture," *Winterthur Portfolio* 17, nos. 2/3 (summer/fall 1982): 135–44. Ettema argued that the antiquarian approach should be abandoned in favor of interpretive methods that placed history and culture, not objects and aesthetics, at the center. The essay provoked a wide range of responses. Some scholars acknowledged Ettema's conclusion that the field was not living up to its potential, some voiced concerns that he was not offering new directions that were in accord with the traditional mission of art museums, whereas others rejected his argument that interpretive strategies based in aesthetics were necessarily more limited than methods grounded in cultural history (see *Winterthur Portfolio* 17, no. 4 [winter 1982]: 259–68, and *Winterthur Portfolio* 18, no. 1[spring 1983]: 80–90.)Wendy Kaplan, "R. T. H. Halsey: An Ideology of Collecting American Decorative Arts," *Winterthur Portfolio* 17, no. 1 (spring 1982): 43–53. For a discussion of the divide between curators and scholars, see Jules D. Prown, "Can the Farmer and the Cowman Still Be Friends" in *Learning From Things: Method and Theory of Material Culture Studies,* edited by W. David Kingery (Washington, D. C.: Smithsonian Institution Press, 1996), pp.19–27.

2. R. T. H. Halsey and Charles O. Cornelius, *A Handbook of the American Wing*, 4th ed. (New York: Metropolitan Museum of Art, 1928), p. xv. Notable examples of earlier scholarship, much of it well researched, include Irving Whitehall Lyon, *The Colonial Furniture of New England* (Boston: Houghton Mifflin Co., 1891); Esther Singleton, *The Furniture of our Forefathers* (New York: Doubleday, Page and Co., 1908); Luke Vincent Lockwood, *Colonial Furniture in America* (New York: Charles Scribner's Sons, 1913); and Frances Clary Morse, *Furniture of the Olden Time* (New York: MacMillan Co., 1917). For a thoughtful overview of early decorative arts installations, see Elizabeth Stillinger, *The Antiquers: The Lives and Careers, The Deals, The Finds, The Collections of the Men and Women Who Were Responsible for the Changing Taste in American Antiques, 1850–1930* (New York: Alfred A. Knopf, 1980).

3. Stillinger, *The Antiquers,* p. 124.

4. "The Editor's Attic," *Antiques* 16, no. 2 (August 1929): 101.

5. *Girl Scouts Loan Exhibition of Eighteenth and Early Nineteenth Century Furniture and Glass* (New York: Girl Scouts, Inc., 1929), preface.

6 Quoted in Stephen Conn, *Museums and American Intellectual Life, 1876–1926* (Chicago, Ill.: University of Chicago Press, 1998), p. 241.

7. See Lawrence Levine, *Highbrow/Lowbrow: The Emergence of Cultural Hierarchy in America* (Cambridge, Mass.: Harvard University Press, 1988), pp. 185–208. Neil Harris, "Museum, Merchandising, and Popular Taste: The Struggle for Influence," in *Material Culture and the Study of American Life,* edited by Ian M. G. Quimby (Winterthur, Del.: Winterthur Museum, 1978), p. 142.

8. Charles Over Cornelius, *Early American Furniture* (New York: Century Co., 1926), p. 16. Henry Watson West and Florence N. Levy, *Catalogue of an Exhibition of American Paintings, Furniture, Silver and Other Objects of Art* (New York: Metropolitan Museum of Art, 1909), p. 29.

9. Thomas Hamilton Ormsbee, *Early American Furniture Makers: A Social and Biographical Study* (New York: Tudor Publishing Co., 1930), pp. 37–38. On the formation of white racial identity and its dependence on the marginalization of the non-white, see Matthew Frye Jacobson, *Whiteness of a Different Color: European Immigrants and the Alchemy of Race* (Cambridge, Mass.: Harvard University Press, 1998).

10. Patricia West, *Domesticating History: The Political Origins of America's House Museums* (Washington, D. C.: Smithsonian Institution Press, 1999), pp. 48–50. On the influence of gender in twentieth-century decorative arts studies, see Catherine L. Whalen, "American Decorative Arts Studies at Yale and Winterthur: The Politics of Gender, Gentility, and Academia," *Decorative Arts* 9, no.1 (fall/winter 2001–2002): 108–44. The emergence of a more masculinized period room aesthetic and an increasing emphasis on the manliness of American craft traditions were associated, as West argues, with the diminished status of female museum professionals throughout the late nineteenth and early twentieth centuries. Yet women, including Helen Comstock and Alice Winchester, played prominent roles as the authors of popular histories and publications of American furniture. Future scholarship on the gender politics of early decorative arts might benefit by examining the connections between the relative prominence of women as authors of decorative arts publications and female dominance of the literary marketplace more generally.

11. Cornelius, *Early American Furniture,* p. 105. On the "elevation of the craftsman" and the link to the founding fathers, see Kaplan, "R. T. H. Halsey," p. 51. Edmund Stratton Holloway, *American Furniture and Decoration Colonial and Federal* (Philadelphia, Pa.: J. B. Lippincott, 1928), pp. 8–9.

12. Paul Dimaggio, "Cultural Boundaries and Structural Change: The Extension of the High Culture Model to Theater, Opera, and the Dance, 1900–1940," in *Cultivating Differences: Symbolic Boundaries and the Making of Inequality,* edited by Michèle Lamont and Marcel Fournier (Chicago, Ill.: University of Chicago Press, 1992), p. 47. David Carr, "Balancing Act: Ethics, Mission, and the Public Trust," in *Museum News* 80, no. 5 (September/October 2001): 29–31. Harold K. Skramstad, Jr., "Interpreting Material Culture: A View from the Other Side of the Glass," in Quimby, ed., *Material Culture and the Study of American Life,* p. 181.

13. For an overview and analysis of the key developments and issues in twentieth-century literary studies, see Paul Lauter, *Canons and Contexts* (Oxford: Oxford University Press, 1991).

14. Gary B. Nash, Charlotte Crabtree, and Ross E. Dunn, *History on Trial: Culture Wars and The Teaching of the Past* (New York: Vintage Books, 1997), p. 40. As Robert F. Trent has suggested, furniture scholarship could be enriched by incorporating post-colonial theory that considers American art and culture as the products of a broader, international colonial context (correspondence with the authors, June 10, 2002).

15. Edward S. Cooke, "Study from the Perspective of the Maker," in *Perspectives on American Furniture,* edited by Gerald W. R. Ward (Newark: University of Delaware for the Winterthur Museum, 1985), pp. 115–16.

16. Albert Sack, *Fine Points of Furniture, Early American* (New York: Crown Publishers, 1950). This formula has since been augmented to include "superior" and "masterpiece." Scholarship in the field could benefit from greater consideration of the role played by the antiques market in the emergence of the American decorative arts canon. A number of the most influential dealers were first or second generation immigrants who sold American antiques to a growing market composed of clients hoping to become part of the cultured classes. Analysis of the emerging market in American antiques might, for example, incorporate recent scholarship on the early film industry, which was in many ways influenced by similar cultural dynamics and desires, or pay closer attention to the broader relationship between the market and the preoccupation in the culture at large with issues related to class, ethnicity, and assimilation. Henry Glassie, *Material Culture* (Bloomington: Indiana University Press, 1999), pp. 1–3. Jules D. Prown, "Can the Farmer and the Cowman Still Be Friends?" p. 20. Glassie, *Material Culture,* pp. 1–3.

17. Laurel Thatcher Ulrich, "Furniture as Social History: Gender, Property, and Memory in the Decorative Arts," in *American Furniture,* edited by Luke Beckerdite (Hanover, N. H.: University of New England Press for the Chipstone Foundation, 1995), pp. 39–69; Amanda Carson Banks, *Birth Chairs, Midwives, and Medicine* (Jackson: University Press of Mississippi, 1999). Kenneth L. Ames, *Death in the Dining Room* (Philadelphia, Pa.: Temple University Press, 1992), pp. 2–6 and passim.

18. Steven C. Dubin, *Displays of Power: Controversy in the American Museum from the Enola Gay to Sensation* (New York: New York University Press, 1999), p. 14. Hilde S. Hein, *The Museum in Transition: A Philosophical Perspective* (Washington, D. C.: Smithsonian Institution Press, 2000), p. 105. One particularly innovative example of re-thinking museum exhibits is the Museum of Jurassic Technology in Los Angeles, a fascinating and, at times, surrealistic place that "deploys all the traditional signs of a museum's institutional authority—meticulous presentation,

exhaustive captions, hushed lighting, and state-of-the-art armature—all to subvert the notions of the authoritative as it applies not only to itself but to any museum" (Lawrence Weschler, *Mr. Wilson's Cabinet of Wonder: Pronged Ants, Horned Humans, Mice on Toast, and Other Marvels of Jurassic Technology* [New York: Vintage Books, 1995], p. 40).

19. Lawrence Levine, *The Opening of the American Mind* (Boston, Mass.: Beacon Press, 1996). This book was written as a direct response to the politically and culturally conservative interpretation in Allan Bloom, *The Closing of the American Mind* (New York: Simon & Schuster, 1987). Ronald L. Hurst and Jonathan Prown, *Southern Furniture, 1680–1830: The Colonial Williamsburg Collection* (New York: Harry N. Abrams, Inc., 1997), pp.142–46. The widely held belief in the non-canonical status of southern furniture makers from the American furniture canon is epitomized in Carl Bridenbaugh, *The Colonial Craftsman* (New York: New York University Press, 1950).

20. Jane Tompkins, *Sensational Designs: The Cultural Work of American Fiction, 1790–1860* (New York: Oxford University Press, 1989), p. xvi.

21. Edward S. Cooke, Jr., "The Social Economy of the Preindustrial Joiner in Western Connecticut, 1750–1800," in Beckerdite, ed., *American Furniture* (1995), pp. 113–14; and Edward S. Cooke, Jr., *Making Furniture in Preindustrial America: The Social Economy of Newtown and Woodbury, Connecticut* (Baltimore, Md.: Johns Hopkins University Press, 1996), pp. 3–12.

22. Henry Louis Gates, Jr., *Loose Canons: Notes on the Culture Wars* (Oxford: Oxford University Press, 1992), p. 9; Lauter, *Canons and Contexts,* pp. 256–70; and Lillian Robinson, "Canons to the Left of Them," in *In The Canon's Mouth* (Bloomington: Indiana University Press, 1997), pp. 120–23.

Figure 1 Cupboard head attributed to John Taylor, Cambridge, Massachusetts, 1640–1670. Oak and pine with pine. H. 31", W. 51", D. 18¾". (Private collection; photo, Jim Schneck.) The panels have lozenges that were carved with a V-shaped parting tool, and rondels and scrolls carved with a gouge. This effective but simple carving has no exact cognate in New England joinery, even though incised lozenges were a common motif throughout the region.

Robert F. Trent and Michael Podmaniczky

An Early Cupboard Fragment from the Harvard College Joinery Tradition

▼ THE UPPER CASE or head of a seventeenth-century New England cupboard (fig. 1) illuminates a thorny interpretive problem in American furniture history, documenting the transition from an early carved phase of mannerism to a later one characterized by the use of applied ornament. A major stumbling block in this quandary is identifying the precise date at which the applied-ornament style was transmitted from London to Boston. Building upon the pioneering research and attributions of Benno M. Forman, Robert F. Trent has asserted that London-trained joiners Ralph Mason (arrived 1635, d. 1678) and Henry Messinger (arrived 1641, d. 1681) and London-trained turner Thomas Edsall (arrived 1635, d. 1676) introduced the style during the mid-1630s. Some scholars have expressed doubt that the earliest Boston pieces with London-style appliqués (see fig. 2) date before the 1650s, but more recent research by Trent supports his hypothesis.[1]

Setting aside this dating controversy, an additional problem resides in assessing the influence of the Boston style on joiners working in surrounding towns in eastern Massachusetts. Many of them came from provincial areas in England and probably were working in the carved style when they arrived in New England in the 1630s or 1640s. Were they or their apprentices influenced by the applied-ornament style in the form of London or Boston case furniture, and if so, when? Answers to these questions may not be forthcoming in every instance. Third-generation colonists commissioned the vast majority of surviving New England mannerist furniture in the heyday of applied ornament. Insofar as many Massachusetts joinery traditions are concerned, no case pieces in this hypothetical earlier carved manner may survive. The cupboard fragment illustrated in figure 1 is a significant exception, expanding both the chronology and vocabulary of the Cambridge joinery tradition.

The Cambridge Paradigm
The furniture attributed to this tradition consists of a small group of cupboards in the applied-ornament style. Trent has asserted that these objects represent the work of three successive Harvard College joiners: John Taylor (arrived 1638, d. 1683), John Palfrey (m. 1664, d. 1689), and Zechariah Hicks, Jr. (1651–1752). As the only group of joiners with an official institutional affiliation, the Harvard College masters were undoubtedly important workmen. According to Taylor's gravestone, he worked as both a joiner and college butler until his death in 1677. At his death, he owned two pounds ten shillings worth of "Joyners Tools" as well as fifty-eight pounds

Figure 2 Chest of drawers with doors attributed to the Ralph Mason and Henry Messinger shop tradition, Boston, Massachusetts, 1635–1650. White oak, red oak, chestnut, maple, black walnut, cedar, cedrella, snakewood, rosewood, and lignum vitae with red oak, white oak, chestnut, and white pine. H. 49", W. 45 3/16", D. 23 3/8". (Courtesy, Mabel Brady Garvan Collection, Yale University Art Gallery.) The turnings on this piece are attributed to Thomas Edsall.

in cash that he kept in a "great cupboard." Taylor and Braintree, Massachusetts, joiner William Savell (arrived ca. 1639, d. 1669) worked on the first college building from about 1638 to 1641. The cupboard illustrated in figure 18 has unusual back construction that is related to work attributed to Savell.[2]

The second joiner, John Palfrey, married Rebecca Boardman, whose father William was college cook. Palfrey subsequently trained his brother-in-law William Boardman (1657–1696), who later lived in and may have built the Boardman house in nearby Saugus. Palfrey assumed the office of college joiner by 1679, when he made "1 doz. Stooles for College Library." Later records confirm his status as the institutional joiner in 1683. Palfrey's inventory taken in 1689 lists "Joyners Tools" and "Timber for Joyner Worke." His daughter Rebecca married carpenter Joseph Hicks whose brother Zechariah Jr., was the third college joiner. Palfrey's other daughter Martha married joiner Benjamin Goddard (1668–1748), and the couple moved to Charlestown in 1712.[3]

Hicks was born into a woodworking family in Cambridge. In 1690, he became the college joiner, and his father Zechariah became the college carpenter. After the elder Hicks died in 1702, Zechariah Jr. assumed responsibility for several building projects in Cambridge including the prison (built ca. 1701–1703) and the courthouse (built ca. 1721).[4]

Figure 3 Cupboard attributed to the Harvard College joiners, Cambridge, Massachusetts, 1660–1670. Oak and maple with pine. H. 51⅝", W. 45", D. 19½". (Courtesy, Concord Museum.)

Figure 4 Rear view of the cupboard illustrated in fig. 3.

A cupboard that reputedly belonged to Gregory Stone (arrived 1637, d. 1672) of Cambridge (fig. 3) is the cornerstone of this attribution. Like all of the cupboards in this group, it displays a curious mix of retrograde and avant-garde construction and ornamental traits. The upper and lower cases are sealed on the rear surfaces with large, chamfered pine boards nailed to the framing members (fig. 4), a less formal alternative to sealing the cases with feathered panels held in grooves. In addition, the sides of each case have one large panel rather than two or more—a conservative feature in seventeenth-century joinery (fig. 5). The drawer construction of the Cambridge cupboards is similar, although not identical, to that of Boston case pieces in the London style. The front corners of the drawers are joined with one large dovetail (fig. 6), and the rear corners are secured with wrought nails. Each drawer bottom is one large chamfered pine board set into a groove in the front and nailed on the sides and back.[5]

Figure 5 Side view of the cupboard illustrated in fig. 3. Some of the side panels are made of pine rather than oak.

Like their Boston counterparts, the Cambridge cupboards also display a full panoply of accomplished turned pillars and applied ornaments such as half-columns and bosses (figs. 7, 8). Although these components could have been purchased from local tradesmen such as John Gove (m. 1658, d. 1704), who had family and professional ties to all three Harvard College masters, the pillars and appliqués are probably the work of Boston turners.[6]

Figure 6 Detail of the dovetailing of a drawer in the cupboard illustrated in fig. 3.

Figure 7 Detail of a pillar on the cupboard illustrated in fig. 3.

Figure 8 Detail of a pair of half-columns on the cupboard illustrated in fig. 3.

The Boston cupboard illustrated in figure 9 has pillars (fig. 10) and half-columns (figs. 9, 11) similar to those on case pieces attributed to the Harvard College joiners, but its construction is quite different. This distinctive object has a trapezoidal storage compartment flanked by turned pillars and a lower case with drawers. The edge and base moldings of the lower case relate directly to those on the earliest Boston chests of drawers, although the cupboard probably dates from the 1670s. The drawers of the cupboard have two dovetails at each front corner (fig. 12), a standard feature on Boston drawers of this height (deeper drawers in related case pieces sometimes have three dovetails at each front corner, and shallow drawers occasionally only have one).[7]

The Boston/Cambridge Quandary

Given the proximity of Cambridge and Boston, it should come as no surprise that metropolitan furniture influenced Cambridge work. In most

Figure 9 Joined cupboard with four drawers attributed to the Ralph Mason and Henry Messinger joinery tradition and the Thomas Edsall turning tradition, Boston, Massachusetts, 1675–1690. Oak, maple, cedar, walnut, and chestnut with oak and white pine. H. 55 5/8", W. 49 1/8", D. 21 3/4". (Chipstone Foundation; photo, Gavin Ashworth.) The frieze ornaments, top of the upper case, several small moldings, and the knobs are modern restorations. The original owners of the cupboard were Isaac (1650–1731) and Elizabeth (Tallman) (d. 1701) Lawton of Portsmouth, Rhode Island, who were married in 1673.

Figure 10 Detail of a pillar on the cupboard illustrated in fig. 9.

Figure 11 Detail of a pair of half-columns on the cupboard illustrated in fig. 9. These small half-columns differ from those found on the Cambridge group, which are similar to those on the upper section of the cupboard illustrated in fig. 9.

Figure 12 Detail of the dovetailing of a drawer in the cupboard illustrated in fig. 9.

instances, the products of the Harvard College joiners are easily separable from those of their Boston counterparts. Two cupboards formerly attributed to Cambridge are exceptions because they have construction details that differ significantly from those of other case pieces in the group. The example shown in figure 13 has a drawer with one dovetail at each front corner, but the bottom has a shallow chamfer along the back edge (fig. 14). Other atypical details include the framed panels that seal the rear facade of the lower case (fig. 15) and the use of two panels on the side frames of the

Figure 13 Joined cupboard, Boston or Cambridge, Massachusetts, 1670–1700. Oak and maple with oak and pine. H. 60", W. 49¾", D. 23¼". (Courtesy, Museum of Fine Arts, Houston; Bayou Bend Collection, museum purchase funds provided by the Theta Charity Antiques Show.) Two corbels, some applied moldings and plaques, the knobs, and the bottoms of the posts are modern restorations. The pillars are slender versions of those on several cupboards that clearly are part of the Cambridge group.

Figure 14 Detail of the dovetailing of a drawer in the cupboard illustrated in fig. 13.

Figure 15 Rear view of the cupboard illustrated in fig. 13. On most of the cupboards in the Cambridge group, the rear façade of the lower case is sealed with nailed-on boards.

Figure 16 Side view of the cupboard illustrated in fig. 13. On most of the cupboards in the Cambridge group, the side frames of the lower case have one panel rather than two.

Figure 17 Chest of drawers attributed to the Ralph Mason and Henry Messinger joinery tradition and the Thomas Edsall turning tradition, Boston, Massachusetts, 1640–1670. Oak, cedrella, cedar, walnut, and ebony with oak. H. 51¼", W. 47³⁄₁₆", D. 23¹⁄₁₆". (Courtesy, Museum of Fine Arts, Boston, bequest of Charles Hitchcock Tyler.)

lower case (fig. 16). The frieze of the upper case, which features three corbels separated by dentil courses, relates most closely to that of an early Boston chest of drawers (fig. 17).[8]

The other cupboard with a related frieze (fig. 18) has a lower case with two doors that are not separated by a muntin; the side frames have one horizontal panel over two vertical ones. The construction of the backs of the upper and lower cases is also unusual. The upper case has one horizontal, feather-edged board that engages grooves on the top and sides and is nailed to an internal rail at the bottom. The lower case has multiple horizontal boards, the outer of which engage grooves in the posts and are nailed to internal rails at the top and the bottom (fig. 19). These nailing rails also function as bearing surfaces for the top of the case and floor of the storage compartment under the drawer. Although the back of this cupboard has no Boston parallel, it relates to the vertically-oriented "clapboard backs" on early oak *kasten* made in the vicinity of New York City and to the backs of chests attributed to the Savell shops of Braintree, Massachusetts. Given their unusual structural and ornamental details, this cupboard and the example illustrated in figure 13 could be Boston products or late Cambridge pieces influenced by that Boston work.[9]

Figure 18 Joined cupboard, Boston or Cambridge, Massachusetts, 1650–1690. Oak, maple, and walnut with oak and pine. H. 61", W. 52½", D. 23". (Private collection; photo, Gavin Ashworth.) The pillars, knobs, and some applied moldings and plaques are modern restorations. The cupboard was reputedly found in Ipswich, Massachusetts.

Figure 19 Rear view of the cupboard illustrated in fig. 18.

A Piece of the Puzzle

The cupboard fragment (fig. 1) provides new information on the Cambridge school and the succession of Harvard College joiners responsible for that tradition. It is in remarkably good condition and appears to have an undisturbed surface with accumulated grime but no later resin coatings. Most of the joints have never been disassembled or re-glued, and all the pins and nails are intact.

The fragment is the upper case of a two-part cupboard, and the front posts of its frieze have holes, presumably for the round upper tenons of large, turned pillars. It is unlikely that the posts had pendants because there is no imprint for them, nor is there any glue residue in the holes. The front edge of the top board has a scratch-stock molding resembling two quarter-rounds and a fillet. This same molding appears on the upper edge of the frieze rail, although it is barely discernible because of the shadow created by the top (fig. 22). The maker may have intended this molding to be on the bottom edge and accidentally inverted the frieze rail during assembly. The frieze rail, the two façade muntins, and the lower front rail have a second scratch-stock molding resembling astragals separated by a flat

Figure 20   Detail of the left door of the cupboard fragment illustrated in fig. 1. Each door hinges on ½" pins set into holes in the top and bottom of the stile. These pins engage holes in the case. The joiner clearly drilled the holes to make the doors recessed on the hinge side and flush with the façade on the other.

Figure 21   Photos showing how the joiner ran the groove for the panel in the outer stile of the left door of the cupboard fragment illustrated in fig. 1.

Figure 22   Detail of the chamfering on the right upper post of the cupboard fragment illustrated in fig. 1. The slight chamfer at the juncture of the top rail and the suspended posts is unusual, but it appears to be the result of a mistake rather than a stylistic conceit. This detail is barely discernible and may represent the joiner's attempt to dress up the posts adjacent to the mistakenly inverted frieze rail.

groove—a profile favored by early joiners in Windsor, Connecticut, and later joiners in the Connecticut River towns of western Massachusetts. The scratch-stock-generated quirked bead on the stiles and rails of the doors and framing members of the sides also has parallels in Connecticut River Valley work.[10]

The chamfering of various structural components is even more distinctive. The stiles and rails of the doors and the side and top edges of the framing members around the central panel have chamfers that taper out at each end, rather than those that terminate in ogee-shaped "lamb's tongues" or shallow V-shaped cuts known as "pips." Seventeenth-century case pieces

Figure 23 Detail of an open mortise-and-tenon joint on the underside of the upper right post of the cupboard fragment illustrated in fig. 1.

with chamfers treated exclusively in this manner are rare. Later cupboards in the Cambridge group differ in having framing members with a combination of edge details including tapered chamfers, stopped chamfers, and scratch-stock moldings. They also have applied mitered moldings on the drawer fronts and the doors and central panels of the upper cases. Whether this departure is the result of Boston influence or indigenous stylistic evolution is not immediately apparent, but simple tapered chamfers are associated with the carved phase of mannerism. This supports the theory that the cupboard fragment represents an early phase of the Harvard College joinery tradition.[11]

Several features of the cupboard fragment link it with later examples in the group. The tenons for the frieze rail and upper side rails are exposed at the top and bottom of each joint (fig. 23). Although these open joints are not visible once the top is nailed in place and the pillars are installed, they are one of the more coarse construction details shared by most of the Cambridge cupboards. Jettied corner posts usually extend below the frieze and side rails, but there is no evidence that the ones on the fragment were shortened at a later date.

Other diagnostic details can be observed in the joinery and orientation of the two doors. Rather than hanging completely in plane with the façade, each door is recessed on the hinged side and is flush on the other (fig. 20). The hinged side is set into a rabbet approximately three-eighths of an inch deep, and the doors rotate on wooden pins. The opposite stile is rabbeted on the back to mate with the rabbet on the adjacent muntin. Three other cupboards attributed to the Harvard College joiners have doors framed and hung in a similar manner (see figs. 3, 24). The panels of the doors are trapped in a conventional manner, but the grooves in the stiles do not extend through the ends as they often do in seventeenth-century New England joinery. Evidently, the joiner chopped the mortises in the stiles and then cut the grooves with a conventional plow plane (fig. 21). He started the groove at the surface at one end and slowly worked the nose of the plow down into the groove, ending the stroke in the opposite mortise. Repeated passes of the plane produced a full-depth groove at the far end of the stroke but left some bulk at the beginning which had to be removed with a chisel. The joiner used the same tool to cut one shoulder of each of the door rabbets, but he appears to have used a grooving plane with a deeper setting to cut the other shoulder.[12]

The use of wide pine boards for the top, back, and bottom of the case is ambiguous in an Anglo-American context, but it does attest to the availability of sawn lumber in New England. More significant is the use of nails to attach the backboards to the rear framing members, a quicker and cheaper alternative to trapping them in grooves in the rear stiles and rails.

Ultimately there is little doubt that this fragment is a carved predecessor of the Cambridge cupboards with applied ornament. Although most of the intact examples resemble the Stone cupboard (fig. 3), there are two important and intriguing variants. The first is represented by a cupboard formerly owned by early Boston collector Dwight Blaney (fig. 24) and a similar one in the collection of the Colonial Williamsburg Foundation. Both pieces have drawers with planed moldings on their upper and lower edges. It is possible that planed moldings preceded applied ones in the development of the Harvard College joiners' vocabulary. The cupboard

Figure 24 Joined cupboard with drawers attributed to the Harvard College joiners, Cambridge, Massachusetts, 1670–1690. Oak, maple, and cedar with oak and pine. H. 52", W. 46", D. 20". (Private collection; photo, David Stansbury.)

Figure 25 Joined cupboard attributed to the Harvard College joiners, Cambridge, Massachusetts, 1670–1700. Oak and maple with oak and pine. H. 53 7/8", W. 46 5/8", D. 20 1/8". (Courtesy, Winterthur Museum.)

Figure 26 Detail of the left corbel of a Cambridge cupboard (overall not illustrated). (Private collection; photo, Gavin Ashworth.) The corbel is decorated with the carved letter "I".

Figure 27 Detail of the middle corbel of a Cambridge cupboard. (Private collection; photo, Gavin Ashworth.) The corbel is decorated with the carved letter "M".

illustrated in figure 25 represents the second variant and is the only Cambridge example with a trapezoidal storage compartment in the upper case and an open shelf below. This design permitted the use of two different pillars—tapering vases above and straight-sided ones below. The use of large panels with V-shaped mitered break-outs and plaques along the centers of all sides is another detail not found on other case pieces in the Cambridge group.

The framing of the storage compartment is also distinctive. To allow the rails to meet the posts at ninety-degree angles, the joiner made the corner posts pentagonal, a technique common on cupboards and trapezoidal joined tables from northern Essex County, Massachusetts. In contrast, the maker of the Boston cupboard shown in figure 9 toe-nailed the rear ends of the horizontal side rails to rectangular rear posts, a crude technique that is surprising in an urban object.

One other Cambridge cupboard conforms to the format of the Stone example (fig. 3) but has three frieze corbels carved with floriated initials (figs. 26–28). These initials resemble mortised initial blocks used in printing, but they also have leafage that relates to the carving on the cupboard fragment (fig. 1). Further analysis of this carving may assist in the identification of other Cambridge case pieces that may surface in the future.

Figure 28 Detail of the right corbel of a Cambridge cupboard. (Private collection; photo, Gavin Ashworth.) The corbel is decorated with the carved letter "B".

Figure 29 Cupboard head illustrated in figure 1 with its restored lower case and upper pillars. The reproduction base and pillars made to display the cupboard fragment are somewhat conjectural, but many features were not difficult to infer; the Stone cupboard (fig. 3) provided the basic design. Decisions about construction and ornament were based on the assumption that the fragment was made before Boston styles influenced the Harvard College joinery tradition. The lower case was decorated with chamfers and carving matching that on the upper case; the drawer front was decorated with planed moldings; and the pillars were based on English examples of comparable date rather than the tapered urns seen on later Boston and Cambridge cupboards. The rear of the lower case was sealed with nailed-on, chamfered boards, and the front corners of the drawer were joined with one large dovetail.

New Insights on Cambridge Joinery

The cupboard fragment with carved decoration probably dates from the working career of John Taylor, the first Harvard College joiner. Presumably, it embodies the style in which he had been trained in England. It also seems likely that the Cambridge school's transition to a Boston-influenced, applied-ornament style occurred when John Palfrey took over as college joiner about 1670–1675. This coincided with similar stylistic shifts in Essex County, notably in the Symonds shop tradition based in Salem and the Ipswich-Newbury tradition responsible for numerous cupboards and other case pieces. With these dating guidelines in place, a more firm chronology for the development of certain Massachusetts joinery styles can be established. One must keep in mind, however, that some shop traditions persisted in making carved mannerist furniture until well into the eighteenth century and that a stylistic shift in eastern Massachusetts does not necessarily provide a model for Connecticut or western Massachusetts.[13]

1. Benno M. Forman, "Urban Aspects of Massachusetts Furniture in the Late Seventeenth Century," in *Country Cabinetwork and Simple City Furniture,* edited by Ian M. G. Quimby (Charlottesville: University Press of Virginia for the Winterthur Museum, 1969), pp. 1–33. Robert F. Trent, "Furniture in the New World: The Seventeenth Century," in *American Fur-*

niture With Related Decorative Arts, 1660–1830 (New York: Hudson Hills Press, 1991), pp. 25–26. Doubts about the early date of this object were raised in Gerald W. R. Ward, *American Case Furniture in the Mabel Brady Garvan and Other Collections at Yale University* (New Haven, Conn.: Yale University Art Gallery, 1988), pp. 125–28.

2. Robert F. Trent, "The Joiners and Joinery of Middlesex County, Massachusetts, 1630–1670," in *Arts of the Anglo-American Community in the Seventeenth Century,* edited by Ian M. G. Quimby (Charlottesville: University Press of Virginia for the Winterthur Museum, 1969), pp. 126–33. Peter Follansbee and John D. Alexander, Jr., "Seventeenth-Century Joinery from Braintree, Massachusetts: The Savell Shop Tradition," in *American Furniture,* edited by Luke Beckerdite (Hanover, N.H.: University Press of New England for the Chipstone Foundation, 1996), pp. 81–104.

3. Trent, "The Joiners and Joinery of Middlesex County," pp. 40, 65. Abbott Lowell Cummings, *Massachusetts and Its First Period Houses* (Boston, Mass.: Colonial Society of Massachusetts, 1979), pp. 184–86.

4. Trent, "The Joiners and Joinery of Middlesex County," pp. 40–41.

5. Ibid., pp. 127–30.

6. *The Concord Museum – Decorative Arts from a New England Collection,* edited by David Wood (Concord, Mass.: Concord Museum, 1996), pp. 1–2.

7. Robert F. Trent, "The Lawton Cupboard: A Unique Masterpiece of Early Boston Turning and Joinery," *Maine Antique Digest* 16, no. 3 (March 1986): 1c–4c.

8. For more on the cupboard illustrated in fig. 13, see David B. Warren, Michael K. Brown, Elizabeth Ann Coleman, and Emily Ballew Neff, *American Decorative Arts and Paintings in the Bayou Bend Collection* (Houston, Tx.: Museum of Fine Arts, Houston, 1998), p. 19.

9. Peter Kenny, Francis Safford, and Gilbert T. Vincent, *American Kasten* (New York: Metropolitan Museum of Art, 1991), p. 43. Follansbee and Alexander, "Seventeenth-Century Joinery from Braintree," pp. 81–104.

10. For more on Connecticut River Valley joinery, see *The Great River: Art and Society of the Connecticut River Valley,* edited by Gerald W. R. Ward and William N. Hosley (Hartford, Conn.: Wadsworth Atheneum, 1985), pp. 192–206; and Philip Zea and Susan Flynt, *Hadley Chests* (Deerfield, Mass.: Pocumtuck Valley Memorial Association, 1992).

11. For a convenient summary of chamfering, scratch-stock moldings, and intersecting framing members, see Victor Chinnery, *Oak Furniture: The British Tradition* (Woodbridge, Suffolk, Eng.: Antique Collectors' Club, 1984), pp. 112–14, 183. When used in combination with more elaborate scratch-stock or planed moldings, chamfers on framing members can intersect in mason's miters, in true miters, or with biased tenon shoulders. When chamfers are supplanted by combinations of edge moldings, the ends of framing members can have run-out moldings that butt against unmolded sections of complementary framing members achieved by run-outs of scratch-stock moldings that are the equivalent of stopped chamfers.

12. A cupboard formerly in the collection of Elizabeth and Miodrag Blagojevich and now owned by the Colonial Williamsburg Foundation also has doors framed and hung like those of the fragment and examples shown in figs. 3 and 25. It is conceivable that the joiner was concerned about the structural integrity of the door stiles, which are 1¼ inches thicker than the upper and lower rails (see fig. 21). He may have been reluctant to rabbet the back edges of the hinge stiles due to the large pin holes and mortises in those framing members. He may also have intended to chop a lock mortise in the jamb stile. Nevertheless, the layout and hanging of the doors in the earlier cupboards is unusual by period standards. Most joiners used a plow plane to cut grooves for panels. The grooves generally run the entire length of the framing members and are visible as voids on the ends of the stiles. Later cabinetmakers often plugged the voids for cosmetic purposes, but most seventeenth-century workmen left them open. Most grooving planes were used in a plow with an adjustable fence. Although this makes it impossible to prove that the workman used two grooving planes with dedicated depths to cut the rabbets, the uniformity of the two shoulder depths throughout the piece suggests that he did.

13. Trent, "The Joiners and Joinery of Middlesex County," pp. 127–28. Michael Podmaniczky conserved the fragment and made the pillars and base.

Book Reviews

Jeremy Adamson. *The Furniture of Sam Maloof.* Washington, D.C.: Smithsonian American Art Museum and W. W. Norton, 2001. xviii + 270 pages, 212 color and bw illus., bibliography, index. $60.00.

Ursula Ilse-Neumann et al. *Made In Oakland: The Furniture of Garry Knox Bennett.* New York: American Craft Museum, 2001. x + 228 pp.; numerous color and bw illus., chronology, artist's statements, exhibition history, bibliography. $75.00.

If scholarly coverage is any accurate measure, then two Californians—Sam Maloof and Garry Knox Bennett—now can be said to rank among the most important furniture makers in American history. They are the subjects of full-length studies published last year by the nation's leading craft museums, the American Craft Museum in New York City and the Smithsonian's Renwick Gallery in Washington, D.C. The books are to be welcomed enthusiastically, for several reasons. First, their sheer size and accomplishment mark them as milestones in the publishing records of the sponsoring institutions. This is particularly true in the case of the American Craft Museum, which has lately distanced itself from a previously cogent identity. At one time, the museum was the only major institution in the country devoted to the enormous subject of contemporary craft. As others have sprouted across the country—first the Renwick in the 1970s and more recently the Mint Museum of Craft & Design in Charlotte, North Carolina—the American Craft Museum has moved away from its mandate. Many of the shows the museum has originated in the past five years have presented such topics as Frank Lloyd Wright's stained glass and early modern European porcelain—topics, in other words, that are done far better elsewhere. So a project devoted to Garry Knox Bennett, an honest-to-goodness studio furniture maker, is a welcome return to the museum's original mission.

That two contemporary furniture makers should have books of length, quality, and seriousness devoted to them is a matter of celebration, and not only for studio craftspeople and their partisans. If furniture history is a meaningful intellectual discipline, it cannot have an end date. Museums across the country typically sever furniture made after a certain date (1820 in some places, 1920 in others) from the steady flow of historical development and influence. These two monographs offer readers the opportunity to see contemporary work that rivals antique furniture in terms of complexity, interest, and quality.

Figure 1 Rocking chair by Sam Maloof, Alta Loma, California, 1977. Walnut. H. 46", W. 27½", D. 44". (Courtesy, Philadelphia Museum of Art; gift of Mrs. Robert L. McNeil, Jr.)

A third attraction of the two books is suggested by their simultaneous publication, which invites comparison. Maloof (see fig. 1) and Bennett (see fig. 2) are antithetical in both personality and style. Maloof is so unassuming and low-key as to be almost precious, and has lived out his long career in a pastoral lemon grove. Bennett is crude and hilarious—both in person and as a designer—and is steeped in the rough urbanism of Oakland. That decorative arts scholars can value such mutually exclusive qualities says a lot for the field. Rigorous and objective analysis has heretofore been the exception rather than the rule in twentieth-century furniture studies. Perhaps it is the legacy of modern design itself that causes historians to take sides "for" or "against," whether the subject is art deco, mass-produced davenports, or handmade studio work. As the historiography of eighteenth-century material demonstrates, however, it is only when advocacy subsides that clarity can be achieved. The old days of "good, better, best" are mostly behind us in the study of the colonial era, at least within the academy. But it is only recently that the heterogeneity of modern furniture has come to be seen positively.

Jeremy Adamson's authoritative study of Maloof is as good a point of entry into that principle as any book ever written on the subject of modern furniture. The account, like the subject, is somewhat old-fashioned. It is both chronological and biographical, describing the arc of Maloof's career from graphic illustrator to beginning designer-craftsman to master furniture maker. Throughout these stages Maloof comes across as an unvarying quantity, a given. Though the tides of fashion shift around him, his work plods unerringly forward from decade to decade. The furniture emanating from the little shop in Alta Loma remains largely unchanged (see fig. 1) except for a few formal developments that are agonizingly slow in the making. Thanks to extensive and glorious photography by longtime Maloof associate Jonathan Pollock, the reader can trace the incremental improvements in the design of a single furniture form over five decades. There are, for example, no less than nine examples of Maloof's two-seater settees illustrated, none of which differs radically from a formula that was formulated in the 1950s: low arms, sculptural back rests, scooped Windsor-type seats. Spindles and upholstery may come and go, and the legs may have more or less flare, but it is astounding how much the walnut settee of 1967 (fig. 122, p. 133) looks like the striped maple settee of 1987 (fig. 192, p. 228).

This would seem to make poor material for an exhaustive study. Indeed, if one only looks at the pictures, *The Furniture of Sam Maloof* can seem like too much of a good thing. But Adamson manages to use Maloof's slow and steady production of forthright, user-friendly furniture as a sounding board for the craft movement as a whole. The original title for the volume was *Sam Maloof and the American Craft Movement,* and it is a pity that the Smithsonian abandoned that wording. It would have implied the catholic breadth that Adamson achieved. Throughout he seems to have assigned himself responsibility not only for the craftsman himself, but for everything that impinged on Maloof's consciousness as well. We get pages of information on seminal moments such as the formation of the American

Figure 2 Chair by Garry Knox Bennett, Oakland, California, 2002. Found metal chairs and plastic ties. Dimensions unrecorded. (Courtesy, Garry Knox Bennett.)

Craftsmen's Council, the 1969 traveling craft exhibition "Objects: USA," and the passage of the critical journal *Craft Horizons* in favor of the more market-oriented *American Craft*. In many cases, Adamson provides the most thorough account of such events that has yet seen print. Partly this can be attributed to the book's foundation of excellent research materials, many of which were collected by Maloof's wife Alfreda over the years. We learn exactly how many pieces of furniture Maloof produced year by year, and how much money he made doing it. We read about the assistants who passed through Alta Loma and their roles in the shop. And we get exhaustive treatments of the response to Maloof in the press and later in museums. Such hard data is very rarely included in monographs on craftspeople; its presence here is an important reminder that the skillful arrangement of facts can be the most effective form of analysis.

But the most important factor in Adamson's success is his method, which is to measure the craft world by the yardstick of how that world measured Maloof over time. The book's balanced account of the shift towards a more "arty" and commercial crafts scene is a good example of this technique. He tells this story through the lens of an ongoing dialectical tension between Maloof's lovely and finely joined functional pieces and the more adventurous sculptural furniture of Wendell Castle. Castle's working technique involved gluing stacks of boards together and then going at them with a chainsaw to make impressive but ungainly behemoths. The contrast could not have been more overt, and yet the two makers were consistently included in the same exhibitions. This tension ended in the late 1970s, when Maloof was "promoted" to the role of éminence grise, a "living treasure" and the reigning "dean of American furniture makers." Of course this beatification was a victory for Castle, or at least for Castle's conception of furniture, because it consigned Maloof to the past. By describing the rhetoric of those who celebrated Maloof at this critical turning point, Adamson conveys more about the issues at stake than he could through more direct means.

There is one significant drawback to this approach, however. *The Furniture of Sam Maloof* circles around an absent center, which is the answer to the question: "What does Adamson really think of Maloof?" This answer never comes, which is hard to pull off in 250 pages of analytical prose. Adamson indicates the contradictions and limitations of Maloof's career, but only by implication. He refuses to judge, letting the reader decide how much to believe in the myth that has been constructed around Maloof. Sometimes, this withholding can be frustrating. Before one has read very far into the book it is evident that Adamson is far too incisive to take at face value the unassuming naïveté for which Maloof is famous. Many readers will become impatient for him to call a spade a spade. This is especially true when Adamson fails to subject the self-promotional 1993 book *Sam Maloof: Woodworker* to analysis, calling it "honest, revealing, and . . . unpretentious" (p. 194); or when he uncritically recounts one of Maloof's favorite chestnuts. Take, for example, the tale of Wharton Esherick's injunction to Maloof to "stick to your convictions and don't stray from the way you work and believe," delivered at the 1957 ACC Asilomar conference (p. 69). Much is obviously at stake here. The story functions as a figurative passing of the torch from one great maker to another, just as the new craft movement is getting underway. It also invests Maloof with the imprimatur of authenticity and moral uprightness; but of course, it is Maloof himself who has propagated the event and made it part of his own legend.

On balance, though, Adamson's decision not to question his subject's motives comes across as a sound one. After all, those readers who are inclined to view the maker's humility as thinly cloaked egotism are tacitly given all the evidence they need. Similarly, those who see Maloof's furniture (wrongly) as little more than warmed-over Scandinavian modern are given ample ammunition. Adamson painstakingly recounts the story of a commission Maloof received from the New York industrial designer Henry Dreyfuss (p. 36). Having ordered one of the Danish designer Hans Wegner's armchairs, Dreyfuss found that it did not fit underneath the dining table he had just ordered from Maloof. He therefore asked Maloof to rebuild the Wegner chair and to also create a set of five exact replicas with lower arms. Most historians would be tempted to pounce on this narrative as a kind of smoking gun, especially since Maloof's furniture immediately took a turn toward more organic lines shortly thereafter. That Adamson does not do this is a measure of the care in his scholarship. For after the Dreyfuss experience, Maloof went on to become a member of a Los Angeles–area community of furniture designers. He thus defined himself more in reference to these lesser-known figures—men like Kipp Stewart, Hendrick Van Keppel, and Ernest Inouye—than Wegner, Aalto, or other far-off Scandinavians. Here, as often, Adamson resists the quick answer, and the book is better for it.

The American Craft Museum's study of Garry Knox Bennett, *Made in Oakland,* is another kettle of fish, but it also achieves a pleasantly indeterminate complexity. In this case, the density of the scholarship is achieved by dividing the book among four writers of profoundly different outlooks: philosopher Arthur C. Danto; decorative arts historian Edward S. Cooke, Jr.; Ursula Ilse-Neumann, the curator of the exhibition accompanying the book; and John Marlowe, an old friend of Bennett's from the heyday of the California subculture. The book opens with an essay titled "Philosophizing With A Hammer" by Danto, who has made himself something of a fixture in the contemporary craft literature. Danto's proper field of study is aesthetics, not art history. Consequently his writings on specific artists and craftspeople often have the breezy enthusiasm of the amateur. He tends to make drastic and sweeping claims about contemporary art, to the chagrin of art historians and the delight of art students and others who need a quick handle on a dauntingly complicated subject. This is true of his contribution here. In fact, the placement of the essay in the book's pole position suggests that it is meant for readers who only want twenty pages of lively commentary before skipping to the pictures. Danto clearly feels no obligation to explore the historical or artistic contexts of studio furniture.

Instead, he emphasizes a few objects, notably Bennett's notorious *Nail Cabinet* of 1979. This is a tall display cabinet made of padouk, with a large nail driven unceremoniously into its front. Danto says, rightly, that Bennett "built the cabinet in order to disfigure it," and that the nail was "a gesture of liberation." Bennett made the piece at a time when fine craftsmanship was in danger of becoming an end in itself among studio furniture makers. The periodical *Fine Woodworking,* beginning in 1975, inaugurated an era in which discussion of technique threatened to overwhelm the conceptual, stylistic, and ideological issues relevant to studio work. Bennett had little patience with this trend. (To this day he gleefully shouts "What kind of glue do you use?" when a furniture maker finishes a lecture.) Danto presents this widely accepted view of the *Nail Cabinet* well. He even passes along an interesting reading by *Fine Woodworking* editor John Kelsey, in which the structure of the *Nail Cabinet* itself is seen as subversive. For the record, none of the supposedly iconoclastic joinery details seem inconsistent with the work of an inexperienced furniture designer, which Bennett was at the time. It is also worth noting that Bennett had a lot of help with the construction from two local cabinetmakers. Nonetheless, one should give credit to Danto for taking a craft-based argument seriously.

It is harder to be patient with his claim that by making the *Nail Cabinet* Bennett "declared that the entire structure of insider criticism was irrelevant to the art of contemporary furniture." This is a problematic assertion. First, the nail was itself a piece of insider criticism, as Danto acknowledges. It was aimed squarely at the prevalent trends in contemporary furniture, and on the basis of Bennett's own testimony does not seem to have been intended to be read as much more than that. It's fine to suggest that the gesture had greater implications than were initially obvious, but Danto's version of Bennett's intentions is just bad art history. Second, the implication that "insider criticism" needed to be cleared from the table, opening the way to full-fledged artistic postmodernism, is disturbing. Currently the studio furniture community is still working hard to develop its internal dialogue, a conversation that will have the sophistication of art criticism but will also specifically address the concerns of furniture. Danto wants to invest Bennett's piece with the paradigm-shattering quality of Duchamp's ready-mades, which is a noble goal. In his haste to do so, however, he implies that furniture will need to escape its own category in order to be interesting—a notion that Bennett's oeuvre flatly contradicts.

The next essay in the book comes from a diametrically opposite position. Edward S. Cooke, Jr., is a longtime supporter of contemporary furniture; he curated a seminal 1989 showing of the material at the Museum of Fine Arts, Boston, and is currently planning a follow-up exhibition. He is also a frequent contributor to this journal and a professor of art history at Yale University. In the interest of full disclosure, I should add that I studied with him there until recently. But I would like to think that if I had never met the author I would still find Cooke's essay, "The Urban Cowboy as Furniture Maker," to be a welcome about-face from Danto's overreaching. Like Jeremy Adamson, Cooke has done his homework. His account of

Bennett's development as a maker steers an unpredictable course, beginning with a brief summary of the west coast arts and crafts movement. He singles out such figures as metalsmith Dirk Van Erp, architect Bernard Maybeck, and ceramist Frederick Rhead as examples of a locally oriented, intentionally simplified style that stood in opposition to the "rigidly academic" work then practiced on the east coast. These values were transmitted to the San Francisco art scene of the 1950s, in which raffish beatniks like Wally Hedrick and Bruce Connor flourished, and thence to the Bay Area's 1960s "Funk" movement in ceramics and sculpture.

It is debatable whether Bennett had ever heard of, much less been influenced by, these historical precursors when he started out. That is not Cooke's point, though. He is establishing groundwork for the argument that Bennett's eclectic and anti-establishment stance is a matter of cultural as well as personal history. It is tempting to see him simply as a radical child of the 1960s, since he built up his wood skills by constructing his own teepee-shaped house and made his money by fabricating and selling drug paraphernalia. But calling Bennett a hippie does not explain the acuity of his mature work. This is where the value of Cooke's carefully laid foundation becomes clear. As we read of Bennett's early use of plastics and painted surfaces, we are reminded of the anti-academic leanings of earlier Bay Area art. And when we learn that he has always avoided making chairs—the traditional test form for any furniture maker—it rings true with what Cooke has described as Bennett's "oppositional attitude," inherited from previous generations of similarly minded artists. Cooke refines this point, however, by putting Bennett into strategic contrasts with other makers. Many of these, such as the comparatively little-known Jack Hopkins, J. B. Blunk, and Sterling King, are also self-styled rebels from the California counter-culture. Many of the others are not, however, and it is enlightening to notice how Bennett's careful handling of his own ideas resembles that of an ostensibly conservative maker such as Judy McKie. This broad studio furniture context gives the reader a balanced account: Cooke presents Bennett not only as an impulsive *enfant terrible* but also a consummate professional, who has adroitly managed his own artistic and marketplace development.

After the analyses provided by Danto and Cooke, the reader is prepared to dive in to the specifics of Bennett's furniture. As curator, Ursula Ilse-Neumann was in a good position to provide that information, and made the intelligent decision to let pictures lead the way in her section of the book. The structure is simple but effective. After focusing attention on a specific example of a form, such as a table or bench, Ilse-Neumann gives us a creatively arranged photo essay on the maker's exploration of that form type. This gives the reader the opportunity to see the development of particular core ideas. Unlike Maloof, Bennett is a fountain of invention, so even the photographs of the finished pieces have something of the air of pages in a sketchbook. The effect is exactly opposite to the similarly exhaustive coverage of Maloof's furniture. A few of the formal and conceptual possibilities evident in Bennett's work are brought to fruition, notably his tendency to base an entire composition around a single joint (as in his trestle tables) or a bandsawn cartoon profile (as in his benches and sideboards).

In many other cases, ideas are picked up, used once, and then abandoned. In *Eames Chair* of 1984, Bennett bisected one of Charles and Ray Eames' iconic LCW chairs with a planar board and painted the halves black and white. In *Tangarry Chest* of 1991, he exploited the syncopated façade of a traditional Japanese *tansu,* placing more than thirty irregular doors and drawers into a single case piece. And in 1996, as if to demonstrate the depths of his creativity, he created one hundred assemblage lamps for a single gallery exhibition. One can imagine the current generation of young furniture makers mining these images for some time to come. The only real regret in Ilse-Neumann's portion of the book is that she is obliged to give special attention to the new work that Bennett created for the American Craft Museum exhibit. These "tablelamps" lack the integration of form and concept characteristic of his work, and in some cases even seem to have been thrown together for the occasion of the exhibition. But, as Ilse-Neumann writes, Bennett will soon "be off in a new direction, and no one can predict where that will lead." Indeed, since the book's publication he has already made a series of chairs that attest to his continued artistic vitality (fig. 2).

The book concludes with a section of back matter that must rank as one of the great documentations of a contemporary craftsperson. The centerpiece is a set of eleven manifesto-like artist's statements written by Bennett's self-described "long suffering friend" John Marlowe in 1986. Bennett used to send these texts to galleries and collectors with an explanatory note, thereby exempting himself from the process of explaining his work himself. It is a measure of the persuasiveness of these texts that many over the years have taken them to be authentic (indeed, Arthur Danto quotes extensively from Marlowe's writings as if they were Bennett's in his essay in this very volume). Designed to be funny, self-contradictory, and provocative rather than informative, they are an apt symbol of Bennett's desire to both rebel against and dominate the contemporary furniture scene.

Also included in the back matter is an exhibition history by Elizabeth Bard, and an extremely helpful illustrated chronology no less than twenty-seven pages long, lovingly compiled by Marlowe. A short note at the end of this timeline reads: "Additional information for this chronology provided by Sylvia Bennett." In fact, this is an absurd understatement, since Sylvia—Garry's wife—preserved the ephemera of her husband's career in a manner rivaling the archival accomplishments of Alfreda Maloof. Unlike Alfreda, who carefully preserved Sam's history but tragically did not live to see the publication of the Renwick volume, Sylvia Bennett also shepherded *Made in Oakland* to publication. It cannot be sufficiently stressed how much both projects owe to these two women. Therein lies an important question for furniture scholars: at what point will we begin to treat contemporary work seriously enough that the family members of the makers do not have the primary responsibility to record the crucial facts? One hundred years from now, historians will know about Maloof and Bennett exactly what we today would like to know about George Hunzinger, John and Thomas Seymour, or the anonymous "Garvan carver" of Philadelphia. So the decorative arts field can be thankful for these two impressive books. But if we do not see them as a challenge, then we have missed the point entirely.

Glenn Adamson
Chipstone Foundation

Clive Edwards. *Encyclopedia of Furniture Materials, Trades and Techniques.* Brookfield, Vt.: Ashgate, 2000. x + 254 pp.; 24 color and 148 bw illus., bibliography. $134.95.

Witold Rybczynski. *One Good Turn: A Natural History of the Screwdriver and the Screw.* New York: Scribner, 2000. 173 pp.; line drawings, glossary, index. $22.00.

One way of measuring the maturity and viability of a field of scholarly endeavor, perhaps, is through an assessment of the number and quality of its standard reference works—those essential tools that should reside on or near everyone's desk. In the field of American furniture, there are not many such works—some general dictionaries of decorative arts, the magisterial but venerable *Dictionary of English Furniture,* some collection catalogues and pictorial surveys, and a few more or less unsatisfactory encyclopedias are all that come to mind quickly. Thus the English historian Clive Edwards has advanced the cause of the study of old (and more recent) furniture tremendously in his new *Encyclopedia of Furniture Materials, Trades and Techniques*. He courageously attempts to define and summarize every subject—from abrasives to zippers—related to the making of "British and American furniture and furnishings of the period 1500–2000." Although the emphasis is mainly on British work before about 1920, the coverage is indeed broad, and the student of American furniture will find much of interest and value here.

The intended audience for this work is the furniture historian, broadly conceived, including collectors, curators, dealers, conservators, and students. It is not a "how-to" manual for the practicing woodworker, nor is it an attempt to summarize the evolution of design and aesthetics for the traditional art historian, although both groups would profit from having the book nearby for ready consultation. Rather, Edwards has provided us with a highly useful guide to furniture woods and other materials; to construction techniques and processes, including joints, adhesives, finishes, and so forth; and to the principal craft specialties within the large umbrella of furniture making, including the carver, joiner, gilder, marquetry worker, frame maker, upholsterer, and others. He also supplies entries for most furniture-making equipment, from hand tools to power-driven machinery. Some style terms, such as art deco, art nouveau, and baroque, are included but are dealt with (in accordance with the book's ground rules) rather quickly. Others, such as mannerism and collector's terms such as Queen Anne and Chippendale, are omitted.

One of the strengths of the book is the grounding of its entries in period sources, allowing for the discussion of a given term to be anchored in time. As might be expected, much of the documentation cited is from English materials. More emphasis is naturally placed on the historical aspects of a given topic than on more recent developments, but the coverage is nevertheless extensive. Carefully chosen illustrations supplement the text, although in some instances (as with the discussion of various joints), the inclusion of line drawings would have enhanced the text. Selected references are given for most of the longer entries, and a useful bibliography of both primary and secondary sources is included at the end of the volume.[1]

Almost every term one could think of finds a definition here, although I searched without success for cake, an upholsterer's term, stack lamination, a process used by studio furniture makers such as Wendell Castle and Jack Rogers Hopkins in the 1960s, drawer blade, and a few others. However, if you want or need to know what a fat bag is (in terms of furniture), or what xulopyrography, domes of silence, atomic wood, or beaumontage happen to mean, this is the place to start.

But perhaps the book's greatest strength is not so much the short definitions of obscure words (which in any event can be found in most good dictionaries), but in its longer narratives that provide capsule summaries of more well-known, but complicated to explain, processes and crafts. These provide a quick spot check of the state of our current understanding of the anatomy of the field, and will be of enormous assistance in manifold ways to students of all kinds. Specialists in various topics may find nits to pick here and there, but overall the *Encyclopedia* accomplishes its audacious goal in a superb manner.

Obviously, most research will not end by checking the *Encyclopedia,* but much of it will begin there. Many of Edwards' subjects, to which he can only devote a page or two, might easily occupy a full volume. Such is the case, for example, with the five paragraphs (p. 191) he gives to screws and screwdrivers, a subject that Witold Rybczynski expands into an entire volume in *One Good Turn*. In the kind of book perhaps only an established and well-known author could get published, Rybczynski rambles on a bit about his attempt, in response to an editor's question, to determine the best tool of the last millennium. After considering a variety of hand tools—most of which date much farther back in antiquity—he settled on the humble turnscrew (as screwdrivers were initially known, although the term doesn't appear in Edwards). He allows us to follow his research, which begins with the *Oxford English Dictionary* and then moves on to many period books, including Moxon, Roubo, and Diderot's encyclopedia. He digresses (always entertainingly) about various side trips along the way, such as his visit to the collection of Henry Mercer at the Mercer Museum in Doylestown, Pennsylvania, or to the arms and armor gallery at the Metropolitan Museum of Art.

Much of his research, however, was book-centered, rather than object related, which is unfortunate, since he could have learned quite a bit very quickly in a few hours with a curator or conservator of old furniture. But it is always a pleasure to follow the thought process of a great scholar, and Rybczynski doesn't disappoint. In fact, he has a good deal of interesting material on various screw types, such as those invented by Peter S. Robertson and Henry F. Phillips, that Edwards simply doesn't have room to discuss.

An astonishing statement made by Rybczynski concerns the screw-making factory established by the brothers Job and William Wyatt in 1776 near Birmingham, England. Using a process they patented in 1760, they developed machinery for making screws that could be operated by children and completely eliminate the workmanship of risk. Thus, he claims, "their factory was the earliest example of an industrial process designed specifically to shift control over the quality of what was being produced from the skilled artisan to the machine itself" (p. 87). Quite an achievement for the humble screw.

Although the Edwards volume and the Rybczynski essay are at opposite ends of the literary spectrum, each reminds us in its own way of the importance of understanding tools, materials, and craftsmanship when evaluating an example of furniture as a work of art or as material culture.

Gerald W. R. Ward
Museum of Fine Arts, Boston

1. The bibliography is weighted toward English sources (no American cabinetmakers' price books are cited, for example) and has its share of minor slips in citations: C. Hummel is given as C. "Humell"; J. L. Fairbanks as "J. C. Fairbanks"; D. Fennimore as "E. Fennimore"; and so forth. The list of periodicals has a curious omission (*The Magazine Antiques*) and doesn't include some more recent technical periodicals, such as *Fine Woodworking* (published since 1975), that contain useful articles on twentieth-century furniture making.

Paul J. Foley. *Willard's Patent Time Pieces: A History of the Weight-Driven Banjo Clock, 1800–1900*. Norwell, Mass.: Roxbury Village Publishing, 2002. xviii + 358 pp.; 638 color and bw illus., biographies, appendices, bibliography, glossary, index. $89.95.

Simon Willard is unquestionably one of the most celebrated names among students of the American arts. He was acknowledged by early generations of popular writers on American decorative arts as "the most famous ... among American clock-makers" (Frances Clary Morse) and "the finest exponent of American mechanical genius" (Wallace Nutting). Willard clocks are pictured in most surveys of American decorative arts, in every survey of American clocks, and have a high profile in museum galleries and in the marketplace.

Willard's patent timepiece, the "banjo clock," is among the most original and successful American innovations in the field of decorative arts. Paul Foley's study of the form, *Willard's Patent Time Pieces,* deserves two places in any library of American decorative arts; first, as the best monograph on the subject of patent timepieces yet produced and, second, as a rich and thorough compilation of biographic references to federal-era craftsmen in the Boston-Roxbury area. The first would constitute an impressive resource on its own, but combined with the second, the reader has the opportunity to construct a vivid and authentic picture of a teeming, productive crafts community that was in the forefront of many aspects of the new American culture.

The study of American clocks can be frustrating. Thomas S. Michie, in his very useful interpretive bibliography, pointed out the scarcity of good interpretive clock studies and the prevalence of anecdote in the literature. In his book, Paul J. Foley combines rigorous connoisseurship, excellent photography, and the research methodology of a social historian to create a document that will serve both as a valuable reference and as an exemplar for future clock studies.[1]

Simon Willard made eight-day clocks and timepieces the way the English made watches. The component parts of Willard's eight-day clocks were fashioned and finished by specialists working in disconnected shops (as far away as Lancashire), and the final product was warranted and sold by the clockmaker. This methodology is in marked contrast to the single-shop or traditional manufacture practiced by makers like Daniel Burnap of Connecticut (1758–1838) or the distinctive and well-documented, vertically integrated Dominy shop on Long Island. The division of labor among many shops is clearly seen in patent timepieces, where the movement, dial, cast brass ornaments, hands, painted glasses, case, and gilt wood ornament were all made in separate shops. Foley has undertaken with admirable success the daunting task of considering the timepiece in its polyglot complexity over a century of production in a variety of New England communities.[2]

Willard's Patent Time Pieces is organized into seven parts, plus six appendices, a bibliography, glossary, and index. Part I, "History and Background," discusses the Willard family of Grafton and Roxbury and some of their timepiece forms that predate the patent timepiece (1802), and introduces and describes the patent timepiece with a splendid early example in the American Clock and Watch Museum. The photograph on page 3 of a timepiece movement is the first of many such views in the book, clearly photographed to allow for easy comparison. For those unused to looking behind dials, these privileged views will be a revelation; the nearly 650 illustrations in this volume will have a lasting value as by far the best visual index of the form in print. On page 9 is a list of eleven journeymen and apprentices who assisted Simon Willard in timepiece production during the patent period (1802–1816), a provocative introduction to the complex shop structure behind these timekeepers.[3]

Part II, "Patent Timepieces: 1800–1840," pictures and describes more than sixty timepieces from a variety of manufacturers, beginning with Simon Willard and continuing with other Roxbury makers; makers from Boston, Charlestown, Concord, and the North and South shores of Massachusetts; from Newport, Rhode Island, and from New Hampshire, Maine, and Vermont. Included in this section are some sidebars, among them an incisive discussion of marketing and prices which is illustrated with the first of many reproductions of newspaper advertisements. These illustrations point out an admirable part of the author's methodology—his scrupulous use of newspapers and court records—and combine (with others in the volume) to form another unique resource of real value.

In parts III and IV Foley addresses some variations on the patent timepiece. Part III includes three patented variations: Lemuel Curtis' patent timepiece, now commonly called a girandole clock; Daniel Munroe's patent suspension, an adaptation of a silk pendulum suspension found on some French table clocks (this variant perhaps was never actually patented); and a remarkable movement by Harrison Gray Dyar that employs helical gears. Part IV includes timepieces with variations in the case design—thermometers in the waist glass, "elegant harp pattern" timepieces, which are commonly called lyre clocks, and timepieces with stenciled cases—and with variations in the movement, including alarm and striking movements. Part V, "Production Timepieces: 1840–1900," includes later timepieces like those made by Howard and Davis in Boston. In the movements of these timepieces may be found evidence for the introduction of machine tools into the clock finishing process.

The first five sections make up a volume well worth having, but are only half of *Willard's Patent Time Pieces.* With parts VI and VII, Foley expands his discussion to include the myriad crafts and craftsmen necessary to timepiece manufacture. Part VI, "Ornamental Painters and Cabinetmakers," is filled with new information on the mostly anonymous hands behind painted clock dials and glasses in New England, many of whom were general ornamental painters who worked on looking glasses and other forms as well. This section is illustrated with more than forty lower glasses from timepieces, and here again the reader has a discrete resource that is not reproduced anywhere in the literature. Foley has been assiduous in his choice of examples to illustrate, and the reader can have a high degree of confidence that those illustrated here are genuine. They deserve careful study. Much of the information on cabinetmakers, particularly in Boston and Roxbury, will be new even to specialized readers.

Part VII, "Biographies of Patent Timepiece Makers, Ornamental Painters, Cabinetmakers, and Allied Craftsmen: 1800–1900," will put any student of American decorative arts of the federal period in Foley's debt. He has assembled from "city directories, newspapers, census records, vital records, family genealogies, account books, town histories, land deeds, probate records, and civil court records" (p. vii) biographical information on more than one thousand New England craftsmen, most of whom worked in the first half of the nineteenth century. This section is illustrated with more than eighty dial signatures carefully chosen for their authenticity. Dial signatures are perhaps even more treacherous than painted glasses, and the reader has another chance here to benefit from Foley's first-rate connoisseurship and superior photography.

Paul Foley's enthusiasm for the subject is evident throughout *Willard's Patent Time Pieces* and, as he points out (p. viii), "[a] study like this is never finished." In the hundreds of excellent photographs of clock movements is a rich trove of evidence about the shop structure underlying these timepieces. On page 41, Foley suggests the reader "[c]ompare the movement in the signed Taber timepiece in Fig. 86 with those in Figs. 95, 98, and 323." The comparison reveals that the same brass clockwork founder, steel forger, and clock finisher or clockmaker was at work on genuine timepieces by Elnathan Taber and Simon Willard, Jr. Similarly, comparison of figs. 36 and 39 reveals, in two genuine contemporary timepieces by Simon Willard, differences in the castings and forge work (great wheel drums, pendulum keystone, T-bridge, and steel click or pawl) and differences in the finishing (plate shape, tooth form, and steel screws). Many similar comparisons can be made in this volume (and at present, nowhere else) because Foley has hunted down the examples, verified their authenticity, removed the dials, and photographed the movements carefully to reveal the salient details. Clock movements can be analyzed in good Morellian fashion as successfully as drawer construction or ornamental carving, since the clock finishers were as subject to the tyranny of training and tools as any other craftsman, but they rarely are; Foley's book will make that exercise possible for a much wider audience.

The heterodyne shop practice revealed in the movements is corroborated in the biographical entries. For example, in the entry (p. 278) for brass founder Thomas Lillie (1789–1848) may be found the information that he advertised clock work as early as 1807; that he was in partnership with brass founder John Andrews making "Castings of any description" including "Clock Work, &c.;" and that "Orders and Patterns for Castings of any kind, left with *Ezekiil Jones*... will meet immediate attention, and where will be kept constantly for sale, Clock and Timepiece Cast Work, superior to English, and at less prices." Ezekiel Jones' (ca. 1788–1826) entry (p. 272) includes the probate inventory of his shop, which included "53 time piece glasses...26 time piece movements...29 time piece Trimming Sides [brass side ornaments]...28 Time piece Tins...24 Patent Time piece cases...128 Empty Boxes for Time pieces," and much more, suggesting his trade was that of a horological supply merchant. Hundreds of such connections are revealed by a study of Foley's entries, creating a vivid image of the true nature of American clockmaking.

Despite their fame and appeal, Willard's clocks continue to occupy a peculiar nether region for historians. British horologists have long regarded clocks of that period as factory-made, and therefore of no interest. American economic historians tend to view them as handmade, and therefore inapplicable to the study of the onset of industrialization, for which they may instead use the example of Eli Terry. Further definition of the niche that Willard and related craftsmen occupied and helped create may well contribute to an understanding of issues like the development of the machine tool industry in New England; the role of capital in this process; the changing nature of labor; rural aspects of New England industrialization; and economic and geographic mobility. For furniture historians, *Willard's Patent Time Pieces* not only belongs at the head of the list of resources to be used in any future study of New England clocks, but will be useful to everyone interested in federal-era decorative arts.

David Wood

Concord Museum

and

Robert C. Cheney
Brimfield, Massachusetts

1. *Decorative Arts and Household Furnishings in America, 1630–1920: An Annotated Bibliography*, edited by Kenneth L. Ames and Gerald W. R. Ward (Winterthur, Del.: Henry Francis du Pont Winterthur Museum, 1989), pp. 283–306.

2. For a helpful overview of English watch making, see Leonard Weiss, *Watch-Making in England, 1760–1820* (London: Robert Hale, 1982); Robert C. Cheney, "Roxbury Eight-Day Movements and the English Connection, 1785–1825," *Antiques* 157, no. 4 (April 2000): 607–15; Penrose R. Hoopes, *The Shop Records of Daniel Burnap* (Hartford: Connecticut Historical Society, 1958); Charles F. Hummel, *With Hammer in Hand* (Winterthur, Del.: Henry Francis du Pont Winterthur Museum, 1968).

3. Foley's glossary at the end of the volume includes many of the terms he uses to describe the timepieces, though not all; readers unfamiliar with clock terminology might also want to consult the glossaries in Philip Zea and Robert C. Cheney, *Clock Making in New England, 1725–1825* (Sturbridge, Mass.: Old Sturbridge Village, 1992) and Stephen P. Petrucelli and Kenneth A. Sposato, *American Banjo Clocks* (Cranbury, N. J.: Adams Brown Co., 1995).

Wendy A. Cooper. *An American Vision: Henry Francis du Pont's Winterthur Museum*. Washington, D.C.: National Gallery of Art; Winterthur, Del.: Winterthur Museum, Garden & Library, 2002. 214 pp.; 150+ color and bw illustrations, checklist, index. $35.00.

Winterthur is a wonderful place. That may sound trite but it is true. There is nothing quite like it. Winterthur has its imitators, surely, but it has no peers. Winterthur is, simply put, the greatest collection of early American decorative arts anywhere.

I had the privilege of working at Winterthur for some seventeen years. Few days go by when I do not wish that I still had access to that extraordinary collection. Even now, when looking at quirky New England eighteenth-century chairs, I can still visualize details of similar chairs at Winterthur that Benno Forman and I examined and argued about in his office a quarter of a century ago. I say all this to alert readers that I was once a Winterthur insider and know something about the place. Furthermore, I am predisposed to think positively about it and, at least at the outset, to give the benefit of the doubt to any product that emanates from it.

An American Vision is a celebratory volume produced to coincide with and serve as a souvenir of an exhibition of Winterthur highlights on view at the National Gallery in Washington from May 5 to October 6, 2002. The timing was not accidental. The year 2002 marked the Winterthur Museum's fiftieth anniversary and the DuPont Company's two hundredth. Appropriately, the company was one of the supporters of the project.

Anniversary ventures are a tricky business. How does a museum with nationally ranked education programs mark such an occasion? What balance of celebration and cerebration is appropriate? Hard to be quite sure. On average, anniversary projects tend to fall a bit short on substance. It may simply be the nature of the genre.

An American Vision was both an exhibition and a publication. I did not see the exhibition at the National Gallery, although I have seen, repeatedly and at close hand, many of the objects included in it. The exhibition may have been quite lovely but, as we all know well and sometimes regret, exhibitions are ephemeral while publications endure. This publication is also lovely, but that, alas, is pretty much the end of it.

The best features of *An American Vision* are easily identified. The first is Winterthur Director Leslie Greene Bowman's graceful biographical sketch of Henry Francis du Pont and of his creation of Winterthur. The second is the superb collection of spectacular photographs, most taken by Gavin Ashworth, adorning the volume. It is a very pretty book and most enjoyable to leaf through.

Reading it is another matter, however. And here we return to the dilemma of what an anniversary publication should be. Wendy Cooper, either of her own volition or someone else's, produced five short thematic essays dealing with, in this order, early settlement, Asian impact on the West, the rococo, the Pennsylvania Germans, and American classicism. A pretty ambitious undertaking for a text of only about eighty full pages, I think, and one that frankly just does not work well. She should have offered either more or less. This is one instance in which the middle option, in contrast to what we learned in childhood from the story of *Goldilocks and the Three Bears,* is not "just right" at all.

I have no desire to dissect Cooper's text in any detail. Suffice it to say that it is superficial, simplistic, and unfocused. The subtleties and nuances of the American historical past are completely and consistently swept away. Sometimes the text is outright wrong, as when it claims that rococo equals Chippendale and that Chippendale equals rococo. And sometimes it is inconsistent or unclear, with historical and art historical commentary interrupted by unnecessary and, I think, inappropriate fawning over H. F. du Pont. Most sadly, the book offers no ideas. And that is both unfortunate and avoidable.

The book did not have to take this form. There are alternatives. One would have been to offer less text and more pictures, to celebrate the visual splendors of the place without the pretense of doing much more. I have in hand a handsome volume that offers a useful model. The long and clearly descriptive title is *A Concise History of Glass Represented in the Chrysler Museum Glass Collection.* Written by Nancy O. Merrill and published by the Chrysler Museum in 1989, this little gem is roughly the same size as the Winterthur publication. Here and there it provides a page or two of historical background or overview, but the bulk of the book is taken up with photographs of objects accompanied by captions, some long and some short. The result is an attractive and useful volume that can also be a handy reference. I think it is demonstrably superior to *An American Vision* and would have required even less effort at Winterthur to produce.

Another route altogether would have been to insert a few ideas into the volume. Now I recognize that there are those in the field of decorative arts who love ideas and those who do not. It is my sense, however, that the museum-visiting public includes a goodly number of educated people who are not afraid of ideas and, indeed, embrace them. These are people who, for example, read the *New York Times,* the small-circulation cultural commentary magazines, and books that are overtly and unapologetically ideational. There are millions of such folk in this country. *An American Vision* could have decided to talk to them.

I am not suggesting a deep philosophical treatise here, just a text that invites its readers to muse, reflect, and contemplate, to make connections between Winterthur and the things in it and their own world. Some of these matters are quite basic. Consider possession, for instance. The text refers repeatedly to H. F. du Pont's buying but does not suggest why possession itself might hold such appeal or what it might mean. Charles F. Montgomery maintained that the best way to learn about a category of goods was to buy one. Still sound advice. Integrating ideas of self-education through acquisition or of a personal odyssey of growth into this text might have added nuance to an understanding of du Pont, who, despite the fawning—or perhaps because of it—does not come off as a particularly attractive character here.

Was du Pont an antiquarian? What is antiquarianism and what might it be all about? Bill Hosley has useful—and typically impassioned—things to say on this topic in his article "Regional Furniture/Regional Life" published in the 1995 volume of *American Furniture* (pp. 3–38). Hosley also talks to the importance of place. Furniture historians and other decorative arts scholars are highly attentive to place. It might have been useful to talk a bit about why this is and what it might mean. Everyone has some understanding of place. The topic is familiar, accessible, and, treated correctly, profound.

Laurel Thatcher Ulrich, writing as an informed and friendly outsider, has brought a new humanistic perspective to the study of American decorative arts. Her chapter (pp. 108–41) on Hannah Barnard's cupboard in *The Age of Homespun* (New York: Knopf, 2001) is a notable achievement, combining local history, genealogy, a sensitivity to the many-layered meanings of objects, and woman's awareness and perspectives. Better than many others, Ulrich has been able to bring people of the past back to the objects they once owned and lived with, creating a picture replete with all the cares and complexities that are part of human lives. Even if Cooper had missed *The Age of Homespun,* she might have extracted something from Ulrich's warm-up piece, "Furniture as Social History: Gender, Property, and Memory in the Decorative Arts," which also appeared in the 1995 volume of *American Furniture* (pp. 39–68). Following Ulrich's model, *An American Vision* might have offered a bit more biography, mused on the importance of memory, or, better still, meaningfully acknowledged difference in the American past.

Ann Smart Martin has a wonderful article in the *Winterthur Portfolio* laying out consumerism as a framework for studying American material culture and decorative arts. Useful ideas could have been extracted. Richard Bushman has written a fine book of several hundred pages about the refinement of American life. Some of the large transformations he describes could have been sketched in here. Richard Lawrence Greene has a provocative article in *Antiques* about fertility symbols on Hadley chests. A bit of that could have been woven it. Maybe most to the point, considering the fact that Cooper wrote an entire section on the rococo, something from the article, "The Rococo, the Grotto, and the Philadelphia High Chest" by Jonathan Prown and Richard Miller in the 1996 issue of *American Furniture* (pp. 105–36) could have been incorporated. In fact, it should have been. But nothing is there. An opportunity lost.[1]

In the end, *An American Vision* is a disappointment. It offers no inspiration, because it takes us nowhere, except maybe backwards. By avoiding virtually all ideational scholarship in and relevant to our field, it trivializes what we do. Instead of summarizing all that is best in decorative arts scholarship, it exemplifies much of what is worst. And that really is unfortunate.

I could write more but my assessment would only grow bleaker, for there is yet more that is disappointing about this publication and, perhaps, the strategies and perspectives behind it. Instead, let me conclude by noting that museums have had a tendency in recent years to grasp at opportunities for funding or publicity that take them away from their appointed courses. These side trips, which often require considerable staff time and additional resources, can have unanticipated consequences, either damaging to reputations or simply, when all is said and done, making no difference whatsoever. The lesson is that sometimes what seems to be a good deal really is not. The trick here, as in so many other aspects of life, is to learn to resist temptation.

Kenneth L. Ames
Bard Graduate Center

1. Ann Smart Martin, "Makers, Buyers, and Users: Consumerism as a Material Culture Framework," *Winterthur Portfolio* 28, nos. 2/3 (summer/autumn 1993): 141–57; Richard L. Bushman, *The Refinement of America: Persons, Houses, Cities* (New York: Knopf, 1992); Richard Lawrence Greene, "Fertility Symbols on the Hadley Chests," *Antiques* 112, no. 2 (August 1977): 250–57.

Compiled by Gerald W. R. Ward

Recent Writing on American Furniture: A Bibliography

▼ THIS YEAR'S LIST marks the tenth such annual compilation that I have prepared for readers of *American Furniture,* representing several thousand books, catalogues, and articles published during the last decade.

This year's list includes works published in 2001 and roughly through August of 2002. As always, a few earlier publications that had escaped notice are also cited. The short title *American Furniture 2001* is used in citations for articles and reviews published in last year's issue of this journal, which is also cited in full under Luke Beckerdite's name.

For their assistance in various ways, I am grateful to Luke Beckerdite, Jonathan L. Fairbanks, Edward S. Cooke, Jr., Kelly H. L'Ecuyer, Pat Warner, Steven M. Lash, Tom Michie, Milo Naeve, and Anne Woodhouse.

I would be glad to receive suggestions for titles that have been inadvertently omitted from this or previous lists, as well as information on new publications. Review copies of significant works would also be much appreciated.

Adamson, Glenn. "More Than Meets the Eye: Tom Loeser's Kinetic Furniture." *Woodwork*, no. 72 (December 2001): 26–34. 30 color and 1 bw illus.

Adamson, Glenn. "The Next Moment in Studio Furniture." In Rick Mastelli and John Kelsey, eds., *Furniture Studio*, vol. 2, *Tradition in Contemporary Furniture*, 100–105. Free Union, Va.: The Furniture Society, 2001. Color illus.

Adamson, Glenn. "A Perfect Match: The Furniture of Charley Radtke." *Woodwork*, no. 78 (December 2002): 24–29.

Adamson, Jeremy. *The Furniture of Sam Maloof.* Washington, D.C.: Smithsonian American Art Museum and W. W. Norton, 2001. xviii + 270 pp.; 212 color and bw illus., bibliography, index.

Albrecht, Donald. "Russel Wright: Creating American Lifestyle." *Newsletter of the Decorative Arts Society* 9, no. 3 (fall 2001): 5–9. 2 bw illus.

[American Craft Museum]. "Objects for Use." *American Craft* 61, no. 5 (October/November 2001): 72–75. 4 color and 4 bw illus.

American Folk Art / Les Primitifs Américains. Paris: Somogy éditions d'art, 2001. 119 pp.; numerous color illus., bibliography. (Text in French; catalogue of selections from the collection of the Fenimore Art Museum, Cooperstown, N.Y., including some furniture; contributors include Russell M. Porter, Laure Meyer, Elizabeth Stillinger, Jacqueline M. Atkins, William C. Ketchum, and Elizabeth D. Garrett.)

American Period Furniture 2 (January 2002): 1–28. bw illus. (The journal of the Society of American Period Furniture Makers.)

"An American Vision: Henry Francis du Pont's Winterthur Museum." *Antiques and the Arts Weekly* (September 13, 2002): 1, 68–71. 18 bw illus.

[Art Gallery of Southwestern Manitoba]. *Canadian Furniture Exhibition: A Juried Exhibition of Contemporary Furniture.* Brandon, Manitoba: Art Gallery of Southwestern Manitoba, 2000. 36 pp.; color illus.

Auction 2002: This Year's Best Handcrafted Furniture… Manchester, N.H.: New Hampshire Furniture Masters Association, 2002. 58 pp.; color illus.

Baarsen, Reinier, et al. *Rococo in Nederland.* Zwolle: Waanders, 2001. 330 pp.; numerous color and bw illus., bibliography, index.

Bacot, H. Parrott. "Living with Antiques: Temple Heights, Columbus, Mississippi." *Antiques* 162, no. 1 (July 2002): 96–105. 12 color illus.

[Baltimore Museum of Art]. "Recent Acquisitions." *Newsletter of the Decorative Arts Society* 9, no. 3 (fall 2001):17–18. 1 bw illus. (Re painted table of ca. 1815 attributed to Thomas Renshaw of Baltimore.)

Banks, Amanda Carson. *Birth Chairs, Midwives, and Medicine.* Jackson: University Press of Mississippi, 1999. 154 pp.; illus., appendices, bibliography, index.

Barter, Judith A., and Jennifer M. Downs. "Shaping the Modern: American Decorative Arts at the Art Institute of Chicago." *Museum Studies* 27, no. 2 (2001): 1–112. Numerous color and bw illus.

Bascom, Mansfield, author and narrator. "Wharton Esherick: Artistry in Wood." Paoli, Pa.: Wharton Esherick Museum, 2001. Video; 25 minutes.

Bates, Elizabeth Bidwell. "Catherine Hoover Voorsanger." *Maine Antique Digest* 30, no. 2 (February 2002): 4A. 1 bw illus.

Beach, Laura. "As Beauty Does: Winterthur Honors Collectors for Their Devotion to the Decorative Arts: du Pont Award Goes to Linda H. and the Late George M. Kaufman." *Antiques and the Arts Weekly* (January 4, 2002): 1, 34–36. 10 bw illus.

Beach, Laura. "Redwood Library Acquires Day Book of Newport Cabinetmaker." *Antiques and the Arts Weekly* (October 5, 2001): 74–75. 9 bw illus. (Re Jonas Berger's day book of the 1920s.)

Beach, Laura. "Sotheby's Auctions Collection of Mr. and Mrs. Lammot du Pont Copeland." *Antiques and the Arts Weekly* (February 1, 2002): 94–96. 16 color illus.

Beckerdite, Luke. "Introduction." In *American Furniture 2001*, xi–xiii. 1 bw illus. (Includes memorial to the late furniture scholar John Bivins and a partial list of his publications.)

Beckerdite, Luke, ed. *American Furniture 2001.* Milwaukee, Wis.: Chipstone Foundation, 2001. xiii + 279 pp.; numerous color and bw illus., bibliography, index. Distributed by University Press of New England, Hanover, N.H., and London.

Benes, Peter, ed. *Textiles in New England II: Four Centuries of Material Life.* Dublin Seminar for New England Folklife, annual proceedings, 1999. Boston: Boston University, [2001]. 272 pp.; numerous bw illus., bibliography, abstracts. (A conference report containing a few articles related to furniture.)

Berlin, Carswell Rush. "'Solid and Permanent Grandeur': The Design Roots of American Classical Furniture." *[Catalogue of] The International Fine Art and Antique Dealers Show* (New York, 2001): 17–26. Illus.

Berry, Ian, with Tom Lewis. *Work: Shaker Design and Recent Work.* Saratoga Springs, N.Y.: Tang Teaching Museum and Art Gallery at Skidmore College, 2001. 52 pp.; color and bw illus., checklist, biographies.

Beyer, Steven, and Maltida McQuaid. *George Nakashima and the Modernist Movement.* Doylestown, Pa.: James A. Michener Art Museum, 2001. 80 pp.; color and bw illus., biographies, checklist.

Binzen, Jonathan. "Fitting In." In Rick Mastelli and John Kelsey, eds., *Furniture Studio*, vol. 2, *Tradition in Contemporary Furniture*,

61–71. Free Union, Va.: The Furniture Society, 2001. Color illus.

Binzen, Jonathan. "Jeff Kellar." *American Craft* 62, no. 4 (August/September 2002): 46–51. Color illus.

Binzen, Jonathan. "Pritam & Eames." *American Craft* 61, no. 5 (October/November 2001): 96–98. 4 color illus.

Bosley, Edward R. *Greene & Greene*. New York: Phaidon Press, 2000. 240 pp.; illus.

Bowett, Adam. *English Furniture from Charles II to Queen Anne, 1660–1714*. Woodbridge, England: Antique Collectors' Club, 2002. 368 pp.; numerous illus.

Bowett, Adam. "A New Chronology for English Walnut-Veneered Furniture." *Antiques* 161, no. 6 (June 2002): 108–15. 9 color and 4 bw illus.

Bowett. Adam. "London Furniture, 1666–1714." *Antiques* 160, no. 6 (December 2001): 786–93. 10 color and 1 bw illus.

Breed, Alan. "The Basics of Turning a Finial." *The Catalogue of Antiques and Fine Art* 3, no. 1 (winter/spring 2002): 304–8. 12 color illus.

[Brooklyn Museum of Art]. "American Identities: A Reinterpretation of American Art at the BMA." *Antiques and the Arts Weekly* (October 19, 2001): 1, 68–69. 10 bw illus.

Brown, Johanna M. "Such Luxuries as Sofas: An Introduction to North Carolina Moravian Upholstered Furniture." *Journal of Early Southern Decorative Arts* 27, no. 2 (winter 2001): 1–50. 33+ bw illus.

Brunk, Andrew. "Classical Tables." *Christie's Magazine* (January/February 2002): 9091. 2 color illus.

Burks, Jean M. "Mystery Revealed: The 'Finished' Chest." *The Catalogue of Antiques and Fine Art* 3, no. 1 (winter/spring 2002): 44. 2 color illus. (Re reproduction Hadley chest.)

Chalfant, Skip. "Tribute: Philip H. Bradley." *The Catalogue of Antiques and Fine Art* 3, no. 2 (spring 2002): 120. 3 color illus.

[Chamblin, Doug.] "Doug Chamblin." *American Craft* 62, no. 1 (February/March 2002): 84. 1 color illus. (Re contemporary furniture maker.)

Chase, Linda, and Karl Kemp. *The World of Biedermeier*. New York: Thames and Hudson, 2001. 416 pp.; 202 color illus.

Collector's Compass: '50s Décor. Bothell, Wash.: Martingale & Co., 2000. 128 pp.; color and bw illus., bibliography, glossary, index.

[Colonial Williamsburg]. "Furniture of the American South, 1680–1830: Collection from Colonial Williamsburg on View at the Atlanta History Center." *Antiques and the Arts Weekly* (March 29, 2002): 1, 68–70. 10 bw illus.

[Concord (Massachusetts) Museum]. "A Distinguished Addition to the Concord Clock Collection." *Concord Museum Newsletter* (fall 2001): 7. 1 bw illus. (Re tall clock by Nathaniel Munroe, with case attributed to William Munroe, ca. 1805.)

[Connecticut Historical Society]. "Connecticut Historical Awarded $150,000 from Luce Foundation: Society Plans Exhibition and Book on 18th Century Connecticut Valley Furniture." *Antiques and the Arts Weekly* (November 30, 2001): 25. 2 bw illus.

[Connecticut Valley Historical Museum]. "Connecticut Valley Furniture." *Maine Antique Digest* 30, no. 1 (January 2002): 10A. 1 bw illus.

[Connecticut Valley Historical Museum]. "Valley Furniture, Valley Tools: Antique Furniture from the Connecticut River Valley on View at the Connecticut Valley Historical Museum." *Antiques and the Arts Weekly* (September 21, 2001): 1, 68–69. 8 bw illus.

Connors, Jill. "Furniture Facts: William Savery as Chairmaker." *The Catalogue of Antiques and Fine Art* 3, no. 2 (spring 2002): 230–31. 1 color illus.

Connors, Michael. "Colonial Furniture of the West Indies." *Antiques* 161, no. 3 (March 2002): 74–83. 20 color illus.

Cooper, Wendy A. "American Painted Furniture: A New Perspective on Its Decoration and Use." *Antiques* 161, no. 1 (January 2002): 212–17. 8 color illus.

Cooper, Wendy A. "George M. Kaufman (1932–2001): A Tribute." *The Catalogue of Antiques and Fine Art* 3, no. 1 (winter/spring 2002): 320. 1 color illus.

Cooper, Wendy A. "H. F. du Pont's Fondness for Furniture: A Collecting Odyssey." *Antiques* 161, no. 1 (January 2002): 158–63. 8 color and 2 bw illus.

Cooper, Wendy A., with the assistance of Tara L. Gleason and Katharine A. John. *An American Vision: Henry Francis du Pont's Winterthur Museum*. Washington, D.C.: National Gallery of Art; Winterthur, Del.: Winterthur Museum, Garden & Library, 2002. 215 pp.; numerous color bw illus., checklist, index.

Corn, Wanda M. *The Great American Thing: Modern Art and National Identity, 1915–1935*. Berkeley: University of California Press, 1999. xxiii + 447 pp.; 321 color and bw illus., bibliography, index.

Cummings, Abbott Lowell. "The Abigail Ball Box: The History of an Initialed Object." In D. Brenton Simons, Peter Benes, et al. *The Art of Family: Genealogical Artifacts in New England*, 191–99. Boston: New England Historic Genealogical Society, 2002. 1 bw illus., 1 table.

"Discoveries." *The Catalogue of Antiques and Fine Art* 2, no. 5 (autumn 2001): 12–14. 7 color illus. (Includes joined Hadley settle of ca. 1730-1740 acquired by Historic Deerfield, Inc.)

"Discoveries." *The Catalogue of Antiques and Fine Art* 2, no. 6 (winter 2002): 10–13. 12 color illus. (Includes early Rhode Island tray-top tea table; English rococo-style looking glass and matching sconces acquired by SPNEA; and a Portsmouth dining table of 1760-1785.)

"Discoveries." *The Catalogue of Antiques and Fine Art* 3, no. 1 (winter/spring 2002): 24–27. 8 color and 1 bw illus. (Includes Shaker tall-case clock, made by Benjamin Youngs at Watervliet, New York, ca. 1800–1815.)

"Discoveries." *The Catalogue of Antiques and Fine Art* 3, no. 2 (spring 2002): 14–16. 7 color illus. (Includes dressing table from Wethersfield, Connecticut, 1750–1760.)

"Discoveries." *The Catalogue of Antiques and Fine Art* 3, no. 3 (summer 2002): 18–19. 4 color illus. (Re chest of drawers by Aaron Miltimore of Weston, Vermont, ca. 1827.)

Doherty, Susannah. "Curvaceous Forms." *Christie's Magazine* (January/ February 2002): 92–93. 3 color illus.

Educational Committee of the Antique Dealers' Association of America, Inc. "A Conversation with Mr. Albert Sack." *The Catalogue of Antiques and Fine Art* 3, no. 2 (spring 2002): 116–18. 5 color and 1 bw illus.

Evans, Nancy Goyne. "A Guide to Eighteenth-Century Windsor Chairs." *The Catalogue of Antiques and Fine Art* 3, no. 2 (spring 2002): 190–95. 7 color illus.

Eversmann, Pauline. "Museum Focus—Winterthur: Celebrating Fifty Years of Inspiration and Education." *The Catalogue of Antiques and Fine Art* 2, no. 5 (autumn 2001): 252–53. 3 color illus.

Eversmann, Pauline. *The Winterthur Guide to Recognizing Styles: American Decorative Arts from the 17th Through 19th Centuries.* Winterthur, Del.: Henry Francis du Pont Winterthur Museum, 2001. 119 pp.; color illus., time line, bibliography. Distributed by University Press of New England, Hanover, N.H., and London.

Feld, Stuart, and Elizabeth Feld. *"Of the Newest Fashion": Masterpieces of American Neo-classical Decorative Arts.* New York: Hirschl and Adler Galleries, 2001. 103 pp.; color and bw illus., bibliography.

Fiske, Betty, and Anne A. Verplanck. "Vernacular Art at Winterthur." *Antiques* 161, no. 1 (January 2002): 194–99. 11 color and 1 bw illus.

Foley, Paul J. *Willard's Patent Time Pieces: A History of the Weight-Driven Banjo Clock, 1800–1900.* Nowell, Mass.: Roxbury Village Publishing, 2002. viii + 358 pp.; 638 color and bw illus., biographies, appendices, bibliography, glossary, index.

Follansbee, Peter. "Unpacking the Little Chest." *Old-Time New England* 78, no. 268 (spring/summer 2000): 5–23. 15 bw illus.

Forsyth, Amy. "Frank Klausz Workshop." *Woodwork*, no. 74 (April 2002): 32–36. 4 color illus.

"Furniture Gallery, Part One" and "Furniture Gallery, Part Two." In Rick Mastelli and John Kelsey, eds., *Furniture Studio*, vol. 2, *Tradition in Contemporary Furniture*, 20–41, 106–27. Free Union, Va.: The Furniture Society, 2001. Color illus.

[Furniture Society, The]. *Furniture Matters: A Periodic Forum of the Furniture Society* (October 2001): 1–16. Bw illus. (Articles and pictures re: contemporary studio furniture.)

[Furniture Society, The]. *Furniture 2001 Program / Furniture Society Directory.* Free Union, Va.: The Furniture Society, 2001. 272 pp.; index.

[Furniture Society, The]. *Furniture 2002 Program / Furniture Society Directory.* Free Union, Va.: The Furniture Society, 2002. 272 pp.; index.

Gadsden, Eleanore. "Surviving the Revolution: A Philadelphia Cabinetmaker's Struggle During the War." *The Catalogue of Antiques and Fine Art* 2, no. 5 (autumn 2001): 262–65. 3 color and 1 bw illus.

Gadsden, Eleanore. "When Good Cabinetmakers Made Bad Furniture: The Career and Work of David Evans." In *American Furniture 2001*, 65–87. 22 color and bw illus.

Galassi, Peter, et al. *Making Choices: 1929, 1939, 1948, 1955.* New York: Museum of Modern Art, 2000. 348 pp.; 162 color and 144 bw illus., index. (Includes a few pieces of furniture.)

Gallagher, Fiona, et al. *Christie's Art Deco.* New York: Watson-Guptill, 2000. 192 pp.; color illus., bibliography, index.

Gallagher, Fiona, et al. *Christie's Art Nouveau.* New York: Watson-Guptill, 2000. 192 pp.; color illus., bibliography, index.

"Gallery." *Woodwork*, no. 72 (December 2001): 54–57. 15 color illus. (Re contemporary furniture.)

"Gallery." *Woodwork*, no. 73 (February 2002): 55–61. 25 color illus. (Re contemporary furniture by Josh Davidson, Cory Robinson, Ryan Legassicke, Mark DelGuidice, and others.)

"Gallery." *Woodwork*, no. 74 (April 2002): 48–55. 25 color illus. (Re contemporary furniture from England, Australia, Hawaii, and Arizona.)

"Gallery." *Woodwork*, no. 77 (October 2002): 40–45. 20 color illus.

"Gallery." *Woodwork*, no. 78 (December 2002): 46–53. 27 color illus.

Garrett, Elisabeth D. Review of Betty C. Monkman, *The White House: Its Historic Furnishings and First Families.* In *American Furniture 2001*, 243–46.

Garrison, J. Ritchie. Review of Luke Beckerdite, ed., *American Furniture 1999.* In *Winterthur Portfolio* 36, no. 1 (spring 2001): 49–59.

Garvin, Donna-Belle. "Reading the Evidence: The Challenge of Furniture Documentation." *The Catalogue of Antiques and Fine Art* 3, no. 3 (summer 2002): 162–68. 10 color and bw illus., biblio.

Garvin, James L. *A Building History of Northern New England.* Hanover, N.H.: University Press of New England, 2001. ix + 198 pp.; numerous bw illus., line drawings, appendix, bibliography. (Although restricted to architecture, a model study of great use to furniture historians.)

Gertz, Harris. *Heywood-Wakefield.* Atglen, Pa.: Schiffer Publishing, 2001. 160 pp.; numerous color illus.

Gilbert, Christopher. *Selected Writings on Vernacular Furniture, 1966–98.* Edited by David Jones. Leeds, England: Regional Furniture Society, 2001. viii + 209 pp.; numerous bw illus. (Re English furniture.)

Gilges, Peggy. "The Wright Stuff." *Christie's Magazine* (December 2001): 118–21. 8 color illus.

Gleason, Tara L. "The Georgia Dining Room Revisited." *Antiques* 161, no. 1 (January 2002): 188–93. 9 color and 1 bw illus.

Gomez-Ibañez, Miguel. "Understanding Tradition." In Rick Mastelli and John Kelsey, eds., *Furniture Studio,* vol. 2, *Tradition in Contemporary Furniture,* 42–51. Free Union, Va.: The Furniture Society, 2001. Color illus.

Gordon, Paul Jacques. "Can Maine Furniture Make Time Stand Still?" *Maine Antique Digest* 30, no. 2 (February 2002): 13E. 4 bw illus.

Greensted, Mary. "Ernest Gimson as a Designer." *Antiques* 161, no. 6 (June 2002: 82–91. 17 color illus.

Gronning, Erik. "Early New York Turned Chairs: A *Stoelendraaier's* Conceit." In *American Furniture 2001,* 88–119. 45 color and bw illus.

Guidice, Anthony. "An Interview with Frank Klausz." *Woodwork,* no. 74 (April 2002): 24–31. 17 color illus.

Gustafson, Eleanor H. "Museum Accessions." *Antiques* 161, no. 1 (January 2002): 42. 4 color illus. (Includes miniature chest over drawers from Chester County, Pennsylvania, 1747, acquired by Winterthur Museum.)

Gustafson, Eleanor H. "Museum Accessions." *Antiques* 161, no. 5 (May 2002):38. 3 color illus.

Hafertepe, Kenneth, and James F. O'Gorman, eds. *American Architects and Their Books to 1848.* Amherst: University of Massachusetts Press, 2001. xiii + 231 pp.; bw illus., index. (A dozen essays on the ownership and use of pattern books, builder's guides, and other architectural books from ca. 1700 to the early nineteenth century; see especially Abbott Lowell Cummings, "The Availability of Architectural Books in Eighteenth-Century New England.")

Halén, Widar. "Christopher Dresser, the Centennial Exhibition, and the Anglo-American Dialogue." *Antiques* 160, no. 3 (September 2001): 354–63. 17 color and 2 bw illus.

Halfpenny, Patricia. "Curator's Choice: New Decorative and Fine Arts Displays at Winterthur." *The Catalogue of Antiques and Fine Art* 2, no. 5 (autumn 2001): 254–55. 3 color illus.

Halpern, Martha. "Curator's Choice: Henry Pratt's Account for Lemon Hill." *The Catalogue of Antiques and Fine Art* 3, no. 2 (spring 2002): 44–45. 3 color illus. (See also Martha Halpern, "Museum Focus: Lemon Hill and Its Gardens," pp. 40–43, in the same issue.)

Handler, Sarah. *Austere Luminosity of Chinese Classical Furniture.* Berkeley: University of California Press, 2001. 425 pp.; 101 color and 221 bw illus., bibliography, glossary, index.

Harding, Deborah, and Laura Fisher. *Home Sweet Home: The House in American Folk Art.* New York: Rizzoli, 2001. 160 pp.; 200 color illus., bibliography, index.

Harris, Eileen. *The Genius of Robert Adam: His Interiors.* New Haven and London: Yale University Press for the Paul Mellon Centre for Studies in British Art, 2001. xi + 379 pp.; 407 color and bw illus., bibliography, index.

Harwood, Barry R. "A Herter Brothers Library Rediscovered." *Antiques* 161, no. 5 (May 2002): 150–57. 9 color and 6 bw illus.

Hawley, Henry. "Plain and Fancy." *Cleveland Museum of Art Magazine* (April 2001): 4–5. 4 color illus. (Re sideboard and cellarette by Duncan Phyfe recently acquired by the museum.)

Hermanson, John B. "Careswell, the Historic Winslow House in Marshfield, Massachusetts." *Antiques* 160, no. 3 (September 2001): 312–19. 13 color illus.

Herr, Donald M. "Joseph Lehn and Lehnware." *Antiques and the Arts Weekly* (August 17, 2001): 1, 68–70. 17 bw illus.

Hewett, David. "All About Banjo Clocks" (review of Paul J. Foley, *Willard's Patent Time Pieces: A History of the Weight-Driven Banjo Clock, 1800–1900*). In *Maine Antique Digest* 30, no. 10 (October 2002): 12B. 1 bw illus.

Hewett, David. "Nutting's 'Finest Piece of Furniture' Sells for Record Price." *Maine Antique Digest* 30, no. 5 (May 2002): 11A. 1 bw illus.

Hewett, David. "Rare Painted Court Cupboard Brings $69,500 at Dawson's." *Maine Antique Digest* 30, no. 3 (March 2002): 9A. 1 bw illus.

Hewett, David. "SPNEA Buys Barrell Family Mirror for $80,300." *Maine Antique Digest* 29, no. 9 (September 2001): 10A. 1 bw illus.

Hewett, David. "Three Rare Wooten Desks Sold . . ." *Maine Antique Digest* 30, no. 1 (January 2002): 11A. 4 bw illus.

"Highlights." *The Catalogue of Antiques and Fine Art* 2, no. 5 (autumn 2001): 24–27+. Color and bw illus. (Includes illus. and discussion of Harold Ionson's re-creations of the Thomas Seymour commode of 1809 in the collection of the Museum of Fine Arts, Boston.)

Hoban, Sally. *Miller's Collecting Modern Design.* New York: Mitchell Beazley, 2001. 160 pp.; 500 color illus.

Hollander, Stacy C., et al. *American Anthem: Masterworks from the American Folk Art Museum.* New York: American Folk Art Museum in association with Harry N. Abrams, 2001. 432 pp.; 293 color and 283 bw illus., catalogue, exhibition history, bibliography, index.

Hosaluk, Michael. "Surface Effects." *Woodwork*, no. 78 (December 2002): 42–45. 10 color illus.

Hough, Romeyn Beck. *The Wood Book*. Köln: Taschen, 2002. 864 pp.; numerous color and bw illus., bibliography, index. (Reprint of Hough's *The American Woods* (1888–1913, 1928].)

Hurst, Ron. "Just Arrived: From the Shop of Williams & Wright." *Colonial Williamsburg: The Journal of the Colonial Williamsburg Foundation* 24, no. 2 (summer 2002): 13. 1 color illus. (Re black walnut desk, made ca. 1750 in the William and Mary style, by Willis Williams [ca. 1710-1765] and John Wright [ca. 1705-1753].)

Husher, Richard W. "Simon Willard (1757–1848) and the Banjo Clock." *NAWCC Bulletin* 44, no. 1 (February 2002): 12–25. 21 bw illus.

Jackson, Anna. *The V & A Guide to Period Styles: 400 Years of British Art and Design*. New York: Harry N. Abrams, 2002. 176 pp.; numerous color illus.

Jeffrey, Michael. *Christie's Arts and Crafts Style*. New York: Watson-Guptill, 2001. 192 pp.; 120 color illus., bibliography, index.

Jobe, Brock. "A Case Study: The Cecil and Lancaster Rooms at Winterthur." *Antiques* 161, no. 1 (January 2002): 164–69. 3 color and 5 bw illus.

Jobe, Brock. "The Lisle Desk-and-Bookcase: A Rhode Island Icon." In *American Furniture 2001*, 120–51. 48 color and bw illus.

Jones, Ted. "Furniture Facts: The Loudon Connection." *The Catalogue of Antiques and Fine Art* 3, no. 3 (summer 2002): 188–90. 3 color illus.

Jones, Ted. "What is it Worth?: Windsor Chairs." *The Catalogue of Antiques and Fine Art* 3, no. 2 (spring 2002): 196–97. 2 color illus.

Joyce, Henry, and Julie Eldridge Edwards. "Three Historic Houses at the Shelburne Museum Reinterpreted." *Antiques* 161, no. 4 (April 2002): 104–13. 17 color and 2 bw illus.

Kane, Patricia E. "Living with Antiques: A Saint Louis Couple Collects." *Antiques* 161, no. 5 (May 2002): 112–23. 15 color illus.

Kenny, Peter M. "Two Early Eighteenth-Century *Schränke*: Rare Survivals of the German Joiner's Art in the Hudson River Valley." In *American Furniture 2001*, 220–42. 24 bw illus.

Kingwell, Mark. "More Beauty and More Deep Wonder." In Rick Mastelli and John Kelsey, eds., *Furniture Studio*, vol. 2, *Tradition in Contemporary Furniture*, 52–60. Free Union, Va.: The Furniture Society, 2001. Color illus.

Kirtley, Alexandra Alevizatos. "New Discoveries in Baltimore Painted Furniture." *The Catalogue of Antiques and Fine Art* 3, no. 2 (spring 2002): 204–9. 9 color illus.

Kline, Katy, et al. *Pointed Pairings: The Valuing of Art*. Brunswick, Me.: Bowdoin College Museum of Art, 2002. 78 pp.; color and bw illus., checklist. (Exhibition catalogue with entries on American furniture by Laura Sprague.)

Kolbe, J. Christian. "Willis Cowling (1788-1828), Richmond Cabinetmaker." *Journal of Early Southern Decorative Arts* 27, no. 2 (winter 2001): 51–75. 9 bw illus., 3 appendixes.

Kramer, Miriam. "Report from Europe: Dutch Rococo." *Antiques* 160, no. 6 (December 2001): 760. 3 color illus. (Re exhibition at Rijksmuseum.)

Lahikainen, Dean Thomas. "A Salem Cabinetmakers' Price Book." In *American Furniture 2001*, 152–221. 47+ color and bw illus., appendixes, facsimile.

Laird, Ross A. *Grain of Truth: The Ancient Lessons of Craft*. New York: Walker and Company, 2001. 188 pp.; illus.

Landis, Scott. "Furniture with a Sense of Place." In Rick Mastelli and John Kelsey, eds., *Furniture Studio*, vol. 2, *Tradition in Contemporary Furniture*, 128–39. Free Union, Va.: The Furniture Society, 2001. Color illus.

Landsmark, Ted. Review of John T. Kirk, *American Furniture: Understanding Style, Construction, and Quality*. In *American Furniture 2001*, 251–54.

Lane, Joshua. "Furniture Transformations." *The Catalogue of Antiques and Fine Art* 2, no. 6 (winter 2002): 142–43. 2 color and 1 bw illus.

Lane, Joshua. "Joined, Carved Settle." *Historic Deerfield* 1, no. 3 (fall 2001): 13–18. 8 color and 5 bw illus. (Also issued as a separate offprint.)

Lang, Christopher. "Hugh Easley, Alabama Cabinetmaker." *Antiques* 161, no. 5 (May 2002): 134–39. 13 color illus.

Laux, Barbara. "The Furniture Mounts of P. E. Guerin." *Antiques* 161, no. 5 (May 2002): 140–49. 11 color and 3 bw illus.

Leben, Ulrich. "The Toilette in the Eighteenth Century." *Antiques* 162, no. 3 (September 2002): 84–91. 15 color illus.

Ledes, Allison Eckardt. "Current and Coming: American Clocks." *Antiques* 162, no. 2 (August 2002): 24. 1 color illus.

Ledes, Allison Eckardt. "Current and Coming: American Neoclassicism." *Antiques* 160, no. 6 (December 2001): 752. 3 color illus. (Re exhibition at Hirschl and Adler Galleries.)

Ledes, Allison Eckardt. "Current and Coming: Modern Living." *Antiques* 160, no. 6 (December 2001): 752, 754. 2 color illus. (Re exhibition about Russell Wright.)

Ledes, Allison Eckardt. "Current and Coming: Winterthur at Home and in New York." *Antiques* 161, no. 1 (January 2002): 24, 26. 2 color and 2 bw illus.

Ledes, Allison Eckardt. "Current and Coming: Winterthur in Washington, D.C." *Antiques* 161, no. 5 (May 2002): 26. 3 color illus.

Ledes, Allison Eckardt. "Design Notes: A New Service for Dating English Furniture." *Antiques* 161, no. 6 (June 2002): 136. 3 color and

1 bw illus. (Re locks made by the Chubb Lock Company, est. 1818.)

Levison, Deanne D. "Living with Antiques: A Collection on the Chesapeake Bay." *Antiques* 160, no. 6 (December 2001): 804–11. 13 color illus.

Levy, Bernard and S. Dean, Inc. *Gallery Catalogue XII: Spring 2002.* New York: Bernard & S. Dean Levy, Inc., 2002. 36 pp.; color illus.

"Lifestyle: Town House of Treasures." *The Catalogue of Antiques and Fine Art* 3, no. 1 (winter/spring 2002): 62–70. 9 color illus. (Re private collection.)

Loeser, Tom. "Finding Your Own Direction: Five Stories of Life After Graduation." *Woodwork,* no. 72 (December 2001): 35–40. 22 color illus. (See also p. 80.)

Lucas, Beverly Johnson. "History in Houses: The Butler-McCook House and Garden in Hartford, Connecticut." *Antiques* 162, no. 2 (August 2002): 88–95. 14 color illus.

Mackay, James. *Antiques at a Glance: Furniture.* New York: Sterling Publishing, 2002. 144 pp.; 120+ color illus., index.

Maeder, Edward F. "'. . . and the pockets were slanted': Clothing of Elisha Barnard." *Historic Deerfield* 1, no. 3 (fall 2001): 2–4. 4 color illus.

Main, Keri K. "Pursuing 'The Things of This World': Mormon Resistance and Assimilation as Seen in the Furniture of the Brigham City Cooperative, 1874–88." *Winterthur Portfolio* 36, no. 4 (winter 2001): 191–212. 14 bw illus.

[Maine State Museum]. "Federal Secretary Comes Back to Maine: Maine State Museum Acquires Dinsmore-Batchelder Secretary." *Antiques and the Arts Weekly* (April 19, 2002): 8. 1 bw illus.

Maresca, Frank, and Roger Ricco. *American Vernacular: New Discoveries in Folk, Self-Taught, and Outsider Sculpture.* Boston: Little, Brown/A Bulfinch Press Book, 2002. 303 pp.; numerous color illus., biographies, index. (Contains a few pieces of furniture.)

Martin, Loy D. "Decoding Studio Furniture." In Rick Mastelli and John Kelsey, eds., *Furniture Studio,* vol. 2, *Tradition in Contemporary Furniture,* 8–19. Free Union, Va.: The Furniture Society, 2001. Color illus.

Mastelli, Rick, and John Kelsey, eds. *Furniture Studio,* vol. 2, *Tradition in Contemporary Furniture.* Free Union, Va.: The Furniture Society, 2001. 144 pp.; numerous color and bw illus., index.

May, Stephen. Review of Rick Mastelli and John Kelsey, eds., *Tradition in Contemporary Furniture.* In *American Craft* 62, no. 2 (April/May 2002): 52.

McKinstrey, E. Richard. "The Byrdcliffe Arts and Crafts Colony." *Winterthur Magazine* (fall 2001): 43–49. Color and bw illus.

[Memphis College of Art]. *Studio Furniture: A Fine Art Invitational, The Biennial Exhibition.* Memphis, Tenn.: Memphis College of Art, 2000. Unpaged; color illus.

[Metropolitan Museum of Art]. *A Walk Through the American Wing.* New York: Metropolitan Museum of Art, 2002. 216 pp.; numerous color illus. Distributed by Yale University Press, New Haven.

Mijuskovic, Ben. "The Collector's Find: The Master's Hand?" *Maine Antique Digest* 30, no. 5 (May 2002): 47B. 5 bw illus. (Re nineteenth-century center table, possibly by the Meeks firm.)

Miranda, D. Hector Rivero Borrell, et al. *The Grandeur of Vice-Regal Mexico: Treasures from the Museo Franz Mayer.* Houston: Museum of Fine Arts, Houston, and Museo Franz Mayer, Mexico, 2002. xi + 367 pp.; numerous color illus., bibliography, index.

Moser, Thomas F., with Brad Lemley. *Thos. Moser: Artistry in Wood.* San Francisco: Chronicle Books, 2002. 192 pp.; numerous color illus.

Muller, Charles R. *Soap Hollow: The Furniture and Its Makers.* Groveport, Ohio: The Canal Press, 2002. vii + 95 pp.; numerous color illus., appendix, index.

[Museum of Early Southern Decorative Arts]. "Table Found, Saved." *Maine Antique Digest* 30, no. 5 (May 2002): 10A. 2 bw illus. (Re Baltimore table, ca. 1798, acquired by MESDA.)

[Museum of the Shenandoah Valley]. "Collection Acquired for Museum of the Shenandoah Valley." *Maine Antique Digest* 30, no. 1 (January 2002): 9A. 1 bw illus.

[Munson Williams Proctor Arts Institute]. "Heavy Metal: Innovative Victorian Furniture." *Munson Williams Proctor Arts Institute Bulletin* (September 2002): 1. 5 color illus.

Neumann, Dietrich, ed. *Richard Neutra's Windshield House.* New Haven and London: Yale University Press, 2001. xxvi + 150 pp.; numerous color and bw illus., appendix, bibliography, index.

Nichols, Michele K. "The National Clock and Watch Museum: Non-Horological Museum Pieces." *NAWCC Bulletin* 43, no. 5 (October 2001): 625. 1 bw illus. (Re portrait of clockmaker Elnathan Taber of Roxbury.)

Niven, Penelope. "Frank L. Horton and the Roads to MESDA." *Journal of Early Southern Decorative Arts* 27, no. 1 (summer 2001): 1–151. 72 bw illus.

Northeast Auctions. *Northeast Auctions by Ronald Bourgeault: Year 2001 in Pictures.* Portsmouth, N.H.: Northeast Auctions, 2001. 12 pp.; color illus.

"Noteworthy Sales." *The Catalogue of Antiques and Fine Art* 2, no. 5 (autumn 2001): 10–11. 6 color illus. (Includes Boston high chest and dressing table of ca. 1740 acquired by the Peabody Essex Museum, and other furniture sold to private collectors.)

"Noteworthy Sales." *The Catalogue of Antiques and Fine Art* 2, no. 6 (winter 2002): 14–15. 6 color illus.

(Re federal-period clocks and Portsmouth one-drawer stand.)

"Noteworthy Sales." *The Catalogue of Antiques and Fine Art* 3, no. 1 (winter/spring 2002): 22–23. 6 color and 1 bw illus. (Re Boston chest of drawers attributed to John Cogswell, ca. 1760–1780.)

"Noteworthy Sales." *The Catalogue of Antiques and Fine Art* 3, no. 2 (spring 2002): 17–19. 13 color illus. (Includes federal-period chest of drawers from Essex County.)

"Noteworthy Sales." *The Catalogue of Antiques and Fine Art* 3, no. 3 (summer 2002): 20–22. 10 color illus. (Includes some furniture.)

Nutting, Wallace. *Windsor Chairs: An Illustrated Handbook*. 1917. Reprint. New York: Dover Publications, 2002. 192 pp.; illus. (With new introduction by Victor M. Linoff.)

Nye, John B. A. "Captain's Table." *Sotheby's Preview* (October 2001): 40–41. 1 color illus. (Re Philadelphia pier table, ca. 1750.)

Nye, John B. A. "Outdoor Types." *Sotheby's Preview* (October 2002): 140–41. 1 color illus.

Nye, John B. A. "The Robert E. Crawford Collection." *Sotheby's Preview* (October 2001): 42. 2 color illus.

Olmert, Michael. "Peering into Rings of Grain." *Colonial Williamsburg: The Journal of the Colonial Williamsburg Foundation* 24, no. 2 (spring 2002): 74–78. 4 color illus. (See also Edward Chappel, "Dendrochronology in Context: Williamsburg's Everard House," pp. 78–79, in the same issue.)

Osgood, Jere. "A Meditation on the Desk." In Rick Mastelli and John Kelsey, eds., *Furniture Studio*, vol. 2, *Tradition in Contemporary Furniture*, 72–83. Free Union, Va.: The Furniture Society, 2001. Color illus.

Owen, Nancy. *Rookwood and the Industry of Art: Women, Culture, and Commerce, 1880–1913*. Athens: Ohio University Press, 2001. xiv + 335 pp.; color and bw illus., appendix, bibliography, index. (Some references to furniture making in Cincinnati.)

"Palley Collection Sold at Sotheby's." *Antiques and the Arts Weekly* (February 1, 2002): 34–36. 18 bw illus.

Perry, Barbara Stone. *On the Surface: Late Nineteenth-Century Decorative Arts*. Charlotte, N.C.: Mint Museum of Art, 2001. 111 pp.; numerous color and bw illus., checklist, bibliography.

[Philadelphia Museum of Art]. "Philadelphia Museum of Art Receives Icon of American Decorative Arts." *Antiques and the Arts Weekly* (March 22, 2002): 65. 1 bw illus.

Pierce, Kerry. *The Custom Furniture Source Book: A Guide to 125 Selected Craftsmen*. Newtown, Conn.: Taunton Press, 2001. 264 pp.; numerous color illus., indexes.

Pollack, Jodi. "The Meeks Cabinetmaking Firm in New York City: Part I, 1797–1835." *Antiques* 161, no. 5 (May 2002): 102–11. 13 color and 4 bw illus.

"Portfolio: Erik A. Wolken." *American Craft* 61, no. 6 (December 2001/January 2002): 70. 1 color illus. (Re contemporary furniture maker.)

Priddy, Sumpter, III. "John Bivins: A Tribute." *The Catalogue of Antiques and Fine Art* 2, no. 5 (autumn 2001): 272. 1 bw illus.

Prown, Jules David. *Art as Evidence: Writings on Art and Material Culture*. New Haven: Yale University Press, 2001. xii + 304 pp.; numerous color and bw illus., bibliography, index.

Rago, David, and John Sollo. *Collecting Modern: A Guide to Mid-Century Furniture and Ceramics*. Salt Lake City, Utah: Gibbs Smith, 2001. 160 pp.; 160 color illus.

Ramaci, Lisa. "Mahantango Marvels." *Sotheby's Preview* (May 2002): 83. 1 color illus.

Ramond, Pierre. *Masterpieces of Marquetry*. 3 vols. Los Angeles: J. Paul Getty Museum, 2000. Vol. 1, *From the Beginnings to Louis XIV*. 150 pp.; numerous color and bw illus., line drawings. Vol. 2, *From the Regénce to the Present Day*. 217 pp.; numerous color and bw illus., line drawings, bibliography. Vol. 3, *Outstanding Marqueters*. 136 pp.; numerous color and bw illus., line drawings. (First published in France in 1996.)

Rapaport, Brooke Kamin, Kevin L. Stayton, et al. *Vital Forms: American Art and Design in the Atomic Age, 1940–1960*. Brooklyn, N.Y.: Brooklyn Museum of Art in association with Harry N. Abrams, 2001. 256 pp.; numerous color and bw illus., bibliography, index.

Reed, W. A. "Charles Radtke Interview." *Woodwork*, no. 78 (December 2002): 30–31. 3 color illus. 17 color illus.

Regional Furniture: The Journal of the Regional Furniture Society 15 (2001): 76. Numerous bw illus. (Seven articles related to English furniture.)

Regional Furniture Society Newsletter, no. 35 (autumn 2001): 1–17. bw illus. (Notes, brief articles, reviews, and illustrations of English vernacular furniture.)

[Renwick Gallery]. "Renwick Gallery to Present Sam Maloof Retrospective." *Antiques and the Arts Weekly* (August 24, 2001): 35.

Richter, Paula Bradstreet. *Painted with Thread: The Art of American Embroidery*. Salem: Peabody Essex Museum, 2001. xxi + 157 pp.; numerous color illus. (Also published as *Peabody Essex Museum Collections* 136 [2000]. Contains some furniture.)

Roberts, Hugh. *For the King's Pleasure*. London: The Royal Collection, 2001. 486 pp.; 486 color and bw illus. (Re furnishings of George IV's apartments at Windsor Castle.)

Robertson, Cheryl. "Decorating the Avery Coonley House: Frank Lloyd Wright and George Mann Niedecken." *The Catalogue of Antiques and Fine Art* 2, no. 5 (autumn 2001): 242–47. 7 color and bw illus.

Roche, Daniel. *A History of Everyday Things: The Birth of Consumption in France, 1600 to 1800*. Trans. Brian

Pearce. Cambridge: Cambridge University Press, 2000. 320 pp.; bibliography, index.

Rousseau, Francis. *The Book of Antique Furniture: An International Style Guide from the 16th to the 20th Century*. Trans. Lisa Davidson. Edison, N.J.: Chartwell Books, 2000. 223 pp.; numerous color illus., chronology, glossary, index. (Devoted to European furniture.)

Sack, Albert. "Exceptions to the Rule." *The Catalogue of Antiques and Fine Art* 3, no. 1 (winter/spring 2002): 300–303. 1 color and 5 bw illus.

Schleining, Lon. *Treasure Chests: The Legacy of Extraordinary Boxes*. Newtown, Conn.: Taunton Press, 2001. 208 pp.; 250+ color illus.

Schwartz, Marvin D., Edward J. Stanek, and Douglas True. *The Furniture of John Henry Belter and the Rococo Revival*. 1981. Reprint. Edina, Minn.: Lise Bohm Publishing, 2000. 88 pp.; 145 color and bw illus.

"Selections from Israel Sack at Sotheby's." *Antiques and the Arts Weekly* (February 1, 2002): 20–22. 17 bw illus.

Shallcross, Gilian Ford. Review of Rosemary Troy Krill with Pauline K. Eversmann, *Early American Decorative Arts, 1620–1860: A Handbook for Interpreters*. In *American Furniture 2001*, 246–49.

Siegel, Kathran. "Art Furniture." In Rick Mastelli and John Kelsey, eds., *Furniture Studio*, vol. 2, *Tradition in Contemporary Furniture*, 84–99. Free Union, Va.: The Furniture Society, 2001. Color illus.

Silberman, Robert. "Sam Maloof." *American Craft* 62, no. 2 (April/May 2002): 62–67. 6 color illus.

"Simon Willard: Clockmaker and Inventor, Roxbury's Clockmaker to Thomas Jefferson." *Forest Hills Flame* 6, no. 2 (autumn 2001): 4–5. 5 bw illus. (Includes images of Willard's gravestone at Forest Hills, carved by Alpheus Carey.)

Simons, D. Brenton, Peter Benes, et al. *The Art of Family: Genealogical Artifacts in New England*. Boston: New England Historic Genealogical Society, 2002. xiv + 336 pp.; numerous color and bw illus., indexes. (See especially the article by Abbott Lowell Cummings cited above, and additional articles by Wendell Garrett, Jane Cayford Nylander, and Laurel Thatcher Ulrich.)

Smith, Paul J., ed. *Objects for Use: Handmade by Design*. New York: Harry N. Abrams, 2001. 366 pp.; numerous color illus.

Smith, R. Scudder. "'American Radiance': Folk Art Illuminated." *Aniques and the Arts Weekly* (December 7, 2001): 1, 38–45. Numerous bw illus.

Smith, Robert. "Abijah Reed." *Woodwork*, no. 77 (October 2002): 22–26. 15 color illus.

Snodin, Michael, and John Styles. *Design and the Decorative Arts: Britain, 1500–1900*. London: V&A Publications, 2001. 480 pp.; 1,080 color illus.

Snyder, John J., Jr. "A Pennsylvania Clock Mystery." *The Catalogue of Antiques and Fine Art* 3, no. 2 (spring 2002): 232–35. 2 color and 1 bw illus.

[Society for the Preservation of New England Antiquities]. "SPNEA Acquires Barrell Family Looking Glass and Sconces." *Antiques and the Arts Weekly* (October 19, 2001): 20. 1 bw illus.

Solis-Cohen, Lita. "The Copeland Sale." *Maine Antique Digest* 30, no. 3 (March 2002): 40D–43D. Numerous bw illus.

Solis-Cohen, Lita. "Eight Philadelphia Side Chairs to Sell at Doyle's." *Maine Antique Digest* 30, no. 3 (March 2002): 9A. 1 bw illus.

Solis-Cohen, Lita. "Godshalk Clock in the Pickering Case." *Maine Antique Digest* 30, no. 10 (October 2002): 1E-3. 15 bw illus. (Re Philadelphia tall-case clock, ca. 1770–1780, with works by Jacob Godshalk and case with paper label of George Pickering, sold at Sotheby's. See also sidebar on "American Clocks from the Time Museum," p. 3E.)

Solis-Cohen, Lita. "The Israel Sack, Inc., Sale." *Maine Antique Digest* 30, no. 3 (March 2002): 28A–30A. 27 bw illus.

Solis-Cohen, Lita. "John Cadwalader's Easy Chair Gift to PMA." *Maine Antique Digest* 30, no. 5 (May 2002): 9A. 1 bw illus.

Solis-Cohen, Lita. "More on Antique Furniture" (review of Luke Beckerdite, ed., *American Furniture 2001*). *Maine Antique Digest* 30, no. 4 (April 2002): 8C. 1 bw illus.

Solis-Cohen, Lita. "Nakashima." *Maine Antique Digest* 29, no. 9 (September 2001): 10A. 2 bw illus.

Solis-Cohen, Lita. "Of the Newest Fashion: Hirschl & Adler Galleries, New York City" (exhibition review). *Maine Antique Digest* 30, no. 1 (January 2002): 44A–45A. 8 bw illus.

Solis-Cohen, Lita. "Select Masterpieces Tell the Winterthur Story: National Gallery of Art, Washington, D.C." *Maine Antique Digest* 30, no. 9 (September 2002): 12B. 8 bw illus.

Sollo, John. *American Insider's Guide to Twentieth-Century Furniture*. Ed. Lita Solis-Cohen. New York: Miller's, 2002. 224 pp.; illus.

Sotheby's. *The American Folk Art Collection of Sandy and Julie Palley*. New York: Sotheby's, January 18, 2002. Sale N07754. 120 pp.; numerous color illus. (Forewords by Gerard Wertkin, Nancy Druckman, Alan Miller, Joan Johnson, and others.)

Sotheby's. *The Collection of Mr. and Mrs. Lammot du Pont Copeland*. New York: Sotheby's, January 19, 2002. Sale N07757. 244 pp.; numerous color illus. (Forewords by Pamela Cunningham Copeland and Wendell D. Garrett.)

Sotheby's. *Important Americana*. New York: October 10, 2002. Sale N07825. 192 pp.; numerous color illus. (Includes furniture deaccessioned from the Davenport collection at the Williams College Museum of Art, lots 236–77.)

Sotheby's. *Important Americana from the Collection of Richard and Joy Kanter.* New York: Sotheby's, January 18, 2002. Sale N07755. 96 pp.; numerous color illus. (Foreword by Nancy Druckman.)

Sotheby's. *Property from the Collection of Gunston Hall Plantation.* New York: Sotheby's, January 20, 2002. N07753. 104 pp.; numerous color illus. (Forewords by Wendell D. Garrett, Susan Borchardt, and Judith C. Herdeg and Thomas A. Lainhoff.)

Sotheby's. *Selections from Israel Sack, Inc.* New York: Sotheby's, January 20, 2002. Sale N07761. 100 pp.; numerous color illus. (Introduction by Wendell D. Garrett.)

[Southern Highland Craft Guild]. *The Chair Show 3.* Asheville, N.C.: Southern Highland Craft Guild, 1999. 46 pp.; color illus. (Includes text by Andrew H. Glasgow and Edward S. Cooke, Jr.)

[Southern Highland Craft Guild]. *The Chair Show 4.* Asheville, N.C.: Southern Highland Craft Guild, 2001. 46 pp.; color illus. (Includes text by Andrew H. Glasgow and David Revere McFadden.)

[Speed Art Museum]. "Early Kentucky Furniture from Noe Collection at the Speed Art Museum." *Antiques and the Arts Weekly* (June 14, 2002): 9.

Spittler, Tom. "Ashwin & Co.: British or American Dialmaker? and the William Jones Connection." *NAWCC Bulletin,* 43, no. 4 (August 2001): 436–445. 19 bw illus.

Spittler, Tom. "The Reading School of Dialmaking, with an Overview of American Dials." *NAWCC Bulletin* 44, no. 3 (June 2002): 305–20. 30 color and bw illus.

Stein, Mark V. *20th Century Modern Clocks: Desk, Shelf, and Decorative.* Baltimore: Radiomania Books, 2001. 255 pp.; 1,600 bw illus.

Stevens, Charlene E. *On Time: How America Has Learned to Live by the Clock.* Boston: Little, Brown/A Bulfinch Press Book, 2002. 256 pp.; 175 color and 50 bw illus., index.

Stillinger, Elizabeth. "Edna Greenwood and Everyday Life in Early New England." *Antiques* 162, no. 2 (August 2002): 62–71. 10 color and 8 bw illus.

Stillinger, Elizabeth. "Historic Deerfield Frontier of Freedom." *The Catalogue of Antiques and Fine Art* 2, no. 6 (winter 2002): 137–39. 2 color and 3 bw illus.

Strazdes, Diana. "The Millionaire's Palace: Leland Stanford's Commission for Pottier & Stymus in San Francisco." *Winterthur Portfolio* 36, no. 4 (winter 2001): 213–43. 26 bw illus.

Sullivan, Timothy M. "In Search of Robert Harrold, Portsmouth Cabinetmaker." *Warner House Newsletter* (winter 2001): 1, 4–5. 3 bw illus.

Talbott, Page. "Continuity and Innovation: Recliners, Sofa Beds, Rocking Chairs, and Folding Chairs." *Antiques* 161, no. 5 (May 2002): 124–33. 11 color and 6 bw illus.

Taylor, Snowden. "Research Activities and News." *NAWCC Bulletin* 43, no. 5 (October 2001): 650–60. 17 bw illus.

Terraroli, Valerio. *Skira Dictionary of Modern Decorative Arts.* Milan, Italy: Skira, 2001. 336 pp.; 300 color and bw illus.

"Thinking Furniture Making." In Rick Mastelli and John Kelsey, eds., *Furniture Studio,* vol. 2, *Tradition in Contemporary Furniture,* 140–41. Free Union, Va.: The Furniture Society, 2001. Color illus.

Thompson, Neville. "Trade Catalogues in the Winterthur Library." *Antiques* 161, no. 1 (January 2002): 206–11. 10 color illus.

Thompson, Neville. "Victorian Advice: *All You Need to Know,* Thomas Webster and Frances Parkes's Encyclopedia of Domestic Economy." *Nineteenth Century* 21, no. 2 fall (2001): 31–32. 2 bw illus.

Three Centuries of New Hampshire Furniture Making: New Hampshire Furniture Masters Association Fifth Annual Exhibition and Auction. Concord: New Hampshire Furniture Masters Association, 2000. 40 pp.; color and bw illus.

Trent, Robert F., Peter Follansbee, and Alan Miller. "First Flowers of the Wilderness: Mannerist Furniture from a Northern Essex County, Massachusetts, Shop." In *American Furniture 2001,* 1–64. 100 color and bw illus.

Trilling, James. *The Language of Ornament.* New York: Thames and Hudson, 2001. 224 pp.; illus.

[Tubman African American Museum]. *Sankofa: A Century of African American Expression in the Decorative Arts.* Macon, Ga.: Tubman African American Museum, [2001]. 17 pp.; bw illus., bibliography.

Ulrich, Laurel Thatcher. *The Age of Homespun: Objects and Stories in the Creation of an American Myth.* New York: Alfred A. Knopf, 2001. 501 pp.; bw illus., index. (See chapter 3, "Hannah Barnard's Cupboard," reprinted here for the third time in revised form.)

Vlach, John Michael. "Roots and Branches: Historical Patterns in African Diasporan Artifacts." In *African Roots/American Cultures: Africa in the Creation of the Americas,* ed. by Sheila S. Walker, 183–205. New York: Rowman and Littlefield, 2001. 14 bw illus.

Ward, Gerald W.R., comp. "Recent Writing on American Furniture: A Bibliography." In *American Furniture 2001,* 255–65.

Warren, David B. "The Arts of Vice-Regal Mexico, 1521–1821: A Confluence of Cultures." *Antiques* 161, no. 4 (April 2002): 120–29. 25 color illus.

Wells, Camille. "Deliberation on Display: An Exhibition Review." *Winterthur Portfolio* 36, no. 1 (spring 2001): 39–47. 5 bw illus. (Re "How Do We Know? Recreating Domestic Interiors," held at The Octagon, Museum of the American Architectural Foundation, Washington, D.C., June–December 2000.)

"Werneke on 78th Street." *Antiques and the Arts Weekly* (February 1, 2002): 55. 2 bw illus. (Includes image of lolling chair made ca. 1780–1785 and signed by William Brown of Boston.)

Westermann, Mariët, et al. *Art and Home: Dutch Interiors in the Age of Rembrandt*. Zwolle: Waanders Publishers for the Denver Art Museum and The Newark Museum, 2001. 240 pp.; numerous color and bw illus., bibliography. (Includes many decorative arts objects and a discussion of interiors, all of significance in relation to American material culture.)

White, Cheryl. "Garry Knox Bennett." *American Craft* 61, no. 5 (October/November 2001): 60–63+. 7 color illus.

White, Karen R. *Donald Lloyd McKinley: A Studio Practice in Furniture*. Oakville, Canada: Oakville Galleries, 2000. 45 pp.; bw illus.

[Winterthur Museum]. "Shells, Scrolls, and Cabrioles: American Furniture from Winterthur at the Winter Antiques Show, January 20–27." *Winterthur Magazine* (December 2001): 35–41. 9 color illus.

[Winterthur Museum]. "Winterthur Museum: 50 Years." *Antiques* 161, no. 1 (January 2002): 1–224. Numerous color and bw illus. (Special issue celebrating the first half century of Winterthur as a museum.)

Woodhouse, Anne. "Conserving the 'Klismos' Fancy Chair." *Gateway Heritage* (The Quarterly Magazine of the Missouri Historical Society) 20, no. 2 (fall 1999): 76–79. 4 color illus.

Woodhouse, Anne. Review of Peter Benes, ed., *Rural New England Furniture: People, Place, and Production*. In *American Furniture 2001*, 249–51.

"Wunsch Collection Traces Early Nesting in New York: Two Centuries of Cultural History as Seen Through Home Furnishings at UBS Paine-Webber Gallery." *Antiques and the Arts Weekly* (September 13, 2002): 102E. 5 bw illus.

Zimmerman, Philip D. "Eighteenth-Century Philadelphia Case Furniture at Stenton." *Antiques* 161, no. 5 (May 2002): 94–101. 14 color illus.

Zimmerman, Philip D. "Queen Anne and Chippendale Chairs in Delaware." *Antiques* 160, no. 3 (September 2001): 330–39. 17 color illus.

Index

Academie or Store-House of Armory and Blazon (Holme), 126, 144n3
Academy of Natural Sciences, 99
Acanthus, 64(fig. 20), 72, 73(fig. 37), 74, 75(fig. 45), 80, 172n16, 194
ACC Asilomar conference, 246
Accessions, 1960, 65
Account books, 146n24
Adams, John, 27–28
Adamson, Jeremy, 243, 247
Addison, Joseph, 185
Adze, 131
Aesthetic, seventeenth-century, 184–187
Affleck, Thomas, 9, 64, 113, 153, 154
Age of Homespun, The (Ulrich), 258
Air pump case, 163(fig. 19)
Alabaster, figures, 24(&fig. 37)
Alexander, John D., 141
Allen, Nathaniel, 151, 172n9
Allen, Robert, 153
Altar tombs, 103(&fig. 16), 122n10
American: armchairs, 68(&fig. 27), 69(fig. 29); candlestands, 75(figs. 44, 45), 79(fig. 53); card tables, 70(figs. 31, 33), 72(fig. 35), 73(fig. 40); dressing tables, 80(&fig. 54), 83–87(&figs.); easy chairs, 61(fig. 11), 62(figs. 13, 14, 16), 63, 64(fig. 19), 65(figs. 21, 22); folding-leaf table, 73–74(&figs. 41, 42, 43); upholstered armchair, 58(fig. 6)
"American Art Worlds and Material Culture," 207
American Clock and Watch Museum, 253
American Craft, 245
American Craft Museum, 243, 249
American Craftsmen's Council, 244–245
American Furniture, 141, 217, 258, 259
American Furniture at Chipstone (Roque), 87
American Furniture: Queen Anne and Chippendale Periods (Downs), 71–72(&fig. 36)
American furniture scholarship: American Wing (Metropolitan Museum of Art) and, 207–208(&figs.); canon of, 207–227; cultural diversity and, 219–221; ethnicity and race and, 209, 212–213, 225n9; Fred Wilson, 219(&fig. 16); gender and, 209, 213–214, 226n10; Girl Scouts Loan Exhibition, 210–211(&fig. 5) and; High Street exhibition and, 210(&fig. 4); material culture studies and, 207, 217, 219; Milwaukee Art Museum exhibits and, 221–224(&figs.); museum catalogues and auctions and, 209–210, 212; museums' display of decorative arts and, 207–225(&figs.); new interpretive models for, 214–219
American Seating Furniture 1630–1730 (Forman), 125, 175
American Vision: Henry Francis du Pont's Winterthur Museum, An (Cooper), 256–259
American Weekly Mercury, 108
American Wing (Metropolitan Museum of Art), 207–208(&fig. 2), 214
Ames, Kenneth, 217
Andrews, John, 255
Annapolis (Maryland): billiard table, 27–28(&fig. 45), 51n44, 51n47; Chase-Lloyd House, 15(&fig. 22); desk-and-bookcase, 19(&fig. 28), 31; shaving table, 21(&fig. 31); walnut desk, 22(fig. 33); writing table, 21(&fig. 32)
Annunciation Tryptich (Campin), 135(fig. 20)
Anthony, Aaron, 45

Antiques, 64(fig. 20), 210, 259
Antiques market, American furniture scholarship and, 55, 226n16
Applied-ornament style, 229–232, 239
Apprentices: caned chair and, 183; among Philadelphia joiners, 150, 151, 152, 169, 173n25; tools made by, 133
Arched crest, 100, 101(&fig. 11)
Arched pediments, 160, 161(figs. 15, 16), 162(fig. 17), 163
Architectural design books, 48n20
Architecture Revised, Designed, and Published by Giacomo Leoni (Palladio), 48n20
Armchairs, 8, 11: American, 68(fig. 27); Baltimore, 32(fig. 52); Boston/Salem, 59(fig. 8); caned, 177(fig. 3), 186(fig. 10), 192(fig. 23), 198(fig. 33), 202(fig. 39); English, 15–16(&fig. 23), 24(fig. 36); fakery and, 65–69(&figs.), 71; New York, 220–221(&fig. 17); Philadelphia, 69(figs.); Portsmouth (New Hampshire), 66–67(figs. 23, 24, 25, 26); upholstered, 7(&fig. 6), 58(fig. 6), 59(fig. 8); Virginia, 220(fig. 18)
Armitt, Stephen, 162, 173n18: desk-and-bookcase, 159(fig. 12), 160
Armoire, 40–41(&fig. 70), 53n68
Arthur, Catherine Rogers, 36
Art Institute of Chicago, American decorative arts gallery, 214(fig. 10)
Artisans, romanticization of, 125–126, 143–144n2, 213–214
Arts and crafts movement, west coast, 248
Arts and Crafts of Newport, The (Carpenter), 63(&fig. 17), 85
Ash, armchair, 32(fig. 52)
Ashworth, Gavin, 257
Astragal elements, 165, 166

Augers, 131
Augustus Lutheran Church (Trappe, Pennsylvania), 103(&fig. 16)
Axes, 129, 131

Backstools, 62(fig. 15), 91n4
Baird, James, 119–120
Baird, John, 117, 124n27
Baird, Michael, 119–120
Balance of trade, 180
Ball-and-claw feet. *See* Claw-and-ball feet
Balls, lawn bowling, 26(&fig. 41)
Baltimore: armchair, 32(&fig. 52); bedroom suite, 44(fig. 77); card tables, 31–32(figs. 50, 51), 33(&fig. 53), 35(fig. 57); chairs, 50n38; chamber table, 37(fig. 62); chest of drawers, 37(fig. 64); clothes press, 30(fig. 49), 31; corner table, 119(fig. 41); cornice, 33(fig. 54); dining table, 34(fig. 55); Edward Lloyd V and, 29–30; handrailing, 36(fig. 61), 37, 52n61; liquor case, 38(fig. 65); secretary, 30(fig. 48); sideboard, 35(fig. 58); sideboard tables, 23(fig. 35), 38(fig. 65), 42(fig. 72); side chairs, 23(fig. 35); sofa, 34(fig. 56), 35; wardrobes, 39–41(figs. 66, 67, 68, 69); writing table, 36(fig. 60)
Banjo clock, 252–256
Banks, Amanda Carson, 217
Baptismal bowl, 104, 105(fig. 20)
Barbon, Nicholas, 181, 183
Bard, Elizabeth, 249
Barker, Robert, 145n12
Barnes, John, 20
Baroque crest, 100(&fig. 10)
Barrett, Thomas, 52n54
Battens, 77–79(&fig. 52)
Bedroom suite, 44(fig. 77)
Beds, bedsteads: 6, 7, 8, 14, 41, 44(fig. 77), 71: canopy, 14(&figs. 20, 21); settee, 6

Beech, 183: armchair, 15(fig. 23); caned armchair, 177(fig. 3); caned side chairs, 178(fig. 4), 179(fig. 5), 188(fig. 15), 189(figs. 16, 17); card tables, 20(fig. 30), 35(fig. 57); side chair, 22(fig. 34), 23; upholstered armchair, 7(&fig. 6)
Beetles, 129
Bellers, John, 184
Bench hook, 127–128, 130–131(&figs. 8, 9, 10)
Bennett, Garry Knox, 243, 244, 245(fig. 2), 246–250
Bennett, Sylvia, 249
Bernard, Nicholas, 69(fig. 28), 80, 82(figs. 56, 57), 113, 114(fig. 33)
Berry, Harry, 32
Biddle, Nicholas, 120(fig. 42)
Biddle family (Philadelphia), 80
Billiard table, 27–28(&fig. 45), 51n44, 51n47
Birch: easy chair, 61(fig. 12); lolling chair, 58(fig. 7)
Birdcage, 77–79(&fig. 52)
Birdsall, Henry, 126
Black walnut: cabinet, 128(fig. 2); chest of drawers, 230(fig. 2)
Blagojevich, Elizabeth, 242n12
Blagojevich, Miodrag, 242n12
Blaney, Dwight, 239
Blin, Peter, 139
Blunk, J. B., 248
Board, 127
Boardman, William, 230
Bolles collection, 208
Bolt, 127
Bombé desk-and-bookcase, 87–89(&figs.)
Bonnell, Hezekiah W., 41
Bonnet top, 172n15
Bonsall, James, 151, 171n8
Bookcases, 15
Book reviews, 243–259: *An American Vision* (Cooper), 256–259; *Encyclopedia of Furniture Materials* (Edwards),

250–252; *Furniture of Sam Maloof, The* (Adamson), 243–246; *Made in Oakland* (Ilse-Neumann et al.), 243, 244, 245(fig. 2), 246–250; *One Good Turn* (Rybczynski), 250–252; *Willard's Patent Time Pieces* (Foley), 252–256
Bookstand, 17(&fig. 25)
Boote, Anne, 139
Bordley, John Beale, 29(fig. 47)
Boston: backstool, 62(fig. 15); caned armchairs, 192(fig. 23), 198(fig. 33), 202(fig. 39); caned chairs and, 189–190, 202–203; caned side chairs, 174(fig. 1), 190(figs. 19, 20), 193(fig. 24), 194(fig. 25), 195(fig. 27), 196(figs. 28, 29), 197(figs. 30, 31), 198(fig. 32), 199(fig. 34), 200(figs. 35, 36, 37), 201(fig. 38); chair makers in, 92n5; chest, 129(figs. 4, 5); chests of drawers, 230(fig. 2), 235(fig. 17); cupboards, 132(figs. 11, 12), 137(fig. 27), 233(figs. 9, 10, 11, 12), 234(figs. 13, 14, 15), 235(fig. 16); desk-and-bookcases, 88(fig. 68), 90–91(&fig. 73); easy chair, 61(fig. 12); federal-era craftsmen in, 253, 254–255; high chest, 223, 224(fig. 24); joined cupboard, 236(figs. 18, 19); leather chairs, 202–203; relation to Cambridge joiners, 229, 232–235(&figs.); upholstered armchair, 59(fig. 8)
Botany Bay oak, 32(fig. 51)
Bottle stands, 6, 7
Bowdrill, 111
Bowen, Jabez, 56
Bowman, Leslie Greene, 257
Boyd, Jeremiah, 52n65
Boydell, John, 25(&fig. 39)
Boydell, Josiah, 25(&fig. 39)
Brace and bit, 134, 135(&figs. 20, 21)

Braintree (Massachusetts): chest, 141(fig. 33); cupboard fragment, 137(figs. 28, 29)
Brass, mantle clock, 37(fig. 63)
Brasses, 80, 86
Bread basket, silver, 9(fig. 10)
Breakfast table, 6
Brian Wilkinson & Son, 113, 122n15
Bronze: deck cannon 10(fig. 12); mantle clock, 37–38(&fig. 63)
Brooks Quarry, 94(fig. 2), 110, 118
Brunetti, Gaetano, 91n4
Bryan, Arthur, 8, 48n22
Bryant, John, 110
Bryne, Humphrey, 133
Buchanan, Franklin (Admiral), 10, 48n18
Buckland, William, 8, 15(&fig. 22), 18, 49n28, 49n29
Builder's Jewell, or Youth's Instructor, The (Langley), 13(&fig. 19), 161(fig. 16)
Builders Companion (Jones), 13
Bulkeley, Peter, 139
Bureau bookcase, 16(fig. 24), 17–18
Bureaus, 8, 15
Bureau table, 54(fig. 1)
Burin, 106, 107(figs. 23, 24), 111
Burke, James, 11
Burnap, Daniel, 253
Bushman, Richard, 259

Cabinets, Symonds shops, 128(fig. 2), 129(&fig. 3), 133(fig. 16)
Cabinet and Chair-Maker's Real Friend and Companion, The (Manwaring), 50n30, 92n4
Cabinet Dictionary (Sheraton), 53n67
Cabinetmaker, as iconographic figure, 213–214
Cabinetmaker and Upholsterer's Drawing Book, The (Sheraton), 19(fig. 28)50n38, 51n41, 51n47

Cabinet-Maker and Upholsterer's Guide, The (Hepplewhite), 25, 50n38
Cabinetmaker's Assistant, The (Hall), 40
Cabriole chairs, 7(&fig. 6), 92n4
Cabriole legs, 91n4, 93n7, 164(fig. 21), 165(&figs. 22, 23), 189–190, 196(&fig. 28), 201
Cadwalader, Elizabeth Lloyd, 6, 7–8(&fig. 5), 10–11, 18, 47n16, 48n19, 51n47, 93n7, 123n23
Cadwalader, John, 6, 7–8(&fig. 5), 9, 10–11, 15, 18, 22, 45, 47n6, 47n16, 48n19, 51n47, 93n7, 113, 123n23, 154
Cambridge (Massachusetts): cupboard fragment, 228(fig. 1), 236–240(&figs.), 241(fig. 29); cupboards, 231(figs. 3, 4, 5), 232(figs. 6, 7, 8), 234(figs. 13, 14, 15), 235(fig. 16), 236(figs. 18, 19), 241(fig. 29); joined cupboards, 236(figs. 18, 19), 239(&fig. 24), 240(figs. 25, 26, 27); joiners, 229–232(&figs.); relation to Boston joiners, 229, 232–235(&figs.). *See also* Harvard College joinery
Campbell, Colin, 176
Campbell, Thomas, 172n8
Campin, Robert, 135(fig. 20)
Candlestands, 74–79(&figs.): American, 75(figs. 44, 45), 79(fig. 53); Philadelphia, 76(figs. 46, 47), 77–79(&figs. 51, 52)
Cane, sources of, 204–205n9
Caned chairs, 41: in America, 188–203(&figs.); armchairs, 177(fig. 3), 186(fig. 10), 192(fig. 23), 198(fig. 33), 202(fig. 39); as expression of mercantilism, 182–184; expression of taste and, 184–187; diffusion model and, 175–176; Dutch model, 179–180; mercantilism, 176–181, 203; side chairs, 174(fig. 1),

178(fig. 4), 179(fig. 5), 186(fig. 11), 187(figs. 12, 13), 188(fig. 15), 189(figs. 16, 17), 190(figs. 19, 20), 193(fig. 24), 194(fig. 25), 195(fig. 27), 196(figs. 28, 29), 197(figs. 30, 31), 198(fig. 32), 199(fig. 34), 200(figs. 35, 36, 37), 201(fig. 38); as text, 175
Cannon, deck, 10(&fig. 12), 48n18
Canopy beds, design for, 14(fig. 21)
Card tables, 8, 15, 51n53: American, 70–73(&figs.); Baltimore, 31–32(&figs. 50, 51), 33(&fig. 53), 35(&fig. 57); London, 19–20(&fig. 30); Newport, 71(fig. 34); New York, 72(fig. 36), 73(fig. 39); painted, 33(&fig. 53)
Carpenter, Joseph, 130
Carpenter, Ralph, 63(&fig. 17), 85
Carpenter, Samuel, 171n2
Carpenter, William, Sr., 134, 145n16
Carpenters, vs. joiners, 129, 131, 145n9
Carpets, Wilton, 6, 8, 11
Carr, David, 214
Carroll, Charles, 15
Carteret, Thomas, 81(fig. 55), 123n19: sideboard table, 110(fig. 30), 111
Carved shell, 84, 86(fig. 65)
Carving: acanthus, 64(fig. 20), 72, 73(fig. 37), 74, 75(fig. 45), 80, 172n16, 194; applied-ornament style, 229–232, 239; caned chair leaf, 190, 195, 196; on desk-and-bookcase, 90(fig. 73); on dressing table, 80, 82(figs. 56, 57); fakery and, 68–71(&figs.); knee, 65(fig. 21), 69(figs. 29, 30), 76(fig. 47), 80, 82(figs. 57, 59); mannerist, 228(fig. 1), 240; Nicholas Bernard, 82(figs. 56, 57, 58, 59); relief, 137; stone, 113; tools and techniques for, 136–137

Case construction, 84(figs. 63, 64), 86(fig. 66)
Castle, Wendell, 245, 251
Cedar: chests of drawers, 230(fig. 2), 235(fig. 17); cupboards, 132(figs. 11, 12), 233(fig. 9); desk-and-bookcases, 157(fig. 10), 159(fig. 12); dressing table, 81(fig. 55); joined cupboard, 239(fig. 4). See also White cedar
Cedar Grove Marble Works, 94(fig. 2), 113, 115
Cedar Grove Quarry, 94(fig. 2), 115
Cedrella: bureau bookcase, 16(fig. 24), 17–18; chamber table, 37(fig. 62); chest, 129(fig. 4); chests of drawers, 230(fig. 2), 235(fig. 17)
Center table, 120(fig. 42)
Chair Maker's Guide, The (Manwaring), 50n30
Chair making: in rural New England, 223; as test of maker's skill, 248
Chairs: Baltimore, 50n38; cabriole, 7(&fig. 6), 92n4; comparison of styles and forms, 221–223; Crim, 23; eighteenth-century designs for, 91n4; elbow, 7(&fig. 6); flag bottom, 8; French, 7(&fig. 6), 15–16(&fig. 23), 49n30, 59(fig. 8), 92n4; grand, 91n4; lolling, 58(fig. 7); remaking, 24; rocking, 42–43(&figs. 73, 75, 76), 244 (fig. 1); state, 92n4; stool easy, 6. See also Armchairs; Caned chairs; Easy chairs; Side chairs
Chair table, 142(figs. 34, 35)
Chambers, David, 113, 123n23
Chambers, William, 123n23
Chamber table, 37(&fig. 62); marble-topped, 52n62
Chamfering, chamfers, 237–238(&fig. 22), 241(fig. 29), 242n11

Charleston furniture, vs. Philadelphia, 172n15
Charleston Gazette, 152
Charter and By-Laws of the Pennsylvania Land and Marble Company, 124n27
Chase, Samuel, 15
Chase-Lloyd House, 15(&fig. 22): door frieze, 18(&fig. 26)
Cherry: armchairs, 67(fig. 25), 220(fig. 18); chest-on-chest, 56(fig. 2); high chest, 223, 224(fig. 23)
Chestnut: bureau table, 54(fig. 1); chest-on-chest, 56(fig. 2); chests of drawers, 57(fig. 3), 230(fig. 2); cupboard, 233(fig. 9); dressing table, 83(fig. 62), 84, 85
Chest-on-chests: Philadelphia, 162(fig. 17), 163, 167(fig. 26), 168(fig. 27), 169; Providence (Rhode Island), 56(&fig. 2)
Chests: Boston, 129(figs. 4, 5); Hadley, 259; Marblehead, 142(figs. 36, 37); Savell shop, 141(fig. 33); Thurston shop, 136(figs. 24, 25). See also High chests
Chests of drawers: Baltimore, 37(&fig. 64); Boston, 230(fig. 2), 235(fig. 17); England, 25(&fig. 38); Newport, 56, 57(fig. 3); Philadelphia, 169(fig. 29), 170(fig. 30)
Chew, Benjamin (Chief Justice), 113
Chicago World Fair, 118
Chimneypiece, 115(figs. 34, 35)
Chinese export platter, 9(fig. 11)
Chinese motif, 205n20
Chippendale style, 257
Chippendale, Thomas, 14(fig. 21), 18(fig. 27), 21, 49n30, 50n31, 59(fig. 8), 92n4
Chipstone, living room, 57(fig. 4), 58(fig. 5)
Chipstone Collection, 55–59: fakes in. See Fakes

Chipstone Foundation, 221
Chisels, 106, 107(fig. 23), 111–112, 127, 128, 129, 131, 137: marteline, 107(figs. 23, 24); mortise, 134(&fig. 18); round-nosed, 107(fig. 23)
Chisholm, Archibald, 8, 21
Chrysler Museum, 257
Churchyards: clouded limestone tombstone, 94(fig. 2), 100–105(&figs.)
Cipolin, 98
Clapboard backs, 235
"Classical Chaos"(Milwaukee Art Museum), 222(fig. 20)
Classical style, 34
Claw-and-ball feet, 60, 63, 76, 87(&fig. 67), 113, 114(fig. 33), 156(&fig. 9), 165
Claypoole, Catherine, 173n25
Claypoole, Edith, 151
Claypoole, Edward, 171n3
Claypoole, George, Jr., 169, 173n25: chest of drawers, 169(fig. 29); chest-on-chest, 167(fig. 26), 168(fig. 28)
Claypoole, George, Sr., 151, 152, 153–154, 163, 170, 172n14, 173n22: chest of drawers, 169(&fig. 29); desk-and-bookcase, 157(fig. 10), 158; dressing table, 166(&fig. 24); high chests, 165(figs. 22, 23), 166(fig. 25)
Claypoole, James, 147–149(&fig. 1), 151–153, 166, 171n1, 171n2, 171n3, 171n6
Claypoole, John, 147, 148(fig. 2), 149, 153, 171n1
Claypoole, Joseph, 110, 122n17, 149–152(&fig. 4), 154(&fig. 6), 163–164, 169, 171n6, 171n7, 171–172n8, 172n9, 172n10, 172n16, 172n17, 173n22: desk-and-bookcase, 157(fig. 10), 158; dressing table, 166(fig. 24); high chests, 155–157(&figs. 7, 8, 9), 165(figs. 22, 23), 166(&fig. 25); retirement of, 156
Claypoole, Josiah, 110–111, 151–153, 154–155(&fig. 6), 169, 172n9, 172n12
Claypoole, Mary Angell, 147
Claypoole, Norton, 149, 171n6
Claypoole, Rebecca Jennings, 152, 172n10
Claypoole, Sarah Jackson, 152, 172n12
Claypoole, Thomas, 153
Cliffton, Henry, 81(fig. 55), 123n19: sideboard table, 110(fig. 30), 111
Clocks: Banjo, 252–256; dial signatures, 254; girandole, 254; lyre, 254; mantle, 37–38(&fig. 63); tall case, 8(&fig. 7)
Closterman, John, 185(fig. 8)
Clothes press, 15, 30(fig. 49), 31, 51n52
Clouded limestone, 94–124 (&figs.): center table, 120(fig. 42); corner table, 119(fig. 41); decline of marble business, 120–121; ecclesiastical monuments and gravestones, 100–106(&figs.); eighteenth-century quarries and dealers, 107–113; geological surveys of, 97–100; nineteenth-century quarries, 113, 115–119; Philadelphia area quarries, 94(fig. 2); in Philadelphia region, 95–97; processing of for furniture, 106–107(&figs.); samples of, 99(fig. 8), 100(fig. 9); sideboard tables, 38(fig. 65), 94(fig. 1), 109(fig. 26), 110(fig. 30), 111(fig. 31), 112(fig. 32), 114(fig. 33), 154(fig. 6); taste for, 119–120; washstand, 121(fig. 44). See also Marble
Coat-of-arms, Lloyd family, 10(figs. 13, 14)
Coffins, 151, 152, 153
Colchester (Connecticut), high chest, 223, 224(fig. 23)

Coldee, Thomas, 107, 111
Cole, John, 123n26
Collection of Designs in Architecture, A (Swan), 48n20
Collections, family vs. institutional, 3
Colonial Furniture in America (Lockwood), 92n4
Colonial Williamsburg, 211
Colonial Williamsburg Foundation, 74, 91n2, 242n12
Colonies Reduced, The (Franklin), 180(fig. 6)
Compass, 127, 128
Comstock, Helen, 226n10
Concise History of Glass Represented in the Chrysler Museum Glass Collection, A (Merrill), 257
Condition, premium placed on, 55
Conifers: bureau bookcase, 16(fig. 24), 17–18; in fakes, 71; knife vases, 36(fig. 59). *See also* Cedar; Pine; White cedar; White pine; Yellow pine
Conn, Steven, 211
Connecticut River Valley, joinery technique in, 237, 241, 242n10
Connor, Bruce, 248
Conshohocken (Pennsylvania), 94(fig. 2), 95
Conshohocken blue, 95
Construction: case, 84(figs. 63, 64), 86(fig. 66); cupboard, 231–232, 235; drawer, 231; errors in, 142–143(&figs.); fakery and, 72–73, 80; nailed, 138–139(&figs.), 190, 231, 234(fig. 15), 239; slab frame, 111
Consumerism, American decorative arts and, 259
Cook, William, 41
Cooke, Edward S., Jr., 216, 223, 246, 247–248
Cooper, Anthony Ashley (third Earl of Shaftsbury), 185–187(&fig. 8)
Cooper, Wendy A., 256

Copeland, Lamont du Pont, 122–123n18
Corbels, 133(fig. 15), 240(figs. 26, 27), 241(fig. 28)
Cornelius, Charles Over, 209, 212, 213
Corner table, 119(fig. 41)
Cornices, 19, 33(&fig. 54): painted, 52n55
Couch, mahogany, 11
Cox, William, 153
Craft Horizon, 245
Craft movement, 244–245
Craftsmen: federal-era Boston-Roxbury, 253, 254–255; romanticization of, 125–126, 143–144n2, 213–214
Crest rail, 65, 66(fig. 24), 67(fig. 26)
Crests: arched, 100, 101(fig. 11); baroque, 100(&fig. 10); caned side chair, 190–199(&figs. 19, 22, 26, 29, 31, 32), 203, 205n20; saddled, 196, 198(fig. 33), 199; tombstone, 100–101(&figs.)
Crim, William, 23
Crim chair, 23
Cromwell, Oliver, 148, 171n1
Cultural diversity, American furniture scholarship and, 219–220
Cultural hierarchies: American furniture scholarship and, 207–208, 209, 211–212, 225n1; caned chairs and, 175, 176, 179, 185–187, 203
Cupboard fragment: Harvard College joinery, 228(fig. 1), 236–240(&figs.), 241(fig. 29); Savell shop, 137(figs. 28, 29)
Cupboards: Boston, 132(figs. 11, 12), 137(fig. 27), 233(figs. 9, 10, 11, 12), 234(figs. 13, 14, 15), 235(fig. 16); Boston or Cambridge, 234(figs. 13, 14, 15), 236(figs. 18, 19); Cambridge (Massachusetts), 231(figs. 3, 4, 5), 232(figs. 6, 7, 8), 235(fig. 16), 241(fig. 29); Cambridge joined, 236(figs. 18, 19), 239(&fig. 24), 240(figs. 25, 26, 27); Hannah Barnard, 217, 258

Curtains, silk, 6, 7, 8
Curtis, Lemuel, 254
Curvilinear elements, 177
Cut card scrolls, 63
Cyma elements, 122–123n18, 165, 166, 196
Cypress, armoire, 41(fig. 70)

Dager, Daniel, 113
Dager, Peter, 113
Danto, Arthur C., 246, 249
David, James, tombstone, 102(&fig. 13)
Davis, John, 139–140
Death in the Dining Room (Ames), 217
Dedham (Massachusetts), chest, 136(figs. 24, 25)
Defoe, Daniel, 184
Denmead, John, 53n66
Dennis, Thomas, 143n1, 146n27, 216
Desk-and-bookcases, 15, 31, 50n32, 50n33, 173n20: Annapolis, 19(&figs. 28, 29); bombé, 87–89(&figs.); Boston, 88(fig. 68), 90–91(&fig. 73); design for, 18(fig. 27); Philadelphia, 157–162(&figs.), 173n20
Desks, 15, 50n36: fall-front, 150(fig. 4); "portable," 36; walnut, 22(&fig. 33); writing, 11. See also Writing tables
Dial signatures, 254
Dictionary of English Furniture, 250
Diffusion model, 175–176
Dimaggio, Paul, 214
Dining tables, 14, 15, 34(&fig. 55)
Distressing, artificial, 60(fig. 9)
Dolomitic marble, 96
Dominy shop (Long Island), 253

Door frieze, Chase-Lloyd House, 18(&fig. 26)
Doors: cupboard, 238–239; desk-and-bookcase, 87, 89(&figs. 69, 70)
Doremus, Mrs. John F., 160
Douglass, Frederick (Frederick Augustus Washington Bailey), 45
Dovetailing, 232(&fig. 6), 233(fig. 12), 234(fig. 14), 241(fig. 29)
Downs, Joseph, 71, 72(fig. 36)
Dressing tables, 6, 7, 15, 51n41, 173n22: American, 80(&fig. 54), 83–87(&figs.); Philadelphia, 81–83(&figs.), 164(figs. 20, 21), 166(&fig. 24), 169
Dreyfuss, Henry, 246
Dukehard, Henry, 39
du Pont, Henry Francis, 28, 215(fig. 12), 256, 257, 258
Dustboards, dressing table, 81(fig. 55)
Dutch caned chairs, 204n1
Dyar, Harrison Gray, 254
Dylander, John, 104, 105(fig. 19)

Eames, Charles, 249
Eames, Ray, 249
Eames Chair, 249
Earle, Peter, 204n3, 205n10
Earl of Shaftsbury, First, 185–186(&fig. 9), 205n15
Earl of Shaftsbury, Third, 185(&fig. 8)
Early American Furniture Makers (Ormsbee), 212
Earnest, C., 99(&fig. 8)
Easton (Maryland), tall clock case, 8(&fig. 7)
Easy chairs: American, 61(fig. 11), 62(figs. 13, 14, 16), 63, 64(fig. 19), 65(figs. 21, 22); Boston, 61(fig. 12); Newport, 92n5; Philadelphia, 93n7
Eaton, Francis, 130, 145n10

Eaton, William, 12, 26
Ebony: card table, 20(fig. 30); chest of drawers, 235(fig. 17)
Eckstein, J., Jr., 116
Eden, Robert, 8
Edes family (Boston), 199
Edge moldings, 76, 77(fig. 49)
Edge tools, 106, 107(figs. 23, 24)
Edsall, Thomas, 229, 230(fig. 2): chest of drawers, 235(fig. 17); cupboard, 233(fig. 9)
Edward Lloyd Family, The (Fairbanks), 28–29(&fig. 46)
Edward Lloyd Family, The (Peale), 5(fig. 3)
Edwards, Clive, 250
"Eighteenth-Century Cabinet Shops and the Furniture-Making Trades in Newport, Rhode Island" (Headley), 126
Elbow chair, 7(&fig. 6)
Elbow stools, 91n4
Elite, American furniture scholarship and, 207–208, 209, 211–212, 225n1
Empire style, 34
Enamel, mantle clock, 37(fig. 63)
Encyclopedia of Furniture Materials, Trades and Techniques (Edwards), 250–252
Engelbreckt, Anthony, 110
England: armchairs, 15–16(&fig. 23), 24(fig. 36); caned armchair, 177(fig. 3), 186(fig. 10); caned side chair, 178(fig. 4), 179(fig. 5), 186(fig. 11), 187(figs. 12, 13), 188(fig. 15), 189(figs. 16, 17); chest of drawers, 25(&fig. 38); knife vases, 36(fig. 59); side chair, 22(fig. 34), 23; as source of America's artistic tradition, 212; upholstered armchair, 7(&fig. 6). *See also* London
England's Treasure by Forraign Trade (Mun), 180

Engraving, silver, 9(fig. 9)
Erp, Dirk Van, 248
Errors, in furniture construction, 142–143(&figs.)
Escritoire, 173n18
Escutcheon plates, 86
Esherick, Wharton, 245
Essex County (Massachusetts), joinery technique, 240, 241
Ethnicity, American furniture scholarship and, 209, 212–213
Ettema, Michael J., 225n1
Evans, Edward, 150(fig. 4), 151(fig. 5)
Evelyn, John, 137

Fairbanks, Jonathan, 28–29(&fig. 46)
Fakes: chairs, 59–71(&figs.); Chipstone Collection and, 55–59(&figs.); defined, 54(fig. 1); desk-and-bookcases, 87–91 (&figs.); tables, 71–87(&figs.)
Fallboard, 89
Fall-front desk, 150(fig. 4)
Family of John Cadwalader, The (Peale), 7(fig. 5)
Fauteuils, 91n4
Farris, William, 8
Feet: claw-and-ball, 60, 63, 74, 75(fig. 45), 76, 87(&fig. 67), 113, 114(fig. 33), 156(fig. 9), 165; desk-and-bookcase, 89(fig. 71), 90(fig. 73); French, 25; gadrooned ball, 91; Marlborough, 14(fig. 20); ogee, 162(fig. 17), 163, 170; pad, 60; paneled, 165(&fig. 23), 166; slipper, 109(&fig. 26), 165; Spanish, 164(fig. 21), 165(&fig. 22), 189; tassel, 189; trifid, 165
Felibien, Andres, 134(&fig. 18), 145n16
Figure marks, 86
File marks, 71(fig. 34)
Files, first-cut, 93n11

Fine Points of Furniture, Early American (Sack), 217(&fig. 14)
Fine Woodworking, 247
Finials, 90(fig. 73)
Finlay, Hugh, 32–33(&figs. 53, 54), 52n55
Finlay, John, 32–33(&figs. 53, 54)
Fireplace surround, 115(figs. 34, 35)
First-cut files, 93n11
First Earl of Shaftesbury, The, 185(fig. 9)
Fish tail pendant, 165(&fig. 23)
Flag bottom chairs, 8
Flags, 127
Fleeson, Plunkett, 11
Fly rail, 71
Folding-leaf tables, 73–74(&figs. 41, 42, 43)
Foley, Paul J., 252
Foliate panels, 136(&figs. 24, 25)
Foliate spray crest, 174(fig. 1), 190(fig. 19), 193
Folwell, Richard, 31
Fore plane, 131, 145n13
Forman, Benno, 125, 175, 188, 229, 256
Forrest Plantation, 11
Four Books of Architecture, The (Palladio), 48n20
Foust and Weaver, 119
Fox, George, 148
France, mantle clock, 37(fig. 63)
Frank Leslie's Illustrated Newspaper, 213(fig. 8)
Franklin, Benjamin, 172n9, 180(fig. 6)
Franklin Marble Mantel Manufactory, 116(fig. 36)
Free Society of Traders, 149, 171n2
Freedley, J. K., 124n27
Freedley, M., 124n27
French chairs, 7(&fig. 6), 15–16(&fig. 23), 49n30, 59(fig. 8), 92n4
French feet, 25
Frieze rail, 228(fig. 1), 236–237
Friezes, cupboard, 233(fig. 9), 234

(fig. 13), 235(& fig. 17), 236(fig. 18)
Fritz, Peter, 115–116(&fig. 36), 123n26
Fritz Quarry, 94(fig. 2), 115, 117, 123n27
Froes, 129, 130(fig. 6)
Front legs, easy chair, 62(&fig. 13), 65(&fig. 22)
Fruitwood, smoothing plane, 132(fig. 14)
"Furniture as Social History" (Ulrich), 258
Furniture makers, contemporary, 243–250
Furniture of Sam Maloof, The (Adamson), 243–246
Furniture painting, 32–33(&fig. 53, 54)

Gadrooned ball feet, 91
Gaines family (Portsmouth, New Hampshire), 66(fig. 23), 67(fig. 25), 93n8
Gale, Mathias, 11
Gambling, 27–28
Garden, Wye House, 26
Gardiner, Charles, 11
Gates, Henry Louis, Jr., 225
Gender, American furniture scholarship and, 209, 213–214, 226n10
Genteel Houshold Furniture in the Present Taste (Society of Upholsterers), 50n30, 92n4
Gentleman and Cabinet-Maker's Director, The (Chippendale), 14(fig. 21), 18(fig. 27), 49n30, 50n31, 59(fig. 8), 92n4
Geological Survey of Pennsylvania (Rogers), 98
Geological Survey of the Environs of Philadelphia performed by the order of the Philadelphia Society for promoting Agriculture (Troost), 97(fig. 5)

Geological surveys, of Pennsylvania clouded limestone, 97–100
Georgian style, 186–187, 199–200, 203
Gerfschaff, 132, 145n13
Gibbs, James, 48n20
Gillows & Company (England), 32
Ginsburg, Benjamin, 55
Girandole clock, 254
Girandoles, 14, 30, 34, 49n25
Girard College, 117(&fig. 37), 118
Girl Scouts Loan Exhibition, 210–211(&fig. 5)
Glass: mantle clock, 37(fig. 63); plateau, 24(&fig. 37)
Glassie, Henry, 217
Gloria Dei Church, 94(fig. 2), 103–105(&figs.)
Glue blocks, 71
Glues, 145–146n18
Goddard, Benjamin, 230
Goddard, Martha Palfrey, 230
Goddard family (Newport, Rhode Island), 223
Godey's Lady's Book, 120(fig. 43)
Goforth, Aaron, 171n8
Goldsborough, William Tilghman, 52n65
Gooch, William, 205–206n22
Good-better-best formula, 217(&fig. 14), 226n16
Goodman, W. L., 127
Gostelowe, Jonathan, 169–170(&fig. 30)
Gouges, 128, 131, 137, 228(fig. 1)
Governor Edward Lloyd V (Bordley), 29(fig. 47)
Graeme Park (Montgomery County, Pennsylvania), 115(fig. 34), 163, 172n16
Grand chairs, 91n4
Graphite, limestone and, 96
Gratz, Bernard, 92n6
Gratz, Michael, 64, 92–93n6
Gratz, Miriam, 64, 92–93n6
Gratz family, 64(fig. 20)

Gravestones, clouded limestone, 100–106(&figs.)
Graveyards: Philadelphia region, 94(fig. 2), 100–105(&figs.); Wye House, 26(&figs. 42, 43)
Great Fire, caned chairs and, 179, 204n3
Great Valley Baptist Church (Upper Merion Township, Pennsylvania), 94(fig. 2), 100–101(&figs.), 121–122n10
Great Valley Presbyterian Church (Chester County, Pennsylvania), 94(fig. 2), 102–103(&figs.)
Greble, Edwin, 116
Greene, Richard Lawrence, 259
Greenhouse, Wye House, 26–27(&fig. 44), 51n44
Greenland, William, 153
Green timber, 137
Grooving planes, 133, 242n12
Grumbling Hive, The (Mandeville), 184
Guilloche, 13(fig. 18), 33

Hadley chests, 259
Half-columns, 135(&fig. 22), 136(fig. 23), 232(&fig. 8), 233(fig. 11)
Half-round, 135–136(&fig. 22)
Half-round plane, 131, 133
Hall, John, 40
Hall, Thomas, 18(&fig. 26), 49n28
Halsey, R. T. H., 209
Hammer, 127
Hancock family (Boston), 203, 206n23
Handrailing, 36(fig. 61), 37, 52n61
Handsaws, 107(fig. 23), 127, 131, 134
Hannah Barnard cupboard, 217, 258
Hardcastle, Henry, 73(fig. 39)
Harding, Martha, 126, 144n4
Harding, Samuel, 80, 93n17, 108(fig. 25), 109

Hargrave, Thomas, 116
Harmanville (Pennsylvania), quarries, 107
Harrison, John, 163(&fig. 19)
Hart, Ware & Company (Baltimore), 44(fig. 77), 53n73
Harvard College joinery: 229–232(&figs.); cupboard fragment, 228(fig. 1), 236–240(&figs.), 241(&fig. 29); joined cupboard, 239(fig. 4), 240(figs. 25, 26, 27)
Harvey, Robert, 117
Harwood, Elizabeth Lloyd, 29
Harwood, Henry Hall, 29
Hatchet, 127
Head, John, 122n14, 165, 173n20
Headley, Mack, 126
Heath, Richard, 171n7
Heckscher, Eli, F., 180
Hedrick Wally, 248
Hein, Hilda S., 219
Hemings, John, 220–221(&fig. 18)
Henderson, John, 117
Henderson Quarry, 94(fig. 2), 100, 117
Henry, David, 107, 111
Hepburn, Andrew, 57
Hepplewhite, George, 25, 50n38
Hicks, Joseph, 230
Hicks, Rebecca Palfrey, 230
Hicks, Zechariah, Jr., 229, 230
Hicks, Zechariah, Sr., 230
High chests, 92n5: Boston, 223, 224(fig. 24); Colchester, 223, 224(fig. 23); Newport, 63(&figs. 17, 18); Philadelphia, 155(figs. 7, 8), 156(fig. 9), 165(figs. 22, 23), 166(&fig. 25); Salem, 223, 224(fig. 24)
High Street (Philadelphia Sesquicentennial Fair), 210(&fig. 4), 211
Hill, Christopher (Sir), 207
Hill, Richard, 151, 171–172n8
Hitner, Daniel, 117
Hitner, Daniel O., 117
Hitner, Henry S., 117

Hitner quarries, 124n27
Hocker, Christopher, 113
Hocker, Jardella, 113
Holdfast, 128, 130(&fig. 8), 131, 136(fig. 26), 137
Holes: draw-bored, 137(fig. 29); plugged, 76, 77(fig. 48), 79
Holland, William, 122n14
Holloway, Edward Stratton, 213
Hollow planes, 133
Holme, Randle, 126, 129, 130(&fig. 6), 132(&fig. 13), 135(fig. 21), 133, 135, 138, 144n3, 144–145n8
Holme, Thomas, 148(fig. 2), 149
Holyoke, William, 206n23
Hooks, 107(fig. 23)
Hope, Thomas, 38(fig. 65), 53n67
Hope Lodge, 163
Hopkins, Jack, 248
Hopkins, Jack Rogers, 251
Hornor, William MacPherson, 150, 171n7
Horseman, Stephen, 8(&fig. 7)
Horton, Frank L., 143n2
Hosley, Bill, 258
Houghton, John, 181
Houguettes, 107(fig. 23)
Household Furniture and Interior Decoration (Hope), 38(fig. 65), 53n67
Howard, Elizabeth Phoebe Key, 4(fig. 2)
Howard and Davis (Boston), 254
Howell, Ezekiel (Major), tombstone, 103(fig. 15)
Hudson Bay Company, 185
Hudson-Fulton Celebration (Metropolitan Museum of Art, 208(&fig. 1), 212(&fig. 7)
Huguenots, caned chairs and, 179, 181
Husks, 63

Ilse-Neumann, Ursula, 243, 246, 248–249
"I" marks, 174(fig. 1), 175, 188–189(&fig. 14)

Inboring planes, 131
Ince, William, 49n30, 92n4
Indentures, set of tools and, 133. *See also* Apprentices
Independence Hall (Philadelphia), 98(&figs. 6, 7)
Independence National Historic Park, 173n20
Indexing pins, 111, 112(fig. 32)
Inouye, Ernest, 246
"IP" mark, 188
Ipswich (Massachusetts): access to timber from commons in, 140; caned chair production in, 196; caned side chair, 195(fig. 27), 196(figs. 28, 29)
Ipswich-Newbury (Massachusetts), joinery technique, 241
Irish furniture, 109(&fig. 26), 122n16, 172n16
Iron: deck cannon 10(fig. 12); smoothing plane, 132(fig. 14)
Iron frower, 144n8
Italian marble, 119: pier table, 119(fig. 40); sideboard table, 108(fig. 25)

James, David, 100(fig. 10)
Jardella, Guiseppa, 113
Jefferson, Thomas, 220
J. Hancock & Company (Philadelphia), 42–43
Jimmals, 126
Joined cupboards, 236(figs. 18, 19), 239(&fig. 4), 240(figs. 25, 26, 27)
Joiners, joinery, 127(&fig. 1): vs. carpenters, 129, 131, 145n9, of fakes, 85; order of work, 140–143; patrons and, 139–140; prices of wares, 140–141; tools and materials, 126–139. *See also* Claypoole, George, Jr.; Claypoole, George, Sr.; Claypoole, Joseph; Claypoole, Josiah
Joiners' and Carpenters' company, 179, 182–183

Joiners' Company, 182–183, 205n10
Joiner's plow, 133
Jointer, 131
Jointer plane, 130(fig. 7,b2), 131, 133
Jonathan H. Duvall Shipping (Baltimore), 41
Jones, Ezekiel, 255
Jones, John, 151
Jones, William, 13
Josiah Child (attr. John Riley), 180(fig. 7)
Journals, American furniture scholarship and, 210
J. Struthers & Son, 117
Jugiez, Martin, 113, 114(fig. 33)
J. W. Berry & Sons (Baltimore), 23–24(&fig. 36)

Kamil Neil, 202–203
Kelsey, John, 247
Kent, William, 91–92n4
Keppel, Hendrick Van, 246
Key, Francis Scott, 29
Key, Mary Lloyd, 29
Keyes, Homer Eaton, 209–210
Kimbal, Richard, Sr., 146n24
King, Sterling, 248
King of Prussia marble, 95
Knee acanthus, 64(fig. 20), 72, 73(fig. 37), 74, 75(fig. 45), 172n16
Knee blocks, 60, 61(fig. 10), 62
Knee carving, 65(fig. 21), 69(figs. 29, 30), 76(fig. 47), 80, 82(figs. 57, 59)
Knife cases, 11
Knife vases, 36(&fig. 59)

Ladles, 107(fig. 23)
Lafayette, Marquis de, 38
Lamb's tongues, 166, 237
Langley, Batty, 13(&fig. 19), 161(fig. 16)
Langley, Thomas, 13(&fig. 19)
Lannuier, Charles-Honore, 220(fig. 17)

Lare, 144n4
Lath axe, 129, 130(fig. 6)
Lathes, 76, 79, 128: pole, 135; slab type, 144n7
Lathe faceplate, 76
Lawn bowling balls, 26(&fig. 41)
Lawton, Elizabeth Tallman, 233(fig. 9)
Lawton, Isaac, 233(fig. 9)
Layton Art Collection, 221
Leaf carving, on caned chairs, 190, 195, 196. *See also* Acanthus
Leath, Robert, 139
Leather chairs, Boston, 202–203
Legg, John, 141
Legs: cabriole, 91n4, 93n7, 164(fig. 21), 165(&figs. 22, 23), 189–190, 196(&fig. 28), 201; front, 62(&fig. 13), 65(&fig. 22); high chest, 63(fig. 18); rear, 62(&fig. 16)
Lehman, Benjamin, 112
Lentz Quarry, 94(fig. 2), 124n27
Levine, Lawrence, 211, 219
Levi-Strauss, Claude, 2
Levy, Bernard, 55
Library Company of Philadelphia, 163(&fig. 19)
Lignum vitae, chest of drawers, 230(fig. 2)
Lillie, Thomas, 255
Lime, production of, 96–97 (&fig. 4)
Linen slides, 25
Liquor case, 38(&fig. 65)
Literary studies, as source of interpretive model for American furniture scholarship, 215–216
Little, Thomas, Sr., 127
Lloyd, Alicia McBlair, 38
Lloyd, Anne Catherine, 10
Lloyd, Anne Rousby, 7, 14
Lloyd, Charles Howard, 4–5(&fig. 2), 14, 21, 23, 35, 36, 44, 45, 47n17, 49n26
Lloyd, Cornelius, 46n2

Lloyd, Edward I, 3, 46n2
Lloyd, Edward II, 8
Lloyd, Edward III, 6–11, 14, 18(fig. 27), 26, 46–47n6, 47n16
Lloyd, Edward IV, 3–4, 6, 8, 11–14, 15–29, 47n6, 48n20, 48n22, 49n28
Lloyd, Edward V, 13–14, 15, 19, 20, 29–38, 37, 48n18: *Governor Edward Lloyd V* (Bordley), 29(fig. 47)
Lloyd, Edward VI, 14, 17, 29, 38–46, 52n65
Lloyd, Edward VII, 4, 44
Lloyd, Edward VIII, 4
Lloyd, Elizabeth, 29
Lloyd, Elizabeth Tayloe, 14, 15(&fig. 22), 16, 20, 47n6, 49n28
Lloyd, Henrietta Maria Neal Bennett, 51n44
Lloyd, Joanna Leigh, 4(fig. 2), 46n3, 48n19
Lloyd, Mary, 29
Lloyd, Mary Donnell, 4–5, 14, 49n26
Lloyd, Mary Lloyd Howard, 4(fig. 2), 44
Lloyd, P., 102(fig. 14)
Lloyd, Philemon, 51n44
Lloyd, Richard Bennett, 6–7, 8, 9, 10, 29, 48n19
Lloyd, Sarah Scott Murray, 29, 44
Lloyd, Thomas, 17n6
Lloyd family coat-of-arms, 10(figs. 13, 14)
Lloyd House, 49n28
Loan Exhibition of Eighteenth and Nineteenth Century Furniture and Glass...for the Benefit of the National Council of Girl Scouts, 70(fig. 32), 71, 92n4, 93n11
Locke, John, 185
Lockwood, Luke Vincent, 92n4, 207
Logan, James, 96(fig. 3), 151(&fig. 5), 158, 160

Logan, Sarah Armitt, 160
Lolling chair, 58(fig. 7)
London: armchair, 15–16(&fig. 23); bookstand, 17(&fig. 25); bureau bookcase, 16(fig. 24), 17–18; card table, 20(fig. 30); desk-and-bookcase, 162(fig. 18); pier glasses, 13(figs. 17, 18); silver and glass plateau, 24(fig. 37); silver bread basket, 9(&fig. 10); silver salver, 8–9(&fig. 9). *See also* England
Long, Robert Cary, 52n65
Lotter, Matther, A., 98(fig. 6)
Lowndes, Anne Lloyd, 28
Lumber, 239
Luxury trade, 183–185
Lyon, Irving P., 143n1
Lyre clocks, 254

Made in Oakland: The Furniture of Garry Knox Bennett (Ilse-Neumann et al.), 243, 246–250
Magazine Antiques, The, 210
Magnesium, limestone and, 96, 100(fig. 9)
Mahogany: armchairs, 8, 24(fig. 36), 32(fig. 52), 68(fig. 27), 220(fig. 17); armoire, 41(fig. 70); bedsteads, 6, 7, 8, 14(&fig. 20); billiard table, 27(fig. 45); bookstand, 17(&fig. 25); bureau bookcase, 16(fig. 24), 17–18; bureau table, 54(fig. 1); candlestands, 75(figs. 44, 45), 76(figs. 46, 47), 78(fig. 51); card tables, 8, 20(fig. 30), 31–32(figs. 50, 51), 35(fig. 57), 70(fig. 31), 72(fig. 35); chairs, 11, 41; chamber table, 37(fig. 62); chest-on-chests, 56(fig. 2), 162(fig. 17); chests of drawers, 25(&fig. 38), 37(fig. 64), 57(fig. 3), 170(fig. 30); clothes press, 30(fig. 49); corner table, 119(fig. 41); couch, 11; desk-and-bookcases, 19(&fig. 28), 31, 88(fig. 68), 90(fig. 73), 157(fig. 10), 158(fig. 11), 159(fig. 12), 161(fig. 15); dining table, 34(fig. 55); dressing tables, 80(fig. 54), 81(fig. 55), 83(fig. 62), 164(fig. 21); easy chairs, 61(fig. 11), 62(figs. 13, 16), 64(fig. 19); handrailing, 36(fig. 61), 37; high chests, 155(fig. 7), 156, 165(fig. 23), 224(fig. 24); knife vases, 36(fig. 59); liquor case, 38(fig. 65); lolling chair, 58(fig. 7); pier table, 119(fig. 40); secretary, 30–31(&fig. 48); shaving table, 21(&fig. 31); sideboard tables, 38(fig. 65), 42(fig. 72), 94(fig. 1), 108(fig. 25), 109(fig. 26), 110(fig. 30), 114(fig. 33), 154(fig. 6); sideboard table frames, 112; side chairs, 8, 11(fig. 15), 22(fig. 34), 23(fig. 35), 41(fig. 71); sofa, 34(fig. 56); tea table, 54(fig. 1); upholstered armchairs, 58(fig. 6), 59(fig. 8); wardrobes, 39(fig. 66), 40(figs. 67, 68), 41(fig. 69); washstand, 121(fig. 44); writing tables, 21(&fig. 32), 36(fig. 60)
Mallets, 106, 107(figs. 23, 24), 109, 111, 129
Maloof, Alfreda, 245, 249
Maloof, Sam, 244–246, 248, 249
Malvern (Pennsylvania), 94(fig. 2)
Mandeville, Bernard, 184
Mannerist style, 229, 241. *See also* Boston, cupboards; Harvard College joinery
Mantle clock, 37–38(&fig. 63)
Manwaring, Robert, 50n30, 92n4
Map, geological, 97(fig. 5)
Mapp of Ye Improved Part of Pensilvania in America, A (Holme), 148(fig. 2)
Maple: armchairs, 32(fig. 52), 66(fig. 23), 67(fig. 25); cabinet, 128(fig. 2); caned armchairs, 192(fig. 23), 198(fig. 33), 202(fig. 39); caned side chairs, 190(fig. 20), 191(fig. 21), 193(fig. 24), 194(fig. 25), 195(fig. 27), 196(figs. 28, 29), 197(figs. 30, 31), 198(fig. 32), 199(fig. 34), 200(fig. 35), 201(fig. 38); card table, 33(&fig. 53); center table, 120(fig. 42); chair table, 142(figs. 34, 35); chest of drawers, 230(fig. 2); cupboards, 132(figs. 11, 12), 231(fig. 3), 233(fig. 9), 234(fig. 13); desk-and-bookcase, 158(fig. 11); dressing tables, 83(fig. 62), 164(fig. 21); easy chairs, 61(figs. 11, 12); folding-leaf table, 74(fig. 41); high chest, 155(fig. 7), 156; joined cupboards, 236(fig. 18), 239(fig. 24), 240(fig. 25); rocking chair, 42(fig. 73); settee, 244; side chairs, 194(fig. 25), 200(fig. 35); upholstered armchairs, 58(fig. 6), 59(fig. 8)
Marble: dolomitic, 96; European, 96(&fig. 3); frame for, 154; Italian, 108(fig. 25), 119(&fig. 40); King of Prussia, 95; marble-topped chamber table, 52n62; sideboard, 217(fig. 15); sideboard table, 42(fig. 72); slab of, 7; techniques for working with, 122n12, 122n13; true, 96; white Carrara, 117, 119. *See also* Clouded limestone
Marble dealers, 107–113
Marble Hall Quarry, 94(fig. 2), 117, 121, 124n27
Marblehead (Massachusetts), chest, 142(figs. 36, 37)
Marble Worker's Manual, Designed for the Use of Marble Workers, Builders, and Owners of Houses, The, 106, 107(fig. 23)
Marketplace: fakery and, 55; scholarship and, 55, 226n16
Marks: caned chair, 188–189(&figs. 14, 18); "I,"

174(fig. 1), 175, 188–189(&fig. 14); "IP," 188
Marlborough feet, 14(&fig. 20)
Marlowe, John, 246, 249
Marmion (Prince George County, Virginia), 208(fig. 2)
Marot, Daniel, 91, 91n4
Marquis, 26
Marsh, Jacob, 8, 9(fig. 8)
Marteline chisels, 107(figs. 23, 24)
Martelines, 107(fig. 23)
Martin, Ann Smart, 259
Martin, James, 30(fig. 49), 31
Maryland Gazette, 51n54
Maryland Historical Society, "Mining the Museum," 219(&fig. 16)
Mason, George, 49n28
Mason, Ralph, 223, 229, 230(fig. 2): chest of drawers, 235(fig. 17); cupboard, 233(fig. 9)
Material culture studies, American furniture scholarship and, 207, 217, 219
Materials: joiners', 137, 138; stock of, 140; woodworkers', 127, 250–252
Mathias Hammond House, 49n28
Maybeck, Bernard, 248
Mayhew, John, 49–50n30, 92n4
Maynard, James P., 27
McCubbin, Richard, 8
McFaddon, William, 51n54
McKie, Judy, 248
Mechanick Exercises; or the Doctrine of Handy-works (Moxon), 126, 128, 130(fig. 7), 132, 134, 144n3
Medfield (Massachusetts), chest, 136(figs. 24, 25)
Mercantilism, 176–181: caned chair as expression of, 182–184, 203
Mercer, Helen, 171n1
Mercer, Henry, 251
Mercer Museum (Doylestown, Pennsylvania), 251

Merchant's Exchange Building, 117(&fig. 38)
Meredith, Margaret Cadwalader, 154, 172n14
Meredith, Samuel, 153–154, 172n14
Merrill, Nancy O., 257
Messinger, Henry, 223, 229, 230(fig. 2): chest of drawers, 235(fig. 17); cupboard, 233(fig. 9)
Metropolitan Museum of Art, 251: American Wing, 208(&fig. 2), 214; Hudson-Fulton Celebration, 208(&fig. 1), 212(&fig. 7)
Michie, Thomas S., 253
Middle-class furniture, caned chairs as, 176. See also Social class
Middleton, Joseph, 8
Midway Plaisance (World's Colombian Exposition), 211
Miller, Alan, 123n19
Miller, Peter, 160
Miller, Richard, 259
Milwaukee Art Museum, 221: American collections gallery, 215(fig. 11), 216(fig. 13), 221–224(&figs. 19, 20, 21, 22)
"Mining the Museum," 219(&fig. 16)
Mint Museum of Craft & Design, 243
Molding planes, 127, 133
Moldings, 13(fig. 19), 133; edge, 76, 77(fig. 49); scratch-stock, 236, 238, 242n11; scroll, 19
Montgomery, Charles F., 258
Monticello joinery (Albemarle County, Virginia), 220–221 (&fig. 18)
Moore, John, 150
Moore, Thomas, 117
Morse, Frances Clary, 252
Mortise-and-tenon joints, 137, 238(&fig. 23)
Mortise chisel, 134(&fig. 18)
Mortising errors, 142–143(&figs. 35, 37)
Moulthrop, Ruben, 177(fig. 2)

Mount Airy, 15(&fig. 22), 49n28
Moxon, Joseph, 126, 128, 130(fig. 7), 131, 133, 134, 135, 144n3, 145n16
Muhlenberg, Henry and Anna Marie, 103(fig. 16)
Mun, Thomas, 180
Munroe, Daniel, 254
Muntins, 236
Murray, Sarah Scott, 29
Museum of Fine Arts (Boston), 211, 247
Museum of Jurassic Technology (Los Angeles, California), 226n18
Museums: catalogues, 209–210, 212; displays of decorative arts, 207–225(&figs.); themed displays, 224–225. See also *individual museums*

Nail Cabinet, 247
Nailed construction, 138–139(&figs.), 190, 231, 234(fig. 15), 239
Nail holes, 60, 61(fig. 10)
Nairne, E., 48n20
Nash, Gary, 216
National Gallery (Washington, D.C.), 256
National Gallery of Art, View of "An American Vision: Henry Francis du Pont's Winterthur Museum," 215(fig. 12)
National Trust for Historic Preservation, 46n3
Navigation Acts, 181
Neat and plain style, 21, 220
Needles, John, 52n62, 53n66
Neoclassical furniture, 20, 30, 34, 220, 221: clouded limestone and, 119; painted, 32–33(&fig. 53)
Neth, Lewis, 31
"The New England Kitchen in the Old Log Cabin," 213(fig. 8)
New Hampshire Historical Society, 188

New Orleans, armoire, 40–41 (&fig. 70)

Newport (Rhode Island): bureau table, 54(fig. 1); card table, 71(fig. 34); chest of drawers, 56, 57(fig. 3); easy chairs, 92n5; high chest, 63(&figs. 17, 18); tea table, 54(fig. 1)

New York: armchair, 220–221 (&fig. 17); card tables, 72(fig. 36), 73(fig. 39); side chair, 41(&fig. 71)

Norman, John, Sr. or Jr., 142(figs. 36, 37), 143

Norris, Charles, 173n20

Norris, Isaac, 151, 171n8

Norristown (Pennsylvania), 94(fig. 2), 99

North, Dudley, 184

Northborough Manor (Cambridgeshire, England), 147(fig. 1)

Norton, Freegrace, 140

Nouveaux Livres di Licts de différentes penseez (Marot), 91n4

Nutting, Wallace, 125, 252

Oak: armchair, 15(fig. 23); Botany Bay, 32(fig. 51); bureau bookcase, 16(fig. 24), 17–18; caned side chair, 193(fig. 24); card tables, 31–32(figs. 50, 51), 33(&fig. 53), 35(fig. 57), 72(fig. 35); carved panel, 127(fig. 1); chair table, 142(figs. 34, 35); chest, 129(fig. 4), 136(fig. 24), 141(fig. 33), 142(figs. 36, 37); chests of drawers, 25(&fig. 38), 235(fig. 17); cupboard fragment, 228(fig. 1); cupboards, 132(figs. 11, 12), 231(fig. 3), 233(fig. 9), 234(fig. 13); desk-and-bookcases, 157(fig. 10), 158(fig. 11), 159(fig. 12), 162(fig. 18); dining table, 34(fig. 55); easy chair, 64(fig. 19); joined cupboards, 236(fig. 18), 239(fig. 24), 240(fig. 25); knife vases, 36(fig. 59); rocking chair, 42(fig. 73); sideboard table, 42(fig. 72); tall clock case, 8(&fig. 7). See also Red oak; White oak

Oak blocks, 156

Oakland Quarry, 118

"Objects: USA," 245

"Of the Maker, By the Maker, and For the Maker" (Milwaukee Art Museum), 223(fig. 22)

Ogee bracket feet, 162(fig. 17), 163, 170

Ogee head, 155(fig. 7), 157–161 (&figs.), 162(fig. 18), 172n15, 172–173n18: high chest, 155(fig. 7)

Old Swedes Episcopal church, 103–105(&figs.)

Oliver, Robert, 49n25

One Good Turn: A Natural History of the Screwdriver and the Screw (Rybczynski), 250, 251–252

Order of work, 140–143

Ormolu mounts, 42

Ormsbee, Thomas, 212

Ornamental painters, of timepieces, 254

Osborn, Danvers (Sir), 160, 173n19

Ottinger, Oliver, 117

Oval table, Philadelphia, 151(&fig. 5)

Ovolo elements, 166

Oxford English Dictionary, 251

Oxley Hancock & Company (London), 24, 25, 50n40, 50n41

Pad feet, 60

Padouk, 247

Painted furniture, 32–33(&figs. 53, 54)

Palfrey, John, 229, 230, 241

Palfrey, Rebecca Boardman, 230

Palladio, Andrea, 48n20

Palleday, William, 160

Paneled feet, 165(fig. 23), 166

Panels: cupboards, 228(fig. 1), 234–235; defined, 145n8; foliate, 136(&figs. 24, 25)

Parlin, Olamus, 104

Parting tools, 107(fig. 23)

Parts, reuse of period, 60–63, 86

Patent suspension, 254

Patent timepieces, 253–254

Payne, William, 113, 123n23

Peale, Charles Willson, 5(fig. 3), 7(fig. 5), 28–29(&fig. 46), 51n47

Peckford, Richard, 108

Pediments, 89(fig. 72): arched, 160, 161(figs. 15, 16), 162(fig. 17), 163; designs for, 18, 161(fig. 16); pitched, 163(fig. 19), 173n20; scrolled, 160, 162(fig. 17), 172n15

Pembroke tables, 15

Pendant, fish tail, 165(&fig. 23)

Penn, Letitia, 121n5

Penn, Thomas, 166

Penn, William, 148, 149(&fig. 3), 171n5, 171n6

Pennsylvania Gazette, 108, 113

Pennsylvania Land and Marble Company, 116–117, 124n27

Pennsylvania State House, 98(&figs. 6, 7)

Pentil holes, 77

Perspectives on American Furniture, 217

Peters, William, 113

Philadelphia: armchair, 69(&figs.); attribution of furniture, 147; candlestands, 76(figs. 46, 47), 77–79(&figs. 51, 52); caned side chair, 191(fig. 21); center table, 120(fig. 42); vs. Charleston, 172n15; chest-on-chests, 162(fig. 17), 163, 167(fig. 26), 168(fig. 27); chests of drawers, 169(fig. 29), 170(fig. 30); desk-and-bookcase, 157–161(&figs.); dressing tables, 81–83(&figs.), 164(figs. 20, 21), 166(&fig. 24); easy chairs, 93n7; fall-front desk, 150(fig. 4); Girard College, 117(fig. 37); high chests, 155(figs. 7, 8), 156(fig. 9), 165(figs. 22, 23), 166(&fig. 25); limestone from region, 95–97.

See also Clouded limestone; Merchant's Exchange Building, 117(fig. 38); oval table, 151(&fig. 5); pier table, 119(fig. 40); Second Bank of the United States, 118(fig. 39); sideboard tables, 94(fig. 1), 108(fig. 25), 109(&figs.), 110(fig. 30), 111(fig. 31), 112(fig. 32), 114(fig. 33), 154(fig. 6); side chairs, 11(fig. 15), 69(figs. 28, 29, 30); washstand, 121(fig. 44). *See also* Claypoole, George, Jr.; Claypoole, George, Sr.; Claypoole, Joseph; Claypoole, Josiah

Philadelphia Cabinet and Chair-Maker's Book of Prices (Folwell), 31

Philadelphia cabinetmakers, sideboard table frames and, 111–112

Philadelphia Centennial, 213(fig. 8)

Philadelphia Gazette, 110, 122n14, 151

Philadelphia Museum of Art, 211(&fig. 6): Gallery 283, 209(fig. 3)

Philadelphia Sesquicentennial Fair, High Street, 210(&fig. 4), 211

Phillips, Henry F., 252

Phyfe, Duncan, 216

Physick House (Philadelphia), 115(fig. 34)

Pianoforte, 25, 51n42

Pickworth, John, 127, 144n6

Piercer, 135

Pier glasses, 7, 11, 12–14(&figs. 17, 18), 18(fig. 27), 48n23, 49n25

Pier table, 119(fig. 40)

Pilgrim Century furniture, 125

Pillars, 232(&fig. 7), 233(fig. 10), 241(fig. 29)

Pine: armchairs, 66(fig. 23), 68(fig. 27); caned side chair, 189(fig. 16); chair table, 142(figs. 34, 35); chest-on-chest, 168(fig. 27); chests, 136(fig. 24), 142(figs. 36, 37); cupboard fragment, 228(fig. 1); cupboards, 231(fig. 3), 233(fig. 9), 324(fig. 13); desk-and-bookcases, 158(fig. 11), 162(fig. 18); dressing table, 81(fig. 55); easy chairs, 61(fig. 11), 64(fig. 19); folding-leaf table, 74(fig. 41); joined cupboards, 236(fig. 18), 239(fig. 24), 240(fig. 25); sideboard table, 110(fig. 30); upholstered armchair, 58(fig. 6)

Pins, 72–73(&figs. 38, 39), 137, 237(fig. 20)

Pips, 237

Pitched pediments, 163(&fig. 19), 173n20

Pitts, William, 24(fig. 37)

PLAN of the City and Environs of PHILADELPHIA, Pennsylvania, 1777, A (Lotter), 98(fig. 6)

Plane irons, 133

Planes, 127, 131, 134(&fig. 18): fore, 131, 145n13; grooving, 242n12; half-round, 131, 133; hollow, 133; molding, 127, 133; plough, 242n12; plow, 134(&fig. 17); round, 133(&fig. 15), 145n13

Planks, 127

Plaster ornaments, 20

Plateau, silver and glass, 24(&fig. 37)

Platter, Chinese export, 9(fig. 11)

Plow, 130(fig. 7), 133–134

Plow planes, 134(&fig. 17), 242n12

Plumley, Charles, 150–151, 171n7

Plumley, Rose, 171n7

Plumstead, Clement, 122n14

Pole lathe, 135

Political Register, The, 180(fig. 6)

Pollock, Jonathan, 244

Poplar: armchair, 68(fig. 27); desk-and-bookcase, 158(fig. 11). *See also* Tulip poplar; Yellow poplar

Porcelain: Chinese export platter, 9(fig. 11); tobacco leaf, 9, 47n17

Portable desks, 36

Portsmouth (New Hampshire): armchairs, 66(fig. 23), 67(fig. 25); lolling chair, 58(fig. 7)

Potthast brothers (Baltimore), 5, 35: side chair, 23(&fig. 35)

Potts, E. Channing, 113

Potts, Robert T., 113

Potts Quarry, 94(fig. 2)

Powel, Samuel, Jr., 122n14

Powell, Samuel, 113

Powell, William (Captain), 38

Preedy, Joseph, 24(fig. 37)

Priestley, Edward, 34(&figs. 55, 56), 35(figs. 57, 58), 36(figs. 60, 61), 37, 38(fig. 65), 52n61, 52n65

Prince, S. F., 124n27

Principes de L'Architecture, Des (Felibien), 134(&fig. 18)

Prints, Boydell, 25(&figs. 39, 40), 30

Probate records, 144n6: determining person's trade from, 126–127, 129–130, 131, 133–134; Edward Lloyd III, 6, 9; Edward Lloyd IV, 22, 23; Edward Lloyd V, 20; Joseph Claypoole, 151, 172n9

Providence (Rhode Island), chest-on-chest, 56(&fig. 2)

Prown, Jonathan, 259

Puncheons, 107(fig. 23)

Quakers, 148–149

Quare, Daniel, 8(&fig. 7)

Quarries: eighteenth-century clouded limestone, 94(fig. 2), 107–113; nineteenth-century clouded limestone, 113, 115–119

Quarter-round tenon, 62(&figs. 14, 15)

Quervelle, Anthony, 119

Quoins, 98(&figs. 6, 7)

R. A. Campbell (Baltimore), 37

Race, American furniture scholarship and, 209, 212–213, 225n9

Race Street between 6th & 7th, Philadelphia, 116(fig. 36)
Rail scalloping, 109(&fig. 26)
Randall, Richard, 188
Randolph, Benjamin, 113, 153, 216: side chair, 11(fig. 15)
Rasps, 106, 107(figs. 23, 24)
Rawlings, John, 20
Rear rail, 71, 72
Red oak: cabinet, 128(fig. 2), 129; caned side chair, 190(fig. 20); chest of drawers, 230(fig. 2)
Reeseville quarry, 94(fig. 2)
"Regional Furniture/Regional Life" (Hosley), 258
Regionalism, 92n5
"Reinventing the Past" (Milwaukee Art Museum), 221(fig. 19)
Renwick Gallery, 243
Reproduction, colonial revival, 5
Restoration furniture, 176–177
Reynals (Reynell, Reynolds), John, 153, 169
Reynolds, James, 94(fig. 1)
Rhead, Frederick, 248
Richard Act V Scene II (Boydell brothers), 25(&figs. 39, 40)
Richard Bennett Lloyd (West), 6(fig. 4)
Rickards, John, 139
Ridge Pike, 120
Ridman, Andrew, 104, 105(fig. 18)
Riley, John, 180(fig. 7)
Riving: tears, 129(&fig. 2); tools, 129
Robb Collection, 93n7
Robertson, Peter S., 252
Rocking chairs, 42–43(&figs. 73, 75, 76), 244(fig. 1)
Rococo style, 20, 21, 91–92n4, 113, 114(fig. 33), 257, 259
"The Rococo, the Grotto, and the Philadelphia High Chest" (Prown & Miller), 259
Rogers, Henry Darwin, 98–99, 121n8

Rondels, 228(fig. 1)
Roney, William, 52n61
Roque, Oswaldo Rodriguez, 87
Rosewood: armchair, 220(fig. 17); chest of drawers, 230(fig. 2); wardrobe, 40(fig. 68)
Ross, William, 44
Round-nosed chisels, 107(fig. 23)
Round plane, 133(&fig. 15), 145n13
Round tables, 6, 8
Royal African Company, 185
Rules for Drawing the Several Parts of Architecture (Gibbs), 48n20
Rutter, Thomas, 173n25
Ruyi, 205n20
Rybczynski, Witold, 250

Saarinan, Eero, 222
Sack, Albert, 217(&fig. 14)
Sack, Israel, 55
Saddled crest, 196, 198(fig. 33), 199
Saint Peter's Church (Chester County, Pennsylvania), 94(fig. 2), 102(&fig. 13)
Salem (Massachusetts): cabinet, 128(fig. 2), 129(fig. 3), 133(fig. 16); high chest, 223, 224(fig. 24); secretary, 55; upholstered armchair, 59(fig. 8)
Salver, silver, 8–9(&figs. 8, 9)
Sam Maloof: Woodworker, 245
Samuel Carpenter's Mansion (Strickland), 149(fig. 3)
Samuel Powell House drawing room, 211(fig. 6)
Satinwood: card table, 20(fig. 30); corner table, 119(fig. 41); lolling chair, 58(fig. 7)
Savalls, 47n16
Savell, William, 230(&fig. 18)
Savell, William, Sr., 127
Savell shop, 235: chest, 141(fig. 33); cupboard fragment, 137(figs. 28, 29)
Savery, William, 22

"Sawing Rooms of J. & M. Baird's Steam Marble Works," 120(fig. 43)
Saw kerfs, 74, 103(fig. 15), 109(&fig. 29)
Saws, 129
Schiller, Elizabeth Lloyd, 5, 14, 24, 28, 32, 34, 44, 46n3, 49n26
Schiller, Morgan B., 5, 46n3
Scholarship, marketplace and, 55
School & Faurest, 117
Schuylkill gray, 95
Scrapers, 107(fig. 23)
Scratch-stock molding, 236, 238, 242n11
Scrolled pediments, 160, 162(fig. 17), 172n15
Scroll moldings, 19
Scrolls, 63, 228(fig. 1)
Sears, William Bernard, 49n29
Sebillas, 107(fig. 23)
Second Bank of the United States, 117, 118(fig. 39)
Second Geological Survey, 99
Second Livre d'Apartements (Marot), 91n4
Secretary: Baltimore, 30–31(&fig. 48); Salem (Massachusetts), 55
Secretary bookcase, 15
Serres, Dominc, 29
Settee bed, 6
Settees, 6, 15, 16, 17, 50n30, 224
"Seventeenth-Century Joinery from Braintree, Massachusetts: The Savell Shop Tradition" (Alexander), 141
S. F. Jacoby and Company, 117
Shagreen case, 8
Shaving table, 21(&fig. 31)
Shaw, John, 21, 27(&fig. 45), 50n32, 50n33, 51n47: desk-and-bookcase, 19(&fig. 28), 31
Shell, B., 117
Shell, J. E., 117
Sheraton, Thomas, 19(fig. 28), 50n38, 51n41, 51n57, 53n67
Shippen, Edward, Jr., 153

Shippen, Joseph, 151, 173n25
Sideboards, 8, 15, 52n66, 122–123n18, 154–155: Baltimore, 35–36(&fig. 58); Victorian, 217–219(&fig. 15)
Sideboard tables: Baltimore, 38(&fig. 65), 42(&fig. 72); Philadelphia, 94(fig. 1), 106(fig. 21), 108–109(&figs.), 110(fig. 30), 111(&fig. 31), 112(fig. 32), 114(fig. 33), 154(fig. 6)
Side chairs, 8, 15: Baltimore, 23(fig. 35); caned, 174(fig. 1), 178(fig. 4), 179(fig. 5), 186(fig. 11), 187(figs. 12, 13), 188(fig. 15), 189(figs. 16, 17), 190(figs. 19, 20), 191(fig. 21), 193(fig. 24), 194(fig. 25), 195(fig. 27), 197(figs. 30, 31), 198(fig. 32), 199(fig. 34), 200(figs. 35, 36, 37), 201(fig. 38); English, 22(fig. 34), 23; New York, 41(&fig. 71); Philadelphia, 11(fig. 15), 69(figs. 28, 29, 30), 71
Side rail, 65(fig. 22)
Signification value, of caned chairs, 178–179, 182–184, 202
"Sign Language" (Milwaukee Art Museum), 222(fig. 21)
Silk: curtains, 6, 7, 8; mantle clock, 37(fig. 63)
Silver: bread basket, 9(&fig. 10); Lloyd family, 8–9, 47n16; plateau, 24(&fig. 37); salver, 8–9(&figs. 8, 9); tea service, 17–18
Silver and glass plateau, 24(&fig. 37)
Simon, Joseph, 93n6
Singer, Joanna Leigh Lloyd, 5
Singleton, William, 32(&fig. 52), 51–52n54
Sixty Different Sorts of Ornament (Brunetti), 91n4
Slab frames, for marble tops, 110–113

Slipper feet, 109(&fig. 26), 165
Sloan, Samuel, 118
Smith, Adam, 180
Smoothing plane, 131–132(&fig. 14)
Snakewood, chest of drawers, 230(fig. 2)
Soapstone, 98
Social class: American furniture scholarship and, 207–208, 209, 211–212, 225n1; caned chairs and, 175, 176, 179, 185–187, 203
Society of Upholsterers, 92n4
Sofa, 15, 34(fig. 56), 35
Spanish feet, 164(fig. 21), 165(&fig. 22), 189
Sparke, John, 133
Spice cabinet, 173n22
Spindle turning, 93n16
Splats, 32(&fig. 52), 50n38, 201
Spoon bit, 72, 73(fig. 39)
Sprig bit, 138
Springs, 138
Square etching needle, 107(figs. 23, 24)
Stanaland, John, 113
Staplefoot, Thomas, 151(fig. 5)
State chairs, 92n4
State Museum (Pennsylvania), 99
Steel: deck cannon 10(fig. 12); mantle clock, 37(fig. 63)
Steinmetz, Adam, 117
Stenton (Germantown, Pennsylvania), 160(fig. 13), 163
Stent panel, 127–129(&fig. 1), 130
Stephen Girard House, 211
Stewart, Kipp, 246
Stiles, 199, 201
Stiles, William, 113
Stillinger, Elizabeth, 209
Stone, Gregory, 231
Stone, Polly, 55
Stone, Stanley, 55, 87
Stone carving, 113
Stone cutters' tools, 106, 107(fig. 23)
Stool easy chair, 6
Stools, elbow, 91n4

Stretcher configuration, on Boston caned chairs, 189
Strickland, William, 117(&fig. 38), 118(fig. 39), 149(fig. 3)
Studio furniture, 243–250
Style terms, 250
Sullivan, Robert, 99
Swan, Abraham, 18, 48n20
Sylva, or a Discourse of Forest-Trees, and the Propagation of Timber in His Majesties Dominions (Evelyn), 137
Symonds, John, 126, 129, 144n6
Symonds, Robert W., 176, 182
Symonds shops (Salem, Massachusetts), 139, 144n5, 241: cabinet, 128(fig. 2), 129, 133(fig. 16)

Taber, Elnathan, 255
Table bases/frames, for marble, 110–113, 154
Tablelamps, 249
Tables: billiard, 51n44, 51n47; breakfast, 6; bureau, 54(fig. 1); center, 120(fig. 42); chair, 142(figs. 34, 35); chamber, 37(&fig. 62), 56n62; corner, 119(fig. 41); dining, 14, 15, 34(&fig. 55); folding-leaf, 73–74(&figs. 41, 42, 43); oval, 151(&fig. 5); Pembroke, 15; pier, 119(fig. 40); round, 6, 8; shaving, 21(&fig. 31); tea, 6, 7, 8, 54(fig. 1), 71, 172n16; writing, 15, 21(&fig. 32), 36(&fig. 60). *See also* Card tables; Dressing tables; Sideboard tables
Table slabs, tool marks on, 106(&fig. 21)
Talbot County (Maryland), rocking chair, 42(fig. 73), 43(figs. 75, 76)
Tangarry Chest, 249
Tansu, 249
Tarr, Edwin S., 41

Tarr, Henry S., 117
Tassel feet, 189
Taste, seventeenth-century theory of, 184–187
Tawley, John, 139–140
Tayloe, Elizabeth, 14, 15(&fig. 22), 16, 20, 47n6, 49n28
Tayloe, John, 49n28
Tayloe, Rebecca, 49n28
Taylor, John, 228(fig. 1), 229–230, 241
Tea service, 17–18
Tea tables, 6, 7, 8, 71: Irish, 172n16; Newport, 54(fig. 1)
Tea waiter, silver, 8–9(&figs. 8, 9)
Tenon, quarter-round, 62(figs. 14, 15)
Terry, Eli, 255
Textiles, Lloyd family, 14, 31, 33
Themed displays, 224–225
Third Earl of Shaftesbury, The (after Closterman), 185(fig. 8)
Thomas, Dalby, 181
Thomas Eden, Christopher Court & Company, 13, 22–23, 25, 26, 49n25, 50n40, 51n42
Thompson, Lewis, 117
Thorp, John, 131, 145n12
Thurston, John, 136(&figs. 24, 25)
Tilghman, Mary Donnell, 5
Timber, 127, 140: green, 137
Tobacco leaf porcelain, 9, 47n17
Tombstones, 100–101(&figs.), 121–122n10
Tompkins, Jane, 221
Tool marks: on clouded limestone, 101(fig. 12), 102–103(&figs. 14, 15), 106(&figs.); saw kerfs, 74, 103(fig. 15), 109(&fig. 29)
Tools: carving, 136–137; joiners', 145n13; making woodworking, 133, 145n14; stone cutters', 106, 107(fig. 23); woodworkers', 126–139, 250–252
Tops, candlestand, 76, 77(fig. 50), 78(fig. 52), 79

Townsend family (Newport, Rhode Island), 223
Tradesmen, attitudes toward their work, 125–126, 143–144n2
Trappe Lutheran Church, 94(fig. 2)
Traquair, James, 113, 123n24
Traquair Quarry, 94(fig. 2)
Trent, Robert F., 226n14, 229
Trifid feet, 165
Troost, Gerhard, 97(&fig. 5)
Tuck, William, 8
Tulip poplar: armchair, 32(fig. 52); armoire, 41(fig. 70); billiard table, 27(fig. 45); bureau table, 54(fig. 1); card tables, 32(fig. 51), 33(&fig. 53), 35(fig. 57), 72(fig. 35); chamber table, 37(fig. 62); chests of drawers, 37(fig. 64); chest-on-chest, 168(fig. 27), 170(fig. 30); clothes press, 30(fig. 49); cornice, 33(fig. 54); desk-and-bookcases, 19(&fig. 28), 31, 157(fig. 10), 159(fig. 12), 161(fig. 15); dining table, 34(fig. 55); dressing tables, 80(fig. 54), 83(fig. 62), 84; easy chair, 64(fig. 19); high chest, 155(fig. 7), 156; liquor case, 38(fig. 65); oval table, 151(fig. 5); secretary, 30(fig. 48); shaving table, 21(&fig. 31); sideboard, 217(fig. 15); sideboard tables, 38(fig. 65), 42(fig. 72), 154(fig. 6); sofa, 34(fig. 56); tall clock case, 8(&fig. 7); wardrobes, 39(fig. 66), 40(figs. 67, 68), 41(fig. 69); writing tables, 21(&fig. 32), 36(fig. 60)
Turner, 127(&fig. 1)
Turner's cross, 76
Turnscrew, 251
Tweed, Richard "Boss," 41
Tweed & Bonnell (New York), 41(&fig. 71)
Tympanum, 89
Ulrich, Laurel Thatcher, 217, 258

Unfinished work, 126–127
United States, caned chair in, 188–203(&figs.)
U.S. Mint, 117
U.S. Naval Academy, 48n18
Universal System of Houshold Furniture, The (Ince & Mayhew), 50n30, 92n4
Upholstered armchairs: American, 58(fig. 6); Boston/Salem, 59(fig. 8); in Chipstone Collection, 59–71(&figs.); England, 7(&fig. 6)
"The Urban Cowboy as Furniture Maker" (Cooke), 247
Use, history of, 60, 62, 74, 77, 79, 85, 93n13

Vambrace, 135
Vases, knife, 36(&fig. 59)
Victorian furniture, 217–219 (&fig. 15)
Virginia, upholstered armchair, 220(fig. 18)
Vogler, John, 125, 143n2
Voids, 242n12
Volutes, 192

Wages, joiners', 140
Wainscot plow, 133
Wallington, Nehemiah, 126, 143–144n2
Walnut: caned side chairs, 174(fig. 1), 186(fig. 11), 187(figs. 12, 13), 201(&fig. 38); chest, 129(fig. 4); chest-on-chests, 167(fig. 26), 168(fig. 27); chests of drawers, 169(fig. 29), 235(fig. 17); cupboards, 132(figs. 11, 12), 233(fig. 9); desk, 22(fig. 33); dressing table, 164(fig. 20); easy chair, 61(fig. 12); fall-front desk, 150(fig. 4); folding-leaf table, 74(fig. 41); high chest, 165(fig. 22); joined cupboard, 236(fig. 18); oval table, 151(fig. 5); rocking chair, 244(fig. 1); settee,

244; sideboard, 217(fig. 15); sideboard table, 94(fig. 1); sideboard table frames, 112; tall clock case, 8(&fig. 7); upholstered armchair, 7(&fig. 6). *See also* Black walnut
Walter, Thomas Ustick, 117(&fig. 37)
Walton, John, 64(&fig. 20)
Wanton, Joseph, 56
Ward, John, 132
Wardrobes, 39–41(&figs. 66, 67, 68, 69), 53n66, 53n67
Ware, Isaac, 48n20
Washington, George, 68
Washstands, 15, 121(fig. 44)
Wayne, William, 113
Wear, history of, 60, 62, 74, 77, 79, 85, 93n1
Wedges, 111, 129
Wegner, Hans, 246
Welch, John, 90(fig. 73)
West, Benjamin, 6(fig. 4), 29, 48n19
West, Patricia, 213
Weyden, Roger van der, 135(fig. 20)
White Carrara marble, 117, 119
White cedar: armoire, 41(fig. 70); chest of drawers, 170(fig. 30); chest-on-chest, 167(fig. 26), 168(fig. 28); dressing tables, 81(fig. 55), 164(figs. 20, 21); fall-front desk, 150(fig. 4); high chest, 155(fig. 7); oval table, 151(fig. 5); sideboard tables, 108(fig. 25), 109(fig. 26); side chair, 11(fig. 15); wardrobe, 41(fig. 69)
White City (World's Colombian Exposition), 211
White oak, chest of drawers, 230(fig. 2)
White pine: bureau table, 54(fig. 1); cabinet, 128(fig. 2); caned side chair, 201(fig. 38); card tables, 31–32(figs. 50, 51), 33(&fig. 53), 35(fig. 57), 70(fig. 31); center table, 120(fig. 42); chamber table, 37(fig. 62); chest-on-chest, 56(fig. 2); chests, 129(fig. 4), 141(fig. 33); chests of drawers, 37(fig. 64), 57(fig. 3), 230(fig. 2); clothes press, 30(fig. 49); corner table, 119(fig. 41); cupboard, 132(figs. 11, 12); desk-and-bookcases, 88(fig. 68), 90(fig. 73); easy chair, 61(fig. 12); fall-front desk, 150(fig. 4); high chest, 223, 224(figs. 23, 24); liquor case, 38(fig. 65); lolling chair, 58(fig. 7); secretary, 30(fig. 48); sideboard, 217(fig. 15); sideboard tables, 38(fig. 65), 42(fig. 72); wardrobes, 39(fig. 66), 40(figs. 67, 68), 41(fig. 69); washstand, 121(fig. 44); writing table, 36(fig. 60)
Whitehead, George, 148
Whitemarsh Township (Pennsylvania) quarries, 94(fig. 2), 107, 111
Wickes, Thomas, 127, 144n6
Widdowfield, John, 151(fig. 5)
Wilkinson, Anthony, 107–108, 111, 113, 122n14, 123n26
Wilkinson, Brian, 109, 113, 122n15
Wilkinson Quarry, 94(fig. 2)
Willard, Simon, 252–256
Willard, Simon, Jr., 255
Willard's Patent Time Pieces: A History of the Weight-Driven Banjo Clock, 1800–1900 (Foley), 252–256
Willdey, George, 148(fig. 2)
Willet, John, 171n8
William and Mary chairs, 176
Williams, James, 17, 39, 41, 50n30, 53n69
Williams, John, 39, 41, 50n30, 52n66, 53n69
Williams, John A., 52–53n66
Wilson, Fred, 219
Wilton carpets, 6, 8, 11
Wimble, 135
Wimble-Brace, 135
Winchester, Alice, 226n10
Windsor (Connecticut), joinery technique, 237
Winterthur Museum, 64(&fig. 20), 65, 93n7, 207, 215(fig. 12), 256–259
Winterthur Portfolio, 259
Winthrop, John, 140, 146n26
Wirgman, John, 9(&fig. 10)
Wistar, Caspar, 165
Wistar family (Philadelphia), desk-and-bookcase, 157(fig. 10), 158
Witness marks, 86
Wolbers, Richard, 48n23
"Womb Chair," 222
Woods: deck cannon 10(fig. 12); planks, 127; reuse in fakes, 71–73, 85, 89; sawn lumber, 239; timber, 127, 137, 140. *See also* Beech; Birch; Black walnut; Cedar; Cedrella; Cherry; Chestnut; Conifers; Cypress; Ebony; Mahogany; Maple; Oak; Pine; Poplar; Red oak; Rosewood; Satinwood; Snakewood; Tulip poplar; Walnut; White cedar; White oak; White pine; Yellow pine; Yellow poplar
Woodworking shop: pace of work, 140, 141; seventeenth-century, 127–129(&fig. 1), 130
Work benches, 127, 129–130 (&fig. 7)
World's Colombian Exposition, 211
Wright, Frank Lloyd, 243
Writing desk, 11
Writing tables, 15, 21(&fig. 32), 36(&fig. 60)
Wyatt, Job, 252
Wyatt, William, 252
Wye Heights, 38, 52n65
Wye House (Talbot County, Maryland), 2(fig. 1), 3–4, 11,

12(fig. 16), 46: garden, 26; graveyard, 26(&figs. 42, 43); greenhouse, 26–27(&fig. 44), 51n44; north side, 43(fig. 74). *See also under* Lloyd

Yale University Art Gallery, American decorative arts installation, 213(fig. 9)

Yellow pine: billiard table, 27(fig. 45); card table, 31(fig. 50); chest of drawers, 170(fig. 30); chest-on-chest, 167(fig. 26), 168(fig. 28); desk, 22(fig. 33); desk-and-bookcases, 19(&fig. 28), 31, 161(fig. 15); dressing tables, 80(fig. 54), 164(figs. 20, 21); high chest, 155(fig. 7), 156; secretary, 30(fig. 48); shaving table, 21(&fig. 31); sideboard tables, 94(fig. 1), 108(fig. 25), 109(fig. 26); tall clock case, 8(&fig. 7); writing table, 21(&fig. 32)

Yellow poplar, sideboard table, 114(fig. 33)

Chipstone Foundation Publications

Order Form

Title	Code	Qty	Price
American Furniture 2002	AF2002	____	$55
American Furniture 2001	AF2001	____	$55
Back Issues Available 1994 – 2000	AFback	____	$55
American Furniture – *2 year subscription*		____	$100
American Furniture – *3 year subscription*		____	$145
Ceramics in America 2002	CA2002	____	$55
Ceramics in America 2001	CA2001	____	$55
Ceramics in America – *2 year subscription*		____	$100
Ceramics in America – *3 year subscription*		____	$145
If These Pots Could Talk	IFTHCL	____	$75
_____	_____	____	____
Shipping			____

U.S. Shipping $5.00 for first book; $1.25 for each additional book.
Foreign Shipping $6.50 for first book; $2.00 for each additional book.

TOTAL _____

Name _____
Tel _____
Address _____
_____
City State ZIP _____

❏ Check payable to "UPNE"
Credit Card
❏ AMEX   ❏ Discover   ❏ Mastercard   ❏ VISA
CC# _____ Expires _____

Please send to:
University Press of New England
37 Lafayette Street
Lebanon, NH 03766
University.Press@Dartmouth.edu

www.chipstone.org   603/643-7110 • 800/421-1561   FAX 603/643-1540   www.upne.com